River *of* Promise

River *of* Promise

Lewis and Clark on the Columbia

David L. Nicandri

Foreword by
Clay S. Jenkinson

wsupress.wsu.edu I wsupress@wsu.edu I 800-354-7360

The Dakota Institute Press
of the Lewis & Clark Fort Mandan Foundation

Library of Congress Control Number
2009941167
ISBN-13 978-098-255-97-0-3 (Hardcover)
ISBN-13 978-098-255-97-1-0 (Paperback)

Distributed by The University of Oklahoma Press
Created, produced, and designed in the United States of America
Printed in Canada

Internal book layout and design by Margaret McCullough corvusdesignstudio.com

The paper in this book meets the guidelines for permanence and durability
of the Committee of Production Guidelines for Book Longevity of the
Council on Library Resources.
10 9 8 7 6 5 4 3 2 1

Cover Images: "No. 2 Great Falls of the Columbia River [Map]
Entry of 22 October-23 October, 1806. Voorhis Journal #4"
Missouri History Museum, St. Louis. State Historical Society of North Dakota,
C3674 (William Clark), C3675 (Meriwether Lewis)

The Dakota Institute Press
of the Lewis & Clark Fort Mandan Foundation
2576 8th Street South West . Post Office Box 607
Washburn, North Dakota 58577
www.fortmandan.com
1.877.462.8535

Mixed Sources
Cert no. SW-COC-001271
© 1996 FSC
FSC

To Dominic, my co-captain in western travel

Contents

Foreword

By Clay S. Jenkinson

The completion of Gary Moulton's edition of the *Journals of the Lewis and Clark Expedition* represents a watershed in the history of Lewis and Clark scholarship. Definitive and comprehensive though they are, the 13 volumes of the University of Nebraska edition of the journals do not represent everything that the seven known journal keepers wrote between 30 August 1803 and 23 September 1806. We know from references in the journals that some field notes and dispatches between the captains were lost in boat accidents, windstorms, and cache seepages. In fact, some pages were probably tossed away unceremoniously as their contents were copied or paraphrased during those "leisure times," as the great Jefferson put it, when the captains were instructed to "multiply... them against the accidental losses to which they will be exposed."

More to the point, thanks to the proprietary hostility of Meriwether Lewis, private Robert Frazer's journal has been lost. Owing to the printing and manuscript conventions of the time, Patrick Gass's original journal has been lost, as well as significant portion of whatever original journal manuscript Joseph Whitehouse produced before his editors cleaned it up. Gass's original journal, we can be certain, was quite different from the polished and embellished print version that appeared in 1807, the first journal-based account published following the Corps of Discovery's triumphant return. Indeed, Gass's *A Journal of the Voyages and Travels of a Corps of Discovery Under the Command of Capt. Lewis and Capt. Clarke of the Army of the United States*, was the world's primary source of information about the Lewis and Clark Expedition until Nicholas Biddle's paraphrase narrative finally appeared seven years later. The *authorized* account, published in Philadelphia in 1814, was entitled, *History of the Expedition Under the Command of Captains Lewis And Clark, to the Sources of the Missouri, thence Across the Rocky Mountains and Down the River Columbia to the Pacific Ocean. Performed During the Years 1804-5-6. By order of the Government of the United States.*

Although few scholars are still willing to believe that the 441 days of missing journal entries by Meriwether Lewis were lost or destroyed, most scholars still *feel* that there is (or was) more Lewis than we now possess. It seems likely that between now and the tercentennial of the Lewis and Clark Expedition, more discoveries will be made like that of the Filson Historical Society of Louisville, which, in October 1988, came into possession of 47 letters written by William Clark to his brother Jonathan between 1792 and 1811, many never before published. The letters were published in 2002 by Yale University Press, edited by James J. Holmberg, under the title *Dear Brother: Letters of William Clark to Jonathan Clark*. The last discovery of actual journals from the expedition occurred in 1953, when a bundle of Clark's field notes were found in an attic in St. Paul, Minnesota, wrapped in an 1805 edition of the *National Intelligencer*. They were published, edited by Ernest Staples Osgood, in 1964. Since then only letters related to the expedition have been discovered.

For the moment, at least, all the journals we have from the Expedition have been published under one roof, using consistent editorial protocols, with lavish annotation, and in several media, including a free and searchable online edition.

The University of Nebraska's 13-volume edition represents the starting point for all future studies of the Lewis and Clark Expedition. Moulton has established the text for our time and laid the foundation for a fresh examination of a chapter in American history so rooted in national mythology that our understanding of it has become strangely detached from the textual record. In other words, the Moulton edition is both a publishing triumph and a summons. The best thing that could happen now is that a fresh cadre of scholars with little or no prior understanding of the expedition would read all 13 volumes as if these remarkable journals had just been discovered for the first time, resulting in a new master narrative (or indeed the principled rejection of the idea of a master narrative), and new conclusions about the purposes, achievements, rhythms, discoveries, and personnel of what James Ronda has called "America's first great road story." The second best thing that could happen would be for the entire existing community of Lewis and Clark scholars, buffs, re-enactors, museum directors, and cultural tourists to read the journals with fresh eyes, like those characters from the *Men in Black* movies who have their brains zapped into *tabulae rasae* by a device that looks like a laser pointer. Who would not wish to read her or his favorite work of literature, *Hamlet* or *My Antonia*, again, in maturity, as if for the first time?

In this book, David Nicandri has attempted to do just that. He has tried to put aside the accumulated mythology of Lewis and Clark, as well as his own lifelong understanding of the expedition, and bring to a fresh reading of the journals a historian's contextual eye together with the exegetical attention of a literature scholar.

River of Promise immediately takes its place as the most important study of Lewis and Clark in the post-bicentennial era. It joins Thomas Slaughter's essay of provocation, *Exploring Lewis and Clark: Reflections on Men and Wilderness* (2003), as the first fruits of the cultural studies approach to reading Lewis and Clark's journals as texts rather than as a straightforward narrative. Both Slaughter and Nicandri—Slaughter often wildly, Nicandri much more carefully—read the journals not only for what they say but for what they don't say, not only for what they reveal but for what they conceal, not just for their utterances, but for their silences. In fact, Nicandri argues that the silences of Lewis and Clark are often extremely significant. Nicandri freely acknowledges that his study is "inherently risky because it involves making unorthodox speculations and reading sometimes literally between the lines of journal entries, directly challenging received wisdom about the expedition," (See page 5).

There is no question that Nicandri is something of an iconoclast. He takes a certain joy in challenging the principal myths of the Lewis and Clark story. He reminds us, for example, that we know very little about Sacagawea, and what little we know does not indicate that she guided the expedition to the Pacific, saved it from starvation, or even served as a kind of good will ambassador among the tribes that the expedition encountered. In Nicandri's view, much too much has been made of Clark's statement, 13 October 1805, that "the Wife of Shabono... reconciles all the Indians, as to our friendly intentions. A woman with a party of men is a token of peace." And a whole legendary career has been extracted from Clark's statement, on his larkish return journey down the Yellowstone River, that "the Indian woman has been of great Service to me as a pilot through this country." Nicandri rightly insists upon Sacagawea's relatively minor contribution to the success of the expedition. The minute we really think about it, we know that a U.S. government reconnaissance expedition was not planned—by the U.S. Army in faraway Washington, D.C.—with an eye to finding, somewhere along the trail, a Native American teenaged mother to take the lead and save the day. Nicandri's sensible but controversial argument is that the Sacagawea legend obscures the work of the expedition's true Indian guides, pilots, and ambassadors—such men as Twisted Hair and Tetoharsky.

In an implied criticism of the late Stephen Ambrose, Nicandri does what he can to deflate the myth that Meriwether Lewis and William Clark enjoyed the "greatest friendship in American history." That they were great friends is certain. Lewis called Clark co-captain in direct contradiction of the War Department's firm insistence that Clark was subordinate in military rank, and after the expedition Lewis insisted that Clark be compensated equally with himself. This too the war department prevented, with the approval, no doubt, of the patron of the expedition Thomas Jefferson. Clark, in turn, not only named his firstborn son Meriwether Lewis Clark (10 January 1809), but, of infinitely greater importance, subordinated his own ego and desire for glory to that of his gifted but troubled and difficult friend. It is not too much to say that Clark spent a portion of his life (1795-1814) first propping up the mercurial and self-destructive Lewis and then cleaning up after him—as, indeed, he had done previously on behalf of his tribulative brother George Rogers Clark.

Even so, too much has been made of the "most perfect harmony" of the friendship between Lewis and Clark. It cannot have been easy for a man of Clark's capacities and ambition to let *his estimable friend* Lewis appropriate the mantle of

Columbus and Captain Cook; to let Lewis thrust ahead, sometimes on the basis of transparently flimsy excuses, whenever the great moments of discovery loomed before the expedition; to be "obliged to attend [to] every thing" (7 October 1805) when Lewis was detached, distracted, or depressed. It seems clear that Clark was angry or miffed at Lewis on at least several occasions where not even his devotion and characteristic journal discipline could altogether squelch his true feelings: when Lewis wasted vitally needed weeks on that Jeffersonian *gimcrack*, his iron framed boat; when Clark's infected feet prevented him from having the singular honor of making first contact with the Shoshone, and for that matter discovering the source of the Missouri River; when Lewis, by committing suicide, left Clark to write (or cause to be written) the book upon which the expedition's historical reputation would rest, without having left Clark the slightest clue about which Pennsylvania artists, illustrators, scientists, and geographers had been secured to perform which tasks for that initially ambitious publication project.

Nicandri is not afraid to place the moments of tension between Lewis and Clark on the table. He centers his discussion on an incident of far greater significance than Clark's frustration over a pet boat experiment: Lewis's assertion, in a journal *dated* 14 August 1805, but apparently *written* much later, that he, Lewis, learned about the troubled geographic landscape west of Lemhi Pass directly from the Shoshone leader Cameahwait. Thanks to Nicandri, the first historian to take up this matter with serious analysis, we now know that it was Clark, not Lewis, who first learned about the jumbled and essentially impassable geography west of the Continental Divide in southwestern Montana and eastern Idaho; that Lewis, driven by his ambition always to be first, appropriated the insights that Clark had acquired with the help of Sacagawea, the Shoshone woman hired precisely for the purpose of helping the expedition get the information, horses, and porters they would need to cross the Bitterroot Mountains. In a key, but prior to Nicandri overlooked interlineation, Clark wrote, in Lewis's notebook entry for August 14th, "This part to come in the 20th [of August] related to Capt. C thro the interpreter." What this means, according to Nicandri, is that Clark was challenging (for the benefit of Nicholas Biddle) Lewis's claim that he had obtained this vital information personally, from Cameahwait, with only the help of the sign language interpreter George Drouillard. In other words, Clark carefully but firmly set the record straight about how the expedition learned that the Pacific watershed was not going to be as hospitable as that of the Missouri, which had led Lewis to marvel, on August 10th, that he did "not believe that the world can furnish an example of a river running to the extant which the Missouri and Jefferson's rivers do through such a mountainous country and at the same time so navigable as they are." If Nicandri's analysis is correct, this incident about who controlled the master narrative of the expedition and who was its principal geographer, reveals more about the relationship between Lewis and Clark than a bucket of *perfect harmony* anecdotes.

Nicandri also challenges the notion that on 24 November 1805, the expedition's leaders staged the first democratic vote west of the Mississippi River. The *vote,* now a pivotal strut in celebrations of the multicultural nature of the expedition, was in fact a non-binding plebiscite conducted by military officers determined to canvass their company of experienced woodsmen before *themselves* making a decision of extraordinary importance to the success of the expedition. The captains clearly wanted to know what the 32 men, including the slave York, and sole woman, thought about the location of winter quarters before making that key decision, but there is no indication that they intended to accede to majority rule or to regard the plebiscite as determinative. If the *vote* at Station Camp has any meaning in modern political parlance, it should be regarded as a focus group or a team-building exercise, not a democratic election at the far edge of the American continent.

Not everyone wants to see the sacred cows of the Lewis and Clark story challenged, or as Nicandri puts it, deconstructed. As James W. Loewen's 1996 study, *Lies My Teacher Told Me: Everything Your American History Textbook Got Wrong,* has shown, Americans like their history agreeable, even when it is historiographically threadbare. Old myths die hard. The bicentennial of Lewis and Clark has come and gone. Hundreds of millions of dollars of commemoration and convention, symposium and signage have been thrown at one of the handful of most popular and compelling stories in American history, and yet as far as one can tell the general public is scarcely more sophisticated in its understanding of the story than it was before all of this "throwing about of brains," as Hamlet puts it. And, what is much worse, the community of Lewis and Clark buffs, amateur scholars, and re-enactors has emerged from the bicentennial with most of its previous notions intact.

The most significant *paradigm shift* of the bicentennial is that Native Americans are now central to any serious discussion of Lewis and Clark. They have been restored to their rightful place in the heart of the narrative, not as merely as hosts but as full participants in a rich, complex often troubling series of cross-cultural encounters. The American Indian perspective is now regarded as essential to any mature understanding of the story, and Indian oral traditions are regarded by most historians as invaluable contributions to the Lewis and Clark conversation.

In the plate techtonics of the national historical consciousness, among those with a genuine interest in the expedition, the scorecard looks something like this: Clark is up, Lewis down. Jefferson is now seen as less of a dreamy American exceptionalist and more of a pre-Jacksonian Indian dispossessor. Sacagawea is no longer quite the guide and savior she was on the other side of the bicentennial, but she is still the heroine of the saga, now cast as an exemplar of pluck and multiculturalism, not to mention Clark's special object of cross-cultural affection and protection. York is now no longer the minstrel and sexual titan of the expedition, but a kind of civil rights figure, and a victim of Clark's post-expeditionary inability to emancipate himself from the mental habits of slaveholding. Indians are now no longer stock figures or extras on the Lewis and Clark stage. Indeed, they are now widely regarded as saviors of the expedition, tolerant, hospitable, and innocent of guile—and unendingly patient with the huff and puff of the expedition's sovereignty agenda.

In pop culture, Sacagawea still guides, saves, feeds, and inspires the expedition. Indeed, she is almost everywhere still *Sacajawea*, in spite of heroic efforts to return her to her textual nomenclatural homeland: Sah-cah-gar-we-ah.

II

River of Promise is in a sense several books at once, or perhaps one book with several interlocking argumentative strategies. It is, first and foremost, a nuanced and insightful examination of the least well known portion of the journey, the transit from Weippe Prairie (the western terminus of the Bitterroot Mountains) to the Pacific Ocean and back again. Nicandri rightly bewails the general falling off of Lewis and Clark historical narratives after the expedition reaches the source of the "mighty and heretofore deemed endless Missouri River," certainly after the expedition begins to float *with* rather than *against* the current. The usual historiographical strategy, to focus on the outbound journey at the expense of the return (mere denouement in most accounts), and to wrap things up pretty quickly after Lewis triumphs, 22 September 1805, over *those tremendous mountains,* has had two serious negative consequences, aside from the obvious shortcoming of ignoring a leg of the trail that deserves its fair share of attention.

First, given our multiculturalist interest in the expedition's encounters with Native Americans, the usual narrative peters out just when things get really interesting, when the expedition reaches a region with dense Indian populations. Historians used to say, a little erroneously, that Lewis and Clark did not encounter a single Indian between Fort Mandan, in today's North Dakota, and the Shoshone on the Montana-Idaho border (a distance of 700 miles, and a temporal span of 128 days). Now, suddenly, in the Columbia basin, Lewis and Clark encounter so many Indians of so many tribes and sub-tribes that it is virtually impossible to keep them sorted out in one's mind, like the characters of Tolstoy's novels. This crowding of the historical stage occurs just when most historians stop paying close attention. *River of Promise* fills the Columbia River void admirably and re-peoples the landscape.

Second, Nicandri argues, rightly I believe, that it is simply impossible to understand the decline and death of Meriwether Lewis in the expedition's aftermath without examining his spiritual exhaustion and the effective collapse of his authority (not to mention authorship) somewhere west of the Continental Divide. Lewis's flurry of journal entries at Fort Clatsop beginning on 1 January 1806, Nicandri states, literally has the feel of a New Year's Resolution. But Lewis proves unable to sustain the project. He writes rather dutifully along the return trail, but there is a palpable falling off of energy, insight, and—above all—good will. The muffling of Lewis's muse on the return journey is deafening. It robs the expedition of its most interesting voice. Clark's return journal makes clear, in a loyal friend's understated way, that Lewis was coming undone on the return journey. Lewis's patience with the strange ways of Indians was effectively at an end. He was now openly voicing his darkest fantasies about the savagery of Indians. His famous outburst on 20 February 1806, ("...never place our selves at the mercy of any savages. We well know, that the treachery of the aborigines of America and the too great confidence of our countrymen in their sincerity and friendship has caused the destruction of many hundreds of us.") was not out of character at all, but a revelation of a deep-seated attitude. Lewis's deep devotion to the Enlightenment President's philanthropic principles and progressive agenda had forced his shadow distrust of savagery and his fundamental racism (what might more generously be called his race distaste) under the radar for much of the outbound journey, but Jeffersonian good will and cheerfulness could not be sustained much beyond the moment when Lewis shed the last integuments of Euro-American civilization as he stood, "a perfect Indian in appearance," face to face with Cameahwait, "completely metamorphosed" by his journey into the heart of American darkness (16 August 1805).

Nicandri's point is that if you want to understand Lewis's post-expeditionary spiral into defiant silence, political squabbling, failure to process his territorial finances in a way that satisfied the War Department, drink, "fusty, musty rusty" lovelessness, and estrangement from even Jefferson, you cannot begin with the hostilities and ineptitude of territorial secretary Frederic Bates and President Madison's Secretary of War William Eustis. If you wish to understand the unraveling of the character of Meriwether Lewis, you must study the journals with microscopic attentiveness to mood and revelation, particularly those written after he left the source of the Missouri River. It can be argued that the greatest days of Lewis's life were passed between 13 June 1805, when he "discovered" the Great Falls of the Missouri, and August 16th, when he exchanged his tricorn hat and his rifle for Cameahwait's tippet. After that, whatever had once made Lewis preen like "those deservedly famed adventurers," Columbus or Captain Cook, diminished rapidly. Nicandri's underlying point is that the Lewis and Clark community's failure to make sense of Lewis's undoubted suicide has as much to do with neglect of the Columbia basin experience as it does with America's distaste for dark endings to otherwise triumphant stories.

Some may think that Nicandri pushes a little too far in trying to pinpoint the experiences that *deconstructed* Lewis, but he is surely right in his larger assertion that to understand the sad death of Meriwether Lewis we must first learn to read the journals, particularly the Pacific watershed journals, with fresh scrutiny and fewer preconceived notions about how an American explorer completes his journey. It is easy enough to reject Thomas Slaughter's melodramatic assertion that Lewis "was already dead; only his body was still alive," by the time he got back to St. Louis. But it is much harder to deny Nicandri's argument that it is irrational and counter-textual to claim, as many, including Stephen Ambrose, have, that Lewis was fully intact when he strode into St. Louis on 23 September 1806, and that his downward spiral during the three succeeding years, the last years of his life, was unrelated to his experiences in the wilderness.

Nicandri's bold book will upset some Lewis and Clark buffs, and more cautious historians will be able to fault him for this or that speculative reading of the journals. Those enamored of the *first democratic vote in the American West,* the Lemhi Pass disappointment trope, the *inexplicable* kidnapping of Lewis's Newfoundland Seaman, Sacagawea's singular pluck and heroism, and the romance of *America's purest friendship* will be disappointed or offended by Nicandri's revisionist toughness of spirit. This would seem to me to be a mistake. It's time that Lewis and Clark studies graduate from mythology to something like undaunted clarity. Ultimately Nicandri's analysis may prove to be a temporary settlement of issues at the core of the Lewis and Clark Expedition. It is far too soon to know that. He has done all of us a service in offering a painstaking and unsqueamish new look at the journals.

Furthermore, it is essential that we understand and appreciate Nicandri's essential playfulness. Although he makes arguments in good earnest throughout *River of Promise,* and surely believes in the validity of his analysis, it is clear from the tone and exuberance of the book that he is also having a good time with his craft. He writes in a prose style that is slightly, often amusingly, recondite. It is impossible not to hear his amusement as he couches his analysis of well known events in a slightly Latinate prose. There is something simultaneously intelligent and arguably parodic in his prose style.

III

In order to make his argument that the journals deserve a closer and more nuanced reading than they have hitherto received, Nicandri takes some time to explore just how the journals came into the form we have them in today. He rejects outright the naïve notion that what we now read in editions of Lewis and Clark, including the Moulton edition, is a simple transcript of unreconstructed daily diary entries written around the camp fire at the end of long days of travel. Internal evidence alone indicates that some entries could not have been written on the day they appear in the "journals." It is clear that the diarists, particularly the two captains, revised their journals when, as the poet Wordsworth puts it, they had the opportunity and leisure to *recollect in tranquility* what they had experienced at some previous moment of the expedition. Nicandri brilliantly differentiates the journal styles of Meriwether Lewis and William Clark. Clark's journal, as we now have it, appears to be closer to his actual day by day entries than that of Lewis, who frequently appears to be writing the first draft of his intended exploration masterpiece *in the manner of* a daily journal. In other words, such famous entries as the 7 April 1805, departure from Fort Mandan, the 13 June 1805, first sighting of the Great Falls of the Missouri River, Lewis's melancholy birthday meditation on 18 August 1805, and dozens of other entries, are almost certainly not what a busy and weary military explorer actually wrote on April 7th, June 13th, and August 18th. If we had the actual field notes upon which the apparently spontaneous, but in fact polished, self-conscious, and heroized, final "journal" entries were based, we would understand much more about the character and the textual strategies of Meriwether Lewis. Nicandri's point is that the journals were *constructed* by men who understood what was expected of explorers, who had read Alexander Mackenzie's *Voyages from Montreal*, who in fact often had Mackenzie's text open before them as they wrote--not simply *jotted* around a flickering campfire at the end of each day's experiences. Individual scholars and readers may quibble with Nicandri's attempt to make sense of this or that entry in the journals, but his general argument—that a naïve reading of the journals as if they were originally written in a *daily diary* fashion obscures as much as it seems to reveal about the journey—seems to me the key insight upon which all future readings of the journals must be based.

No study of Lewis and Clark can make sense without some explanation for the silences of Meriwether Lewis. In their recent biography of Lewis, Thomas Danisi and John Jackson, for example, attempt to prove that Lewis was not irresponsible; he was just extremely busy fulfilling other, more compelling, Jeffersonian imperatives, while leaving the relatively unimportant daily log to William Clark. This is certainly true up to a point. An understanding of the task list that Lewis dutifully attempted to fulfill on behalf of Jefferson certainly makes him seem *less irresponsible* than abstract journal statistics suggest. But no amount of special pleading can rescue Lewis from his unmistakable failure to communicate, before, during, and after the expedition. After all, Clark was equally busy, *obliged to attend to every thing*, and yet he managed to maintain his journal with almost astonishing dutifulness.

Nicandri's view would seem to be that at any given moment Lewis was silent for one of three reasons. 1. He was ill or hurt. This is particularly true when the expedition completed the Bitterroot Mountain transit and lurched out onto Weippe Prairie in late September 1805. Lewis also quit writing, on the return journey, one day after he was shot in the buttock by his own man during an elk-hunting excursion in today's North Dakota. Without apology he writes, on 12 August 1806, "as wrighting in my present situation is extreemly painfull to me I shall desist until I recover and leave to my frind Capt. C. the continuation of our journal." The last five words of this sentence are essential to any understanding of the dynamics of the journals of the expedition.

2. He was bored. Because he liked to think of himself as a heroic explorer in the tradition of Christopher Columbus or James Cook, Lewis seems to have regarded the expedition's first year of travel, from St. Charles to the Mandan and Hidatsa villages, a distance Clark calculated at 1610 miles, as little more than the transportation of the flotilla to the staging area for genuine discovery. In Lewis's mind, the real work of exploration would begin *west* of the five earthlodge villages that had been visited by Europeans for at least 62 years, and with genuine frequency (and thus familiarity) for more than 20 years. Alternatively, Lewis may have regarded the first year of travel as a shakedown cruise, during which, *Dirty Dozen*-like, the captains whipped a group of raw, often foreign, recruits into a tough "corps of discovery."

Under this reading, the captains spent the first year of travel learning how to navigate the treacherous Missouri River, learning how best to pack the keelboat and the two pirogues, discovering what parts of their immense equipage were most and least valuable, practicing their Great Father sovereignty rap with the mostly-pliable Indians of the lower Missouri. And—when they encountered the Brule Sioux in today's South Dakota—proving that they had the right stuff to conquer the continent.

Fascinating as all of this is to us, it was pretty jejune to America's Captain Cook. He left the daily log to the expedition's project manager Clark, and spent his creative time on shore with his gun, his dog, and especially his notebook, studying the increasingly unusual flora and fauna of the Great Plains. The field notes that essayed the bioregion of the plains have apparently mostly been lost. The moment the true *discovery phase* of the expedition began, on 7 April 1805, Lewis rumbled back into life as a journal keeper as his "little fleet" left Fort Mandan and the Corps of Discovery walked off the end of the map of the known world. He was able to maintain a continuous journal for 142 days, until 27 August 1805, by which time his main objective, discovering the source of the Missouri River, had been achieved.

3. He was spiritually exhausted. This explains Lewis's descent into silence following the Bitterroots transit, and his silence through much of the winter at Fort Clatsop (except when he was writing drafts of the natural history volume he would publish when the expedition returned), not to mention the nearly absolute post-expeditionary silence that bewildered and exasperated the U.S. War Department, his Philadelphia publisher, and—most of all—Thomas Jefferson.

Lewis is not a reliable journal keeper when any of the above factors is operative. To put it in other terms, Lewis *is* a reliable journal keeper when any one of three factors is present. 1. When he is engaged in what he (not we) regard as true discovery. 2. When he is on the Missouri River west of Fort Mandan (the last outpost of "civilization" in 1804-05). 3. When Clark is somewhere else and Lewis believes he must keep a journal to make sure that the expedition's activities do not go unreported. In other words, it is misguided to try to make sense of Lewis's silences by way of a simple diagnosis of manic depression, or even Jefferson's claim that in Lewis there were "sensible depressions of mind." There is a kind of logic to the dynamics of Lewis's journal-keeping. Those dynamics are much more complex than has hitherto been appreciated. Nicandri's analysis of the way the journals were *constructed* is not the last word on the subject, but all future studies of the dynamics of the journals will benefit from his occasional returns to this subject. It is little short of astonishing that Lewis and Clark scholars have paid so little attention to this issue. The great book on the dynamics of the journals has yet to be written. When it appears, it will instantly revolutionize our understanding of the expedition.

The simple truth is, as everyone knows, that some people have the discipline to keep a diary and most don't. It is true that Lewis was under direct orders from the President of the United States to keep a travel journal and that, if we now possess anything like a complete set of Lewis's writings from the expedition, he failed miserably. But two essential considerations lighten the charge of dereliction of duty.

First, the expedition as an aggregate entity, a corporate generator of prose, fulfilled the President's instructions admirably. No day of the expedition proper, i.e., 14 May 1804 to 23 September 1806, is unaccounted for by one or more of the expedition's journal keepers. In fact, there is sufficient redundancy in the journal record to more than satisfy Jefferson's insistence that Lewis guard against "the accidental losses to which they [the journals] will be exposed." The expedition's third in command, the undervalued John Ordway, was so reliable a journal keeper that he never missed a day for 28 months. The man of duty, William Clark, failed to write in his journal on only ten days—during a blizzardy hunting trip that he led in today's sub-arctic North Dakota—and he dutifully summarized those ten days on the eleventh when he had the opportunity to warm his hands before the fire at Fort Mandan. The captains wisely instructed the sergeants to keep journals and apparently encouraged privates to do so too. By any measure, the accumulated written record of the expedition is superb. Or rather, by any measure but one: when Lewis is silent, we inevitably lose the most lyrical, philosophical, erudite, precise, bemused, and searching voice of the expedition. The other voices are all interesting, and Nicandri rightly restores the "lesser diarists" to their rightful place in the narrative, but there is only one Meriwether Lewis and he, unfortunately, was the least reliable journal keeper of the expedition. Dr. Johnson said of Milton's *Paradise Lost*, "No one ever wished it longer." Nobody who has studied the journals of Lewis and Clark ever wishes Meriwether Lewis had written less.

Second, it is clear from any close reading of the expedition record that a sensible *modus operandi* of journal keeping evolved in the course of the tour. It seems clear that at the beginning of the journey Lewis believed he would keep a daily journal. So would Clark. Danisi and Jackson are surely right to argue that the list of desired Enlightenment information Jefferson outlined for Lewis on 20 June 1803, would have represented a profound challenge to any expedition leader, particularly to one so moody and erratic as Meriwether Lewis. At some point early on, when the press of duties began to tax Lewis's ability to keep up, the two captains seem to have come to an overt or perhaps tacit agreement, that *somebody*, one of the two captains, needed to account for each day of travel. Ideally both would indite. In every situation, one of the two would write. When push came to shove, Clark would be the fallback journal keeper. But when Clark was otherwise engaged, Lewis would see to it that the journal was faithfully maintained. In other words, early on the two captains came to some sort of agreement that while a proliferation and individuation of journals would be desirable, what was *required* was a kind of *captain's log*, and that if one of the two captains was making a daily journal entry, the President's expectations were being met.

Furthermore, students of the expedition have failed to read Jefferson's instructions carefully. Undoubtedly Jefferson wanted Lewis to keep records as assiduously as did he. Jefferson, America's most fully realized exemplar of the Enlightenment, maintained five daily diaries: an account book; a letter log; a farm book; a garden book; and a weather log. Jefferson was one of the best record keepers of his time, as well as the most organized of the Founding Fathers. *Jefferson* would not have missed a day of journal keeping on the trail, and he would have lugged along his polygraph, too. But in his famous instructions of 20 June 1803, Jefferson was not so much insisting upon journal keeping as upon painstaking recording of latitude and longitude.

In those instructions, after discussing the diplomatic efforts that had paved the way for Lewis's expedition, Jefferson turned to his prime instruction. "Beginning at the mouth of the Missouri," he wrote, "you will take observations of latitude and longitude at all remarkable points on the river...." Two paragraphs later, Jefferson returned to this theme to make sure that Lewis perfectly understood his duties. "Your observations [of latitude and longitude] are to be taken with great pains & accuracy to be entered distinctly, & intelligibly for others as well as yourself.... Several copies of these *as well as of your other notes*, should be made at leisure times, & put into the care of the most trustworthy of your attendants... [emphasis mine]."

It is clear from a careful reading of these words that what Jefferson principally wanted Lewis to record was latitude and longitude, that he wanted Lewis to make multiple copies of that data "at leisure times," because that was the information he most wanted to protect against accident. After Lewis's death, Jefferson nagged Clark about the longitude and latitude data, and insisted that Clark's map of the expedition was of limited value without precise latitude and longitude of key places on the trail. Historians have routinely misread these paragraphs to mean that Jefferson was instructing Lewis to keep a travel journal of the sort all students of the expedition rely on. In fact, what Jefferson wanted more than anything else was global positioning data that virtually all historians find uninteresting. The journals as we know and treasure them are all delineated by Jefferson in his nonchalant, even dismissive, phrase "your other notes."

Lewis probably spent more time on the expedition trying to ascertain his latitude and longitude than he did writing the journal entries that have established his literary fame. There are great ironies here. First, we may be judging Lewis by standards that his patron Jefferson never set for him, while he faithfully attempted to fulfill Jefferson's principal desideratum, and to compete successfully with the achievement of Alexander Mackenzie.

Second, though Lewis dutifully took celestial observations in fair weather and foul, no matter how busy the expedition was with other matters or adventures, those notations proved to be unintelligible to mathematician Ferdinand Hassler of West Point. Lewis's herculean efforts to put "mouths of rivers... rapids... islands & other places & objects" on the planetary grid proved to be mere futility. Third, while Lewis was (in our historical view) wasting his time making celestial observations that reveal nothing of interest *to us* about the expedition, he was, as

Danisi and Jackson rightly argue, not writing the prosaic journal entries for which we most hunger.

This much is true. Gary Moulton's stupendous achievement gives all of us an opportunity to reexamine the Lewis and Clark expedition by way of exploring with fresh eyes the complex, problematic, and unstable texts the expedition constructed. Every other document relating to the expedition deserves a fresh reading, too, including Jefferson's instructions, the letters collected by historian Donald Jackson—all set, as Nicandri rightly suggests, in the larger context of the explorations of James Cook, Zebulon Pike, John Ledyard, David Thompson, and above all Alexander Mackenzie.

One of the things that makes *River of Promise* rich and valuable even when the reader is unconvinced by some of Nicandri's conclusions is the way in which he draws out of the journals, particularly those of the lesser diarists, phrases and descriptions that have not until now received sufficient critical attention. *River of Promise* is a veritable anthology of revealing two to ten word phrases that illuminate the expedition's travels in fascinating, sometimes startling, ways. In other words, Nicandri delivers on his promise to provide the closest reading so far of the journal texts, and all students of Lewis and Clark are indebted to him for work that will inspire and pave the way for other scholars.

Clay S. Jenkinson

Preface

> "*The real voyage of discovery consists not in
> seeking new landscapes but in having new eyes.*"
>
> —Marcel Proust

The western third of the Lewis and Clark trail, what might be called Columbia River country, is both the most underanalyzed segment of the captains' journey and home to some of the expedition's most mythologized episodes. There is a correlation of effect here. The lack of regional treatment has provided fertile ground for mythmaking and fostered several interpretive misunderstandings. This book deconstructs the myths and corrects some misunderstandings by re-examining several of the expedition's key trail experiences. Among these are Meriwether Lewis's vaunted first glance into Columbia country while standing astride the Continental Divide; William Clark's understated response upon reaching the main stem of the great river itself; the expedition's tumultuous encounter with the Northwest coastal environment at trail's end; the "vote" at Station Camp; and the physical and emotional toll the return trip up the Columbia took on Lewis.

Furthermore, by examining the stresses imposed upon the expedition by the Pacific Northwest's complex and often challenging geography, and by analyzing the manner in which certain noteworthy passages found in the journals of Lewis and Clark were composed and sometimes edited, I provide a fresh reading of their exploratory account—one that relates a story different than the conventional, accepted one. In addition to describing the "dynamics" of the journals and their sometimes subtle implications, I also attempt to place the expedition within the context of Enlightenment-era scientific exploration. Once we divest ourselves of the simplistic notion that the journals are a straightforward objective account of events recorded at each night's campfire, and that the main themes recounted therein were unique, we have a new way of seeing the Lewis and Clark Expedition.

While there is a vast literature about the expedition, most of it has a remarkably narrow focus. I refer not merely to the pervasive ethnocentric emphasis on the explorers to the exclusion of indigenous people. Fortunately, a major correction of that deficiency has been underway for some time, going back to James Ronda's *Lewis and Clark among the Indians,* published in 1984. I endeavor in this book to make my own contribution by showing how, in Columbia River country more than any other part of the voyage, interaction between the explorers and Native guides made the Lewis and Clark Expedition a true joint venture of exploration.

Beyond ethnocentricity, however, the literature of the expedition shares another serious limitation—one that persists despite the renewed interest generated by the recently celebrated bicentennial of the expedition (2003–2006). Little in the way of truly new research came out of the observance, and what did was largely derivative of standard interpretations. The principal shortcoming of conventional narratives has been a tendency to limit study of the expedition to its internal corridors of time and space, when in fact Captains Clark and Lewis did not explore in a vacuum. Their minds were no more tabulae rasae than were the landscapes of the northern West they investigated. Looming especially large in the backdrop of their mission was the Scotland-bred fur trader and explorer Alexander Mackenzie, who in the employ of the Montreal-based North West Company established a route west to the Pacific Ocean only a few hundred miles to the north of the path Lewis and Clark would carve a mere a decade later. It is no exaggeration to say that the Lewis and Clark Expedition cannot be fully understood outside the parallel contexts of time, space, literary tradition, and imperial rivalry with Great Britain that Mackenzie's experiences, written account, and national loyalty embodied. Indeed, Mackenzie's *Voyages from Montreal,* published in 1801, serves as a "prequel"—an essential "fourteenth volume"—to the thirteen-volume modern edition of the journals of Lewis and Clark. Many of Mackenzie's stories rhyme with those of Lewis and Clark's narrative of the approach to and travel beyond the Continental Divide. They share certain archetypal features that make the Lewis and Clark voyage seem less exceptional, and in other aspects there is a direct causal relationship between the two expeditions.

Structurally, this book utilizes two concurrent methodologies. Each chapter covers a segment of the story, thus establishing a baseline chronology, and also explicates a larger thesis or two through a deconstruction of the journals' literary content. By intertwining these strategies we begin to redress the neglect of textual information that has allowed the propagation of a formidable mythology about Lewis and Clark, one that poses them as cast-in-bronze heroes and not real people. This approach facilitates, in particular, access to both a new understanding of the explorers' Columbia River story, but also insight into such elusive topics as the controversial death of Meriwether Lewis.

If the Lewis and Clark Expedition played out in the wide expanses of Indian Country, with an overlay of imperial and personal rivalry with Mackenzie and others working for British interests in the West, it also played out within the close confines of a company of individuals. A careful study of the personal interrelationships within the party of American explorers thus yields a host of new perspectives. The journals are not merely a gateway to self-evident narrative content. Their composition, complementarities, inconsistencies, and even their silences are a story unto themselves and an important one that I tell episodically.

In the end, however, exploration is a personal experience, lived by real human beings and not legendary figures. During the recent bicentennial many tried to replicate the journey of Lewis and Clark. This was futile in my view; for the most part we can't see what they saw or even hear what they heard. But maybe, by reading what they read and what they wrote, we can discover them.

David L. Nicandri
March 10, 2009

PROLOGUE   The Voice of
             Meriwether Lewis

ON 12 AUGUST 1805 CAPTAIN MERIWETHER LEWIS AND A
small squad of men crossed the Continental Divide at Lemhi Pass (on the present
border between Montana and Idaho) and descended "to a handsome bold running
Creek of cold Clear water. [H]ere I first tasted the water of the great Columbia
river," Lewis reported. The exhilaration was short-lived. The next day, Lewis later
claimed, (I look more closely at his assertion in chapter two), he learned "unwelcome
information" from Shoshone chief Cameahwait about the difficulties inherent in
following those Columbian waters "to the great lake where the white men lived,"
meaning the Pacific Ocean. Lewis inscribed in his journal for August 14th that the
Shoshone account of lands and rivers west "fell far short of my expectation or wishes."
This all-important observation could serve as the epigram for the entire western
third of the route traversed by the "Expedition for Northwestern Discovery," (as the
venture should be more properly titled). In Columbia River country the command
that Lewis shared with Captain William Clark would face the most formidable
physical obstacles and suffer the worst privations of its mission. The challenge posed
by Columbia country geography is the single most distinguishing feature of the
Lewis and Clark Expedition west of the divide.[1]

    In mid-August Lewis could only imagine the difficulties ahead. By 22
September, they were lived experience. On that day Lewis and the trailing unit
of the detachment stumbled out of the woods of the Bitterroot Mountains onto
Weippe Prairie, in today's north central Idaho. The expedition's oft-told Lolo Trail
story is central to understanding the experience of Lewis and Clark in the Pacific
Northwest. The difficulties of that traverse led, more particularly, to the development that, more than any other factor, has thrown the Columbia River leg of the
expedition into the shadow of better-known segments east of the divide. During
the last half of the Bitterroot crossing, game had grown scarce at the elevated
heights surrounding the pass. Clark led a vanguard ahead of the main party to
hunt for food, and Lewis followed with the main unit. Before eventually reaching Weippe Prairie, Lewis's unit encountered Private Reubin Field, one of the

expedition's most capable hunters and frontiersmen. Field had been sent back up the trail by Clark with some dried fish, roots, and berries secured from a band of the Nez Perce tribe. After gorging on these provisions, Lewis's team proceeded to the Nez Perce village.[2]

Upon his unit's arrival at the village, Lewis recorded the following reflection in his journal: "[T]he pleasure I now felt in having tryumphed over the rocky Mountains and decending once more to a level and fertile country where there was every rational hope of finding a comfortable subsistence for myself and party can be more readily conceived than expressed, nor was the flattering prospect of the final success of the expedition less pleasing." After two more sentences, Meriwether Lewis's journal of westward exploration ceases. Except for some ever-so-brief passages when he was again separated from Clark while searching for an overwintering spot on the Pacific Coast, we do not hear again from Meriwether Lewis until 1 January 1806, by which time he and the party were at Fort Clatsop.[3]

What precipitated this silence is made starkly clear in a succession of observations found in William Clark's journals, beginning the very next day:

September 23rd: "Capt. Lewis & 2 men verry Sick this evening."

September 24th: "several 8 or 9 men Sick, Capt Lewis Sick... . Capt Lewis Scercely able to ride on a jentle horse which was furnished by the [Nez Perce] Chief, Several men So unwell that they were Compelled to lie on the Side of the road for Some time."

September 25th: "Capt Lewis verry Sick."

September 26th: "Capt Lewis Still very unwell."

September 27th: "Capt Lewis very Sick."

September 29th: "Cap Lewis very Sick, and most of the men complaning very much of ther bowels & Stomach."

October 1st: "Capt Lewis getting much better than for Several days past."

October 4th: "Capt Lewis Still Sick but able to walk about a little."

October 5th: "Capt Lewis not So well to day as yesterday"[4]

From this we can only conclude that Lewis was too sick to carry out his duties as commander, including writing his journal. Clark reported on October 6th that he himself was "taken verry unwell with a paine in the bowels & Stomach, which is certainly the effects of my diet." Nevertheless, he mustered sufficient strength to record this and other observations associated with the expected departure by canoe via waters that would take them to the Pacific Ocean. On 7 October 1805 the expedition "Set out." As for his own personal circumstances once the voyage resumed, Clark made a key point: "I continu verry unwell but obliged to attend every thing," a crucial reference to the even more diminished capacity of Lewis.[5]

While the malady (what Clark called a "*Lax* & heaviness at the Stomack") befell many—it appears at times most—members of the expedition, Lewis seems to have been the most severely affected. A safe deduction from Clark's account holds that from September 25th until at least October 7th Meriwether Lewis was laid prostrate by the effects of a change of diet from meat to that of roots and dried fish, or exposure to bacteria on the salmon, quite possibly in combination with physical and mental exhaustion. Two years earlier, Henry Dearborn, Thomas Jefferson's Secretary of War, upon learning that Lewis had succeeded in gaining senior accompaniment, told the president that Clark's addition to the roster contributed "very much to the ballance of chances in favour of ultimate success." Indeed, Dearborn's observation betrays a foreknowledge of Lewis's limitations. Jefferson amplified Dearborn's insight in a letter to Lewis that reached him while he was still encamped on the Mississippi in late 1803. The president told Lewis that having Clark with him now meant the expedition was "double manned, & therefore the less liable to failure." As it would turn out, Clark was constantly vital to the success of the entire expedition, but the insurance value of having a second commander was never more important than during the journey from the Nez Perce villages on the Clearwater River to the Pacific Ocean.[6]

In *Undaunted Courage*, now the interpretive standard for the expedition if only because of its immense popularity, Stephen Ambrose was riveted by the question of *why* Lewis was an inconstant writer. Ambrose's solution to this conundrum became one of his book's lasting legacies. Gaps in Lewis's journal-keeping, Ambrose argued, evidenced a manic-depression illness that ultimately led to his suicide as well, a topic to which we will return later in this book. Whatever the reason for Lewis's silence, the loss of his "voice" coming out of the Bitterroot Mountains of northern Idaho has had the important effect of diminishing the interpretive potency of the expedition's story westward from the Nez Perce villages. Correspondingly, a significant shortcoming in the literature of the expedition has been the relatively small amount of analysis given to the voyage down the Snake and Columbia Rivers compared to the Missourian phases.[7]

Lewis *may* have stopped writing because of some psychological disorder, as Ambrose posits, but there are other cases to be made. The triumphant passage he wrote as he emerged from the mountains at Weippe Prairie connotes a belief that the expedition would now inevitably be successful, or that the hard part was behind them; in other words, it portends a kind of emotional let-down. Or, as suggested earlier, Lewis may have dropped his pen because he could not cope with the gastric distress that befell him. In any event, contrary to Ambrose's assertion that Lewis was "as active as always" as soon as the downriver voyage from the Nez Perce homelands commenced, a fair reading of the journals indicates that Lewis played a diminished and distinctly secondary role to Clark's for weeks thereafter. Until, in a quest for Pacific glory, he bolts from the balance of the company marooned at Dismal Nitch, Lewis comes across as a markedly lesser figure in the expeditionary narrative on the Snake and Columbia.[8]

As we shall see later at length, it was a characteristic of Lewis's literary flair that he always made himself the central figure of the story. For example, leaving Fort Mandan in April 1805, Lewis was not shy about likening his venture to famous explorers such as Columbus or James Cook. As Stephen Ambrose said in

Undaunted Courage: "It is through Lewis's eyes and words that we see the White Cliffs, the Great Falls before the dams, the Gates of the Mountains, Three Forks, the Shoshones. Wonderful portraits, all. Vivid. Immediate. Detailed." His poetic description of the Great Falls of the Missouri is justly considered a classic in American literature.[9]

In contrast, the narrative for the whirlwind and often dramatic trip down the Snake and Columbia Rivers is absent the literary touch Lewis lent to the Missouri River stories mentioned above. William Clark, neither poet nor practiced word-smith, became by default the principal chronicler of the end of the outbound voyage. Despite his no-frills style, however, Clark's understated journal entries, if properly mined, provide a rich account. Gary Moulton, editor of the modern edition of the *Journals of Lewis and Clark,* granted that, while of the two Lewis was the more stylish, and Clark's writing "lacked polish," neither Clark's vocabulary "nor his ideas were those of a backwoodsman." [10]

Lewis had such natural talent as a writer that historians have found it easier to interpret the parts of the expedition he describes with his muscular and occasionally florid prose, to the neglect of segments or stories narrated by others. One of the major goals of this book is addressing that neglect and rebalancing posterity's view of William Clark as an explorer, both as field commander and scientist. Furthermore, if William Clark's modest, at times disjointed, and undervalued text needs greater visibility, then so do the frequently overlooked contributions of Sergeants Patrick Gass and John Ordway, and especially those of Private Joseph Whitehouse.[11]

One result of broadening the textual base beyond Lewis is a more nuanced understanding of the dynamics of the expedition and the journals that document it. As James Ronda has recently noted, the Lewis and Clark story is usually told "with one set of voices reading from the same script and without any chance that other words and lines might be possible." Accidents or miscalculations "never quite make it into our thinking," Ronda states. My aim is to present an unvarnished history of the expedition from the Continental Divide to the Pacific Ocean and back to the crest of North America. With a close reading of *all* the journals, one finds that there is more to the story of Lewis and Clark in the Northwest than readily meets the eye.[12]

Above all, I have tried to tell the Lewis and Clark story west of the Continental Divide with the same sense of contingency the explorers themselves lived with. Ronda reminds us that the study of Lewis and Clark has lost what they had—"a sense of uncertainty" about what the expedition would accomplish or discover. "We have smoothed out the rough places and rounded off the sharp corners," Ronda observes. "Doing that," he continues, "we deny the past and what we accept most about the present"—wondering about how it's all going to turn out.[13]

It may seem that a field with as voluminous a literature as Lewis and Clark studies, which burgeoned during the recently concluded bicentennial, is over-labored. Indeed, it's been argued that the journals of Lewis and Clark have already been mined for all they are worth. This argument is premised on the naïve assumption that the journals of the captains' have been read critically. A number of commentators, including Ronda, have called for "fresh readings of the Lewis and Clark journals." Such work, it must be said, has only begun and is much in need. Clay Jenkinson suggests that "new close readings of the journals" will result in "liberation from the conventional (and largely mythic) national master narrative that has been permitted to pass for real history for so long." [14]

In preparing this book I've attempted the new readings of the journals that Ronda and Jenkinson have called for. At salient points in this analysis I will attempt to contrast trail lore—what Jenkinson has termed the "self-enclosed universe of LEWIS & CLARK"—with new insights gleaned from a reading of the journals as subjective texts (a casting of the story by the explorers for reasons associated with personal privilege or sentiment) and not empirical writ (indisputable truth). In so doing I hope to supplant the conventional perspective—"being in the shoes of Lewis and Clark"—with what Mark Spence denominates as the bold new one: getting "inside their heads." Doing so is inherently risky because it involves making unorthodox speculations and reading sometimes literally between the lines of journal entries, directly challenging received wisdom about the expedition. [15]

Perhaps the one aspect of the story most in need of being unpacked and looked at from this new perspective is the dynamic between the captains. Lewis and Clark may have engaged the same landscapes and native people, but they were not interchangeable in their responses. There has been a formidable "rounding off the sharp edges" (to use Ronda's idiom) in the common understanding of Clark's relationship to Lewis, as several episodes recounted in this book will indicate.

Essential to getting "inside the heads" of Lewis and Clark is an understanding of the intellectual environment that was their milieu. James Ronda observes that, while Lewis and Clark are fixtures in the history of the American West, "they have yet to be put in the wider context" of Enlightenment-era exploration. The most important figure in this regard was Alexander Mackenzie, the fur trader and explorer for the North West Company operating in British Canada. Mackenzie's travel narrative, *Voyages from Montreal,* was, in John Logan Allen's estimation, the most extensively promoted exploratory account up to the time of its publication. The geopolitical origins of what became known as the Lewis and Clark Expedition, many of the captains' tactics, and, I believe, their greatest disappointment, were all tied to the precedence of Alexander Mackenzie. It is only within the context of what might be called the Mackenzian paradigm that we take Lewis and Clark out of their isolation and achieve a more faithful understanding of their lives as explorers. Providing an effective American exploratory response to, while also living up to the expository standards of, British imperial agents like James Cook, George Vancouver, and above all Mackenzie, was a daunting physical and intellectual challenge for the captains, especially for Meriwether Lewis. This was a responsibility, frankly, that Lewis failed to meet, and his inability to become an Enlightenment figure like Cook or Mackenzie contributed mightily to his physical dissolution. [16]

This book, then, is a history of a particular set of people—the Expedition for Northwestern Discovery—their encounters with native people and the troublesome geography of the Pacific Northwest, and their narrative response to it. It's a story of ideas, human foibles, and place, or really, many places—the snowfields, thick forests, raging waters, arid plains, and rocky canyons of the Columbia River watershed. The physical environment of the Northwest and its aboriginal inhabitants are not a mere backdrop to the history of the expedition in this region—they are central to the story. Comprehending and coping with this land was Lewis and Clark's most demanding physical and mental challenge.

CHAPTER I

The Great River
of the West

BY AUGUST OF 1805, MERIWETHER LEWIS WAS DESPERATE
to find the Shoshone Indians. Lewis had long deemed the Shoshones and their
horses essential for the portage across the Continental Divide. Once beyond
the divide, Lewis expected to find the waters that would take the expedition to
their ultimate destination—the Pacific Ocean. Lewis, accompanied by George
Drouillard and John Shields, jumped ahead of William Clark and the rest of
the party who were struggling to bring the heavily laden canoes up the shallow
headwaters of the Missouri. By August 12th Lewis's squad had traveled nearly to
the crest of the continent on their scouting mission. The Shoshones were briefly
sighted, but eluded actual contact. Their trail over Lemhi Pass, however, was very
evident. For that reason Lewis recorded in his notebook that he "did not dispair
of shortly finding a passage over the mountains and of taisting the waters of the
great Columbia this evening." [1]

Had Lewis known that over the next two months his efforts to understand
the complex geography of the Columbia River basin would be thoroughly confounded, he may indeed have despaired. To appreciate the challenges Lewis faced
in making sense of the tangled Columbia watershed let us first explore the hazy
understanding he and Clark had of the promise of this Great River of the West
plus its origins and course on the verge of their first encounter with its waters.

Geographical lore from the time of seventeenth-century French explorers
Marquette, Hennepin and LaSalle posited a single mountain chain in the western
interior, beyond which a great river flowed west to the Pacific Ocean. British cartography in the early eighteenth century reinforced the early French theory with
speculative depictions of a river with hydraulic capacity equal to the Missouri that
coursed to the Pacific from heights the rivers shared in common. Closer to Jefferson's
time, Peter Pond, an American employed by the North West Company of Montreal
who had travelled in the western interior, presented the United States Congress
with a map in 1784. This map adhered to the erroneous French theory about a single
range of western mountains, a notion that had misled generations of armchair and

practical geographers about the true complexity of the Rocky Mountain system. Faithful to the orthodox view, Pond's map showed a westward flowing river emanating from a narrow ridge opposite the headwaters of the Missouri. Remarkably enough, Pond speculatively placed the common wellspring of these great rivers at the 45th parallel—precisely the latitude of a mountain crossing that would be first charted by Lewis and Clark and later named Lemhi Pass.[2]

Pond's guesswork was soon followed by American fur trader Robert Gray's actual discovery of the mouth of the Columbia River in 1792, and the more purposeful explorations conducted by George Vancouver and Alexander Mackenzie, working on behalf of British interests. Through their combined efforts actual geographic information about the great western river finally began to supplant hopeful theorizing. Gray and Vancouver established the Columbia River's mouth at the 46th parallel, a promising development since it was nearly the same latitude theorized (by Pond and others) for the headwaters of the Missouri, and the presumed gateway to the Pacific from the interior of the continent. Alexander Mackenzie complemented the work of the maritime explorers in 1792 with his 1793 discovery of a sizable, southward flowing stream that he reasonably believed to be the great "River of the West's" principal northern fork, if not the main stem. Despite the fact that Mackenzie found his river not opposite the Missouri, but in today's north central British Columbia, in American circles the mythic ideal of the Missouri sharing adjoining sources with a major stream flowing due west held sway as the last great hope for the fabled Northwest Passage.[3]

The unsettled and contested state of geographical knowledge about the West can be seen in President Thomas Jefferson's message to Congress on 18 January 1803 requesting funding for what would become known as the Lewis and Clark Expedition. In his request, Jefferson didn't even mention the Columbia by name. Instead, he hypothesized the more general notion of a great western river by which an "intelligent officer with ten or twelve chosen men, fit for the enterprize and willing to undertake it… might explore the whole line, even to the Western ocean." It's worth noting here that the size of the detachment Jefferson established as the requisite was modeled by Alexander Mackenzie during his preceding explorations.[4]

In his ensuing correspondence with friends and confidants in Philadelphia's scientific community Jefferson repeatedly stated that the Missouri was to be explored along with "whatever river," flowing, like the Missouri, from deep within the interior of the continent, ran to the Pacific Ocean. Jefferson's field instructions to Lewis, prepared later that spring, clarified this picture only by the slightest of degrees. "The object of your mission," the president directed, "is to explore the Missouri river, & such principal stream of it, as, by it's course and communication with the waters of the Pacific ocean, whether the Columbia, Oregan, Colorado or any other river may offer the most direct & practicable water communication across this continent for the purposes of commerce."[5]

The vagueness found in Jefferson's communications at the outset of the enterprise was rooted not only in geographic uncertainty but also diplomatic discretion (given that Louisiana had yet to be acquired from France), and domestic circumstances. In regard to the latter, Jefferson, as a strict constructionist, was concerned that his partisan opponents would object to the thin constitutional foundation for an exploratory venture into the West sponsored solely by the executive branch. Furthermore, the lack of geographic specificity in Jefferson's definition of mission scope is attributable to the fact that, Mackenzie's presumed northern fork notwithstanding, only the lower-most section of the Columbia was indisputably "fixed." The river was named by Gray after his ship, *Columbia Rediviva*, in May 1792, but the little that was generally known about its western extent was actually attributable to the efforts of an Englishman, Lt. William R. Broughton, in service of Captain George Vancouver, commander of the *Discovery*. In a cutter and a larger launch from the *Discovery's* escort, the *Chatham,* anchored near the ocean, Broughton and a squad of men rowed up the Columbia in October 1792 as far as Cottonwood Point near today's Washougal, Washington. Broughton's certain geographic findings combined with Mackenzie's speculative conclusions, as engraved by the influential British cartographer Aaron Arrowsmith, eventually found their way into a map prepared by the American government for Lewis's use in the field. Drafted by Nicholas King, this map's pertinent feature was the "River Oregon" which, east of Mounts Rainier and Hood (named by Vancouver and Broughton respectively) split into northerly and east/southeasterly branches of equal size. The latter filled an entire quadrant of King's map otherwise devoid of imagery all the way to the Rocky Mountains. This fork was properly denoted as "conjectural" since no Euro-American had ever seen such a stream. The imperially neutral name "Oregan," which King borrowed from Arrowsmith, in contradistinction to the Americanist "Columbia," shows how ephemeral Gray's finding was even among his own countrymen, a point which would loom large with Lewis and Clark when they reached the main stem of the great river themselves.[6]

The northern fork of the "Oregan" on first Arrowsmith's map and then King's, headed in today's British Columbia. Close to its source the river bore the name Tacoutche Tesse, as denominated by Native informants to Alexander Mackenzie. This North West Company fur trader turned scientific explorer came upon a large southward flowing river during his cross-continental trek in July 1793, coincidentally the same month Gray returned to his home port of Boston, and Broughton to his in England. While we are not certain of the extent to which Gray and his corporate sponsors privately touted the geographic and related commercial prospects attendant upon his discovery of the Columbia River, we do know that press reaction to Gray's return to port could not have been more perfunctory. The *Independent Chronicle* of Boston, on 1 August 1793, reported: "Last Friday arrived at this port the ship *Columbia*, Capt. Gray, from *China*, which she left the 9th of February." Analyzing this account, Robert Ruby and John Brown observed that "Gray's second journey had created a lesser stir on the east coast than it had on the west" among the Chinook Indians. The discovery of the long-sought Great River of the West warranted no mention in this first report of Gray's voyage.[7]

Meanwhile, because of imperial considerations, the British Admiralty wanted to control the release of information from Vancouver's coastal reconnaissance, at least until such time as Vancouver himself returned to Great Britain, which turned out to be October 1795. Vancouver's three-volume *Voyage of Discovery* was published in late August or early September 1798 and included an inset map of Broughton's Columbia River survey on plate 5 of the Atlas. Consistent with Vancouver's narrative, the Atlas refers to the "River Columbia." However, a separate map engraved by Arrowsmith was published in November 1798 titled: "Plan of the River Oregon from an Actual Survey." This, of course, was a reference to Broughton's work, and it pointedly avoided the American-derived nomenclature "Columbia." Though Vancouver himself graciously conceded the appropriateness of Gray's place name for the river, this was a difficult concession for imperial interests in London to make. As Arrowsmith and his patrons saw it, most of the exploration of the river's lower extent and seemingly its upper reaches as well had been conducted by His Majesty's agents. All of this jockeying of names took place within the context of what jurist Robert Miller has delineated as the "Doctrine of Discovery," the prescriptive path by which European powers could preemptively claim title to lands occupied by indigenous people, the fundamental but not sole criterion of which was the first sighting and naming of a part of the world no other person of European ancestry had visited.[8]

Mackenzie did not return to Upper Canada from his western explorations until the late summer of 1794. In a letter written on September 10 of that year from the settlement that was to become Toronto, Mackenzie reported to John Graves Simcoe, a British colonial official, that after crossing the Continental Divide in the northern latitudes he'd made his way to the "Tacoutch Tesse." This river, Mackenzie wrote, took "too much a Southern Course to bring me to the sea as soon as I expected, and from the best information I could procure judged it did not discharge itself to the northward of the River of the West; a Branch if not the whole I take it to be." In other words, without any conceivable knowledge of the explorations of either Gray or Vancouver, Mackenzie assumed that he had discovered the long-sought-after river that in some measure corresponded to geographic lore. Only later, either by word of mouth circulating within commercial fur trade circles or from British colonial sources, would Mackenzie learn of the Gray/Broughton/Vancouver geographic discourse and the name of the river, Columbia, that he too presumed to have discovered, albeit by land from Canada and at its northern extremity. This post-expeditionary knowledge led Mackenzie to conclude that his Tacoutche Tesse was indeed the Columbia of Gray, or a tributary thereto, an insight he incorporated into his narrative, *Voyages from Montreal*, published in Great Britain in 1801. With this publication Mackenzie laid the foundation for a British counterclaim to the Columbia and otherwise prompted Jefferson into action. However, unbeknownst to all at the time, Mackenzie had actually stumbled upon what is now known as the Fraser River, a misidentification that would not become evident until 1808, two years after Lewis and Clark reached the Pacific Ocean and returned to the United States.[9]

King's conjectural southeastern branch of the Great River of the West flowed out of the Rockies from a point conveniently adjacent to the imagined location of the headwaters of the Missouri River. Here King was adhering to the traditional supposition that the West's major river systems flowed from the heights of a common source area. King's southern fork was an act of pure invention, but it had the appeal of fulfilling the then-reigning theory of symmetrical geography and counterpoise. These classic notions held that the earth's architecture required continental landmasses and river systems to mirror or balance one another. Thus, Mackenzie's northern fork required a sizable southern branch of equal dimension. Furthermore, as we shall see later, King's conjectural river reified two American imperial desiderata. First, a large *southern* fork would trump Mackenzie's claim in the north. Second, and better yet, a southern fork of the Columbia that shared a source with the Missouri promised an "All American" trade route to the Pacific that would avoid British entanglements altogether. King's map was commissioned by Secretary of the Treasury Albert Gallatin, the cabinet member who seems to have most identified with Jefferson's geographic ambitions for the venture. Indeed, in a review of the president's instructions to Lewis, Gallatin observed that exploring the Columbia River was "the principal object of this voyage." [10]

While Mackenzie had published a brief sketch of the presumed northern fork, George Vancouver's description of Broughton's explorations was the only extensive account of the Columbia River available when the Lewis and Clark Expedition began. Broughton himself believed the Columbia's source was in the vicinity of Mount Hood. Thus neither British account when published juxtaposed Columbian headwaters with the Missouri. Natives residing in what's now the Portland metropolitan area told Broughton of falling water further upstream, probably a reference to the Cascades or the rapids at Celilo. Given his belief that Mount Hood was the probable source of the river and considering the obvious height of the mountain, Broughton probably did not find the Native reports of falling water exceptional, nor did he grasp the Indians' likely intended message: that the river ran a long distance into the interior. Edward Bell, clerk on the *Chatham* who accompanied Broughton on the Columbia reconnaissance, speculated that in their estimated 127-mile voyage upstream they had probably traversed half the river's length. Vancouver himself, summing up his lieutenant's decision to end exploration and return to the *Chatham* at the estuary, stated: "Mr. Broughton gave up the idea of any further examination, and was reconciled to this measure, because even thus far the river could hardly be considered as navigable for shipping." [11]

Donald Jackson asserted that Thomas Jefferson was familiar with but did not own a set of Vancouver's multi-volume *Voyage of Discovery*. Given the large number of references to Vancouver in the Columbia River portion of the American expedition's journals, we can assume Lewis had access to Vancouver's account when he was interning in Philadelphia; certainly he was familiar with the atlas. One of Jefferson's regular correspondents, the French naturalist Bernard Lacépède, was intimately familiar with Vancouver's narrative, and offered the president an

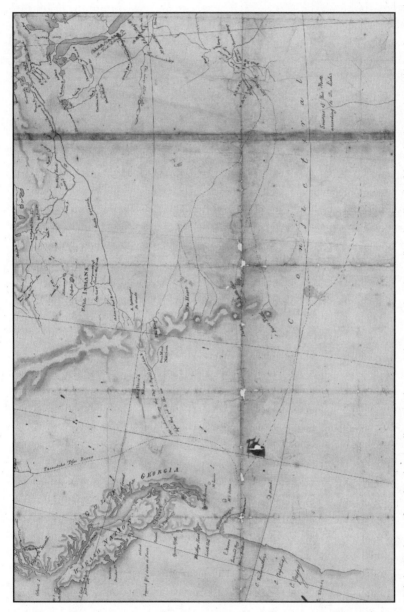

Nicholas King's map of 1803, based principally on British cartography, projected a conjectural southern branch of the Columbia (see lower right quadrant) mirroring the northern fork presumed to have been visited by Alexander Mackenzie. Based on decades worth of geographical speculation and American imperial fantasy and not field observation, King's imaginary southern fork originated near the headwaters of the Missouri River. It was drawn carefully so as to equal the length of the northern branch thought to have been discovered by Mackenzie. (Library of Congress, Geography and Map Division)

interpretation of its significance in a letter received in Washington, DC, in July 1803. The planned American expedition to the West (of which Jefferson had written earlier), Lacépède said, "could well [find] the *Colombia*" at the promised spot opposite the headwaters of the Missouri River. Lacépède correctly gauged that where the British voyagers turned around, the Columbia was "still far from its source," a deduction he came to as a function of the great depth of the river where Broughton terminated exploration. But, as it had for Broughton, Mount Hood also challenged Lacépède's ability to comprehend continental structure. Such an eminence, Lacépède told Jefferson, was a likely "dependence of the *Stony mountains*." The notion of a single range of western mountains was so axiomatic in the minds of this generation of geographers that the possibility of another major chain of mountains running north/south to the west of the Rockies had not yet been conceived of, let alone fully discerned. [12]

Jefferson promptly forwarded Lewis a digest of Lacépède's geographic analysis, including the key provision that where Broughton left the Columbia it was "far then to it's head." Since the Missouri had its origins in the Rocky Mountains of which Lacépède imagined Mount Hood was a part, any number of conjectures could have crowded Lewis's mind upon receiving this letter from the president. How far west was the fount of the Missouri? Was the Columbia a long river or a short one? What were its flow and speed? And what was the extent, that is, the breadth, of the Rocky Mountains? [13]

W. Kaye Lamb, the modern editor of Vancouver's *Voyage,* was critical of the various geographic deductions accompanying Broughton's decision to turn back. Lamb noted that "Broughton would have been astonished to learn that he had left over a thousand miles of the Columbia unexplored." Lamb also says Broughton "should have" known better than to ascribe the profusion of driftwood found at the limits of his exploration to the effects of "an unusually high tide," rather than spring freshets. However, these criticisms, and by analogy today's ubiquitous claims of what Lewis and Clark *should have* known about the world west of the Continental Divide, are modern anachronisms. In 1803, Thomas Jefferson and Meriwether Lewis understood only that Robert Gray's Columbia was a river of significant magnitude, but were far from certain about its origins and courses, given Broughton's brief reconnaissance, Lacépède's armchair geography, and Mackenzie's (mistaken) notion that he had discovered its northern and possibly main fork. The only Europeans, it turns out, who had actually *been* on the Columbia thought the river was about 250 miles in length. [14]

Thus, Lewis and Clark arrived in the vicinity of St. Louis for the winter of 1803–04 with a hope, based on a combination of actual exploration, theoretical conjecture, and mistaken identification, of following the Missouri to a fountainhead near the 45th parallel and, close by, making contact with what they projected to be the major southern fork of the Columbia, a stream that would take them, in turn, to the Pacific Ocean. Meriwether Lewis himself summed all this up in a recently discovered letter sent to his friend James Findley after having launched the voyage up the Missouri in 1804. Presumably citing such authorities as Lacépède, King, and the principles of theoretical geography, Lewis told Findley there "are substantial grounds for a belief that these rivers [i.e., the Missouri and Columbia] derive their sources from the same quarter of the continent; and I think it not improbable that some of their navigable streams may pass contiguous to each other." Here we see that the conjectural construct of Nicholas King had become a practical necessity, certainly an expectation. [15]

Upon reaching St. Louis, Lewis and Clark entered a zone of enhanced understanding about western rivers. The principal and most comprehensive information available at the time about the Missouri River, its upper reaches, and supposed connection to the Great River of the West was derived from the 1795-97 expedition of James Mackay and John Evans. These men were British expatriates enlisted in a last ditch effort by Spanish colonial officials to re-impose their sovereignty over the Missouri River basin. The Spanish were specifically concerned about the presence of British fur traders (which Mackay had once been) working in and around the Mandan Indian villages in today's North Dakota. Mackay, the leader of this expedition as it headed out from St. Louis, only made it up the Missouri as far as present-day Nebraska. Evans, however, was dispatched from that point upstream with the goal of not merely reaching the Mandans and Hidatsas, but traversing the entire width of the continent to the Pacific and back. In the end Evans, too, cut short his venture, turning at the Mandan villages, but in getting that far he accessed detailed Native insights into western topography covering almost the whole of Montana, and hints about the country west of there. [16]

Evans prepared several maps showing the route of the expedition from St. Louis to the Mandans, but of greatest interest to our story is one showing the far western extent of the Missouri. From his Mandan and Hidatsa informants, Evans learned of a western landscape considerably at odds with the lore of armchair geographers, including the estimable Thomas Jefferson. Evans' projection of Native understandings, for example, showed the Missouri coursing by or through four ranges of mountains, whereas Jefferson, in his message to Congress requesting an appropriation for the expedition, seemed to promise a simple ridgeline and a short portage from the Missouri to a river flowing to "the western ocean." This would have been Lewis's naïve expectation as well, upon leaving Jefferson's company. [17]

Lewis and Clark came into possession of a set of Evans' maps and related information in St. Louis. We know this because of the large number of references to this cartographic record made during the lower Missouri phase of their voyage, including the telling fact that Clark scrawled the word "Conjecturall" on a copy of Evans' map depicting the upper Missouri near the Continental Divide. Raymond Wood, the foremost scholar of the Mackay-Evans Expedition, says Clark's one-word note revealed his "pessimism about the map's precision." Curiously, Clark's wording replicated Nicholas King's terminology about the Columbia River. It may also be said that Clark's "editorializing" reflected wishful thinking because Evans' map cracked the long-standing image of an easy portage across the Continental Divide and therefore the prospective utility of the route he and Lewis were hoping to establish for the United States.[18]

Evans' journal contained equally interesting detail complementing his map. Based on his sources, Evans stated, the Missouri River initially ran from its head in a northerly direction (true), then "between the chains of the Rocky Mountains" (true) consider this the Gates of the Mountains in Lewis and Clark nomenclature, near Helena, Montana) until it approached the 49th parallel where it turned east (true), whence "it falls over the East chain of the mountains" and then across the plains until it reached the Mandans (true). "This fall," by which he meant the Great Falls of the Missouri, was said to be "an astonishing height" (also correct). Evans' journal also spoke intriguingly about the plains continuing as far as the falls (true), west of which "the Country then begins to be Absolutely Covered with trees (partly correct), even upon the Rocky Mountains and it is probable these trees extend to the Pacific Ocean." Only the very last observation is less than completely accurate, and its construction suggests that it is a deduction Evans made, as opposed to what the Mandan and Hidatsa Indians told him with remarkable accuracy. Lewis and Clark took their lesson about the country west of the divide from the same Native sources a mere seven years later.[19]

Once Lewis and Clark established Fort Mandan as their interior post for the winter of 1804–1805, they quizzed the Hidatsa and Mandan villagers for intelligence about western topography at every opportunity, gleaning additional information about a westerly flowing river interfacing with the Missouri. In the first published account of the expedition paraphrased from the journals into a continuous narrative by Nicholas Biddle, a map of the upper reaches of the Missouri River was deemed a more precious gift from a chief than the sexual favors of his wife. Meriwether Lewis, in his comprehensive summary of geographic findings for the first year of exploration (May–October 1804) written at Fort Mandan, concluded with a forecast of the Missouri River's tributaries expected to be encountered during the forthcoming season of discovery. The "information has been obtained on this subject," Lewis wrote, "in the course of the winter, from a number of individuals questioned seperately and at different times. [T]he information thus obtained has been carefully compared, and those points only, in which they generally agreed, have been retained." Characteristically, William Clark was slightly more circumspect on these matters. In a letter to his brother-in-law written less than a week before the expedition headed west from Fort Mandan, Clark said: "Country and River above this but little Known. Our information is altogether from Indians collected at different times and entitled to some credit." This last statement was not altogether true in that Clark had previously seen Evans's "Conjecturall" map. Even a modest man like Clark did not want to be seen, even by his family, as reliant on the work of other explorers.[20]

What, precisely, did Lewis and Clark know (or presume to understand given the vagaries of translation) about the Columbia River while at Fort Mandan? Above the Great Falls of the Missouri, the Medicine River (today's Sun River) flowed into it. The Medicine River had its source in the Rocky Mountains "oppo-site to a river which also takes it's rise in the same mountains and which running West to the Pacific Ocean discharges itself into a large river, which passes at no great distance from the Rocky mountains, running from N to South." Promising as this prospect may have seemed at first, Lewis and Clark were not disposed to take what would prove in the end to be a more direct route between the Missouri and the Columbia via the Clark Fork and the Bitterroot Valley, because this west-ward-flowing stream opposite the Medicine was said to pass through "a moun-tainous, broken and woody country." In this description we can hear the echo of Evans' journal about the far west being "Absolutely Covered with trees." Worse yet for voyageurs, this interface with the Medicine was thought "not navigable in consequence of its rapidity and shoals." Besides which, Jefferson's instructions to Lewis had been clear on the matter of source-hunting, as both lore and theory promised that tracing the Missouri to its headwaters would reveal a connection with the Columbia or another stream that could take them to the Pacific. Lewis's letter to his friend Findley, cited earlier, said as much.[21]

The Medicine River, which Lewis assessed on the return trip in 1806, was not explicitly referred to at Fort Mandan as a connector between the Missouri and the Columbian waters. Evans never learned of the Medicine River, indicating that the native sources he had in common with Lewis and Clark did not invest this route with much significance. In any event, Lewis and Clark were inclined to believe that one had to reach the ultimate extent of the Missouri in order to reli-ably rendezvous with the Columbia, and the Hidatsa themselves gave the captains specific directions to the great western river. To access it, the Hidatsa said, the Americans would have to go up the Missouri to its three forks and then over the dividing ridge. On the other side of the crest separating "the waters of the Atlantic from those of the Pacific ocean," Lewis wrote, was yet another "large river which washes [the mountains'] Western base, running from S to N." Since this descrip-tion perfectly reflected the expectations created by Pond and later by Nicholas King, Clark and Lewis concluded that the Indians at Fort Mandan must surely be talking about the Great River of the West—the Columbia—their route to the Pacific. For the moment, Mackenzie's discovery and its implications were conve-niently forgotten, perhaps suppressed, supplanted by a more hopeful geography.[22]

Given that the Medicine River route was actually a shortcut to the Bitterroot Valley west of the Rockies, why didn't the Hidatsa put this option forward more forcefully? After all, when Lewis and Clark eventually reached Traveler's Rest, the Salish-Kootenai Indians there humbled the explorers by pointing out the distinct-ly shorter Medicine River link between the Missouri and Columbia's waters. First, the Hidatsa were probably more familiar with the three forks route, home of the more easily manipulated Shoshone Indians, than they were about the Medicine River which coursed through the homelands of the far more formidable Blackfoot Nation. The experiences of Sacagawea (a Shoshone woman taken captive by the Hidatsa who, years later, joined the expedition at the Mandan villages as

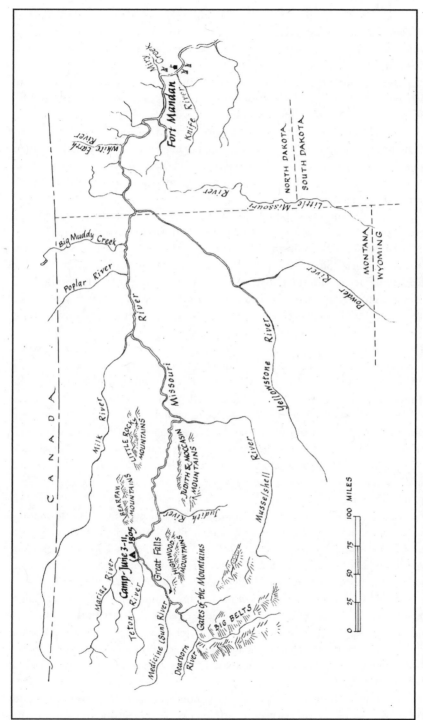

This map shows the major tributaries of the Missouri west of Fort Mandan and the arrangement of mountain ranges in north central Montana. (from *Lewis and Clark and the Image of the American Northwest* by John Logan Allen, courtesy Dover Publications, Inc.)

an interpreter) reflect, in part, the balance of military power on the plains. Second, trade considerations may have been at play. British fur traders had long been established on the upper Missouri and had been bad-mouthing Lewis and Clark to the local tribes. Indeed, it would take another twenty-five years after Lewis and Clark passed through the region for American fur traders to gain parity with the British in terms of commercial relations with the tribes of the northern plains. The British fur man, Alexander Henry, visiting the vicinity of Fort Mandan in 1806, claimed the Hidatsa were "disgusted at the high sounding language the American captains bestowed upon themselves." Though Henry would have had his own reasons for propagating this perspective, the Hidatsa may have withheld some information about western topography from the Americans out of loyalty to their preferred trading partners.[23]

Indirectly, yet another tribe of Indians may have influenced the expedition's eventual route. Unbeknownst to the captains until their return trip, members of the Nez Perce Nation were in the Mandan villages shortly after Lewis and Clark left those precincts. Since we must presume this was *not* the first time the Nez Perce had interacted with the Hidatsa, as a Columbia River tribe they would have had occasion to inform the Plains Indians about the streams and lands west of the divide. The Hidatsa themselves, Lewis reported, never went farther west in their "war exurtions" than "the top of thes[e] mountains."[24]

There is evidence of Nez Perce geographic intelligence embedded in Lewis's Fort Mandan summary. The great river running from south to north at the western base of the dividing ridge, Lewis noted, was "at no great distance" from the "*Flat head* Indians [who] live in one considerable village on the western border of this river." Uncertainty reigned, then as now, as to which tribes the term "Flathead" encompassed and the origin of the name. Nevertheless, we know that the captains, as evidenced in the subsequent use of the terminology, (as in "Flatheads of the Kooskooske," the explorers' name for the Clearwater River in Idaho) were normally referencing the Nez Perce by this name, and likely so in their Hidatsa geography lesson.[25]

Furthermore, the Nez Perce would have been the obvious source of information about the great northward flowing river on the Pacific side of the divide and the terrain to the west. This country, Lewis and Clark learned at Fort Mandan, was "open & level plains like the [Hidatsa] inhabit, with a number of barren sandy nobs irregularly scattered over the face of the country." This we must surmise is a reference to the hills, buttes and scablands of the Palouse country and Snake River plains. Hereby Lewis and Clark acquired a novel and accurate insight about the Columbia River and the adjoining country in contrast to John Evans's mistaken impression about a forested landscape running from the Rockies to the Pacific Ocean.[26]

Most convincingly, the "Flatheads" of Lewis's cognizance at Fort Mandan partook of a "large fish, which they take in the river on which they reside." This is a clear reference to the then-prodigious salmon fishery on the Snake River and its tributaries. It could *not* have been a reference to the Salish-Kootenai of the

Bitterroot and other western valleys in Montana. As Lewis and Clark would discern in September 1805, impediments on the Clark Fork/Bitterroot tributaries to the Columbia did not allow salmon to pass to Salish-Kootenai homelands. Finally, the Hidatsa reported that the Shoshone visited this same "Western river at certain seasons of the year, for the purpose of taking fish which they dry in the sun and transport on horses to their villages on the three forks of the Missouri." All this geographic intelligence about a river west of the divide that ran south to north towards a possible junction with Mackenzie's northern fork led Lewis to a bold conclusion. "This river we suppose to be the S. fork of the Columbia, and the fish the Salmon, with which we are informed the Columbia river abounds. [T]his river is said to be rapid but as far as the Indian informants are acquainted with it is not intercepted with shoals." [27]

William Clark's cartographic complement to Lewis's narrative explication, including a summary table of western rivers he composed at Fort Mandan, conforms to Lewis's assessment. Their expedition would first have to proceed above the Missouri's great falls, past the Medicine River, and proceed through the rocky defiles at the first gate of the mountains to the three forks of the Missouri. From there Clark projected the course "to a large River on the west of the mountain." With that, Clark's catalogue of western information ends. Clark's map, which was to be sent back down the Missouri to President Jefferson when the bulk of the party headed west in the spring of 1805, had been a work in progress for many months, presumably in tandem with his table of western rivers. Beginning as early as 16 December 1804 with an Indian sketch of the upper Missouri provided by North West Company trader Hugh Heney, Clark began pulling his thoughts together. His map was underway by the first week of January. The Mandan Chief Sheheke provided a sketch "as far as the high mountains." Later Clark attempted to persuade a Hidatsa chief out of attacking the Shoshone and in so doing coaxed out of him "a Chart in his way of the Missourie." By early March 1805 Clark had completed his map. [28]

The last word on the captains' geographic assessment of the Great River of the West at Fort Mandan was contained in a letter Lewis wrote to his mother, Lucy Marks, the week before the expedition left their winter confines. One passage is worth quoting in full:

> The Indians in this neighbourhood inform us, that the Missouri is navigable nearly to it's source, and that from a navigable part of the river, at a distance not exceeding half a days march, there is a large river runing from South to North, along the Western base of the Rocky mountains; but as their war excurtions have never extended far beyond this point, they can give no account of the discharge or source of this river. We believe this stream to be the principal South fork of the Columbia river, and if so we shall probably find but little difficulty in passing to the Ocean. [29]

For present purposes, the key phrasing in this passage is *not* the oft-cited naiveté Lewis had about the extent of a portage across the Continental Divide, nor its companion notion about how easy it would be for the expedition to reach the ocean. The former had long been an axiom of geographical speculation. The latter may have represented a son simply trying to reassure an anxious mother. Rather, more noteworthy and usually overlooked is the degree to which this description reflects the expectation that there was a large, probably a great, river flowing south to north immediately west of the Rocky Mountains. As noted earlier, Nicholas King's map had speculated on this point, but the actual native residents of the West now seemed to confirm what had heretofore been deemed "conjectural." Lewis's letter, much like Clark's summary of western rivers cited above, seemed to promise that any river running south to north to the west of the Rockies was also the main fork of the Columbia. In coming to this conclusion Lewis was countering the premise laid down by Mackenzie that the northern fork was possibly the main branch, and in this act we see the dynamic of imperial geography at work. This is a theme to which we shall return in a later chapter. [30]

In correspondence with Jefferson, Lewis does not elaborate on this great western river of which he has learned, except to state that if the Columbia River should "not prove navigable where we first meet with it, our present intention is, to continue our march by land down the river untill it becomes so, or to the Pacific Ocean." This would prove prophetic. [31]

As the explorers gradually wound their way up the Missouri in the spring of 1805, the appearance of tributaries the Hidatsa had (for the most part) predicted reaffirmed Lewis and Clark's confidence that they were on the right track to the headwaters of the Columbia. As early as the Yellowstone-Missouri confluence, reached on 26 April 1805, Lewis recollected geographic intelligence provided by the Indians during the previous winter and speculated that the Yellowstone, as well as the Missouri, shared its source with "the South branch of the Columbia river." Curiously, Clark did not replicate this reference to the Columbia in his notebook, as would have been his normal practice when Lewis was keeping a journal. This is almost certainly a function of Clark making his copy of Lewis's remark well after the relative sizes of what might be termed the British and the American branches of the Columbia were discerned in October of that year, the central episode in chapter six. [32]

Indeed, as will be discussed at length in the ensuing chapter and periodically throughout the entire book, one must always be careful about the chronology of events as found in the captains' accounts. Many readers of the journals, including some eminent scholars, have tended to view the narrative provided by Lewis or Clark as a faithful diary of daily occurrences. In fact, what we see in the journals contains a good deal of retrospective editing and synthesis based on intervening experiences. Consider the illuminating example found in Clark's notebook for 25 May 1805. The expedition was then in the heart of the Missouri Breaks, but Clark's journal contains a comparison between the antelope found in that area and those of the "Columbian Plains." The latter term was not even used as a place name by Clark until he was at Fort Clatsop, a year later, a sure clue that Clark recorded his account of Missouri River travel well after the fact. Thus, in the aforementioned instance of Clark ignoring Lewis's reference to the "South branch" of the Columbia, Clark dropped the allusion to the Great River of the West in light of subsequent geographic insight based on actual exploration of the Columbia basin. The significance of Clark's editing out references to the Columbia River in his journals will also be explicated at length in chapter six.[33]

At the confluence of the Marias and Missouri Rivers in early June 1805, where Lewis and Clark famously tried to determine which fork was the main stem, the necessity of reaching the Columbia River loomed large. Making the right choice was pivotal to the success of Jefferson's venture because, as Lewis explained, the Indians at Fort Mandan promised them that the true or main stem of the Missouri came "very near to the Columbia river." If the captains made the wrong choice and bungled their rendezvous with the Columbia, they risked losing a whole season of exploration. Such a development, Lewis wrote, "would probably so dishearten the party that it might defeat the expedition altogether." Every man in the detachment, except Lewis and Clark, thought the northern (Marias) fork was the true Missouri. At this storied junction, Lewis wrote that the men "said very cheerfully that they were ready to follow us any wher we thought proper to direct but... were affraid that the South fork would soon termineate in the mountains and leave us at a great distance from the Columbia." [34]

These memorable lines are usually presented as evidence of the captains' decision-making skills, their powers of geographic deduction, and the command's esprit de corps. Surely they are also testament to the importance Lewis and Clark placed on the issue of finding the headwaters of the Columbia and establishing the location of *its* main stem. The unvarnished journal of Pvt. Joseph Whitehouse clarified and confirmed this concern, as his candid reckoning of affairs so often did. According to Whitehouse, Lewis communicated the view that this northern fork of the Missouri (the Marias) went too far north to be the true Missouri. If a mistake was made "we Should have more mountains to cross & further to go by land to git to the Columbia River, which we have to descend to the west." Besides the risk of additional miles in rough country, heading north at this fork, and perhaps the next option in the form of the Medicine River route, were both problematic in another respect. As the captains understood western geography, both the Marias and Medicine corridors ran the risk of taking them closer to waters tributary to Mackenzie's Tacoutche Tesse, and not to a hoped-for main Columbia River to their west or southwest. In short, the formula appeared to be: determine the main stem of the Missouri River and you will find the companion feature of the Columbia.[35]

The need to find a passage to the Columbia River was brought to bear once again at the Great Falls of the Missouri. In a fretful entry largely describing the poor health of Sacagawea, Meriwether Lewis was concerned not merely for her personal well being, but the fate of the expedition, now for the second time in two weeks. Lewis wrote of his dependence upon her for productive negotiations with the Shoshone Indians "on whom we depend for horses to assist us in our portage from the Missouri to the columbia River." Still later, at the three forks of the Missouri, Lewis took consolation from his perception that the southwesterly tributary, propitiously named by him the "Jefferson," could head only "with the waters of any other river but the Columbia." Sergeant John Ordway recorded in his journal that the elusive Shoshone had left that district and gone over to the "Columbian River." Whitehouse provided the rationale; the Shoshone left "to fish & c.," probably a surmise gleaned from Sacagawea.[36]

The first practical planning of actual travel to the Columbia occurred a week later, on 8 August 1805. In a bold passage, borne of continued frustration in not encountering Sacagawea's people, Lewis wrote about proceeding with a small party "to the source of the principal stream of this river and pass the mountains to the Columbia; and down that river untill I found the Indians." Two days later, Lewis laid out the details for the final assault on the Continental Divide from his position on the Beaverhead River (a tributary to the Jefferson River, south of present-day Dillon, Montana). With his mind this particular day reeling with a multitude of geographical visions, Lewis concluded that nowhere in the world was there an "example of a river running to the extent which the Missouri and Jefferson's rivers do through such a mountainous country and at the same time so navigable." Lewis continued, wishfully he would soon learn, that "if the Columbia furnishes us such another example, a communication across the continent by water will be practicable and safe." But on reflection Lewis stemmed his optimism. Given the principles of continental architecture, he knew a "practicable and safe" passage down the Columbia ran contrary to his "knowledge of its having in it[s] comparitively short course to the ocean the same number of feet to decend which the Missouri and Mississippi have from this point to the Gulph of Mexico." [37]

Lewis's topographic deduction foretold fast water, rapids, and falls. Geographer John Logan Allen terms this "a remarkably prescient observation" and evidence of Lewis's sophisticated understanding of hydrological principles. However, James Mackay's instructions to John Evans, written from a far more distant remove on the lower Missouri River a decade earlier, fully anticipated this putative insight of Lewis's. Recollect that Mackay had the expectation that Evans was headed all the way to the Pacific Ocean. Mackay projected the relative proximity of the Rocky Mountains to the Pacific. This, he concluded, created a condition wherein the Great River of the West was likely "to be very rapid or else to have great falls, in comparison with the distance which exists between the sources of the Missouri," which ran over a much longer stretch of terrain before it reached sea level at the Gulf of Mexico. Lewis's supposedly brilliant deduction, it would seem, was actually a conventional topographical understanding and, given his personal familiarity with Evans, may even have been borrowed intelligence.[38]

In any event, as Meriwether Lewis approached the Continental Divide in August of 1805, the true scope of the Great River of the West and its connection to the Missouri was, after decades, perhaps centuries, of speculation, about to be revealed.

Armchair geographers like Thomas Jefferson had the intellectual license to formulate hypotheses. Cartographers like Nicholas King were allowed aesthetic latitude in their construction of elegant and rational forms. Explorers like Lewis and Clark agreeably labored to find out what was really there. We have reviewed in this chapter what the captains thought they knew about or expected to see in Columbia country. What they would actually encounter—multiple, complex mountain ranges, a tangle of rivers, and a Columbia that had its headwaters not opposite the Missouri's, but in territory first explored by an agent of the British Empire—would confound and disappoint them. The perplexing watershed that Lewis and Clark were about to enter would not be fully comprehended for the better part of a decade after they left its precincts, and much of its promise would be tarnished.

CHAPTER 2   Lessons in
Continental Geography

IN WHAT CLAY JENKINSON REFERS TO AS THE "SELF ENCLOSED
micro-universe of LEWIS & CLARK," the master narrative reaches its crescendo
on 12 August 1805, with the now-familiar story of Meriwether Lewis's traverse of
the Continental Divide at what came to be known as Lemhi Pass. It is based on
the following journal entry:

[A]t the distance of 4 miles further the road took us to the most distant fountain
of the waters of the mighty Missouri in surch of which we have spent so many
toilsome days and wristless nights. thus far I had accomplished one of those great
objects on which my mind has been unalterably fixed for many years, judge then
of the pleasure I felt in allying my thirst with this pure and ice cold water which
issues from the base of a low mountain or hill of a gentle ascent for ½ a mile.
the mountains are high on either hand leave this gap at the head of this rivulet
through which the road passes. here I halted a few minutes and rested myself. two
miles below McNeal had exultingly stood with a foot on each side of this little
rivulet and thanked his god that he had lived to bestride the mighty & heretofore
deemed endless Missouri. after refreshing ourselves we proceeded on to the top
of the dividing ridge from which I discovered immence ranges of high mountains
still to the West of us with their tops partially covered with snow. I now decended
the mountain about ¾ of a mile which I found much steeper than on the opposite
side, to a handsome bold running Creek of cold Clear water. here I first tasted the
water of the great Columbia river.[1]

The foregoing passage is the most storied of any to be found in the journals
of the Expedition for Northwestern Discovery. Adhering to what is now narrative convention, historians, filmmakers, and novelists alike have all made Lewis's
ascent of Lemhi Pass and his gaze west from the saddle in the Rocky Mountain
gap the pivotal moment of the expedition. The central phrase, around which all
the supposed drama revolves, is Lewis's description of "immence ranges of high
mountains still to the West of us with their tops partially covered with snow."

Popular interpretations, especially melodramatic film and video visualizations, invest this scene with an atmosphere of great disappointment, some actually portraying Meriwether Lewis physically sagging at the sight of more mountains to his west. In addition, almost every modern scholarly account of the expedition addresses the supposed "Lemhi Disappointment," with the consensus that Lewis and Clark's imaginative geography was dashed at Lemhi.[2]

This is odd because, as anyone who has actually stood at Lemhi Pass can attest, the vaunted view *west* from the divide is not particularly more daunting than the view *east* from whence Lewis had just traveled. Furthermore, the westward perspective could hardly have been totally surprising because several weeks earlier, from an eminence 200 miles away, east of the Great Falls of the Missouri, Lewis discerned that the Rocky Mountains at the divide were several ranges deep.[3]

This supposedly axiomatic reaction to the landscape—Lewis's "Lemhi Disappointment" it might be called—has its roots in John Logan Allen's magisterial work of historical geography, *Lewis and Clark and the Image of the American Northwest*. Allen's seminal study, first published now many decades ago, is one of the two or three most influential books ever written about Lewis and Clark. Allen argues that "the view from the ridge had been anything but what Lewis had expected." More accurately, the scene was not what *Thomas Jefferson* might have hoped Lewis would find. A century's worth of geographic lore had previously suggested to students of western geography like Jefferson that the passage from the Missouri headwaters across the divide to those of the Great River of the West would be an easy portage. Thus, as Allen phrased it, "The presence of the peaks of the Lemhi range on the western horizon must have come as a great shock." However, by the summer of 1805 Jefferson's man Lewis was a field-tested and knowledgeable explorer, experienced in reading and anticipating landscapes. Coming over the crest of the continent, Lewis would have been *more* surprised to see a placid Columbia flowing westward to the sea than he was to see another range of mountains.[4]

That the geography of the Columbia River watershed from Lemhi Pass to the Pacific Ocean would ultimately lead to significant disappointment on the part of the company is well-documented. However, whether these coming difficulties were intuitively obvious to Lewis at Lemhi Pass on August 12th and the few days immediately thereafter remains a matter of some speculation. As Stephen Ambrose observes, "whatever Lewis felt as he first saw the Bitterroot Range of the Rocky Mountains, he never wrote about it." Dayton Duncan states: "If Lewis paused to absorb that deflating vista and to contemplate its profound consequences, he doesn't mention it in his journals." Maybe, as Duncan says, the surprising scene at Lemhi Pass left Lewis "speechless." "Perhaps," Duncan continues, "the disappointment was simply too great for words." Such a reaction, however, would be out of character for Lewis who, in so many previous instances where his journal points to disappointment or a bleak prospect, quickly rebounded with a profession of optimism about overcoming obstacles.[5]

View East

View West

These two photos recently taken at Lemhi Pass, the saddle of the Continental Divide where Meriwether Lewis first gazed into the Columbia River watershed, show that the view west is not even slightly more daunting than the view to the east; that is, through the country the expedition had just previously traversed in the summer of 1805. (Katie Bump, USDA Forest Service)

A careful look at the documentary record suggests that, while Meriwether Lewis may have left Jefferson's company in July 1803 believing the lore about a single range of mountains dividing the continent in the western interior, by the time he left Fort Mandan Lewis knew better than to trust that hoary mythology, and would have been neither surprised nor disappointed at the moment of his first glance into Columbia country. In a letter sent to Thomas Jefferson as he was about to leave Fort Mandan in April 1805, Lewis told the president that, should the Columbia "not prove navigable where we first meet it, our present intention is, to continue our march by land down the river untill it becomes so, or to the Pacific Ocean." [6]

This contingency plan may well have been grounded in Lewis's "Summary view of the Rivers and Creeks, which discharge thems[elves] into the Missouri," one of a set of documents, now deprecatingly termed the Mandan Miscellany, sent downstream to President Jefferson concurrent with the expedition venturing into the west. Lewis's summary, in many respects a restatement of findings reported by John Evans in 1797, referenced *five* separate ranges of mountains on the *east* side of the Continental Divide. Lewis noted first that the Musselshell River flowed into the Missouri below the Great Falls, taking its head in a range of mountains running in a transverse line from near the falls to the Yellowstone River. Next, above the falls and to the west, the Medicine River originated "in the rocky Mountains." The Missouri itself then coursed through what Lewis termed serially, the "first connected chain of the Rocky mountains," a "second chain," and finally the "third chain of very high mountains." The last was near where the Missouri, the Hidatsa told Lewis, divided itself "into three nearly equal branches." [7]

Knowing that the terrain *east* of the Continental Divide was so complex as to hold five distinct sub-ranges, Lewis could not possibly have been surprised to find that the Columbia River cut through a complex topography *west* of the divide. Additionally, the very existence of snow-capped volcanoes like Mount Hood relatively close to the Pacific Ocean would have raised questions about their relationship to the Continental Divide and the makeup of terrain between Hood and the headwaters of the Missouri at the divide. Bernard Lacépède's hypothesis that Mount Hood was an appendage of the Rocky Mountains would only have reinforced the expectation of a complicated geography west of the divide.

Of course, the antipode to this "complex" western geography was the widely presumed "simple" physiographic structure of the Appalachians. Even here, however, reality intrudes on the casual assurances of a "myth within the myth." While the Appalachians are neither as high nor wide as the Rockies and do contain the Cumberland Gap and other saddles bridging watersheds, they are not the single fold in the landscape they were once believed to be, and that some had imagined the western mountains to be. [8]

Finally, and remarkably, historians have overlooked a passage in the journals that in and of itself demolishes the notion of Lewis being surprised or disappointed at Lemhi. When Lewis and a few other men jumped out ahead of Clark and the main party in search of the Great Falls of the Missouri and accompanying glory, they had the opportunity to ascend a high ridge adjacent to those cascades. However, prior to reaching the falls, in a passage seemingly lost in its juxtaposition to Lewis's famous meditations on the sublimity of the Missouri's great cataracts, he reported that "from this hight we had a most beatifull and picturesk view of the Rocky mountains which wer perfectly covered with Snow and reaching from S. E. to the N. of N. W." To this Lewis added the probative observation that the mountains "appear to be formed of *several ranges each succeeding range rising higher than the preceding one* untill the most distant appear to loose their snowey tops in the clouds; this was an august spectacle and still rendered more formidable by the recollection that we had them to pass" (emphasis added).[9]

While the foregoing evidence suggests Lewis was neither surprised nor disappointed by the rugged country he beheld upon crossing the Continental Divide, the question remains of when, exactly, he understood the true nature of the eastern Columbia watershed to the degree that he abandoned his hope of a relatively quick and easy journey by water to the main stem of the Columbia. Answering that question requires a reexamination of the other enduring myth associated with Lewis's crossing of the divide, what historian Jim Merritt has termed "Cameahwait's Geography Lesson." Lewis's notebook journal entries for 13–14 August 1805 are particularly detailed and well composed, with an extensive record of his supposed discussions with the famed chief of the Shoshone and Sacagawea's brother, Cameahwait. If one is to take Lewis's record at face value, as some scholars have, a logical conclusion would be that, if Lewis's hopes of an easy journey by water weren't dashed by his first glimpse of the forbidding landscape west of the divide, they certainly would have been in the two days that followed, during which Lewis claims to have received the fabled "geography lesson." A close reading of the record, however, proves we can trust neither that conclusion, nor, indeed, the record itself.[10]

In his notebook entry for August 13th, the day after crossing the divide, Lewis commented a second time that the range of mountains to his west, were "partially covered with snow." Again, this observation is not vested with any particular significance and certainly no apparent stress. In fact, Lewis found more noteworthy that the hills on the western side of the pass were "better clad with pine timber than we had been accustomed to see." This was no doubt a mental note about the now tangibly improved prospects for making canoes for a voyage down the Columbia. For this same reason, Lewis walked down to the Lemhi River for an inspection. He found it "40 yards wide very rapid clear and about 3 feet deep," flowing from south to north, as predicted by geographic lore, the Hidatsa, Nicholas King, and American imperial ambition. The days of relying on such lore about the Great River of the West—whether from French, English, or American mapmakers, Spanish colonial agents, British fur traders, or Indians—were over. Lewis was finally on westward-flowing waters, and soon thereafter Clark would be too.[11]

Contrary to expedition legend and lore, it was William Clark, not Meriwether Lewis, depicted here in this painting by Olaf Seltzer, who experienced the first "distant view" of the Rocky Mountains. Both Lewis and Clark discerned that the Rockies were several ranges deep weeks before Lewis reached Lemhi Pass. ("Lewis' First View of the Rockies" by Olaf Seltzer, Gilcrease Museum, Tulsa, OK)

On first encountering Cameahwait and sixty other Shoshone mounted warriors later that same day, Lewis took a page out of James Mackay's instructional playbook for John Evans, brandishing an American flag and slowly closing the distance between them and him. After "smoking a few pipes" and distributing some presents, Lewis got down to business. "I now informed the chief," Lewis inscribed in his August 13th entry, "that the object of our visit was a friendly one, that after we should reach his camp I would undertake to explain to him fully those objects, who we wer[e], from whence we had come and wither we were going." [12]

Later the same day, Lewis's August 13th entry states, the "geography lesson" began. What information did Cameahwait supposedly convey? A few items stand out in Lewis's account. First, he says he learned that the small stream he was on (the Lemhi River) flowed into one twice as large coming in from the south and west. This reference to the Salmon River would have been additional confirmation of the Hidatsa's understanding of the hydraulics of the great western river—namely, that it ran from south to north at the western base of the Rocky Mountains. Better yet, Cameahwait confirmed that this river flowed "to the great lake where the white men lived," probable confirmation that Lewis was on a fork of the Columbia. No doubt in response to an inquiry about canoes for river voyaging, Cameahwait said there was no better timber below than what was to be found on the Lemhi River. However, to Lewis's supposed dismay Cameahwait said it was impossible to run this larger stream by either canoe or land because the river "was confined between inacessable mountains." This, Lewis recorded, was "unwelcome information," but, the captain posited, it served as a delaying tactic intended to keep him in the Shoshone's midst. At this point in the narrative Lewis gives every indication of being far more concerned with the size of the trees "that would answer the purpose of constructing canoes" than he is with mountains partially covered with snow.[13]

After the initial dialogue with Cameahwait, Lewis espied the Shoshone horse herd. He wrote, much as he had to Jefferson from Fort Mandan, that "if we are compelled to travel by land over those mountains" the Shoshone herd was sufficient to provide an adequate supply of mounts. Any doubts he had about the route he was contemplating evaporated when he ate some roasted salmon. This meal, Lewis said, "perfectly convinced me that we were on the waters of the Pacific Ocean." Lewis then retired for the night while the other few men with him went on to "amuse themselves with the Indians." [14]

Cameahwait, according to Lewis's account, conducted an even more encompassing lesson on western geography on August 14th, the captain's third day west of the divide. The chief's description of the country to the west "fell far short of my expectation or wishes," Lewis wrote. In an elaborate narrative, running over 1,700 words in length, Lewis describes the complex geography of the Lemhi/Salmon River system and the "vast mountains of rock eternally covered with snow through which the river passed." The terrain was so uninviting that Cameahwait professed none of his people had ever ventured through it. However, the chief knew of the

"persed nosed [Nez Perce] Indians who inhabit this river below the rocky mountains [and] that it ran a great way toward the seting sun and finally lost itself in a
great lake of water which was illy taisted, and where the white men lived." [15]

Southwest of Lewis's position the country was even less hospitable. Based on
Cameahwait's information, Lewis described the Snake River plain of southern
Idaho as a land of "horrors and obstructions." Game was scarce and the Indians
lived off roots or the carcasses of horses that strayed into the area. The rare pools
of water in that "dry and parched sandy desert" had, at that time of the year,
evaporated. However, running through the center of this plain was a "large river
[the Snake]... which was navigable but afforded neither Salmon nor timber." In
any event, by this account of things Lewis became more convinced these variously
described streams were the "southern branches of the Columbia." The challenge
was finding a way to "intercept" the large navigable fork (the Snake) without
engaging in a traverse of the desert to his south, especially if, as the Shoshone
insisted, there was no passable route directly west by way of the Lemhi River. The
only solution to this puzzle was revisiting the question of the Nez Perce Indians
and their path of travel east of the divide. [16]

The Shoshone shared the buffalo plains on the upper Missouri and Yellowstone
Rivers with the Nez Perce. Accordingly, they knew the Nez Perce route to those
fat plains, one that ran through the mountains to the north of the Shoshone
lodges on the Lemhi River. Lewis maintained that insights about this northern
road—the Lolo Trail as it has become known—were shared with him on the 14th.
He reported that the road "was a very bad one" because of its thickly forested
terrain and limited sustenance. Nevertheless, Lewis insisted in his journal "my
rout was instantly settled in my own mind."—adding the somewhat contradictory
proviso that the Indian account of the river he was on needed to be confirmed
"on an investigation of it, which I was determined should be made before we undertake the rout by land in any direction." Snow-covered mountains, deserts, and
fallen timber aside, the notion of a voyage down the Columbia had clearly not
yet perished. Even if such a voyage did not prove practicable, Lewis now had an
overland option. He speculated smugly that if the Nez Perce Indians "could pass
these mountains with their women and Children, that we could also pass them."
It's worth noting again, for reasons that will soon become evident, that Lewis
claims in his notebook to have been informed of both the impassibility of the
Lemhi route and the existence and nature of the Lolo route, by August 14th, his
third day over the divide. [17]

Lewis's "geography lesson" is an engaging story, and for that reason it is well
known in scholarly and popular renditions of the expedition. Lewis's time with
Cameahwait is conventionally regarded as one of the captain's more perceptive periods. But whose knowledge was Lewis relying on? Easily overlooked in the journals,
as published in the modern edition, is William Clark's post-expeditionary interlineation posted at the outset of Cameahwait's "lesson" in *Lewis's* notebook for the
14th of August. Clark wrote: "This part to come in the 20th [of August] related to

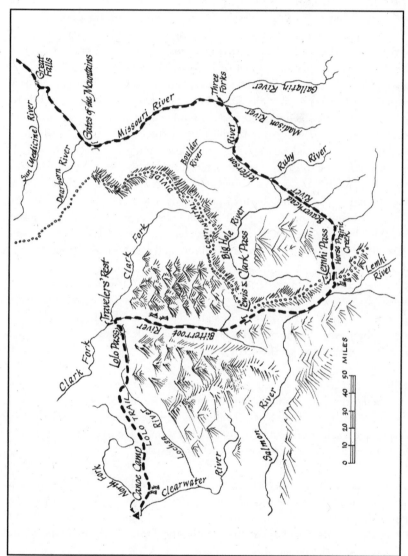

The complex geography of the Rocky Mountains, coupled with the President's imperative that Lewis find the source of the Missouri River, took the expedition on a circuitous route first to Lemhi Pass, then to "navigable" waters that flowed west to the Pacific Ocean. (from *Lewis and Clark and the Image of the American Northwest* by John Logan Allen, courtesy Dover Publications, Inc.)

Capt. C thro the interpreter." Clark's syntax obscures the meaning of the first part of this phase (his intention was to say "starting here what you read is information I gleaned"), and his last referred to Sacagawea, who accompanied Clark over the pass a few days after Lewis first did. Several pages later, at the end of Lewis's geographic discourse, Clark writes again: "as low [in the text] as this in the 20th of the mon[th]: Spoken to Cap C," meaning Clark was the originator of this information.[18]

Clark's pointed reference to the role of Sacagawea as "the interpreter" who stayed with him rather than accompanying Lewis on his initial crossing, raises two questions. Why wasn't Sacagawea with Lewis when her designated role (conversing with the Shoshone) was finally at hand; and, conversely, without her, how were Cameahwait and the other Shoshone Indians supposed to have been able to convey the sophisticated geographic notions rendered by Lewis in his notebook entry for August 14th? The answer to the first of these is, in part, exploratory convention—the brave and perhaps lonely explorer doing civilization's work, a theme we shall develop at greater length later in this book. For now, suffice it to say that any explorer being accompanied by a Native woman at the apex of his narrative would have been unorthodox in the extreme in the literary world of the early nineteenth century or at any point in premodern exploration. Furthermore, Sacagawea had by this time fallen under the protectorate of William Clark. When Lewis left Clark behind to search for the Columbia, he necessarily left Sacagawea behind too.

The answer to the second question, Lewis would have us believe, is that lacking the interpretive services of Sacagawea, Lewis relied upon George Drouillard, a half-Shawnee mixed-blood proficient in sign language, as the master translator. Before describing what he purportedly learned from Cameahwait, Lewis drafted a prefatory paragraph that set the scene:

> The means I had of communicating with these people was by way of Drewyer who understood perfectly the common language of jesticulation or signs which seems to be universally understood by all the Nations we have yet seen. it is true that this language is imperfect and liable to error but is much less so than would be expected. the strong parts of the ideas are seldom mistaken.[19]

Lewis's assertion notwithstanding, there is specific evidence in the journals that calls Drouillard's now-amplified role as interpreter into question. First, the record provides precious little indication prior to this juncture of Drouillard's effectiveness as a translator. For example, at the showdown with the Teton Sioux of September 1804, the hassle was exacerbated, Clark wrote, "for the want of a good interpreter," either of the linguistic variety or one able to communicate by signing. At Fort Mandan through the ensuing winter, visiting fur traders Pierre Dorion, Rene Jessaume, and Toussaint Charbonneau did the translating. Indeed, when Lewis and Clark returned to the Mandan villages in the summer of 1806, they dispatched Drouillard to find Jessaume "to Come and enterpret for us." In short, although Drouillard was cited as a sign talker, he had never truly been called on in that capacity until the occasion of Lewis's geography lesson with Cameahwait. In the course of the expedition he was, rather, more routinely cited as a scout and hunter/trapper.[20]

Complicating the matter of Drouillard's putative effectiveness as an interpreter is recent scholarship suggesting that the tribes of the Rocky Mountains like the Shoshone did not use gesticulation for language. As Sally Thompson has pointed out in her analysis, if Drouillard was not competent to translate on the Missouri, he could hardly have been capable of doing so on the upper Columbia. Certainly it would have been possible for Lewis, with or without Drouillard, to have gleaned some basic geographic information from Cameahwait. However, the full extent of Lewis's geographic understanding as initially related in the journals was not the product of a sign language vocabulary, notwithstanding his feint in Drouillard's direction.[21]

Lewis inadvertently admitted as much in two later journal entries. First, Lewis wrote for August 16th: "I had mentioned to the chief several times that we had with us a woman of his nation... and that by means of her I hoped to explain myself *more fully than I could do by signs*" (emphasis added). On August 17th, when Lewis and Cameahwait joined Clark and the main party still struggling up the Missouri headwaters, and therefore the company of Sacagawea, Cameahwait was once again enjoined in conversation. Once Sacagawea is on the scene, Thompson notes, "no further mention is made of signing as a means of communication." Via Sacagawea on the 17th, Lewis conducted an elaborate discussion with Cameahwait, setting in motion the portage across the mountains and touching on such topics as agriculture and trade.[22]

The second journal entry that casts doubt on the role of Drouillard as translator is Lewis's account of how, on 22 August, some young Shoshones ran off with Drouillard's gun. Drouillard was able to run them down with his horse and signed that he meant no harm, a notion easy to communicate with body language to this day. However, when Drouillard asked for his gun, Lewis wrote, "the only part of the answer which he could understand was pah kee which he knew to be the name by which they called their enemies." In this story Drouillard is trying to communicate orally with the Shoshone, but if he wanted to communicate, why not convey the meaning by sign which Lewis professed would be "understood perfectly?"[23]

Lewis's account of Cameahwait's "geography lesson" puts the nature, context, and sometimes hidden value of the expedition's journals into sharp relief. First, from the internal construction of Lewis's notebook, it's clear that his account is not a same-day "campfire" record of proceedings written on the spot but was instead composed well after the fact. The most obvious evidence for this is that Lewis's record of the days when he was separated from William Clark (August 9–17, inclusive of the "geography lessons" on August 12–14) contains reports on Clark's whereabouts and the doings of the main party dozens of miles away back over on the Missouri headwaters. Similarly, Lewis's extended scientific discursions

into the nature of various berries and succulent plants would have required studied seclusion and access to his traveling library. These volumes are extremely
unlikely to have been in Lewis's possession on the vanguard movement over the
Continental Divide. Further evidence of Lewis's after-the-fact composition comes
from descriptions of activities, such as doffing his moccasins during pipe ceremonies, in which Lewis added the phrase "I afterwards" learned some aspect of the
phenomena he describes proving he is writing with a retrospective glance.[24]

Jim Merritt has identified some of the historiographical ramifications of
Lewis's editorial sleight of hand. Scholars relying on the earlier Thwaites edition
of the journals properly have Clark learning the complex geography west of the
Continental Divide from Cameahwait. Those not paying close attention to the
annotation in Moulton's modern edition, where Lewis is the pupil, can be led
astray. Merritt gives Lewis a very generous benefit of the doubt by stipulating that
Cameahwait covered the same ground with both captains: Lewis via Drouillard
and Clark with Sacagawea. However, this theory is based on the somewhat
questionable notion of Drouillard as the essential medium plus complete faith
in the authenticity of Lewis's first-person narrative. Ignoring Lewis's penchant
for putting himself at the center of every story of import, Merritt believes that if
"Cameahwait had talked geography only with Clark, Lewis—following his usual
procedure—would have placed that discussion in his entry for the 20th and identified Clark in the third person." Merritt argues that Lewis did not do so, Clark's
later edits in the journals notwithstanding, because it was a repeat of what Lewis
learned on the 14th. There is a simpler explanation, however: Lewis claimed Clark's
knowledge as his own. In order to construct a credible narrative on how he came
to the full understanding of transmontane realities as revealed in the Shoshone
"geography lesson," Lewis deleted Clark from the narrative while simultaneously
exaggerating his own role. The retrospective rather than real-time composition of
the journals allowed this type of legerdemain.[25]

Later, when Clark was editing Lewis's journals in the service of Nicholas Biddle,
who was preparing them for publication after Lewis's death, Clark saw that Lewis
had expropriated geographic knowledge that Clark had actually learned the week
following Lewis's first crossing of the divide. Clark took sufficient exception to
Lewis's proto-narrative that he corrected the record, without the discomfiture of
confronting his deceased partner. Accordingly, Biddle's paraphrased account, issued in 1814, places the "geography lesson" with Clark on the 20th, not with Lewis
on the 14th. Of the 1,700-word narrative found in Lewis's notebook, Biddle used
but little for his description of Lewis's activities on August 14th. To wit: "In order
to give time for [Captain Clark and] the boats to reach the forks of Jefferson river,
Captain Lewis determined to remain here and obtain all the information he could
collect with regard to the country." [26]

Besides revealing the nature of the composition of the journals, an analysis of
the Lemhi saga, perhaps most important of all, provides great insight into the relationship between the captains and a dose of realism that serves as an antidote to

romanticist notions about their friendship. The above example of Lewis's "creative" reconstruction of the events and Clark's correction forces us to confront what is certainly the central truism of LEWIS & CLARK lore—*the two captains never disagreed*. As Clay Jenkinson asserts, the absence of overt evidence of quarreling "is hardly proof of profound harmony. The more one studies the individual characters and leadership styles of Meriwether Lewis and William Clark," Jenkinson adds, "the less harmony one discerns." [27]

Both Clark and Lewis knew the latter was indisputably the lead figure in the one pivotal aspect of the expedition—writing the account of discovery. Clearly, however, Clark felt Lewis went too far with this prerogative in the telling of what was sure to emerge as the prime event of the whole venture, and he responded by editing Lewis's journal so that the story would reflect his own contributions. In that very human sense, Clark was settling a score with his beloved but departed colleague. Here we see that by viewing the journals dynamically, a whole new story about Lewis and Clark is revealed.

The "geography lesson" also underscores important issues regarding how historians evaluate evidence generally and the reliability of the journals of Lewis and Clark specifically. Barbara Belyea reminds us that in the review of any discovery narrative, "the reader responds not to the events recorded but to the record of events." Historians are particularly vulnerable in situations where the subject is ostensibly the only source of information, such as Lewis at Lemhi Pass. Thus, what an explorer like Lewis reported is not a mirror of reality but rather a filtering of it. One of the first scholars to appreciate this distinction was Clay Jenkinson, who perceived an obvious "artificiality" to the Lemhi Pass saga as composed by Lewis.[28]

The shortcomings of travel literature as a documentary record were highlighted more than a generation ago by Percy Adams. Explorers, Adams argued, had several incentives that led them to engage in periodic, if not wholesale, deceptions. Of these motives, the one most relevant to the study of Lewis's character is vanity—the urge to show off one's knowledge. The travel genre, as Cook, Vancouver, and Mackenzie had proved, had strong associations with European and Atlantic America's adoption of Enlightenment values about geographic comprehension of the world. As a literary style, successful exploratory accounts conformed to certain conventions. For example, observant travelers occasionally engaged in adventure or encountered the exotic. Lewis's incentive for literary inventiveness was that it enhanced the prospects for a compelling narrative that would satisfy the requirements for such accounts, including making the author into the hero of his own story.[29]

As alluded to earlier, the Lemhi "geography lesson" and its related facets demonstrate that the journals of Lewis and Clark, contrary to popular impression, are not a pure, transparent source, but rather, as Thomas Slaughter calls them, "honed reflections." The factual character of the journals is also complicated, in some measure compromised, because many passages in the journals were *not* written on the days to which they purport to correspond on the calendar. That flawed relationship between narrative and reality makes these texts a more dynamic and elusive element, opening up the prospect of a retrospective casting of events in contrast to the facile presumption of forward-looking linearity. For that reason historians must ask critical questions of these journals, and especially so in the case of Meriwether Lewis because he had the burden of having to compose a constructed narrative at the end of the venture. Lewis's Lemhi Pass discourse is a case in point. The polished notebook in which this story appears gives all evidence, both from its literary construction and its physical appearance, of having been composed well after the fact in a studied setting and intended as the first draft of a forthcoming publication. The pages are nearly pristine, with no crammed writing, worn edges, or stains that one would find in "campfire" notes. Lewis even had time to employ the then-customary practice of the publishing trade of placing on a separate line at the bottom of a page the first word to be carried over to the top of the next page of text. Lewis's notebooks read more like a proto-manuscript akin to Alexander Mackenzie's published account than a daybook or diary.[30]

In contrast, the journals of William Clark, when they are not the so-called verbatim copies of what Lewis originally prepared and Clark dutifully transcribed, typically read much more like field logs "taken in the moment." In this respect, Clark's text typically bears a closer resemblance to the Columbia River journals of his contemporary David Thompson than to the Mackenzie/Lewis style. Readers looking for a dramatic recounting from Thompson won't find it in the density of his daily course-and-distance log but rather in his published narratives. Accordingly, Clark's field notes, when they occur in the published editions of the journals, are very much the proverbial "first drafts" of history and therefore closer to being a primary and more reliable source. Furthermore, tellingly—and in distinct contrast to Lewis—the differences between Clark's field notes and his finished notebooks are negligible when we have both. Not having Lewis's burden of making the whole story hang together, Clark did little by way of revision or rethinking of occurrences. Conversely, as with the "geography lesson," changes in Clark's "verbatim" recounting of Lewis's narrative are *always* noteworthy.[31]

Lewis probably kept a "campfire" record of the traverse of Lemhi Pass and the ensuing few days, indeed about many other trail segments that did not survive, or were destroyed. These field notes served as an aide-memoire from which he later composed the polished notebook account we see today. In an instance such as this, when Lewis was separated from the main party, he surely did not risk the security of the already completed notebooks by bringing them with him. Lewis's Lemhi Pass field notes are lost to history, and so is any more immediate insight into his thinking at the Continental Divide. Nicholas Biddle addressed this issue in his introduction to the first published edition of the journals. Drawing on conversations with Clark, Biddle observed that the record of the expedition was "revised and enlarged at the different periods of leisure which occurred on the route." Biddle's reference to revisions goes to the heart of the dynamics of the journals' creation and the attendant ambiguity created by that practice.[32]

As evidence, then, not all passages in the journals of Lewis and Clark are of equal value. Explorers' field notes are like daily "snapshots" of reality. More carefully composed texts, like Lewis's notebooks, or published narratives like those of Mackenzie or Thompson, were transformed by the perspective that hindsight affords. Knowledge of intervening events, or "how the story turns out," makes narrative explanation a far simpler task for the explorer. As Tom Chaffin has noted, the tales of explorers are written with the "tacit conceit that, at each turn, its author doesn't know what lies ahead" in order to preserve the prospect for drama.[33]

The fundamental premise of exploratory travel accounts—the isolation of the storyteller—vests the narrator with a beguiling authority. This is what gives the genre much of its appeal. Nevertheless, the reader's trust, Bruce Greenfield observes, is at risk when an explorer modifies "the order of events recorded in his journal in light of the actual outcome of the journey and his understanding of its meaning, making the record of his observations into the story of his discoveries." When, as James Ronda says, Lewis or Clark began to shape their experience into "formal history," they entered "the territory of narrative and commentary." At those junctures they ceased being "explorers" and became "explainers." Thus, first-generation texts can be edited retrospectively into a second generation of information to meet literary conventions, the narrative purposes of the expedition, or, for that matter, to obfuscate things, like disappointments or disagreements. Anything embarrassingly self-revelatory about the stature or competency of an explorer was likely, in the end, to be excised from the record or suppressed. It certainly would not find its way into print.[34]

For example, in Alexander Mackenzie's field journal of exploration in 1789, he wrote of being "at a loss" as to whether the river he was on would take him to the Pacific or not. By contrast, in his book Mackenzie is ineluctably on a course to reach the Arctic instead. In the case of Lewis and Clark, the "illusion of precision," Thomas Slaughter states, "has misled readers for two centuries about what the journals reveal." To create a more faithful reconstruction of the Lewis and Clark story, the historian must critically deconstruct the meaning of certain journal passages that are not unvarnished fact but instead a dressed-up narrative the explorers wished to be believed. Where a text reposes within the typology of exploratory discourse is a leading indicator of its ability to enhance understanding or degrade it. The more immediate a text is, meaning unselfconscious of narrative requirements, the more transparent and therefore more reliable it is likely to be. In descending order of immediacy and transparency, the primary source materials for explorers are: (1) first impressions in the field that are thought or felt but not necessarily recorded to paper; (2) the field note, daybook, or "campfire" journal that serves as an aid to memory for a subsequent iteration of information; (3) the reflective note or proto-manuscript; (4) the published account.[35]

The journals of Lewis and Clark are less reliable than some suppose, but this limitation does not diminish their value. Like any other piece of evidence, historians simply have to be prudent in their use of them. Oddly enough, the weakness of the journals on the evidentiary scale can actually reveal more significant, perhaps profound, insights. Oral historians have noted that what their informants tell them may have less to do with the facts than their ambitions or idealizations. By finding and analyzing self-edits and inventions the historian is able to transcend mere fact and gain rare glimpses into the historical figure's internalized view of the world. These "creative errors" are the form and process by which individuals come to see themselves in history. Correspondingly, Thomas Slaughter writes, "reading the journals is a creative act, just as writing them was." [36]

There can be no doubt that Meriwether Lewis saw himself in history as a great explorer—the American counterpart to Alexander Mackenzie. His literary deception—the expropriation of William Clark's geographic findings—must be considered within this context. Lewis was publicly indebted to Jefferson as a mentor and to Columbus and Cook as role models, but his enterprise was always quietly preoccupied with Mackenzie. What became known as the Lewis and Clark Expedition can be said to have begun on 8 January 1802 when Philadelphian Caspar Wistar wrote to his friend Thomas Jefferson and asked: "Have you seen McKenzie's account of his journeys across the Continent & to the Northern Ocean?" Jefferson ordered a copy and read it that summer. Mackenzie's imperial vision for British domination of the global fur trade and continental preeminence through control of the Columbia River spurred the president into action. [37]

Mackenzie's account had an influence on Lewis as well. Indeed, an examination of certain aspects of Mackenzie's *Voyages from Montreal*—more specifically, the style and content of certain stories–make Lewis's literary flair and many of his experiences seem appreciably less exceptional than legend has made them out to be. We will review the relationship between the two texts at length in a later chapter, but for now consider that Mackenzie's saga reached its narrative crescendo in his description of how he came to understand the geography west of the Continental Divide, where he first entered it in today's British Columbia. Indeed, the Scotsman's description of his first week across the divide could almost serve as a script for Lewis's Lemhi narrative. In Mackenzie's account, he first approached the Sekani Indians in a self-described "adventurous" manner. He thought the Sekani would reciprocate friendship when there was no longer "any apparent possibility... that a communication with me was not a service of danger." When at last two Indians did approach, Mackenzie signed for them to come over to his side of the river, "and as an inducement, displayed looking glasses, beads, and other alluring trinkets." In a scene later almost perfectly replicated by Lewis at the divide, one of Mackenzie's hunters advanced at an inopportune time, creating alarm among the Sekani. After calm was restored, Mackenzie's hunter, like Drouillard twelve years later, commenced a discussion about the geography of the country, in which, Mackenzie reported, the hunter and Indian "perfectly understood each other." Lewis said after his first few days with the Shoshone: "every article about us appeared to excite astonishment in their minds." Mackenzie had written of his first Native western interlocutors: "During their short stay, they observed us, and every thing about us, with a mixture of admiration and astonishment." [38]

In his ensuing account, Mackenzie crossed the stream (what he considered the headwaters of the Columbia but was actually the Fraser River) to the Sekani encampment. After another distribution of presents to the adults and sugar to the children, he instructed his interpreter "to collect every necessary information in their power to afford me." The Indians then gave an at times enticing and at others negative report on the course of the river. White people inhabited the mouth of the river, they said, but at three places downstream from Mackenzie's position the river was "altogether impassable, from the falls and rapids... that were much higher, and more rugged, than any we had yet seen, and would not admit of any passage over them." Much like the Shoshone account that Lewis (actually Clark) would record, the Sekani tried to dissuade Mackenzie from following the river any further. Mackenzie observed that this "account of our situation... was sufficiently alarming, and awakened very painful reflections." Nevertheless, a confident Mackenzie stated that Indian reports about a difficult route "did not operate on my mind so as to produce any change in my original determination" to proceed to the ocean. A boastful Meriwether Lewis would later evince similar sentiments when the expedition's mountain guide, Old Toby of the Shoshone, pointed out the Nez Perce route to the Clearwater. [39]

In a day's time, after consulting with a small number of Shuswap Indians visiting the Sekani, Mackenzie would concede to geographic reality. His position was at the 55th parallel. Though the Fraser River debouches into the Pacific just north of the 49th parallel, Mackenzie's field judgment, informed by the same geographic lore influencing Jefferson and Lewis, led to him to conclude that he was on the northern-most extent of "the River of the West." Conjecture prior to the actual findings of Gray and Vancouver in 1792, of which Mackenzie could not possibly have been aware until he returned to Upper Canada in 1794 (or later), placed the mouth of the great western river at 45 degrees north. Mackenzie, thinking he had to traverse 10 degrees of latitude and return upstream the same distance in addition to a recrossing of the divide back to his starting point on Lake Athabasca, reconsidered his route. "Such were my reflections, at this period," Mackenzie wrote, "but instead of continuing to indulge them, I determined to proceed with resolution, and set the future events at defiance." Instead of following the great river south, Mackenzie decided "to penetrate with more safety, and in a shorter period, to the ocean by the inland, western communication." [40]

Thus, *all* of the essential elements of Lewis's narrative in crossing the Continental Divide may be found in Mackenzie's preceding account, including unexpected geography, a handy translator to engage local informants, and the decision to take an alternate route overland to the west. Another mythic element in Lewis's story is also found in Mackenzie's experience as well. The Scotsman found a Sekani woman who had been taken prisoner by the Cree Indians from east of the mountains. Unlike Sacagawea, this woman had escaped on her own. The Sekani woman's appearance in the Mackenzie narrative deflates the legendary quality of the supposedly astonishing incident wherein Sacagawea was reunited with her brother, Cameahwait. Stephen Ambrose said this was an episode which no novelist "would dare invent," but it seems not to have been as improbable as he suggested.[41]

The eminent Lewis and Clark scholar Donald Jackson once observed, regarding the second-draft nature of Lewis's notebooks, that certain scientific information was posted therein not because it was observed the day in question but out of convenience. If this was true of botanical and faunal data, the same editorial principle could apply to *any* element of the narrative. Such appears to be the case with Lewis's "geography lesson" gleaned from Clark's fieldwork and discussions with the Shoshone. If, in his private reflections, Lewis ever pondered his limitations as a writer or failures as an explorer, then, as Jackson writes, he would have had "little point in announcing it to the world." In the same vein, as Tom Chaffin avers in his biography of John C. Frémont, exploratory reputations rarely profited by acknowledgement as to being "guided by the footsteps of others." In Lewis's case, this could apply equally to Mackenzie, Clark, or Sacagawea. [42]

Strange as it may seem to modern readers bathed in the romanticized "Lemhi Disappointment" thesis, Mackenzie's account could have proved reassuring to Lewis. After all, the great Nor'Wester prevailed despite a troubling transmontane geography and overcame "the dangers and difficulties" of navigating western rivers, even if his portage over the Peace/Fraser River divide would prove to be shorter than that of Lewis's on the Missouri/Columbia. What mattered more than the length of the portage was the navigability of the western river. After his initial foray with the Shoshone, Lewis may well have had some modest disappointment. He might have said as much in his now-missing field notes and then edited that sentiment away in the more reflective notebook entry we see today. But if we adjust for the fabrications of the time and place of the "geography lesson" it becomes evident that once Lewis was reunited with Clark and the main party on August 17th he stood in a position no worse than Mackenzie's when the Scotsman was at the limit of navigability on his western river in June 1793. Furthermore, a triangulation of the reports found in the journals of other members of the expedition indicates that the mood at the main party's Camp Fortunate on the upper Missouri upon Lewis's return from across the divide was anything but resigned or disappointed.[43]

At his camp of August 16th, near the forks of the Beaverhead River and in the company of a host of Shoshone Indians, Lewis was indeed gloomy. However, the source of Lewis's concern was not Columbian geography. Rather, he was worried about whether he could keep the suspicious Shoshone and their horses in tow long enough to meet up with Clark and the bulk of the expedition so that the portage across the divide could commence. He slept but little that night for a reason that was in complete contradiction to what his notebook ostensibly stated relative to Cameahwait's lesson on Columbian geography—his frustration in being unable to communicate with the Shoshone! "I had mentioned to the Chief several times," Lewis wrote, "that we had with us a woman of his nation who had been taken prisoner by the [Hidatsa], and that by means of her I hoped to explain myself more fully than I could do by signs." (Compare this with Lewis's earlier claim about Drouillard being "universally understood.") [44]

If the Shoshone were "transported with joy" when they learned Lewis had been telling them the truth about Clark and a larger party proceeding up the Missouri headwaters, the captains struck a pose only slightly less animated. Lewis found being amongst a friendly tribe with horses, and an effective translator (Sacagawea), a "flattering prospect." Notwithstanding the appearance of mountains to the west of the dividing ridge, Lewis was of a mind to proceed by land "should that by water *be deemed* unadvisable" (emphasis added). Obviously from Lewis's construction of the latter proposition, the navigability of the Columbia was still very much an open question when he reunited with Clark. [45]

Late on the afternoon of 16 August, through the consecutive translation of Francois Labiche, Charbonneau, and Sacagawea, an extensive parley was held. In Lewis's terminology, the explorers communicated "fully" on a host of topics. Among these was the request for a "pilot" to conduct them through the mountains west of the divide, "if we could not decend the river by water." (The pilot would prove to be Old Toby and here again the navigability of the Lemhi/Salmon/Snake system has not been ruled out.) Lewis's immediate objective was cajoling the Shoshone into providing "as many horses as were necessary to transport our baggage to their village on the Columbia." As to western geography, Lewis reported that the information communicated in this conversation "was only a repetition of that they had given me before." Nevertheless, we can deduce from the "concerted measures for our future operations" that Lewis and Clark formulated, plus accounts from the journals of the enlisted men, that a confident optimism, not pessimism about coping with mountains west of the divide, was the operative mood. [46]

First, consider Clark's report of the Camp Fortunate reunion with Lewis. Cameahwait tied shells in Clark's hair, a valued decoration procured "from the nations resideing near the *Sea Coast*." The grammatical emphasis was added by Clark, as he did again later in remarking that "Capt Lewis informed me he found those people on the *Columbia* River" about forty miles to the west. Clark's recounting of the inquiry into the nature of the Columbia River country, now aided by Sacagawea, was "verry unfavourable," with stories of rapids, narrow defiles impenetrable to passage, and a scarcity of game and timber to make canoes. "This information (if true is alarming)," Clark wrote. However, substantiating the view that the report of Columbian geography found in Lewis's notebook for August 14th was extrapolated after the fact, Clark then states, "I deturmined to go in advance and examine the Countrey, [to] See if those dificueltes presented themselves in the gloomey picture in which [the Shoshone] painted them." In case the Indians were being overly pessimistic, Clark ordered eleven men to accompany him with their axes and other woodworking tools "Soutable to build Canoes." [47]

Clark's plan was "agreeable" to Lewis, though the latter seems to have amended the mission by suggesting that Clark take Charbonneau and Sacagawea along.

(This proved to be wise counsel though it also suggests that Lewis did not want to cope with the Charbonneau family.) Upon his eventual arrival at the Shoshone camp west of the divide, Clark left the Charbonneaus at the village so that they might "haisten the return of the Indians with their horses to this place," meaning the main camp on the Missouri side. Clark, as Lewis phrased it, was to "proceede himself with the eleven men down the Columbia in order to examine the river and if he found it navigable and could obtain timber to set about making canoes immediately." Concurrently, Lewis would manage the portage over the divide. By the time the captains were reunited again on the Columbian side of the Rocky Mountains, Lewis expected his co-captain "would have sufficiently informed himself with rispect to the state of the river & c. as to determine us whether to prosicute our journey thence by land or water." [48]

Whatever impression Lewis had taken from his first gaze west into Columbia country, it was not as formidable as interpretive myth has made it. Otherwise, how to explain Clark taking some of his best woodworkers to make canoes for a voyage down the Columbia? The rest of the men in the expedition were also sanguine. Sgt. John Ordway recorded Lewis's reunion with the main party on August 17th matter of factly: "Capt. Lewis informed us that he had been over the dividing ridge or mountain to the head waters of the Columbian River & that it is only about 40 miles from this place." Lewis's vanguard, Ordway wrote happily, "drank at the head Spring of the Missourie & went only about a mile and drank at the head Spring of the Columbian River which ran west." Nothing along the lines of impassable barriers or other alarming news was conveyed to Ordway. As for the country to the west of the divide, the sergeant understood from the Shoshone, via Lewis, that there was no timber for canoes on the Columbia or much in the way of game, "but we do not believe them." In short, confidence reigned. On the morning of August 18th Clark and his eleven men set out "to See if possable to make canoes for us to descend the Columbian river to the western ocian." [49]

Pvt. Joseph Whitehouse matched Ordway's understanding of Lewis's first impression of the divide and Columbia country. When Lewis rejoined the Missouri detachment at Camp Fortunate, Whitehouse reported that he "informed us that he had been over the mountain on the head waters of Columbian River." Like Ordway, Whitehouse restated the insight "that their is no timber large enofe for canoes on the head waters." Clark, of course, was determined to verify that point. However, Whitehouse provided still more geographic intelligence than Ordway did. Both referred to the Columbia River's headwaters, strongly suggestive of the view that the fork Lewis had been on was the principal one. Whitehouse expanded on this point by noting that the Shoshone Indians had brought with them some salmon they had brought "from the main Columbia river." Like Ordway's report of Lewis's sojourn on the Columbia, Whitehouse recorded many details about how his captain had initially hailed the Shoshone. Lewis had obviously regaled the detachment with this saga. However, neither Whitehouse nor Ordway records any information from Lewis about expedition-compromising geography west of the divide. [50]

Lastly, there is Sgt. Patrick Gass's journal to consider. Gass had the least to say about the reunion on the Beaverhead and western geography. Gass stated that Lewis "had been as far as the waters of the Columbia river," where he met the Shoshone. Of Lewis's traverse, Gass stated simply that it was forty miles "and the road or way said to be good." Gass also noted that Captain Clark was going over the ridge "to search for timber to make canoes for descending the Columbia." [51]

The combined effect of the journals of Clark, Gass, Ordway, and Whitehouse relative to Lewis's reunion with them at Camp Fortunate demolishes the Lemhi disappointment thesis, at least as popularly conceived. True, the Shoshone at one time or another had intimated the existence of a challenging topography. However, Lewis himself, as we saw earlier, had effectively known about this circumstance for a month, going back to his ramble on the heights above the Great Falls of the Missouri. The main problem by 18 August when Clark headed west with the woodworkers was the uncertain navigability of the Columbia River and whether the timber on the headwaters was big enough to make canoes. This can be confirmed by the fact that in short order every journal keeper would find himself in position to take in the same, initial view west of the divide that Lewis had. William Clark was first among this number, crossing the crest on August 19th in the company of the canoe makers. Of this passage Clark said, with no sense of climax, that his detachment "proceeded on up the main branch with a gradial assent to the head and passed over a low mountain and Decended a Steep Decent to a butifull Stream." [52]

Patrick Gass was in Clark's unit. He wrote about dining "at the head spring of the Missouri." To his south, Gass sighted "snow on the top of a mountain." He did not find this in any way extraordinary since he quickly added that although there had been a frost that morning, the sun was shining that day and the weather was warm. After lunch Gass, Clark, and the others proceeded to the dividing ridge. The only note Gass makes about his first gaze into Columbia country is that two friendly Indians met them there. "We proceeded on through the mountain," Gass wrote, "passed some fine springs and encamped." [53]

Ordway and Whitehouse crossed Lemhi Pass with Lewis and the portage crew on August 26th. The sergeant, like many others, engaged in the now-ritualized drinking of water from the fount of the Missouri River. Lewis said of this activity that the men "consoled themselves with the idea of having at length arrived at this long wished for point." Replicating the act on a Columbian spring, Ordway then looked about and recorded a few unremarkable notes about hills covered with lodgepole pine and fir, ravines, and springs "all makeing west," the desired direction. Ordway did see "considerable of Snow on the mountain near us which appear but little higher than we are." Whitehouse's text replicates Ordway's in all its understated particulars. After drinking from both wellsprings, Whitehouse stated that the heights to the southwest had "Some Spots of Snow on them." The pine and fir, he noted, were "verry tall," a reference to their potential as canoes. [54]

The portage was Lewis's second traverse of Lemhi Pass. With two weeks now elapsed to reflect on the significance of the view from the ridge, even further informed now by some early Shoshone intimations about the Columbia River country, the entirety of his observation of this landscape the second time through reads as follows:

> [T]he tops of the high and irregular mountains which present themselves to our view on the opposite side of this branch of the Columbia are yet perfectly covered with snow; the air which proceeds from those mountains has an agreeable cool-ness and renders these parched and South hillsides much more supportable at this time of day it being now about noon.

The vaunted snow in view at Lemhi did not pose a threat but rather had taken on a salutary quality. This scene is a modest amplification upon his note for August 12th and is hardly the crushing perspective of LEWIS & CLARK legend, especially when we consider that Lewis had yet to hear the results of Clark's reconnaissance of the Salmon River.[55]

August 20th was William Clark's first full day west of the divide. His intended objective was to find a guide in the Shoshone village on the Lemhi River. He was looking for someone who could accompany him farther downstream on a mission to test the river's navigability. The pilot would prove to be an elderly man referred to later in the journals as Old Toby. Cameahwait had apparently recommended his services. From Clark's edits recorded in Lewis's notebook (much like his aviso about the origin of the "geography lesson") we see that conversations in the Shoshone village were the initial sources of Clark's understandings of western topography, later expropriated by Lewis. Everything Clark asked or said through Sacagawea was repeated by Cameahwait to the whole village. Late in the day Clark left the Charbonneaus behind with Pierre Cruzatte to facilitate the gathering of horses that would assist Lewis and the portage. Clark and the balance of his squad, guided by Old Toby, set off on what was truly the first substantive exploration of the Columbia River watershed conducted by any member of the expedition.[56]

Clark's reconnaissance of the Salmon River began to pay conclusive dividends on August 23rd. Early in the day Clark's squad proceeded "with great dificuelty as the rocks were So Sharp large and unsettled and the hill sides Steep that the horses could with the greatest risque and dificulty get on." After a few miles Clark reached a point where the horses could no longer continue without stepping into the river, which was becoming confined within a narrow canyon. Clark took three of his men plus Old Toby for an additional twelve-mile hike down a wolf path "to examine if the river continued bad." [57]

During this traverse Clark found the river to be "almost one continued rapid," the passage of which by canoe was "entirely impossible." The water, Clark confided, ran between huge rocks with "the Current beeting from one against another for

Some distance below." Worse, at one juncture the rapids and mountains came to such proximity so as to "prevent a possibility of a portage." Clark concluded from his survey that to proceed down the Columbia it would be necessary to cross at every bend in contest with an unrelenting current. Such a venture would be hazardous in the extreme. Upon inquiry, Old Toby told Clark that the river continued in the same fashion for many more miles. The water ran "with great violence from one rock to the other on each Side foaming & roreing thro rocks in every direction, So as to render the passage of any thing impossible," Clark concluded.[58]

Climbing up out of the canyon, the party reached a vantage where Old Toby showed Clark the difficulties of which he spoke. From this eminence, as Clark described the scene, the guide "Shewed me a road from the N Which Came into the one I was in which he Said went to a large river which run to the north on which was a Nation called Tushapass, he made a map of it." The "Tushapass" were the Flathead or Salish-Kootenai Indians. Thus, it was during Clark's trip of August 23rd, not August 12th when Lewis crossed the divide, nor the supposed Lewis/Cameahwait "geography lesson" of the 14th, that the true complexity of Columbian topography, including the escape route from the Lemhi Valley became fully discernible. Concurrently, it was here that the promise of a quick portage from the Atlantic side across the divide and down the Great River of the West to the Pacific began to die. It happened two weeks later than LEWIS & CLARK legend has it. Ironically, this denouement was fatefully similar to the disappointment Mackenzie had faced twelve years earlier.[59]

Confirmation that August 23rd was the day of topographical revelation can be found in the diary of Patrick Gass. Among the handful of men whom Clark had left behind with the horses at the Shoshone village on the Lemhi while he proceeded down the Salmon River with Old Toby, Gass was still making notes as late as the 23rd about "timber large enough to make canoes." Meriwether Lewis's own notebook offers further affirmation as to the value of William Clark's reconnaissance. "Capt. C. being now perfictly satisfyed as to the impracticability of this rout either by land or water, informed the old man [Toby], that he was convinced of the varacity of his assertions and would now return to the village from whence they had set out where he expected to meet myself and party." Thus, in real time, as opposed to Lewis's fabricated chronology, it was Clark who provided geographic findings to Lewis, who was at this time still on the Missouri side of the ridge negotiating for horses. Clark did this via a letter to Lewis written on August 24th.[60]

With reality having fully and finally replaced the promise of a "single portage" separating the waters of the Missouri and the Columbia, it fell to Clark to develop alternate scenarios for proceeding west. He tendered several options in his communiqué to Lewis. In one scheme a portion of the detachment would be sent down the Salmon River while a complementary land force attempted to stay within hailing distance from the adjoining ridgelines. Clark's last option, and the one eventually adopted, called for securing as many horses from the Shoshone as possible. Then, guided by Old Toby they would "proceed on by land to Some navagable part of the *Columbia* River, or to the *Ocean*, depending on what provisions we can procure by the gun aded to the Small Stock we have on hand depending on our horses as the last resort." This was a prescient description of the path the expedition took across the divide northward into the Bitterroot Valley and in turn over the Lolo Trail. Clark's comments foreshadowed the provisioning issue as well, right down to killing horses for food. [61]

Ironically, Clark found trees on August 24th that if tied together two at a time would have served the expedition as canoes. He had held out the hope for a river voyage down the Columbia to the last. "[E]very man," Clark wrote, "appeared disheartened from the prospects of the river," highlighting once again that his reconnaissance was the true moment of disappointment in the mountains, not Lewis's ascent to the crest on August 12th. Lewis gamely maintained the narrative fiction of the August 14th geography lesson by recording in his notebook for the 24th that Clark wrote him "a discription of the river and country, and stated our prospects by this rout *as they have been heretofore mentioned*" (emphasis added). As before, when Clark later came upon this dismissive language in Lewis's notebook, he made two interlineations hinting at his divination of this geographic intelligence, including the recourse to the Lolo Trail employed by the Nez Perce. Gass's journal is in conformance on this issue, noting on August 24th that Clark sent a letter to Lewis pointing out it would not be possible to go down by water "without much risk and trouble." Gass quickly added that Clark's guide, Old Toby, knew another route to a navigable portion of the river.[62]

John Colter was the means by which Clark's findings were relayed to Lewis and the larger party. On August 26th, when Lewis finally arrived at the Shoshone village on a "branch of the Columbia" [Lemhi River], he found Colter waiting. As Lewis recorded the moment, Clark's letter gave him an account of Clark's "perigrination and the description of the river and country as before detailed;" that is, in Lewis's pretentious notebook entry for August 14th. Clark later once again objected to Lewis's denigration of his laborious reconnaissance. For the third time, coming upon Lewis's expropriations, Clark corrected the record for Biddle's benefit. Clark edited Lewis's notebook for August 26th by noting that it was he and his guide, Old Toby, who had developed the fallback strategy of pursuing the "*road to the North & c.*" Clark pointedly crossed out Lewis's "we had formed" the plan to follow the Lolo Trail to "*Capt C had recommended*" doing so (emphasis in the original). John Ordway's journal for August 26th confirms Clark's version, as it is only on this late date that the expedition's senior sergeant shows any understanding of the troublesome geography ahead. Ordway, who was helping Lewis with the portage, wrote of finding Colter at the Shoshone village. The latter "had been with Capt. Clark a long distance down this River," Ordway recorded. Colter told him that the river was not navigable and game scarce. Ordway concluded his entry: "Capt. Clark Sent Capt. Lewis a note and Says he will meet us here & determine whether we follow the River or go across by land to the wtn. ocean." [63]

Clark and Lewis would not rejoin each other's company in the Lemhi River Valley until 29 August 1805, by which time the latter had ceased writing—a gap in journaling that would last until September 9th. With the hope of an immediate river voyage now dashed, the attention of both captains turned to the matter of securing a sufficient number of horses to pursue the northern road. On August 28th Clark had received a note back from Lewis in which, Clark states rather sharply, Lewis secured 22 horses "for our rout through by land on the plan which I had preposed in which he agreed with me in." Clark's strategy was to get a sufficient number of horses from the Indians to carry all the baggage and a few others "for Some of the men to ride occasionally." Notwithstanding Meriwether Lewis's repeated attempts at narrative grandstanding, it was William Clark's continued display of good judgment that stands out in the Lemhi Pass/Salmon River saga. Elliott Coues, in an observation obscured by the bicentennial hagiography of Meriwether Lewis at Lemhi Pass, said that Clark's work in late August 1805 "saved the expedition." [64]

With this second transmontane reunion of the captains, the stark realization of what now faced the expedition began to sink into the mental outlook of all of the men. Joseph Whitehouse said Clark's party "informed us that the mountains which they crossed were amazing high & rough; and that they thought it an impossibility, to go down the Columbia, from the place they were at, from the number of steep Clifts & Rocks, and that the Columbia River, was very rapid & full of rocks, and that it was dangerous for Canoes to descend that River." This is the *true* language of expeditionary disappointment, not the mythical conflations derived from Lewis's line of text describing a range of mountains to the west of Lemhi. It was, thus, August 29th, more than two weeks after Lewis's supposed revelation at the crest or later with Cameahwait, or even the first reunion at Camp Fortunate on the Missouri, that a junior man such as Whitehouse learned of the trouble ahead. And he learned it from Clark, not Lewis. "The whole of our party were employed in packing up the Indian Goods & baggage," Whitehouse wrote with a tinge of both resignation and trepidation, "in order to get ready to start tomorrow, on our way to go round, or between the Mountains, in order to find the Columbia River, a distance below where Captain Clark & his party had been, if possible." [65]

Similarly, John Ordway was frustrated by being unable to "find the ocean [via] the course we want to go." Ordway's account, however, reflected the encouragement the expedition took from having a Shoshone guide and his recommendation of the "road to the North." Ordway understood from Old Toby the road would be rough, but in a mere ten days they would be able to return to a point on the river where it would be navigable. An even more enticing prospect was the promise that from said juncture (the Clearwater/Snake confluence) "the River would be navigable or in about 15 days we could go to where the tide came up and Salt water. So we concluded to go that road," Ordway concluded, with more than a hint that the captains vetted the strategy on how to proceed with the sergeants if not, indeed, with everyone in the expedition. By Ordway's calculation the party would be at the approximate location of today's Beacon Rock, or perhaps even the Columbia River estuary, by September 24th. In reality, they would by that date have just ended the traverse of the Bitterroot Mountains they were about to begin.[66]

The Expedition for Northwest Discovery's first two weeks in Columbia River country had been eventful and revealing. To the detriment of scholarly and popular understanding of the expedition's history, the successive editing of the journals has robbed the story of its Columbia River associations, making it a saga about the Rocky Mountains or the Continental Divide. As we have seen, the journalists themselves, particularly Ordway and Whitehouse, routinely refer to the westering headwaters as being those of the Columbia. Even the captains, after a long two years on the Missouri, delighted in the novelty of being on the waters named for Robert Gray's ship. Clark was especially fond of emphasizing the words "Columbia" and "ocean" in his notes. Elliott Coues established an editorial trend with his annotated version of the Biddle paraphrase of the journals in 1893. He routinely eliminated references to the Columbia, replacing them with such euphemistic or anachronistic phrases as "the Pacific watershed," "Lemhi River," or "Salmon River." The annotation of both Reuben Gold Thwaites and more recently Gary Moulton regularly explains away the expedition's contemporaneous understanding that they were on the Columbia River.[67]

The editors, relying on latter-day understanding of the continent's hydraulic architecture, surely did so with the reader's interest in mind. Their goal was to place the story within the bounds of geographic knowledge as revealed with the passage of time. Barbara Belyea, the editor of David Thompson's journals, agrees with this necessity but argues that while "no text can be read except by interpretation, the process can be usurped by the editor." Within this editorial and interpretive framework, the price paid for modern geographic clarity in the case of Lewis and Clark on the upper Columbia is that it has become hard to see the intellectual, temporal, and physical contingencies that the explorers thought, saw, and felt in real time. Conjoined with Lewis's exploratory ego and editorial practices plus his spotty journal-keeping, the Columbia River experience of the Lewis and Clark expedition has become consistently enigmatic from beginning to end.[68]

The story of the expedition as it approached and then entered the Columbia River watershed reveals a more nuanced and ambiguous relationship between the captains. Surely Lewis and Clark were and remained steadfast friends to the end. However, by the time Clark sat down with Nicholas Biddle to edit the journals, if not in real time, Clark's devotion to Lewis was delimited by a measure of resentment at having to play second fiddle to his friendly rival. And as we shall see later in this book, Clark would have to prop up his fragile colleague. This textured relationship was obliterated by the bicentennial's hagiography of both men.

CHAPTER 3   Half Starved

THE TREK TO THE COLUMBIA VIA THE "NORTHERN ROAD" began the first week of September 1805 with a traverse of what is now called Lost Trail Pass. This route connects the Lemhi/Salmon River watershed with the Bitterroot River valley of today's western Montana. The trail crosses a complex aggregation of ridges and nearly intersects with the Continental Divide, which in this vicinity runs east to west. Because of its relatively short length, it would not prove as difficult a passage as the Lolo Trail still ahead, but mile for mile it was as severe a test.[1]

Sgt. John Ordway considered this country a dismal and "verry lonesome place." When the expedition approached the crest of the pass on September 3rd and then camped, Ordway said the detachment "lay down wet hungry and cold." Pvt. Joseph Whitehouse stated the party had "a dissagreeable days march of only 11 miles with much fatigue and hunger." When they crossed the ridge into the Bitterroot valley on the morning of September 4th, the ground was covered with snow. Whitehouse noted the frozen moccasins of his mates, and he said "our fingers aked with the cold." Early in the day there was nothing to eat. Descending the northern slope of the pass into the valley, the hunters finally enjoyed some good shooting. The expedition was "revived" by this success, Whitehouse wrote, "however in all the hardship that they had yet undergone they never once complained, trusting to Providence & the Conduct of our Officers in all our difficulties."[2]

Coming down from the mountainside to the banks of the Bitterroot River, part of a watershed Clark later named for himself in a postdated journal entry, the captains were presented with a puzzle. Geographic lore, including information from the Hidatsa Indians secured during the previous winter at Fort Mandan, suggested, or was interpreted by the captains to mean, that there was only *one* river running south to north on the west side of the Continental Divide. The Bitterroot River was now the second the company had discovered, after the Lemhi/Salmon fork. Their journals describing the approach to, and stay at, the Traveler's Rest campsite of 9–10 September 1805, located a few miles south of present-day

Missoula, show them grappling with this problem. In his notes Lewis referred to the Bitterroot as the "Flathead river," evidence that Clark's act of naming it for himself, as reflected in his own journal, took place appreciably later.[3]

Lewis's first impression of the Bitterroot River, with its low bank and gravel bed, was that "the stream appears navigable, but from the circumstance of their being no sammon in it I believe that there must be a considerable fall in it below." Upon inquiry as to where the "Flathead River" met the Columbia, Old Toby told Lewis that it continued north "and that not very distant from where we then were it formed a junction with a stream nearly as large as itself." This disclosure opened an even more intriguing prospect because the latter took its rise in the Rocky Mountains to the east. This new stream, latterly known as the Blackfoot River, is a tributary to the Clark Fork River, which itself receives the Bitterroot at Missoula, the combined stream being an affluent of Lake Pend Oreille. Of high strategic interest to Lewis, the Blackfoot River passed through an open valley of prairie country "which forms an excellent pass to the Missouri." This was in fact the route the Nez Perce took, via the Medicine and Dearborn River corridors, to their hunting grounds on the buffalo plains in the Missouri watershed, rather than passing through Shoshone homelands via the Lost Trail and Lemhi Passes. It was also the route that had led Old Toby to disclose the existence of the Lolo trail in the first place. From Traveler's Rest, Old Toby told Lewis, it might take only four days to reach the Missouri at a spot thirty miles above the Gates of the Rocky Mountains, between today's Great Falls and Helena, Montana.[4]

These findings held a host of implications, both for the next leg of the journey and for the one just completed. First, the possibility of a waterfall downstream considerable enough to stymie Pacific salmon raised doubts about the navigability of the "Flathead River," reinforcing Old Toby's original recommendation to William Clark—that the expedition take the Nez Perce (Lolo) Trail over the Bitterroot Mountains, whose massive peaks loomed over the shoulders of the expedition at Traveler's Rest. Second, the newly encountered shortcut to the Missouri offered a superior route over the divide than Lemhi Pass. The practicability of this shortcut as a trade route would be probed on the return trip in 1806. The discovery of the shortcut also revealed to Lewis and Clark that they had come to Traveler's Rest through a very roundabout method, a startling revelation that immediately raised questions about the cartographic presumptions the American explorers had carried around in their heads, and called for a reassessment of what they thought they had learned from the Hidatsa.[5]

Lewis and Clark now had to wonder whether the Hidatsa description of a northward-flowing river at the western base of the Rocky Mountains indeed referred to the Lemhi/Salmon River system, as they had believed up to this time, or the newly encountered Bitterroot. Lewis claimed in his journal at Traveler's Rest that the Hidatsa had told him and Clark that the "Medicine River" (today's Sun River of Montana), a tributary of the Missouri above its great falls, approached the sources of a large river west of the Rockies that flowed *south to north*. In fact, however, this contradicted a note Lewis composed at Fort Mandan wherein he recorded that the stream associated with the Medicine west of the mountains (the Blackfoot River) ran initially west and then flowed into a larger river headed *north to south*. One or the other of these notes about Hidatsa information was probably a simple mistake in memory or inscription at Fort Mandan, though of these two an error in the field seems more likely. Alternatively, this textual inconsistency could be an example of the typical practice of explorers never wanting to seem surprised: once the captains faced the Bitterroot River running south to north they recalibrated the entry from Fort Mandan. In any event, as we have seen earlier, it's clear from the route Lewis and Clark took that the Hidatsa did not specify the Medicine as the path to follow, having recommended the three forks of the Missouri and Lemhi Pass track, a suggestion that reinforced Jefferson's directive to go source-hunting.[6]

To help sort out these issues, Lewis and Clark consulted Alexander Mackenzie's *Voyages from Montreal* and probably Nicholas King's map too. The latter was based to a considerable degree on the Nor'Wester's explorations and his cartographer Aaron Arrowsmith. King's map shows a truncated and speculative system called the "Great Lake River," probably an evocation of Flathead Lake in Montana or Lake Pend Oreille in Idaho. The wellspring for this stream was the Continental Divide at a more northerly latitude, and it ran in a southwesterly direction eventually connecting with Mackenzie's Tacoutche Tesse above its junction with the great southern fork that the Americans were seeking. Lewis concluded that the enlarged stream created by the combination of the "Flathead River" (the Bitterroot) and the "Valley plain river" (the Blackfoot/Clark Fork) eventually turned west, like the "Great Lake River" in King's map, and fell into the "Tacootchetessee." This latter stream, of course, was Mackenzie's name for the northerly fork of what the Scot mistakenly concluded was the Columbia River. And indeed, the Blackfoot/Bitterroot/Clark Fork system, subsumed under the "Flathead/Valley plain" river system of Lewis's hydraulic lexicon, redirects the northerly trajectory of the Bitterroot into a more westerly flow.[7]

Lewis's deduction conveniently preserved the prospect that the Lemhi/Salmon fork of the Columbia, if they could simply reach it across the mountains to the west via the Nez Perce trail, would be navigable to the ocean, unlike *two* forks of Mackenzie's "Tacoutche Tesse." Mackenzie had himself proved the most northerly stem was impracticable to canoe travel. Similarly, the "Flathead River," which, presumably, salmon could not pass because of a large waterfall, was likely impassible to watercraft too. Based on his conclusions, Lewis made a recommitment to the Hidatsa-based understanding of Columbia River navigability, a view reinforced by one of the Nez Perce the party encountered at Traveler's Rest. This Nez Perce acquaintance subsequently "agreed to continue with us as a guide," Lewis wrote, "and to introduce us to his relations whom he informed us were numerous and resided in the plain below the [Bitterroot] mountains on the columbia river, from whence he said the water was good and capable of being navigated to the sea."

Indeed, this short-lived Nez Perce guide (he would abandon the expedition after one day on the Lolo Trail) said one of his relatives had been to the sea itself and saw there manufactured goods much like the explorers had in their possession. Thus, as Lewis probably conceived it, his expedition, unlike Mackenzie's, still preserved the prospect of reaching a navigable portion of the Columbia River and possibly its main stem. And, if Lewis had to cross still more mountainous terrain than the short portage originally expected on the basis of geographical lore and Hidatsa insights, at least he now had the potential reward of the "Valley plain river" route, which the expedition would explore on the return trip. This shortcut from and to the Missouri could shave a month's travel time and hundreds of miles off the commercial route to the Pacific that Jefferson had charged Lewis with establishing. This path was eventually deemed by Lewis "a good road" and part of the "practicable rout" linking "the navigable branches of the Missouri and Columbia Rivers." [8]

In imperial terms, Lewis would have acknowledged the "Flathead" and "Valley plain" Rivers (i.e., today's Bitterroot/Clark Fork system) as tributaries of the "Tacoutche Tesse" of Mackenzie. On the other hand, he still regarded the Lemhi/Salmon Rivers found in Shoshone homelands as the headwaters of the Columbia. Lewis would rejoin the Columbia via the northern road of the Nez Perce, as previously recommended by Old Toby to William Clark. If this understanding was not fully explicated in Lewis's journal, confirmation of this theory can be found in the notes of one of the enlisted men.

As so often proves to be the case in trying to access the subtext of the expedition's history, the journals of Joseph Whitehouse prove indispensable. At thirty years of age in 1805, Whitehouse was only a year younger than Lewis and about the median age for the detachment as a whole. He was a Kentuckian with a somewhat independent streak as evidenced by the disciplinary trouble he got into over the winter of 1803–04 at River Dubois. We know the captains were openly working through geography problems with at least some of the men at Traveler's Rest because Whitehouse was aware of their thinking. Upon entering the Bitterroot valley, Whitehouse did not have any sense of a place name having been granted to the stream, which was simply referred to as "this large Creek or small River." Near present-day Stevensville, Montana, Whitehouse recorded seeing snow on the mountains to his left, a chain he knew the party was expected to cross. Ahead lay the "high Barren hills" that envelope Missoula. On September 10th, Whitehouse's field journal concludes with this curiously constructed passage: "our guide [Old Toby] tells us that these waters [the Bitterroot] runs into Mackinzees River as near as they can give an account, but he is not acquainted that way. So we go the road he knows." [9]

Clearly Whitehouse had developed a hybridized understanding out of several threads of geographic intelligence, starting with Old Toby. Lewis and Clark had to have been the source of the reference to Mackenzie. The fair copy of Whitehouse's journal (a polished version of Whitehouse's "campfire" record finished after the expedition and therefore informed by topographical discernment not yet apparent at

Traveler's Rest) also addresses this new geography lesson in a somewhat muddled manner. Therein, Whitehouse reported that several hunters had proceeded to the confluence of the "Flathead" and "Valley plain" rivers and considered themselves, thereby, to have been "in sight of the Columbia River this day." When replicating the combined judgment of Lewis and Old Toby, Whitehouse repeated the view that "these Waters, runs into Mackenzie's River," meaning the northern fork of the Columbia.[10]

Whitehouse provides other insights into the expedition's understanding of their location and situation now deep into the Northwest. First, the Americans deduced that any river they encountered west of the Rockies was a tributary to the Columbia in some fashion. Like Lewis, Whitehouse displayed some ambivalence about whether this new fork of the Columbia was the one the Hidatsa had intended for them to take. Measured in hydrological terms like volume or navigability, the Lemhi/Salmon fork still held a superior status for him as the desired outlet to the Pacific Ocean. It's also important to emphasize how the imperial shadow of Alexander Mackenzie loomed large in all these calculations. Lewis surely studied his situation in juxtaposition to the Scotsman's explorations and shared his conclusions with the others. We see this in the way Whitehouse identified the northern fork of the Columbia with their British competition. We shall return to this theme in later chapters.[11]

Late on the afternoon of 11 September 1805 the expedition left Traveler's Rest and "set out on our Journey again," as Whitehouse phrased it, heading west up Lolo Creek. It's also worth noting that on this day William Clark commenced what is commonly referred to as his "Elkskin-bound Journal," running through 31 December 1805. This daybook or "campfire" compilation is unquestionably the most direct and primary source of information about the expedition from this point west to the Pacific Ocean.[12]

The traverse of the Lolo or Nez Perce Trail is a legendary story in the lore of LEWIS & CLARK. Perforce, this episode has been subject to considerable exaggeration via theatrical presentations and in print. That the trail was exacting and unusually difficult, there can be no doubt. But the journalists in the expedition writing about this crossing going west and again on the return, with the exception of one short segment, describe the care and control of the horses and *not* the physical safety of the party itself as being the greatest risk. Joseph Whitehouse often suggested that the trail was far more difficult for horses than the men. On September 15th, William Clark reported that "Several horses Sliped and roled down Steep hills which hurt them verry much." One of these pack animals carried Clark's portable desk. It is only during Meriwether Lewis's journal for September 19th that we find a description of the road being "excessively dangerous" from which precipice "if ether man or horse were precipitated they would inevitably be dashed in pieces."[13]

However, it is not the danger of the ride but the supply of food along this road that is the source of the Lolo legend. Historians with their own narrative requirements for effective storytelling have inflated a temporary scarcity of game, one both anticipated and recognized by the expedition as transitory, into the Bitterroot Mountains starvation myth. The hyperbole began with Elliott Coues who suggested that the party had barely avoided freezing or starving to death in the mountains. "The situation was grave," Coues averred. Modern authors and film-makers have used such expressions as the "starving time," "near starvation," "severest of threats to existence," "nearly starved," and "more dead than alive" to describe a supposedly barely-avoided demise of the expedition on the Lolo Trail. It is no doubt true that provisions were in considerably shorter supply than the party had been accustomed to on the Missouri, and that such a situation could only have exacerbated the perception of scarcity in the mountains. But those fatted plains were already a month or more distant by the time the expedition hit the Lolo Trail. Though much is made of William Clark's hunting vanguard once the party was well into the depths of the Bitterroot Mountains (addressed later), riflemen were sent out in advance of the main party from the very first day upon leaving Traveler's Rest. In fact, Clark said the practice was common during the entire course of the expedition.[14]

Studied as an exception and in isolation, Lewis and Clark's travails in present-day northern Idaho appear quite dramatic. However, the circumstances the expedition found itself in during the traverse of the Lolo Trail, though straitened, were hardly unique in the history of western exploration. They certainly pale against the bona fide desperation that threatened cannibalism among the Astorians. Less dramatically, John C. Frémont, during his 1842 expedition to South Pass, after venturing out from the depot at Fort Laramie, observed that his party was "on the threshold of danger." He told the men they had ten days worth of provisions but, even absent finding some game along the way, he reassured them "we had our horses and mules, which we could eat when other means of subsistence failed." Crossing the Sierra Nevada Mountains south of Lake Tahoe in February 1844, Frémont wandered in terrain and weather not unlike Lewis and Clark's experience in the Bitterroots but for an even longer period—eighteen days. In that instance Frémont sought recourse to horsemeat for the undernourished men. He even butchered his mascot, the dog "Tlamath," an extreme measure that Lewis was fortunate to avoid. [15]

For a people of plenty like modern-day Americans, the difference between being hungry—feeling discomfort or weak from want of food—and starving—to die or nearly so—may be indistinct. One historian opines that Lewis, despite "nearly starving," conducted "a remarkable flurry of ornithology." Sensibly, a man who was actually starving would not take the time or be able to maintain sufficient focus to write a lot about birds. Rather than starvation, it was the relative uncertainty of where the next meal was coming from and anxiety over the delayed appearance of the Columbia plains that dispirited the party's outlook. The Shoshone and Nez Perce had warned the captains about the supply of food in the mountains. Surely by now Lewis may have thought better of the boast he made in Shoshone country that if the Indians could make it over the Lolo Trail, then so could his party.[16]

It wasn't until September 14th, the fourth day of the mountainous trek, that there was even a hint of concern about food. Back when first describing Old Toby's northern road and formulating his recommendations to Lewis, Clark had anticipated the need for extra horses—not for drayage but for food "as the last resort." This day the party killed one of their colts "for the want of meat," as contingency planning had anticipated. The remnant of that carcass also provided the main meal on the 15th.[17]

At what would prove to be the halfway point across the mountains, six to eight inches of snow compounded the difficulties of passing over the thickly timbered hillsides. The packs on the horses were constantly rubbing up against the low, snow-burdened limbs of the trees. Though the exceptionalist lore of LEWIS & CLARK trumpets these privations, they were far from extraordinary in wilderness travel. In 1807 David Thompson, during his initial foray across the Rockies into Columbia country, arrived at Kootenay Lake "extremely hungry & fatigued, so that we were hardly able to paddle." The next day Thompson's party happened upon a wild horse and made a meal of it. John C. Frémont, four decades after Lewis and Clark, wrote similarly about being forced off ridgelines by heavy snows. The Sierra's slopes "were steep, and slippery... and the tough evergreens of the mountains impeded our way, tore our skins, and exhausted our patience." His men, like Lewis and Clark's earlier, also complained about their moccasins not being able to keep feet dry and warm. A cold and wet Lolo Trail prompted Clark to proceed ahead about six miles with another man to make a fire for the expected arrival of the larger party (a tactic Frémont also later employed). A second colt was killed for supper that night "which we all Suped hartily on and thought it fine meat," Clark reported, using language hardly suggestive of scarcity or meagerness. [18]

The legend of Lewis and Clark's "starving time" is grounded in the events of 18–19 September 1805, the eighth and ninth days of the eleven-day Lolo transit. Exercising classic leadership skill, Clark ventured forward a second time, joining the hunters. The want of deer, elk, or bear meat, Clark later explained to Nicholas Biddle, combined with the rough going in the mountains "dampened the Spirits of the party." Clark's plan was to advance west to the open plains where prospects for finding game were considerably better. Lightened of the burden of conducting baggage across those peaks, Clark's small band of hunters made thirty-two miles on horseback on the 18th compared with the fourteen miles the whole detachment had averaged per day for the previous week. Even Lewis's trailing unit made eighteen miles the same day, still higher than average. Lewis said he was "determined to force my march." [19]

Twenty miles into his ride, Clark's strategy started to pay dividends because from an elevated vantage he secured "a view of an emence Plain and leavel Countrey to the S W. & West." These were the Camas and Nez Perce prairies near today's Grangeville, Idaho. That night, Clark and his squad set up camp on a stream he called "*Hungery Creek*" (emphasis in original). Drouillard had shot at a deer but could not bag it. Accordingly, in this instance, and for truly the only time during the Bitterroot traverse, some subset of the expedition had nothing to eat. However, had the situation called for it, Clark could have killed one of the hunters' horses. He did not because the targeted plains were in view. (For this reason the stream is not named "Starvation Creek.") [20]

The core text for the starvation legend is the party's recourse to the "portable soupe." A precursor of dehydrated food, it was nutritious enough as to convince the diet-conscious Captain Cook of its efficacy. This substance formed the midday meal and supper for the main party on September 18th. Although fairly described by Lewis as "skant proportion," a reference probably as much to its taste as to its nutrient potency, the more pressing requirement that day was not meat but water. Though much is made in the lore of LEWIS & CLARK regarding Lewis's short checklist of provisions then on hand—portable soup, bear's oil, and "candles"— less noticed is the captain's pointed assertion that the party still had its guns and horses. Lewis nonetheless affirmed that the guns were "but a poor dependance in our present situation" where all they could shoot at was a few grouse, squirrels, and blue jays. That the horses remained as a last resort went unstated but neither did the situation call for their use. For Clark and the hunters up ahead, relief came early on the 19th when they stumbled upon a stray horse from the herd of the Nez Perce. This animal was quickly butchered and eagerly eaten for breakfast, a meal "which we thought fine" Clark averred. The bulk of the carcass was "hung up" for Lewis's trailing unit. Also promising, Clark later noted for the benefit of Nicholas Biddle, was that as they descended from the mountains the heat from the Clearwater valley and plains below became "more proseptable every mile." [21]

On September 19th Lewis and the larger detachment came into view of the same prairie Clark had sighted on the 18th, to the captain's "inexpressable joy." Old Toby had told Lewis that beyond the plain lay "the Columbia river." By this the Shoshone guide meant what we know today as the Clearwater or Snake Rivers, but the more important point is that the day after the captains split their forces because of a dampened mood, the end of their travail was already in sight. The prairie was merely a day away, Toby said, and its appearance, Lewis stated, "greately revived the sperits of the party already reduced and much weakened for the want of food." On this day the portable soup again had to suffice. [22]

William Clark and the hunters made it out of the woods on September 20th, the tenth day after leaving Traveler's Rest. Around noon this vanguard stumbled unexpectedly into a camp of Nez Perce Indians on Weippe Prairie. After a quick distribution of presents to allay fears, Clark and his men were conducted to a lodge where they were fed buffalo meat, dried salmon, and some "beries & roots in different States" and bread made from camas root. Of this meal, Clark wrote, the party ate "hartily." For Clark and his squad, the issue of sustenance was over, but they knew Lewis still needed help, and for that reason the hunters were sent out. Meanwhile, Clark began inquiring about the geography of this new region. [23]

Lewis was apparently not overly concerned about the state of provender on September 20th, as this was the day of his aforementioned ornithological foray.

In short order Lewis's detachment came upon the carcass of the stray horse that Clark had left for them. Lewis and his party "made a hearty meal on our horse beef much to the comfort of our hungry stomachs." At camp that night there was but little grass for the pack horses, "however we obtained as much as served our culinary purposes and suped on our beef." It is easy to see in this level of provision how Lewis could afford to make botanical and other scientific observations. The expedition may have been hungry, but they were anything but close to starvation.[24]

On the 21st Lewis found one of Clark's earlier campsites and a glade where there was forage at last for the horses. They fixed a meal for themselves consisting of some grouse, coyote, crayfish from a nearby creek, and "the ballance of our horse beef," meaning that there had been a nominal surplus of meat from the previous day. All in all this was a serviceable diet under the circumstances but not entirely satisfactory because Lewis entered a passage in his journal that has been seized upon to sustain the starvation myth: "I find myself growing weak for the want of food and most of the men complain of a similar deficiency and have fallen off very much." Surely Lewis and the others were facing a nutritional shortage, but this was not his sole, if indeed his principal, preoccupation as reflected in a corresponding journal entry. "I saw several sticks today large enough to form eligant perogues of at least 45 feet in length," he wrote. The long-delayed voyage down the Columbia beckoned.[25]

William Clark was also beginning to make plans in this regard, securing from the headman of the Nez Perce village on Weippe Prairie "a Chart of the river & nations below." Still concerned for Lewis, Clark dispatched Reubin Field back up the Lolo Trail with a "horse load of roots & 3 Sammon." Lewis, for his own part, was determined to get out of the mountains on the 22nd, having ordered the picketing of the horses the night before to allow a quick start on "a forced march" to the open prairie ahead. Despite well-laid plans, "one of the men neglected to comply," pleading ignorance about Lewis's order, holding back the departure until almost noon. After a short 2½ miles of travel down the trail, Lewis's detachment met Field on his way up the mountain with food. Lewis wrote, "I ordered the party to halt for the purpose of taking some refreshment. I divided the fish roots and buries, and was happy to find a sufficiency to satisfy compleatly all our appetites." One meal was all it took. After another 7 ½ miles Lewis was also out of the woods, arriving at the Nez Perce village on Weippe Prairie around dusk. Contemplating his deliverance Lewis composed one of his most memorable passages:

> the pleasure I now felt in having tryumphed over the rocky Mountains and descending once more to a level and fertile country where there was every rational hope of finding a comfortable subsistence for myself and party can be more readily conceived than expressd, nor was the flattering prospect of the final success of the expedition less pleasing.

Two sentences later the westering voice of Meriwether Lewis turns silent. He would not resume regular journal-keeping until 1 January 1806, over three months later.[26]

When William Clark returned to Weippe Prairie after an initial reconnaissance of the Clearwater River, he "found Capt Lewis & the party Encamped, much fatigued, & hungery, much rejoiced to find something to eate of which They appeared to partake plentifully." Here we find the origin of the corollary to the starvation myth—that the Nez Perce Indians saved the expedition. The Nez Perce were unquestionably hospitable to the expedition both upon their first emergence from the wilderness in the fall of 1805 and during an even more cordial stay in the spring of 1806. One of the foundational elements of Clay Jenkinson's lore of LEWIS & CLARK typology—that "the expedition would not have survived without the help of American Indians"—is assuredly grounded in the food provided by the Nez Perce in September 1805. The larger assertion, Jenkinson states, is "hard to establish," and its durability and serviceability has more to do with modern cultural politics—"solidarity with Indian communities through which Lewis and Clark passed"—than reality. In any event, according to Clark, the party looked "much reduced in flesh as well as Strength," wording that suggests the men had lost weight and their endurance was sapped. Clark learned that the horse he had hung up was well placed, for it was found "at a time they were in great want" and that Reubin Field's mission was also deemed to have been well calculated for positive effect.[27]

The Lolo traverse had indeed been difficult, but it is important to keep it in perspective. The expedition always knew where it was going, it was always on the move, always had recourse to some degree of nourishment, and no one, perforce, was ever close to expiring. If anything, the physical condition of the expedition worsened *after* emerging from the mountains. As William Clark noted at Canoe Camp on the Clearwater, many of the men were so debilitated they were unable to work on making the craft intended for the float down the Columbia. The men, Clark reported, were still "complaining of their diat." On September 30th, a week after exiting the mountains, Joseph Whitehouse noted, "the party in general are So weak and feeble that we git along Slow with the canoes." Indeed, in a scene reminiscent of the mountain passage just concluded, Clark and the hunters went out on the hills looking for game and returned with "nothing excep a Small Prarie wolf" (coyote). Whitehouse reported "the party are So weak working without any kind of meat, that we concluded to kill a horse… and we eat the meat with good Stomacks as iver we did fat beef in the States." The expedition was not again fully healthy, "fit to do their duty" or in "high spirits," again until 6 October 1805, on the eve of their descent by canoe down the Clearwater River.[28]

The inflation of the real but survivable deprivation the party experienced into the Lolo starvation myth is also partially grounded in John Ordway's single phrase—"proceeded on half Starved"—expressed in passing. Similar verbiage was also employed once by William Clark the following spring when reflecting on the prospect of the expedition having to re-pass the mountains. This figure of speech, common in everyday parlance to this day, was and is intended to convey a limited extent of provision, not the literal prospect of facing death.[29]

To place this usage in context, consider the single instance during the expedition when one of its members went almost two weeks without any food. In the late summer of 1804 on the Missouri River, Pvt. George Shannon was out searching for horses and came to believe that the keelboat was ahead of him when in fact it was to his rear. Frantic to catch up, Shannon proceeded ahead, succeeding only in putting himself still farther in front of the expedition. Lewis and Clark caught up with him only when he eventually tired and stopped. William Clark, mockingly, said Shannon "in a plentifull Countrey like to have Starvd," showing once again the figurative usage of the word. Shannon had been gone sixteen days, twelve of them without provision except for a few grapes and one rabbit. When Shannon "became weak and [feeble he] deturmined to lay by and waite for a tradeing boat… Keeping one horse for the last resorse," meaning food.[30]

The narrative of Joseph Whitehouse is always a reliable method for placing other journal entries into context. In his account of the Bitterroot Mountains crossing, the difficulty of the terrain was readily conceded, the food was in short supply, but eating the colts was described as satisfying. To Whitehouse, certain Lolo Trail landscapes presented a "delightful prospect," with the weather sometimes stormy, at others pleasant. As for having to resort to the portable soup, Whitehouse said the men went to their rest that first night of its use "seemingly content." Whitehouse later returned to this phrasing in his entry for the trail's most difficult day, September 19th. He professed that the men were getting weak and suffering pangs of hunger, yet they "still seem contented; & flatter themselves of soon getting out of the Mountains." The Bitterroots extended farther west than any of them imagined, but Whitehouse, like Clark and Lewis, took considerable comfort from sighting the prairie off to the west. This was "where we expect is the Columbian River," Whitehouse wrote, "which puts us in good Spirits again." [31]

The spirits of Meriwether Lewis, however, took a longer time to recover, as evidenced by the fact that he did not resume regular journal-keeping until they reached Fort Clatsop, hundreds of miles to the west. His own last testament at Weippe, where he exulted in having "tryumphed over the rocky Mountains," provides the foundation for some possible explanations for this lapse. It is well-known among oral historians that an informants' historical consciousness may be stymied when recounting climactic moments in their personal experience. The stressful passage through the Bitterroots may have been such a moment for Lewis. Another possibility, explored in greater detail in a later chapter, is that having reached the Columbia, a river previously explored by Euro-Americans, Lewis temporarily lost interest, certainly in comparison to his previous fixation on the upper Missouri. A final possibility is that Lewis was simply (and literally) both sick and tired and therefore did not have the energy required to maintain a journal.[32]

Lest we see the temporary dispiritedness of the men during the passage over the Lolo Trail as exceptional, it bears mentioning that such lapses in morale were not at all unusual in the annals of exploration of the Columbia River. David Thompson, the fur trader/explorer advancing British commercial interests, noted in his journals that morale weakened among his men when they encountered snow while crossing Athabasca Pass. "The Courage of part of my Men... is sinking fast," he wrote in January 1811. Later at Boat Encampment on the upper Columbia in today's British Columbia, Thompson named a nearby creek coming in from the Athabasca summit "Flat Heart Brook," as a function of "the Men being dispirited." This was an act of place-naming not unlike Clark's *"Hungery Creek."* [33]

Thompson believed that "when Men arrive in a strange Country, fear gathers on them from every Object." Thompson also observed that when his men were on the verge of panic, seeing him safe and composed "encourage[d] them to think the same also." Surely the field leadership of William Clark in the Bitterroot Mountains qualifies for a meritorious citation in this regard. Twice he ventured ahead in vanguard movements, first to prepare camp and a fire during a snowstorm, and then again on the quest for provisions. If, as Elliott Coues has said, Clark's work of geographic discernment on the Salmon River saved the expedition, no less can be said of his stewardship of the party's interests on the Lolo Trail. [34]

CHAPTER 4   Not One
Stick of Timber

THE ORDERING OF WILLIAM CLARK'S PRIORITIES ONCE OUT
of the Bitterroot Mountains is clear from his journal entry of 21 September 1805.
After dispatching the hunters to help provision Meriwether Lewis and the larger
number of men in the trailing detachment, he "delayed with the Indians... to
acquire as much information as possible." The geographic intelligence proved rich
and detailed. A map drawn for Clark's benefit showed the location of Indian
nations along the river system below his position, including important information
of a "falls below" [Celilo] where white men could be found and from whom the
Indians "got white beeds cloth &c." Fur traders, including the Americans Robert
Gray and John Kendrick, had been plying the inlets of the Northwest coast for
the preceding fifteen years.[1]

Late on the afternoon of the 21st, Clark's advance party wound its way down
a steep hill to the Clearwater River. When Clark first saw this river he was
uncertain of its significance. In his field notes he described descending from
Weippe Prairie and discerning a stream coming in on his left, "and I suppose
it to be [blank] River." Was this the Columbia or was that name to be saved
for some river into which this stream flowed? Clark had become cautious about
such matters because the helpful Weippe Prairie village chief told him that
at "a long distance below" Clark would find "2 large forks one from the left
& the other from the right." There is no hint here as to which of these forks
(at what we know today as the Snake/Columbia confluence) was larger. Was
the river he now beheld part of a tributary system or the main stem? Later
that night Clark arrived at the Clearwater encampment of another hospitable
Nez Perce chief, Twisted Hair. Described as "a Chearfull man" about 65 years
of age, Twisted Hair resided on an island in the middle of the river. In his
recapitulation of course and distances, Clark left another blank spot for the
name of the river which joined the Clearwater a short distance below Twisted
Hair's camp—known today as the North Fork of the Clearwater. Surely Clark
was hedging his toponymic bets, pending further hydrological information and

imperial considerations related thereto. Clark eventually settled on the name "Kooskooske" for the Clearwater, but not until October 6th at the earliest.[2]

Accompanied by Twisted Hair, Clark returned to the village up on Weippe Prairie where he found Lewis and the main party. Clark started out with Twisted Hair and the chief's son on a single horse, but the impracticality of that arrangement resulted in Clark getting thrown three times. Clark resorted to a foundering colt and then another horse of Twisted Hair's before finally pulling into the village. With Lewis now present, Clark prevailed upon Twisted Hair to draw a map of the river downstream from his Clearwater camp. Twisted Hair drew it on a white elk skin, according to Clark, "with great cherfullness." [3]

Twisted Hair's map showed both forks of the Clearwater that merge below Orofino, Idaho, and further downstream a "large fork on which the *So So ne* [Shoshone] or Snake Indians fish." In this fashion the Snake River eventually got its identity despite the captains' best efforts later in the expedition to name it after Lewis. The Snake River was "2 Sleeps" from Twisted Hair's island in the Clearwater. Below the confluence of the Snake and Clearwater, Twisted Hair's map revealed that "a large river which falls in on the N W. Side and into which The *Clarks river* empties itself is 5 Sleeps." The "large river" Twisted Hair was alluding to was the main stem of the Columbia River, though at the time Clark did not and could not know this. "Clarks river," which flowed into the large fork, was a term that was either later inserted in a space left blank in the original transcript of the dialogue with Twisted Hair or over an erasure that was likely "Flat head river." (A field map dated several weeks later while Clark was on the Snake used that nomenclature.) The "Flat head river" represented what's now understood to be the Bitterroot/Clark Fork/Pend Oreille combination that came under scrutiny at Traveler's Rest and reaches the Columbia above its junction with the Snake. Significantly, though noted as being "large," nothing in Twisted Hair's map and related discourse with Clark suggested that this northern fork was a bigger river than the one upon which the expedition was about to embark. The important point, as John Ordway noted, is that when William Clark rejoined the larger party at Weippe, he told them he "had been on a branch of the Columbia River where he expected it is navagable for canoes and only 15 or 20 miles from this place." [4]

Clark understood from Twisted Hair that at Celilo Falls, below the big forks, there were "Establishments of white people &c. and informs that great numbers of Indians reside on all those fo[r]ks as well as the main river." If Twisted Hair was correct, an encounter with whites, perhaps some of the party's American countrymen, was less than two weeks away. Though ship-borne commerce was becoming routine on the Northwest coast, most scholars have concluded that prior to Lewis and Clark no people of European ancestry had reached any farther upstream than the vicinity of today's Washougal, Washington. However, historians Robert Ruby and John Brown found evidence that Samuel Hill, captain of the *Lydia* hailing from Boston, in 1805 proceeded as far up the Columbia as the "Great Rapids," meaning what came to be known as the Cascades of the Columbia.

While it would be another six years after Lewis and Clark before a permanent fur trading "establishment"—Fort Astoria—would be founded at the river's mouth, recent archaeological data recovered at Station Camp—coincidentally or not the expedition's terminal westward camp, within view of the Pacific Ocean—reveals this place as the site of an early and significantly scaled maritime fur trading "post." Surely something like the "post" archaeologists uncovered at Station Camp is what Twisted Hair was alluding to. In any event, this latest in a series of native "geography lessons" provided an early hint of Twisted Hair's formidable knowledge of the Snake and Columbia Rivers. The Nez Perce fished and traded with other Indians at The Dalles, and there they would have learned about white traders on the lower Columbia and the goods that were secured in trade with these strangers over the sides of their ships or from ephemeral stations on land. Sgt. Patrick Gass understood that trade goods emanated from "white men at the mouth of this river; or where the salt water is." [5]

In his journals Clark left no hint of excitement at the thought of meeting the first whites since they left Fort Mandan the previous April, nor what this intelligence portended about Indian demography. If anything, Clark remained somewhat in doubt about these disclosures, evidenced by the fact that he asked other Nez Perce "of note" to verify what he had learned from Twisted Hair about "the Country & river with the Situation of Indians." These additional maps "varied verey little." [6]

Nicholas Biddle, the first editor of the expedition's journals, later quizzed Clark about whites on the Columbia. Biddle's notes relayed Clark's eventual understanding that no white men had ever visited above the falls. Nor, Clark reported, had the expedition met an Indian who had ever seen the ocean until they arrived at Celilo Falls. On the return trip in 1806 Clark met Shoshone and Nez Perce Indians who had been taken prisoner by Chinookan bands and saw whites once they had "gone down to [the] Ocean" with their captors. However, during the westward trip on the Columbia reports of imminent contact with white men were ever elusive. Even as far downstream as Celilo itself the misunderstanding persisted. Joseph Whitehouse understood Indian sign language to mean that the white traders had just left the falls and were "four or 5 days journey further down." The Indians probably meant to suggest white people could be found in four or five days travel below the Cascades, which was entirely possible. [7]

On September 24th the entire expedition vacated Weippe Prairie and headed for the Clearwater River. It was a difficult time for the party, as dietary distress in the form of a doleful combination of indigestion and diarrhea, brought on by the sudden change in diet to salmon and roots, hit the detachment with full force. Meriwether Lewis was "Scercely able to ride," and several others were so sick they "were Compelled to lie on the Side of the road." Others were "obliged to be put on horses." This was not a glorious march for the Army, but duty called the irrepressible Captain Clark. Once again, as he had on the Salmon River and more recently on the Lolo Trail, Clark ventured ahead a few miles with his newfound friend Twisted Hair and two other young Nez Perces. They went downstream to the junction with the North Fork of the Clearwater to "hunt timber for Canoes." The long-promised Columbia River voyage was finally at hand. Joseph Whitehouse said the expedition was ready to leave its horses in the charge of the Nez Perce while he and his mates would "go down by water to the ocean." [8]

A "Canoe Camp" was formed on the Clearwater on 26 September 1805, just opposite the junction with its northerly fork west of today's Orofino, Idaho. The next day work started on five canoes, made by hewing pine logs with axes and then burning the cavities to hollow them out more. During the ensuing week Clark noted repeatedly that the weather was warm. Though he did not say so, Clark probably thought it was unseasonably hot since the party had encountered ice as early as 4 September and weathered a snowfall on the 16th when passing through the Bitterroots. Slowly the good health of the men returned, including Lewis, who by 4 October was able to walk about the canoe camp "a little." Sustaining themselves, with some grumbling, on a diet of camas roots and dried fish and an occasional fresh one, Clark was able to celebrate the launching of the first two canoes on the 5th. His friend Lewis, however, suffered a relapse of dietary distress that day.[9]

With the canoe building proceeding apace and a new river voyage about to commence, the expedition arranged for the Nez Perce to care for their horse herd. Their saddles plus some of their lead and gunpowder were cached. On October 7th the newly finished canoes were placed in the water, loaded, and the flotilla started down the Clearwater River, but temporarily without Twisted Hair and another Nez Perce chief named Tetoharsky. Both had previously agreed to accompany Lewis and Clark's small fleet (four large dugout canoes and a smaller one to serve as a pilot craft), but they were not present at the departure from Canoe Camp. The temporary absence of the chiefs is explicated in a later chapter.[10]

The expedition's first two days on the Clearwater proved tumultuous and gave the explorers a foretaste of what lay ahead on the voyage to the ocean. Lewis and Clark were, by now, experienced and capable river men, but paddling their bulky, unwieldy craft down through Columbia whitewater was nothing like their voyage up the strong but flat Missouri. The re-embarkation story is best told from the perspective of Private Whitehouse. "The Canoe that our Officers went in," he reported on the day of departure, "leaked so bad, that they were forced to unload it, & put their baggage into another Canoe, for fear of getting their Mathematical Instruments & baggage wet." The second day was even more dramatic. According to Whitehouse the canoes were passing through some rapids when one of them "struck a rock, and wheeled round, where she again Struck another rock and Cracked the bottom of it, & was near splitting in two." The steersman was thrown overboard, but

> with great difficulty got to her again. This Canoe soon filled with water & hung on the rock in a perilous situation. Some of the Men on board of her, could not swim; & those Men that could, had no chance of saving themselves, the Waves ran so high, and the current was so rapid, that they must have been dashed against Rocks... & in all probability must have drownded.

All hands were saved through a rescue put into effect by one of the Nez Perce Indians who "came to their assistance with a small Canoe & One of our Canoes went also, & took out some of the loading & landed it safe on the Shore." [11]

The party laid over a day to caulk the damaged canoe and dry the dampened baggage. When the voyage resumed on 10 October 1805 circumstances began to take a more favorable turn. Lewis was getting stronger, which meant that Clark would no longer have to attend to "every thing" as he had remarked several days earlier. The Nez Perce Chiefs Twisted Hair and Tetoharsky, who earlier had promised to accompany them to the "Great rapids," finally joined the fleet in a separate, small canoe, making six in all. At midday they met "an Indian from the falls" who claimed to have seen "white people" there, a now recurring report which clearly intrigued the explorers. Around 5:00 p.m. they reached the Snake River, the Columbia's largest tributary, which presented itself from the south, at a virtual right angle to the Clearwater flowing west. In his field log Clark said the Nez Perce called this large river "*Ki-moo-e-nem.*" Curiously, Clark did not state what *he* called this river. [12]

The confusion and puzzlement about western rivers starting at Traveler's Rest made Clark more cautious in setting his thoughts down on paper. The previous week at the Canoe Camp he had cryptically referred to the "Grat River South of us" and "the main South fork." This characterization imputed considerable hydrologic stature to the Snake River, but Clark now seemed unwilling to dare call it the Columbia. His hesitancy may have been precipitated by the geographical information he received from Twisted Hair at Weippe. Recall that Clark had now reached a spot only "5 Sleeps" from the confluence of this southern fork he was on with one coming in from the northwest. And as he had done after first sighting the Clearwater, when Clark reached this now even bigger river (today's Snake) he again left the space for the stream's name vacant, to be filled in later when conclusions could be more safely drawn. [13]

However, the October 10th journal entries of Sgt. John Ordway and Pvt. Joseph Whitehouse fully exemplified the durability of the original geographic image of the Columbia dating back to Fort Mandan. When Ordway first reached the Clearwater River he unabashedly referred to the stream as a fork of the "Columbia River." Ordway did so again on the 10th when he wrote of reaching the "great columbia River" at the site of the Clearwater/Snake confluence. Ordway's "Columbia," he expanded, was "wide and deep" and "afords a large body of water and of a greenish coulour." Whitehouse also referred to the Clearwater as a "fork of Columbia River" and on reaching its confluence with the Snake referred to his location as "the forks of the Columbian river." [14]

For his part, Clark inscribed two significant passages in his notebook entry for October 10th at the Clearwater/Snake confluence. First, he immediately concluded that the "large Southerly fork" in front of him was "the one we were on with the *Snake* or *So-So-nee* nation." By this he meant the Shoshone Indians of Cameahwait's village visited nearly two months earlier. As we now know, by way of a sequence of affluences Clark was quite right. The Lemhi is a fork of the Salmon River, which is itself a tributary to the Snake at a point fifty miles upstream from the latter's confluence with the Clearwater (and therefore not immediately discernible to Clark). Gary Moulton says that Clark came to this geographic insight "from guesswork or Indian information." John Logan Allen considers Clark's detective work more favorably, calling it "a masterful bit of geographic deduction." As Allen notes, "it was remarkable that the explorer was able to see the river as the same one that had formed the first hope of the short portage." It would be many years more before the full complexity of the Snake River—its origins south of Yellowstone Lake and the long, twisting course to where Clark first saw it—would be fully understood by Euro-Americans.[15]

More immediately, Clark, the expert topographer, was beginning to discern a landscape that the expedition would shortly come to know well and which he was the first to describe, however sparingly, in English. Intimations of physiographic revelation came with his introduction to the countryside adjoining the Clearwater/Snake confluence, which he described as an "open Plain." Clark elaborated on this observation by noting it was "worthey of remark that not one Stick of timber on the river near the forks and but a fiew trees for a great distance up the River we decended." Though neither Lewis nor Clark could have known it, the expedition established their 10 October 1805 campsite at the very center of the entire Columbia River basin. Specifically, they were at the edge of a subregion known today as the Palouse. Later at Fort Clatsop, when writing their geographical memoirs and in Clark's composite map, the captains would call this district the "Columbian Plains" or "the great plains" of the Columbia.[16]

As we saw earlier at the Continental Divide and in the Bitterroots, William Clark was again adept at discerning changes in the landscape, capably piecing together topographical clues once presented to him. John Logan Allen stipulates that the Great Columbian Plain was "a region that did not exist in the geographical lore of the early nineteenth century." In the preceding decades rife with speculation about the wonders of the continental interior, no one imagined a semi-arid biome at that latitude and longitude. Allen says this landscape was "as exotic as it was unknown" and taxed Clark's lexicon. Allen argues that Clark did not have a vocabulary up to the task of explaining or understanding "the unusual and otherworldly physiography" of steep canyons, basaltic outcrops and bluffs, coulees, vast open plateaus, and highly variegated weather patterns. But it did not escape his attention. Whatever Clark's presumed or real limitations may have been, as the principal journalist at this point in the voyage he was still sufficiently adept in his descriptive abilities to begin categorizing this surprising topography into a distinct region. In the cartographic catalogue of "new lands" encountered by Lewis and Clark, only the complexity of the Rocky Mountains would supersede the Great Plain of the Columbia in significance.[17]

If Clark was deficient in the depth or full articulation of his topographical gaze, he compensated for it with the power of repetition. On the first full day of

Expedition geographer William Clark repeatedly referred to the dry, treeless plains of the Columbia. (Robert Reynolds)

the voyage down the Snake River, he described the country on either side of the canyon as "an open plain leavel & fertile" with "not a tree of any kind to be Seen." On October 12th, or the third day on the Snake, he wrote "no timber in view." On the surface, Clark had a strictly utilitarian imperative in mind—a supply of firewood for cooking as well as warmth. Only a few willow bushes and drift trees presented themselves on the river's edge. Ditto on the 13th where this terse journal entry summarizes the treeless landscape: "open plain no timber." However, at a deeper level of analysis, Clark's text can also be read as cultural coding. As Pamela Regis has trenchantly observed, in the tradition of eighteenth- and nineteenth-century natural classification, "trees growing on the land formed a short hand for determining the land's agricultural worth, the standard value that measured 'use.'" Lewis and Clark were late in discerning the fertility of this region so evident today. They did not reach such a conclusion until the return trip in the spring of 1806.[18]

The scarcity of wood along the Snake had become so pronounced that for the campfire on the night of October 14th, the men expropriated the boards of a disassembled Palouse Indian house. The Indians had hidden these precious planks under stones. In his field log Clark implies that he or Lewis sought the permission of their Nez Perce guides before taking the wood. Clark's more reflective notebook journal entry evidenced a greater cry of conscience about this episode. After stipulating that he and Lewis "have made it a point at all times not to take any thing belonging to the Indians even their wood," the stark environment of the Snake River country compelled them to "violate that rule." As Clark explained, no other wood was to be found "in any direction." [19]

Yet again on October 15th Clark recorded in his notebook: "no timber of any kind in Sight of the river, a fiew Small willows excepted." That evening some members of the expedition raided the Indian fishing platforms for wood. Curiously, Clark reported: "here we were obliged for the first time to take the property of the Indians without the consent or approbation of the owner." Actually, it was the second time and on consecutive days, by his own account and that of Private Whitehouse. This suggests that Clark considered the first taking as having had the approbation of the Nez Perce chiefs, and thus did not qualify as theft. In any event, the desiccated physical environment was making a strong impression on Clark, punctuated by the characterization John Ordway gave this country, which he continually referred to as "barron" or "the barrons." [20]

Correspondingly, the adjoining plains offered comparatively little in the way of game. Their first night on the Snake River, Clark observed, "our diet extremely bad haveing nothing but roots and dried fish to eate, all the Party have greatly the advantage of me, in as much as they all relish the flesh of the dogs, Several of which we purchased of the nativs for to add to our Store of fish and roots." Other than snagging a few ducks and geese that flew by, this became their Snake River routine. The difficulty with provisioning was compounded by the fact that the party was routinely confined to the bottom of the canyon, as opposed to the more expansive prairie on the plateau above them. However, even the one hunting foray conducted on the bordering plain yielded no sign of the antelope they knew the Indians hunted. Clark's general adherence to the dictate of respecting Indian property was substantiated when they discovered a buried cache of dried fish, but they were "Cautious not to touch." [21]

The Snake River itself presented a whole different set of challenges. The water was swift and the rapids numerous, much as Lewis had predicted when he studied the matter while still on the Missouri the previous August. On October 11th they passed nine sets of rapids in a single day. Islands and rocks "appeared to be in every direction." The expedition shot through or steered around most of these obstacles. Joseph Whitehouse captured the speedy essence of this experience when he graphically remarked that canoes on the Snake ran "Swifter than any horse could run." Clark suggested they would have been prudently inclined to take more portages were it not for the fact that the season was "advanced and time precious with us." Clark made this comment on October 13th. If he compared their Snake River situation to his Missouri River timetable of 1804, Clark would have remembered that the previous fall on this date the expedition was on its final approach to the homelands of the Mandan Indians where they would spend the winter. [22]

William Clark was fully cognizant of two circumstances obviating some of the stress he might otherwise have felt due to the lateness of the travel season. First, the stream flow in the Snake in the fall was at its ebb. Where the Palouse River meets the Snake, Clark, describing the narrow, rocky channel bordered by rugged basalt rocks, observed with relief: "This must be a verry bad place in high water." Better still, the expedition benefited from the comprehensive knowledge the Nez Perce chiefs had of the river, combined with their inclination to freely share it. Sgt. John Ordway referred to the craft holding Twisted Hair and Tetoharsky as "our Small pilot canoe." [23]

On October 12th, at a site just below today's Little Goose Dam, Clark detailed an incident wherein the Indians had warned of rapids that were "verry bad," a phrase that was to take on the quality of a refrain. Twisted Hair and Tetoharsky knew of a specific course with "maney turns necessary to Stear Clare of the rocks, which appeared to be in every direction," as Clark described it. The Indians demonstrated this safe passage, and then the expedition's smallest canoe followed them through. Being late in the day, the captains determined to camp before the balance of the flotilla made the attempt. The next morning the men who could not swim conducted a portage for the rifles and instruments while the now-lightened canoes remaining upstream "passed over this bad rapid Safe." [24]

The expedition's most dramatic whitewater adventures occurred on October 14–16. Clark counted seven rapids during the twenty miles of river travel on the 15th. As the party approached what would have been the eighth (known as Fish Hook Rapids near today's park of the same name), they found Twisted Hair and Tetoharsky plus several other Palouse and Nez Perce Indians waiting on the bank. (One of them, Apash Wyakaikt, whom Lewis and Clark identified by name on the return trip as the Big Horn Chief, had been following the expedition's progress on horseback.

The expedition used hastily made, somewhat unstable dugout canoes to run the many rapids in the Snake River canyon of eastern Washington. ("The Race to the Pacific" by Roger Cooke, Washington State Historical Society)

He would help Twisted Hair and Tetoharsky pave the way for the expedition's arrival at the forks of the Columbia, as related in a later chapter.) As Clark recounted the episode, "our 2 Chiefs had proceeded on to this place where they thought proper to delay [and] warn us of the difficulties of this rapid." The value of this intelligence was more clearly revealed when Clark examined these rapids from land and found them "more dificuelt to pass than we expected from the Indians information." [25]

The true test of the danger that was averted is revealed in Clark's account of events from the next morning when the voyageurs "deturmined to run the rapids." Clark took two precautions. First, he and Lewis "put our Indian guide in front [of] our Small Canoe next the other four following each other." The first few passed safely, but the last one got stuck on a rock midstream. With assistance from other members of the party and the Indians who were "extreamly ellert[,] every thing was taken out and the Canoe got off without any enjorie further than the articles which it was loaded all wet." Clark's second safety measure was succinctly stated: "I walked around this rapid." [26]

Passing the Fish Hook Rapids was the second time the Nez Perce chiefs had gone well beyond mere piloting to help the expedition. On 14 October, below today's Lower Monumental Dam, a canoe steered by George Drouillard struck a rock and foundered in the water. The craft actually sunk, but the men held on to the canoe from their rocky outpost while many articles disappeared or floated away. Of their "great Cause to lament" was the potential or actual loss of bedding, shot pouches, tomahawks, and "all our roots prepared in the Indian way, and one half of our goods." The stranded men were brought to shore, and most of the buoyant material was recovered in about an hour's time. Clark noted that one of the Nez Perce chiefs "Swam in & Saved Some property." The worst and most ironic loss, which William Clark termed "verry Considerable," was the roots. As food, it was never relished by the men and only reluctantly eaten. Unlike the equipment, it spoiled before it could be dried. [27]

The one salutary side effect from this upset was an enhanced geographic understanding, as the next morning, while Clark was supervising the drying of powder and provisions, the now-recovered and ambulatory Meriwether Lewis climbed the canyon walls for a walk on the plain above. This was a rare opportunity to get out of the daylight tunnel the expedition had been in for five days, and Lewis made several observations. Among them, as Clark recounted it, was a mountain range running diagonally to their course, from the southeast to the northwest. Lewis was viewing the Blue Mountains of southeast Washington and northeast Oregon on his left, and in front of him, to the west and northwest he absorbed the distant view of Rattlesnake Mountain—what serves now as the dramatic backdrop to the Hanford Nuclear Reservation. [28]

Lewis's ramble also provided an interesting perspective on the surrounding countryside. Confined to the river at the base of the canyon, Lewis and Clark had only rare glimpses over the top. They knew open terrain adjoined the Snake, but until Lewis's walk the face of the country adjoining the river had little texture ascribed to it. After Lewis returned to camp, Clark recorded his colleague's perception in typical minimalist fashion: "Plain wavering." Even the briefest of texts, however, can take on significance by repetition and isolation. In his extended notebook entry of October 15th Clark twice reiterated Lewis's finding of a "wavering Plain" on each side of the river. For the entire outbound trip this would be the sum and substance of Lewis and Clark's scientific analysis and aesthetic appreciation of the western limit of the rolling hills of the Palouse—one of the world's richest agricultural districts, though initially perceived by the expedition as barren because of the absence of trees.[29]

CHAPTER 5   The New Sacagawea Myth

DURING THE MIDDLE THIRD OF THE TWENTIETH CENTURY, historians turned a critical eye to one of the great themes established on the occasion of the *centennial* of the Lewis and Clark Expedition—the legend of Sacagawea, trail guide. The mythmaking reached its apogee in 1933 with the publication of Grace Raymond Hebard's *Sacajawea: a Guide and Interpreter of the Lewis and Clark Expedition*. This volume became the principal source for a host of encyclopedia entries, textbooks, statuary, films, and popular publications. Though the original *centennial* legend would eventually come unraveled, a new *bicentennial* myth took root late in the twentieth century—Sacagawea: Native American diplomat.[1]

The essence of the original myth had Sacagawea guiding Lewis and Clark not merely through her Rocky Mountain homelands but all the way to the mouth of the Columbia River. One account even had the young Shoshone woman showing carpenters how to make the wheels for the carriages that would carry the expedition's baggage on the portage around the Great Falls of the Missouri. While Lewis and Clark routinely referred to male Native Americans as pilots and guides, they only once used that terminology to describe Sacagawea, whereas Hebard the mythmaker carefully avoided any mention of other Shoshone and Nez Perce guides in order to puff up the imagined role of her heroine.[2]

C. S. Kingston, the first notable critic of the Hebard school, concluded: "Sacajawea had done nothing to guide or influence the course of the expedition" on its way from the Mandan villages to the Pacific and back to the eastern side of the Rockies. On the upper Missouri, as Lewis and Clark entered her native homeland, Sacagawea "had occasionally recognized certain landmarks," Kingston averred, but this did not amount to advice on which route to take. The genesis of the "Sacagawea-as-guide" legend came on the return trip when Clark was leading a detachment, which included the Charbonneau family, toward the Yellowstone River. At the Three Forks of the Missouri, Clark was presented with several possible courses through the mountains to his east that, once traversed, would put him on the headwaters of the Yellowstone. In making a selection, Clark noted, "The indian woman who has been of great Service to me as a pilot through this Country recommends a gap in the mountains more South which I shall cross." She later also pointed to a road out of a beaver marsh.[3]

Kingston asserted that Clark's comment about Sacagawea as pilot "is to be understood more as an expression of good natured and generous congratulation than a sober assertion of unadorned fact." Here the mythbuster may have overplayed his hand. More equitably, Gary Moulton states that when Sacagawea discerned a route from the upper Missouri to the Yellowstone through what became known as Bozeman Pass, she "did indeed act as a guide, as legend has her doing much more extensively." Nevertheless, when William Clark finally parted company with Sacagawea at the Mandan villages in August 1806, he cited only her services as an interpreter.[4]

Ronald W. Taber analyzed the social and cultural context of the early twentieth century that made the Sacagawea legend such a powerfully attractive story in the first place. Many of the earliest proponents of the Sacagawea-as-guide myth were activists in the woman's suffrage movement. Eva Emery Dye, who first popularized the legend in a historical novel published in 1902, was also chair of the Clackamas County chapter of the Oregon Equal Suffrage Association. It was Dye, Taber argued, who conceived a Sacagawea strategy that was to be incorporated into the larger effort aimed at securing women the right to vote. Sacagawea was foremost among several "strong women of the past" (including Pocahontas, Molly Pitcher, and Susan B. Anthony) who were envisioned as heroines for the movement. In reference to her book, *The Conquest: The True Story of Lewis and Clark*, Dye later said, "I created Sacajawea." Dye portrayed Sacagawea as "that faithful Indian woman with her baby on her back, leading those stalwart mountaineers and explorers through the strange land." [5]

The notion of Sacagawea as a woman whom suffragists might emulate in their "efforts to lead men through the Pass of justice" was more fully explicated by Anna Howard Shaw. The National American Woman Suffrage Association (NAWSA) met in Portland in conjunction with the 1905 Lewis and Clark Centennial Exposition. This was one year before a scheduled statewide vote on a women's suffrage amendment to the Oregon constitution. Shaw, president of NAWSA, seized on the virtues and accomplishments of Sacagawea in her address to the convention: "At a time… when the hearts of the leaders [Lewis and Clark] had well nigh fainted within them, when success or failure hung a mere chance in the balance, this woman came to their deliverance and pointed out to the captain the great Pass which led from the forks of the Three Rivers over the Mountains." Hyperbole of this sort sustained the effort to install a monument to Sacagawea on the grounds of the exposition.[6]

Susan B. Anthony, a veritable living legend at that time, seconded Shaw's themes as did Abigail Scott Duniway, arguably the Northwest's foremost women's rights activist. The men of Oregon—a state, Anthony asserted, "made possible by a woman" —had a chance to reciprocate "the assistance rendered by a woman in the discovery of this great section of the country." Duniway said Sacagawea was a "feminine Atlas" who had helped create "a Pacific empire" for America. Though helpful as a rallying point, the Sacagawea strategy did not carry the suffragist proposition at the polls. It did provide, however, a lifetime's worth of inspiration for Grace Raymond Hebard. Her work, replete with inventions and purposeful omissions, was in time largely repudiated by scholars, but she gave sufficient propulsion to the notion that Sacagawea died on the Wind River Indian Reservation of Wyoming in 1884 that this aspect of the early myth still has currency.[7]

Oddly enough, it was Hebard's critic C. S. Kingston who planted the seed for a second myth about Sacagawea—the bicentennial version—in the treatise he wrote that weakened the first legend. Crediting the young Shoshone woman as a useful "but not an indispensable" interpreter, Kingston said her "presence with the white men was of greater importance in that it confirmed the confidence of her people in the good intentions of Americans." Regarding the Shoshone Indians, this is indisputably credible, but the sentimentality of the notion has been expanded and much amplified in recent times. Even Thomas Slaughter, the scholar most critical of Lewis and Clark mythmaking, posits that Sacagawea was "a symbol of peace who distinguished the explorers from a war party." The modern bi-gendered multicultural sensibility of the bicentennial era re-established a market for an indigenous heroine.[8]

The original Sacagawea myth needed a ledge in the documentary record from which to sprout, as does its modern variant—Sacagawea as the "symbol of peace." A century ago, for the suffrage movement in search of model women who could lead men, it was Clark's comment about Sacagawea as "pilot" through Bozeman Pass. The new legend is grounded in Clark's field note of 13 October 1805 when the expedition was on the Snake River. He observed that the presence of Sacagawea "reconsiles all the Indians, as to our friendly intentions.[A] woman with a party of men is a token of peace." Clark's intended reflection upon a regionalized phenomenon has been conflated by scholars and popularizers into a generalized role for the entire extent of the journey. In one recent account, an author suggests Lewis and Clark brought Sacagawea along precisely *because* she would be perceived as a goodwill ambassador.[9]

Contrary to LEWIS & CLARK lore suggesting that Sacagawea had a calming effect whenever and wherever Native people saw the expedition, the first appearance of this phenomenon in the record occurred on the Snake River in southeastern Washington. The initial occasion is somewhat surprising because the party had encountered only a handful of Indians that day, indeed that whole week. Broadly put, Clark's observation about Sacagawea was celebrated during the recent bicentennial because of its supposedly savvy insight. However, it was common knowledge in the late eighteenth and early nineteenth century West that female companionship offered certain advantages on the trail in Indian country. Fur trader James Mackay's instructions to John Evans when the latter left for the Mandan villages on the upper Missouri in 1795 contained this advice: "You will take heed not to fall in with some parties of savages, where there are neither women or children, as they are almost always on the warpath." [10]

Clark's comment about the Indian woman was prompted by hints that Indian diplomacy was coming to the fore on the Snake River voyage. Joseph Whitehouse's journal for October 12th, the day *before* Clark mentioned Sacagawea's capabilities "as a token of peace," noted that the tour through the "flat head nation" (by which he meant the Nez Perce homelands) had ended. He learned this from the Nez Perce chiefs Twisted Hair and Tetoharsky, who told the Americans that in two more days travel they would "come to another nation at a fork which comes in on the St[board] [i.e., northern] Side of the Columbian [actually the Snake] River." (That this northern fork was in reality the main stem of the Columbia was a fact of continental geography that would elude Lewis and Clark until their arrival at the confluence, as discussed in the next chapter.) Clark's description of Sacagawea's prospective role was probably a function of the same discourse Whitehouse recorded the previous day. The comment about Sacagawea's power to reconcile the newcomers to host tribes appeared on the same page of Clark's field log as a map depicting the soon-to-be-reached northern fork. On October 14th, in anticipation of the encounter with the new nation as initially recorded by Whitehouse, Twisted Hair and Tetoharsky proceeded ahead to the forks "to inform those bands of our approach and friendly intentions towards all nations," Clark said. [11]

As close readers of Alexander Mackenzie's *Voyages from Montreal,* Lewis and Clark would have learned the great value of having Native people proceed ahead of the exploring party to soften the impact of the sudden arrival of strangers. Mackenzie referred to these indigenous intermediaries as "conductors." Indeed, on several occasions Mackenzie would not proceed with his voyage unless he had taken care of this fundamental requirement. Before embarking on his final push to the Pacific in 1793 Mackenzie wrote: "My first object, therefore, was to persuade two of these [Native] people to accompany me, that they might secure for us a favourable reception from their neighbours." The Nor'Wester stated further that "attempting the woods, without a guide, to introduce us to the first inhabitants… would be little short of absolute madness." [12]

Mackenzie had his "conductors" sent ahead with great regularity "to notify to the different tribes that we were approaching, that they might not be surprised at our appearance, and be disposed to afford us a friendly reception." Not engaging in such an "embassy of friendship" could have frightful consequences on both sides of the encounter. Mackenzie described one such scene a few days before he reached the Pacific Ocean.

> As we approached the edge of the wood, and were almost in sight of the houses, the Indians who were before me made signs for me to take the lead, and that they would follow. The noise and confusion of the natives now seemed to encrease, and

when we came in sight of the village, we saw them running from house to house... as if in a great state of alarm. This very unpleasant and unexpected circumstance, I attributed to our sudden arrival, and the very short notice of it which had been given them.[13]

Lewis and Clark relied on Twisted Hair and Tetoharsky as both river guides and "conductors" in equal measure. Indeed, it is likely that the Nez Perce chiefs themselves conceived what might be termed the "Sacagawea strategy" to dissipate apprehensions similar to those Mackenzie described. Though the Yakama and Wanapum who lived near the forks were Sahaptian-speakers like the Nez Perce emissaries, the latter were relatively far from home and recognized the obligation of establishing goodwill before entering the lands of others. They would have done this both for themselves and the Americans. Twisted Hair and Tetoharsky simply apprised Lewis and Clark of the added value of having Sacagawea with the expedition and used the strategy when circumstances called for it. As Whitehouse shows, the rudiments of all of this were explicated well in advance of the party's arrival at the forks of the Columbia.[14]

News about these strangers from the east had preceded them to the forks. The Nez Perce chief Apash Wyakaikt, who had paced the voyageurs on horseback, joined Twisted Hair and Tetoharsky at the confluence and "harranged" the local villagers. Clark's colloquialism, which sounds obnoxious to modern ears, meant to suggest that Apash Wyakaikt confirmed the peaceful intentions of the expedition and secured for them a "friendly reception." We can thus see fully how these Nez Perce chiefs' role and reputation as ambassadors have suffered through history at the expense of the romance about Sacagawea. The Nez Perce men gathered some driftwood, willow, and reeds to make a fire after which, Clark reported, hundreds of men from the neighboring village a quarter-mile upstream on the Columbia visited en masse, beating their drums and dancing while "keeping time to the musik," forming a welcoming circle of song.[15]

On the expedition's second day down the Columbia below the forks, in the vicinity of today's Plymouth, Washington, Clark and a handful of men called on a large Indian village. He stated that he "found the Indians much fritened, all got in to their lodges and when I went in found Some hanging down their heads, Some Crying and others in great agitation, I took all by the hand, and distributed a few Small articles which I chanced to have in my Pockets and Smoked with them which expelled their fears." Then, in a startling, and for William Clark an anomalous passage, he wrote in his field log: "I am confident that I could have tomahawked every Indian here." [16]

Even with a Mackenzian-styled early warning system, incidents like this were not uncommon. After crossing the Continental Divide into Shoshone country the previous August, Clark came upon a village unannounced because Old Toby was temporarily lagging behind. Described in Nicholas Biddle's post-expeditionary paraphrase as a collection of families "who had not been previously acquainted

with the arrival of whites," all the women in this village fled "in great consterna-
tion." The men offered up food and possessions, and Clark recorded in his journal
that it was not until Old Toby came up that he "passifyed… those fritened people."
The women and children, Clark reported, "Cried dureing my Stay of an hour at
this place." Though far less tumultuous, when Clark first arrived at the Nez Perce
village on Weippe Prairie after crossing the Bitterroot Mountains, his appearance
raised similar concerns. The women, especially, evidenced "much apparent Signs
of fear," Clark wrote.[17]

Initially, to Clark's dismay, none of the Indians at this Columbia River village
would come out and smoke with him. When Lewis arrived with the larger party
including the Nez Perce chiefs, Clark reported, one of the chiefs hailed the Native
village "as was their Custom to all we had passed." Biddle, in his rendering, having discussed the episode with Clark, reports that none of the Indian men left
their lodges "till the canoes arrived with the chiefs, who immediately explained
our pacific intentions toward them." It was not until a short time later, Biddle
reported, that "the interpreter's wife [Sacagawea] landed." From Clark's journal
we learn that Twisted Hair and Tetoharsky, sensing the fear and distress on shore,
quickly pointed to Sacagawea in one of the canoes, thereby implementing a strategy that had been worked out earlier on the Snake River. With his now-heightened
understanding of the Nez Perce technique, Clark recorded in his notebook: "This
Indian woman… confirmed those people of our friendly intentions, as no woman
ever accompanies a war party of Indians in this quarter." In other words, the Nez
Perce chiefs had done the principal work at pacification and Sacagawea offered
secondary assurances. Donald Jackson once said of Sacagawea that her "valor
and stolid determination" couldn't be doubted, but that her contributions to the
expedition have been magnified out of proportion. Such seems to be the case
related to her role as a diplomat. Her service in this manner only worked when
mediated by Twisted Hair and Tetoharsky, and in the present instance her presence removed only the last vestiges of concern in a village already calmed by the
Nez Perce chiefs.[18]

Historian William Lang has offered several interpretations of Clark's comportment with the "Fritened Indians" (a term for the subject village that appears on
one of his maps). This "curious incident," as Lang calls it, may have represented
"either braggadocio or perhaps an unfulfilled but genuine threat." More likely,
Lang argues, Clark was showing frustration with the passivity of these Indians.
Alternatively, but more speculatively, Lang suggests that life on the Columbia had
"begun to take its toll on" Clark. Surely, as Lang states, this was "one of the most
mysterious episodes in the entire journey," and Clark's nominally hostile expression does beg for an explanation.[19]

Just prior to crossing the river to visit the village of "Fritened Indians," Clark
had shot a crane out of the sky. Afterwards, as Clark later observed in his notebook entry, the alarmed Natives communicated to him their belief that he and his
compatriots "came from the clouds" and were "not men" of this world. A possible

Nez Perce chiefs Twisted Hair and Tetoharsky were principally responsible for conducting the expedition's diplomatic relations with the tribes on the upper Columbia River. This illustration reinforces the legend of Sacagawea as frontier diplomat. ("From the Clouds" by Roger Cooke, Washington State Historical Society)

meaning for this is that the villagers thought Clark and the others to be super-natural beings or, in James Ronda's phrase, "sky gods." Clark later told Biddle that this perception was enhanced by the fact that the Indians at this village had never heard gunfire before. Plus, they were amazed at Clark's ability to light his pipe with a "burning glass." All of this was explained to Clark by one of the Nez Perce chiefs, "by whose mediation we had pacified them." This last statement alone establishes the credit for successful Columbia River diplomacy on the shoulders of the Nez Perce chiefs, not Sacagawea.[20]

Clark did not repeat in his notebook the chilling observation he'd made in his field log about the ease with which he could have killed the "Fritened Indians." He may indeed have thought better of it. And despite the violent image, his friendly intentions are reflected in the preceding inscription where he states that he "took all by the hand" when he entered their lodges, a gesture which, combined with a few token presents, "expelled their fears." As Roberta Conner observes, the senti-ment behind Clark's anomalous expression is not hostility but more innocuously that Clark felt the absence of the vulnerability he normally would have experi-enced as a stranger visiting another nation's homeland. Though the incident with the crane was perceived to have precipitated the extreme submission on the part of the Indians, Clark, Whitehouse and Gass had all noticed similar behavior by Indians on the river's islands and banks after leaving their camp at the Snake-Columbia confluence two days earlier. Gass's comment from the previous day—that the Columbia River Indians seemed "shy and distant"—and Whitehouse's observation that the Indians living in the Wallula Gap "hid themselves" prefig-ured Clark's encounter of the following day.[21]

As for Lewis and Clark as "sky gods," such perceptions had ample precedent in the history of exploration. The most famous instance, one much debated in scholarly circles, involves Captain James Cook's arrival in the Hawaiian Islands. As historian William Goetzmann writes, Cook received a tumultuous welcome at Kealakekua Bay, where, "to his bewilderment he was made a god"—at least in his own estimation and that of his mates. In contrast to Clark, who seemed somewhat embarrassed by Native deference, Cook is thought by some to have treasured being co-identified with a deity. Greg Dening, a scholar of Oceania's cultures, says Cook became susceptible to this delusion because of the rigors of many years of exploration compounded by extensive "hero worship at home." (Clark, of course, had yet to experience such adulation.) Dening's analysis of Cook's experience seems applicable to the story of Clark's gunfire and the crane. What the explorers perceived as a worshipful posture was instead merely indigenous "respect for pow-ers that are not yet known." [22]

Like Cook, Alexander Mackenzie was also very conscious of arrival protocols and the costs of ignoring them. The Scotsman's *Voyages* included a scene and lan-guage that Clark may have remembered when called upon to describe the incident below Wallula. In July 1793 Mackenzie surprised a village with the predictable result of "horrid shrieks" from the women and children, and one man "so agitated with fear as to have lost the power of utterance. It is impossible," Mackenzie continued, "to describe the distress and alarm of these poor people, who believing that they were attacked by enemies, expected an immediate massacre." Similarly, in the Biddle narrative Clark sums up his opinion on the matter by stating he could not "blame them for their terrors, which were perfectly normal." [23]

Just six years after Lewis and Clark's encounter with the "Fritened Indians," David Thompson had comparable experiences on the Columbia, the first one at the head of the Rock Island Rapids near Wenatchee, Washington. When Thompson's party arrived at the large village of 800 Sinkowarsin people, he was greeted by five men who appeared distressed and confused by his appearance. Like Clark, Thompson conducted a few rounds with the pipe, which assuaged anxiety. Soon the whole village was invited to gather around. The initial nervousness eventually gave way to excitement and exultation. As William Layman tells it, the villagers placed presents of berries and roots before Thompson, "clapping their hands and extending them to the sky." When Thompson resumed his voyage down the Columbia, within a few days he arrived at or very near the same village as Clark's unsettling encounter. Thompson met with precisely the same cultural response Clark had. This alone disproves the notion that Clark, aside from his mere presence, had done something purposeful to precipitate the terror. "All the signs I could make gave them no confidence," Thompson reported. Indeed, the Lewis and Clark Expedition had a similar episode a mere eleven days later. When the party surprised a Chinookan village near the Cascades of the Columbia yet another group of Natives conveyed the observation via sign language that, as Joseph Whitehouse recorded it, "they thought that we had rained down out of the clouds." [24]

The last chapter of Indian diplomacy involving Twisted Hair and Tetoharsky occurred on the approach to the Great Falls of the Columbia at Celilo. Now in their third week of service to Lewis and Clark, the chiefs reported overhearing some Indians from farther downstream planning to attack and kill the expedition that night. This news spread quickly through the encampment. Although the commanders had all arms "examined and put in order," Clark testified that the detachment was "at all times & places on our guard" and were "under no greater apprehention than is common." This view was confirmed by Whitehouse who said the party was alert "but we were not afraid of them for we think we can drive three times our nomber." Nevertheless, Lewis and Clark had every reason to trust Twisted Hair and Tetoharsky, and so that evening, when the local Indians decamped earlier than what Clark thought normal, he saw it as a "Shadow of Confirmation" of what they had learned about the looming threat. Clark's journal ended on a worrisome note. The "two old Chiefs," he wrote, "appeared verry uneasy this evening." [25]

At the break of dawn on October 24th the Nez Perce chiefs apprised Lewis and Clark of their intention to return to their home on the Clearwater. The reasons were several, but all revolved around the prospect of hostilities. They told the captains that their people never proceeded farther downstream than the falls and consequently were unable to converse with the inhabitants along the river below that point. In short, Twisted Hair and Tetoharsky were trying to assert that their days as interpreters, guides, and "conductors" were at an end. The expedition had reached a cultural divide between the Sahaptian-speaking tribes, such as the Nez Perce, and the Chinookan-speaking people downriver, a divide every bit as important to an understanding of the peopled Columbia as the falls were to the physiographic one. This language barrier precluded any prospect of re-employing the Sacagawea strategy utilized with such success upstream, even presuming the peaceful symbolism of a woman traveling with a party transcended the limits of the Columbia Plateau. Ironically, precisely at the juncture when Lewis and Clark supposedly needed a token to prove their peaceful intentions, neither Sacagawea nor any other device could have sufficed. As Clark phrased it, since "the nation below had expressed hostile intentions against us, [they] would Certainly kill them [the Nez Perce chiefs]; perticularly as They had been at war with each other." Associating with Lewis and Clark had become dangerous for the Nez Perce chiefs.[26]

Euro-Americans coming down the Columbia River would not have been a welcome sight for the Chinookan villagers below the falls. White men appearing from the east would have represented a significant threat—a rival source of manufactured goods to which the inland tribes could avail themselves, undercutting the lower Columbia market they monopolized by virtue of their stations near the ocean frequented by maritime fur traders. For this reason, it would have been to the *advantage* of the Nez Perce to flaunt their alliance with Lewis and Clark so as to impress upon the Chinookans that they now had other sources of trade. That may have been the reason Lewis and Clark were successful in cajoling Twisted Hair and Tetoharsky into staying with them an extra two days. The captains' motives for the imploring the Nez Perce chiefs to continue with them were threefold. First, they knew they were about to face more rough water. Second, now that the party was on guard against Native attack, Twisted Hair and Tetoharsky could serve as an early warning system. Third, the commanders arrogantly believed they could broker peace between these tribes, oblivious to the prospect that the Nez Perce might have been using *them* as a wedge.[27]

In the service of their self-imposed obligation, Lewis and Clark mediated what was termed a "good understanding" between their Nez Perce guides and the chief of the Wishram village between the Short and Long Narrows. Clark confided in his notebook that "we have every reason to believe… those two bands or nations are and will be on the most friendly terms with each other." The evening ended with Pierre Cruzatte playing his fiddle and the men dancing, "which delighted the nativs, who Shew every civility towards us," Clark wrote. This now-enlarged community of residents and voyageurs smoked "untill late at night." The festivity of this evening suggests that the fear of an attack had now dissipated entirely. If, in fact, that prospect was ever imminent, Lewis and Clark had either somehow forged a temporary peace that allowed them and the Nez Perce to pass, or Twisted Hair and Tetoharsky had been manipulating the situation for their own purposes.[28]

With their terms as guides and "conductors" temporarily extended, the chiefs proceeded ahead of the expedition, as they had so many times before, to a village below the Long Narrows "to Smoke a friendly pipe." Twisted Hair and Tetoharsky were returning upstream when they met Lewis and Clark at the last of the three "basons" that Clark depicted in his notebook map the present location of Spearfish, Washington. (The Indians told Clark and Lewis that in this vicinity they could "take the Salmon as fast as they wish.") At this place the Nez Perce chiefs were having yet another smoke with a party of Indians who were returning from a hunting trip and heading to their home upriver. This band had just brought their horses across to the north side of the river below the last of the narrows forming The Dalles, where the "old Chiefs," as Clark habitually called the Nez Perce guides, encountered them.[29]

Lewis and Clark joined the parley and smoked with the chief of this new band, whom they found to be a "bold pleasing looking man of about 50 years of age dressd. in a war jacket a cap Legins & mockersons." From him they learned of a recent encounter with a war party of "Snake Indians" in the watershed drained by the Deschutes River. But more noteworthy is that this intersection of trail, river, and tribal cultures became the point at which Twisted Hair and Tetoharsky left the party. Far from home, they found this chance meeting with Indians in posses-sion of horses irresistible, and so they traded robes for steeds. After a last "parting Smoke," Lewis and Clark bid adieu to their "two faithful friends." [30]

The unsentimental Clark did not take the time to elaborate on the contribu-tions of the Nez Perce chiefs. Nor Whitehouse, who said simply: "These Indians left us at this place, after taking a friendly leave." However, a faithful reading of the journals for the Snake and Columbia River voyage to The Dalles can only lead to the conclusion that Tetoharsky and Twisted Hair played far more valuable roles as guides and diplomats than the supposedly indispensable Sacagawea of legend. Even her supporting role as emblem of peace was one the Nez Perce chiefs were required to explicate when it mattered.[31]

Proceeding downriver below The Dalles the explorers came to the village of the "Chil-luc-it-te-quar" (possibly Klickitat) Indians, one of the Wishram-Wasco bands of the Upper Chinookan language group. If the Nez Perce chiefs were to be believed these Indians, living near today's Lyle, Washington, were the ones lying in wait to attack the party. On the contrary, however, Clark found these people to be "friendly." The cordial reception the expedition was given could have been a function merely of the Nez Perce having parted company. Clark recalled seeing the chief of this village fishing at the Long Narrows. The explorers were welcomed to land by a gift of fish, berries, nuts, and root bread for breakfast. The hospitality was so impressive, Clark wrote, that "we Call this the friendly Village." After buying twelve dogs, four sacks of pounded fish, and dried berries, the expedition "proceeded on." Complementing the goodwill they encountered at the "friendly village" was the reception granted to the newcomers at the next Native commu-nity four miles downstream. After smoking the pipe of peace with these villagers, Clark says, "we found those people also friendly." [32]

Clearly the Nez Perce warning above Celilo had heightened Clark's consciousness about equable relationships. But in retrospect the whole notion of threats from "the nation below" Celilo proved chimerical. First, all the reports were second- or third-hand. Second, as Twisted Hair and Tetoharsky had themselves communicated, the Nez Perce did not speak the language of the Chinookan people who lived below The Dalles nor did they regularly travel into their country, so there may be some doubt whether they properly understood whatever they might have overheard. In subsequent years the Wishram and other tribes near The Dalles would resist incursions from white fur traders who challenged their pivotal trade position. Indeed, on their return trip up the Columbia the following spring Lewis and Clark would have a great deal of trouble with the Natives in the vicinity of The Dalles. But on balance, the implied threat in the fall of 1805, James Ronda asserts, had less to do with Lewis and Clark than "relations between the Nez Perces and the Chinookans." Ronda concludes the "alleged preparations for an attack on Lewis and Clark may have been rumormongering or an effort to justify the desire of the Nez Perce guides to leave the party." [33]

As for Sacagawea, she was, as C. S. Kingston phrased it, "a young woman of fine qualities." She has a well-deserved reputation for courage, presence of mind, endurance, inquisitiveness, and industriousness, to say nothing of her obvious competence as a parent. As a genuine historical figure she needs neither legends nor myths, whether as guide or ambassador, to make her a sympathetic figure. [34]

CHAPTER 6   Forks of the Columbia

THE FINAL PUSH TO THE SNAKE RIVER'S CONFLUENCE WITH
the Columbia commenced on the cool morning of 16 October 1805. The arrival of
strangers in the Columbia Basin was creating a sensation among the residents of
the region. Indians on the south bank watched the expedition float by, while five
others came running up the north bank "in great haste." The captains stopped for
a while to share a smoke with these scouts and gave them tobacco to take back to
their people downstream. As Clark noted, the Indians ran "as fast as They Could
run as far as we Could See them." [1]

The excitement exhibited by the Natives was not shared by the explorers.
William Clark's journal entry documenting their arrival at the long-sought
Great River of the West was written in the deadpan manner of a surveyor at
work: "S. 28 W. 6 ½ miles to the Junction of Columbia R." One imagines that
if Lewis had been the one recording this significant geographic accomplishment
it would have been marked with a great rhetorical flourish. As the expedition
is conventionally understood, only crossing the Continental Divide or reaching
the Pacific Ocean would have surpassed this moment in importance. Even on
reflection, as evidenced in an entry he wrote later, Clark could muster little in
the way of exploratory enthusiasm. For their final course that day, he wrote,
the expedition "proceeded on Seven miles to the junction of this river and the
Columbia which joins from the N. W." [2]

In the estimation of John Logan Allen this was indeed the moment when Lewis
and Clark reached what had been "the goal of trans-Missouri exploration since 1673."
In that year French explorers Louis Jolliet and Jacques Marquette had first sighted
the Missouri at its confluence with the Mississippi. In a great leap of imagination
that became ingrained in geographical lore, Marquette theorized that the Missouri
drained much of the interior of the continent. Furthermore, it came to be believed
that the source of the Missouri shared a height of land forming a divide from which
a great western river flowed to the Pacific Ocean. Finding the wellsprings of both
streams would reveal a pathway to the fabled riches of the Orient. [3]

Over a century ago Elliott Coues noted that the captains, upon arriving at the "long-sought Columbia" River, would naturally have been expected to show "some sign of feeling." At this presumably momentous junction, however, he found Clark strangely "unmoved," while Lewis, as already mentioned, had stopped writing altogether. Decades later John Logan Allen leapt into this breach with a theory accounting for what he referred to as Clark's "singularly unemotional" description of "the final discovery" of the Columbia River. In Allen's view, a sense of anticlimax, born earlier that summer when Lewis and Clark realized there was no easy connection between the Missouri and the Columbia rivers, now infused the outlook of the party. In other words, Lewis and Clark had come to the realization that Jefferson's dream of a water route across the continent was illusory, and thus there was no significance to be attached to having reached the great Columbia River.[4]

An alternate explanation for Clark's profound reserve may be found in the revealing journal entries of John Ordway and Joseph Whitehouse. Upon reaching the confluence Ordway referred to "the large River" coming in from the north as being "wider than the Columbia River." In a manner both more direct and more elaborate, Private Whitehouse wrote: "Towards evening we arrived at a large fork that came into this River from a Northerly direction & was much large[r] than *the fork which we descended which we supposed to be the Columbia River*" (emphasis added). As noted in a previous chapter, Whitehouse consistently used the words "Columbia" and "Columbian" to refer to the hydrology from Shoshone country onward. Indeed, on October 12th, two days below the Clearwater/Snake confluence, Whitehouse reported that Twisted Hair and Tetoharsky "tell us that in 2 days more we will come to another nation at a fork which comes in on the St[arboard] [the north] Side of the *Columbian River*" (emphasis added). The inference to be drawn from Ordway and Whitehouse is bold and clear: the Expedition for Northwestern Discovery was surprised to find that, contrary to the promise of speculative geography, it had *not* been on the primary branch of the Columbia River after crossing the Continental Divide! The expedition's moment of greatest geographic dismay is to be found not in Lewis's verbose and semi-fictitious "geography lesson" at Lemhi Pass, but in the nearly mute William Clark at the great forks of the Columbia River.[5]

The sentiment behind Clark's silence was not anticlimax rooted in a two-month-old realization, but something more akin to mortification. The ultimate geographical hope that Lewis and Clark had cultivated from the winter of 1805 forward was not simply that a single, short portage divided the Missouri from the Columbia, but that upon reaching the Great River of the West at the continental crest they would find the *headwaters of its principal stream*. Imagine, then, their shock and disappointment to find, when they finally reached the forks, that as near as they could determine Alexander Mackenzie, working for British commercial interests, had already done so, some twelve years earlier. Ubiquitous annotations by the several editors of the published versions of the journals that the explorers were *mistaken* in their geographic determinations regarding Columbia River hydrology are based on a normative interpretation that only became settled "truth" well after Lewis and Clark were in the field. Anachronistic perspectives have had a beguiling effect on historians and their readers. To take but one example, the noted and influential Bernard DeVoto once wrote about Lewis and Clark heading "down the Snake till at last they reached the river for which they had set out." [6]

As James Ronda writes, for Lewis and Clark "the road ahead was never as clear as we have imagined it was. Their uncertain future has become our seemingly predetermined path." Anachronistic thinking obscures the contingent nature of exploration in general and the specific fact here that geographic chance upended Lewis and Clark's world. Whereas the "decision at the Marias" had been an ephemeral issue, discernment of the main stem at the forks of the Columbia had immediately apparent and profound imperial consequences. The Ordway and Whitehouse statements regarding reaching the forks of the Columbia express a sense of surprise and disappointment that Clark's laconic account hides. The contrast between the astonishment implied in the journals of the enlisted men and Captain Clark's dry course-and-distance entry provides a genuine moment of insight into the nature of real-life exploring. Ronda sensibly avers that it is the "surprise and accident" in the past that gives it "life and vitality." [7]

There are clues in Clark's own record that substantiate the more explicit conclusions of Ordway and Whitehouse. A map appearing in juxtaposition to Clark's field notebook for 13 October 1805, three days *before* he reached the forks, clearly names the river being traversed as "Columbia." Another stream called the "Big River" flows into it. The map's appearance the day after Whitehouse says the Nez Perce chiefs told the captains they were coming to a new Indian nation at a big fork suggests that Clark may have drawn it in his field log concurrent with that discussion. Furthermore, upon arrival at the forks, Clark does not refer to reaching the Columbia, but rather, as did Whitehouse, reaching the "Junction" of the river. For that matter, neither Clark's field sketch showing the Columbia from the forks to and through Wallula Gap nor his plotted segment map showing the confluence, prepared the following winter at Fort Clatsop, lends a name to the main stem. In the latter chart, the Indian name for the Snake River is used—*Ki moo-e nem*—(later to be struck over and named "Lewis's River"), but what we know as the Columbia River goes unnamed. [8]

It's clear from Clark's field journal of October 17th (the second day at the "Junction") that he was perplexed by the problem this larger river from the north created. He refers to the campsite as being at the *"Forks of Columbia,"* but this term in itself is not specific enough to be probative. Clark next mentions going "high up the Columbia river" (the main stem above the Snake) to yet another "forks," which the Indians assured him was but a short ways upstream. Proceeding north about ten miles Clark came to a river entering on his left, that is to say from the west. We know this today as the Yakima River. In his log Clark concluded that this stream was Mackenzie's "Tarcouche tesse." The river emerged from a "hilly countery"

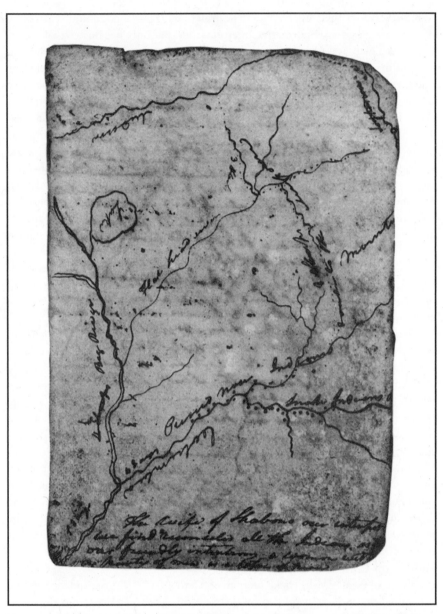

The inscription at the bottom of this page from Clark's field log contains the famous comment about Sacagawea's capacity to "reconcile" Indian tribes to the expedition by her mere presence. Perhaps more significantly, the map, if turned upside down, clearly shows the word "Columbia" adjoining the river Lewis and Clark had descended from the Shoshone and Nez Perce homelands. (Missouri History Museum, St. Louis)

(the Horse Heaven Hills) and emptied into the "Columbia." From the construction of his notes it is readily apparent that Clark was looking for a geographic solution that would mitigate the unwelcome implications of the previous day's discovery. By conceiving the Yakima as Mackenzie's "Tarcouche tesse," Clark momentarily preserved two hydrological and related imperial prospects. First, if the Yakima was Mackenzie's "Tarcouche tesse" then the stream Clark's expedition had navigated to the main Columbia was equal in significance to the Scotsman's. That is, both Mackenzie in British Columbia and Lewis at the Lemhi had been on minor tributaries of the Great River of the West, in which case neither the British nor perhaps the Americans had yet been on the main stem itself, a fact that would in effect neutralize both parties' right of First Discovery. Secondly—and more affirmatively, as one deconstructs Clark's geographical musings: if it turned out that Mackenzie's and Lewis's discoveries were not headwaters but tributaries, and thus cancelled each other, then the "Flat head river" from the vicinity of Traveler's Rest (the Bitterroot/Clark Fork/Pend Oreille River system) would thereby be preserved as the true headwaters of the Columbia, or contributory thereto. *That* river the Americans had been on first to the exclusion of any other Euro-American explorer.[9]

Clark's notebook for October 17th confirms the centrality of Mackenzie in the captains' thinking about the Columbia River. We know Clark consulted Mackenzie's *Voyages from Montreal* directly because he plagiarized its content. Mackenzie, when he was on what he mistakenly thought to be the Columbia River in 1793, described a woman who was said to be a native of the seacoast. "This woman," Mackenzie wrote, "was more inclined to corpulency than any we had yet seen, was low of stature, with an oblong face, grey eyes, and a flattish nose." Clark, on his voyage up from the forks to the junction of the Yakima/Tacoutche Tesse described the native women he saw as "more inclined to Copulency than any we have yet Seen, with low Stature broad faces, heads flatened." Mackenzie's subject "was decorated with ornaments of various kinds, such as large blue beads, either pendant from her ears, encircling her neck, or braided in her hair: she also wore bracelets of brass, copper, and horn." Clark's subjects were ornamented with "large blue & white beeds, either pendant from their ears or encircling their necks, or wrists & arms.[T]hey also wore bracelets of Brass, Copper & horn." Mackenzie noted that "Age seemed to be an object of great veneration among these people." The people Clark saw on the Columbia "respect the aged with veneration." Clark's account here is a virtual copy of Mackenzie's narrative.[10]

Taken unawares on 16–17 October 1805 by the appearance of the larger stream entering from the north, Clark, and probably Lewis too, paged through Mackenzie's *Voyages* looking for clues and solutions to their predicament. Mackenzie had described his "Tacoutche Tesse or Columbia River" as being "confined by the immense mountains that run nearly parallel with the Pacific Ocean, and keep it in a Southern course." In his notebook for October 17th Clark willed Mackenzie's Tacoutche Tesse into a "western fork" (today's Yakima River), which emerged, so far as Clark could tell, from a range of hills between the ocean and the "main Columbia river," or precisely as the Scotsman had described the stretch of the river he had seen and described. In his field log Clark's guard is down when he refers to Mackenzie, but the more reflective leather-bound notebook entry composed much later makes no mention of his British competitor. There the Mackenzian or "western fork" of the Columbia was now referred to as the "Tap teel River." Of late, Lewis and Clark have been taken to task for avoiding Indian place names that might "stand in the way" of their cultural imperialism, but in this case, at least, where the alternative was letting Mackenzie's denomination endure, an aboriginal name had certain advantages.[11]

Today we understand that the "northern fork" of the Columbia is larger than the southerly Snake, and though an obvious modern fact to us, it was *not* something Lewis and Clark could have known until they reached the junction. Clark's narrative reserve regarding the "final discovery" of the Columbia was a literary mask intended to finesse surprise and dismay. On the approach to the forks, Lewis and Clark were not emotionally prepared to be making any more important discoveries, which in itself may explain why Lewis laid down his pen after emerging from the Rockies. James Ronda's general insight that the "Lewis and Clark story is a study in ambiguity and uncertainty" seems especially true here at the forks of the Columbia River. "What looks like success," Ronda writes, may actually hide "abject failure." In this case, what in retrospect should have been perceived as an achievement, as Coues noted so long ago, was instead one of the most disappointing moments of the entire voyage. Silences, Clay Jenkinson writes, can sometimes be "as important as statements." William Clark's silence on reaching the main stem of the Columbia is deafening.[12]

Thomas Slaughter trenchantly observes that "companions create narrative problems for the explorer." In this case, the candor of John Ordway and Joseph Whitehouse, enlisted men not burdened with the pretense of being prescient "explorers," provides a powerful insight into how a discovery narrative can be constructed—actively, or by omission. Whereas John Logan Allen once questioned whether Lewis and Clark "ever fully accepted this great southern branch of the Columbia" as shown on the map of Nicholas King, there can be no doubt from Ordway and Whitehouse's view of the world that the captains were fully invested in the promise of King's theory.[13]

On October 17th, the day of Clark's reconnaissance of the Yakima/Tacoutche Tesse above the Columbia's forks, Ordway wrote: "the River which we came down looses its name and is now Called Kimo e num." He continued by stating "the North fork which is the largest is Called the Calumbia River." Whitehouse, an even more junior man, stated the proposition more bluntly: "Our officers were of the opinion that the River which we descended, & *which we all took, to be the Columbia River* should lose its name at this place and that the North fork being the largest should be called the Columbia River, & the South fork of the River... which we had descended, should be named Lewis's River or after the name it bears among the Indians which is Ki-o-me-num River" (emphasis added).[14]

John Ordway had no expectation that his notes would serve as anything but an aide-memoire to Lewis, and was certainly not keeping an alternate or hidden history of the expedition. Nevertheless, like Whitehouse, he freely recorded many occurrences overlooked or consciously ignored by the captains. In July 1804, for example, Clark's notes were blown overboard, into the Missouri River, an event he failed to mention in his journals. On the return voyage, after Pierre Cruzatte inadvertently shot Meriwether Lewis in the buttock, Ordway said Lewis fainted when Clark dressed the wound. This bit of "conscientious reporting" went unrecorded in Clark's journal. Lewis stopped writing altogether in the wake of this latter incident.[15]

Both Elliott Coues and, later, Gary Moulton noted that neither Lewis nor Clark tended to dwell on episodes where one or both of them failed to perform in some respect or were caught in some embarrassing scenario. We saw earlier that Clark made no mention of his and Lewis's canoe taking a spill on the Clearwater. We know of this episode only because Whitehouse mentioned it. Coues stated, regarding Lewis's frustration with the construction of the iron-frame boat above the Great Falls of the Missouri, that Clark maintained "a discreet silence on the subject, and attends imperturbably to his portage, till Captain Lewis should get tired of his toy." [16]

Clark could hardly have been expected to trumpet a message of defeat or frustration at the forks of the Columbia. Instead, over the course of the ensuing winter he quietly corrected the hydrological errors that had crept into his text and maps. Working in the literary idiom of the travel account, Clark at the Columbia's forks, like Lewis at Lemhi Pass, chose what to write, and what *not to write*, in his journals. The minimalist narrative he recorded upon reaching the Columbia is a purposeful riddle. In the face of such puzzles, it is the job of the historian to make sense of the narrative by discerning the interests and motivations of the storytellers. Though oral historians bemoan the fact that their sources are discounted because of suspected simplification or selectivity, the fact remains that even written records, like the journals of Lewis and Clark, are constructed with similar flaws. They need to be analyzed critically and cannot be taken at face value.[17]

Like Lewis's "geography lesson" at the Continental Divide, Clark's selective narrative at the forks of the Columbia is indicative of the extraordinarily high stakes at both junctures: the dreams of Jefferson and Lewis and the promise of a Missouri/Columbia trade route were on the line. Alessandro Portelli argues that "the most precious information may lie in what informants hide, and in the fact they do hide it, rather than what they tell." Narrators, whether in written or oral form, prefer an "affirmative discourse." These success stories emerge from the narrative ready-made and well articulated. A "discourse of negation," on the other hand, is fugitive, ephemeral, and frequently has to be pieced together after the fact by the historian.[18]

The naming of streams by Lewis and Clark west of the Continental Divide is just such a "discourse of negation," literally as well as figuratively. The captains had every advantage with the naming business going up the Missouri—the quintessential "affirmative discourse." The only modestly difficult assignment, the decision at the Marias, was resolved by strict adherence to Euro-American principles of hydrology. Whichever affluent had more water was named the main stem. As Joseph Whitehouse phrased it at the time, the south fork was "entitled to the Name of the Mesouri River, it being by far the largest." Later that summer on the Jefferson River, Whitehouse again reported on the captains' decision that beyond the Three Forks "the Missourie Should loose its name." [19]

Hydraulic concepts were obviously much harder to employ going down a river and particularly dangerous to the reputation of the voyaging geographer. In the downstream mode an explorer had to operate on faith and with guesswork because hydraulic primacy could only be empirically determined retrospectively. Complicating matters further, Lewis and Clark's Indian guides—Old Toby, Twisted Hair, and Tetoharsky—thought of rivers in a completely different, non-hydraulic manner. Someone like Twisted Hair, Clark's principal informant about the Clearwater/Snake/Columbia system, was far more conscious of where a river's water could take him (Celilo Falls, for example) than its hydrologic structure. To Twisted Hair the rivers that coursed through his and neighboring homelands were an organic unit, not a hierarchical system of affluents. [20]

We know, furthermore, that Lewis and Clark's penchant for hydraulic comprehension made a lasting impression on the Nez Perce. An overland detachment from the United States Exploring Expedition commanded by Charles Wilkes visited the Nez Perce homelands in the summer of 1841. Lt. Robert E. Johnson struck the Clearwater River in the course of his reconnaissance of the Columbia Plateau near present-day Lapwai, Idaho. The river was still running strong late into the season, and accordingly Johnson characterized the Clearwater as "a powerful stream." He went on to note that Lewis and Clark "fell upon this river about forty-five miles above this place, and it is not difficult to imagine how they were induced to suppose that they had reached the great river flowing to the west, so totally different is it from the Ohio and Missouri." More directly, Lieutenant Johnson learned from Protestant missionaries then living among the Nez Perce that the Indians remembered Lewis and Clark. The captains' confusion about the relationship between the tributaries, Johnson maintained, was due to the fact that the Nez Perce had names for places along the rivers but none for the rivers per se. Whether or not that's true, surely the Nez Perce did not think of their waters in terms of hydraulic carrying capacity and thus could never give Clark the precise information he was looking for. [21]

The realization by Clark and Lewis that they had not been on the main fork of the Columbia precipitated a cascade of changes in the original record documenting travel west of the divide. The journals contain a veritable torrent of erasures, strikeovers, and filling-in of blank spaces as a function of inserting "Lewis's River" into the record retroactively. Dozens of these can be found in the text, but the most graphic one is Clark's map of the Continental Divide where the word

Clark's field map of the Continental Divide shows, upon close inspection, that "Lewis's River" has been superimposed over spaces previously carrying the inscription "Columbia." (Yale Collection of Western Americana, Beinecke Rare Book and Manuscript Library)

"Lewis's" is unmistakably scripted over a not fully erased "Columbia." In doing so Clark was not so much manipulating the document or engaging in a cover-up as he was performing his duty as a good geographer. Nevertheless, it couldn't have been a responsibility he welcomed.[22]

The eminent Lewis and Clark scholar Donald Jackson once asked, "What if British explorer Mackenzie had found the Columbia River instead of the Fraser, which he only *thought* was the Columbia?" For Lewis and Clark in October 1805 this was *not* a rhetorical question. Based on their evolving comprehension, it seemed to them that Mackenzie just might have discovered the headwaters of the Columbia. This mortifying prospect meant that Lewis and Clark had not strengthened the mercantile interests of the United States as much as they might have had they linked Gray's crossing of the bar of the Columbia with a corresponding discovery of the river's wellspring. Lewis and Clark knew about Mackenzie's vision—the mere articulation of it had prompted the countermeasure they commanded—and they knew now that their explorations had not forged an image of the Columbia as an "All-American" stream. Their remaining hope, as they faced the prospect of the final push to the sea, was that the Yakima River was Mackenzie's Tacoutche Tesse, and if not then where the "Flat head" and "Valley plain" river system met the Columbia above the main forks that its combined flow was larger than Mackenzie's stream coming in from the north.[23]

Lewis and Clark could do little about this at that moment. Winter was approaching, and there were still many miles to pass before reaching the ocean. But on the return trip, in the spring of 1806, the captains revisited this problem by seeking mitigating information from the plateau's Native inhabitants. Two maps of the Columbia River system were sketched by Indians but denominated by Clark, who assiduously avoided use of the term "Columbia." A third map names the Columbia above "Lewis's River" but the word is carefully situated to appear below the "Clark's River" affluent. Correspondingly, a set of maps prepared by Clark himself, probably during the slack time of their stay with the Nez Perce on the return trip, cagily employs the same strategy, preserving the potential of a Discovery claim for the United States. That is, "Columbia" appears on the greater north fork but the script scrupulously avoids appearing north of the confluence of the "Flathead" or "Clark's River." Visiting the Nez Perce at that time were three "Skeets-so-mish" (Coeur d'Alene) Indians. Intrigued, Lewis learned of their residence to the north on a "river discharging itself into the Columbia," via "Clark's River" as it was by this time officially named. Lewis stipulated that the "Flathead river" terminology used previously was to be retired, concurrent with the renaming of the present-day Deschutes River of Oregon. This latter stream had been named "Clark's River" in October 1805 but now took an Indian designation "To-wannahiooks river."[24]

There was an obvious imperial value to naming the northerly system of rivers after Clark. As Patrick Gass noted, no one from the expedition had seen, or was to see, where Clark's fork entered the Columbia. Thus, there was no way to determine which of two streams was larger at that forks—the one the Americans had been on near Traveler's Rest or Mackenzie's. Since "no whiteman but ourselves" had been on the "Flathead river" or "it's principal branches," Lewis exercised the presumptive naming rights "in honour of my worthy friend and fellow traveller Capt. Clark." Furthermore, the river these "Skeets-so-mish" lived on took its flow from a "large lake in the mountains." This was probably a reference to Lake Coeur d'Alene and the Spokane River that empties it, but in Lewis's contemporaneous cartographic framework, this geographic feature was reminiscent of "the river which Fidler calls the great lake river." [25]

Lewis was referring to Peter Fidler, a surveyor for the Hudson's Bay Company. Traveling in the Canadian West, Fidler had developed sketches based on Native intimations of a "Great Lake River" which flowed toward the Pacific. Fidler's speculative geography found its way into the maps of Aaron Arrowsmith, which showed a "Great Lake River" flowing into Mackenzie's "Tacoutche Tesse." Lewis conceded that Fidler's river "may possibly be a branch of [Clark's River] but if so it is but a very inconsiderable branch and may as probably empty itself into the Skeetssomish as into that river." (Here we find Lewis having trouble differentiating between the two complex lake/river systems of northern Idaho and eastern Washington (the Lake Coeur d'Alène/Spokane and the Clark Fork/Lake Pend Oreille/Pend Oreille River known heretofore in the lexicon of the expedition as the Flathead or Clark's River.) In any event, by wishing away a potential affluent to Mackenzie's northern fork, Lewis built the case for the prominence of the fork of the Columbia named for Clark. In this fashion a fanciful imperial hydrology temporarily survived the disappointment at the forks of the Columbia in October 1805 and even the explorers' return to the Columbia Plateau in 1806. [26]

William Clark's initial reserve at the forks combined with the tendentious geography of Meriwether Lewis the following spring shows that the captains and Jefferson did not consider Robert Gray's "discovery" of the Columbia River to be a decisive moment in American statecraft. The research and writing of legal scholar and jurist Robert Miller provides a helpful explication of this point. Miller claims that the Lewis and Clark Expedition "was expressly designed to strengthen the United States Discovery claim" to the Columbia country. Miller explains that a "First Discovery," like Gray's at the mouth of the river he named or Mackenzie at its head, did not in itself establish a complete title. An initial geographic find, whether an island, a new shore, or a previously unseen land, according to Miller, had to be "perfected" in some fashion so as to preclude other imperial powers from intruding into or competing with the claim. This could be done in several ways, including the establishment of a fort or some other kind of settlement or by proving contiguity to adjoining lands over which there was no dispute. With regard to Lewis and Clark, both of these factors came into play—Fort Clatsop in regard to the former, and the Missouri/Columbia nexus made feasible by the American purchase of Louisiana. [27]

According to Miller the "Doctrine of Discovery is one of the earliest examples of international law" whose concurrent values, he avers, were to regulate diplomacy

This inset from Mackenzie's "track map" published in his *Voyages from Montreal* (1801) depicts the Scotman's route to the Arctic Ocean in 1789, and what he determined to be the principal north fork of the Columbia River encountered on his trek to the Pacific Ocean in 1793. (Washington State Historical Society)

and minimize conflict between imperial nations, while, in practice, isolating and limiting the rights of Native peoples. In Miller's reading of Jefferson's interpretation of the ill-defined northwestern boundary of the Louisiana Purchase, the president concluded that the Columbia country might be considered an extension or appendage to the territory recently acquired from France. According to this line of reasoning, given the weakness of the Spanish contiguity claim north of California, a Missouri/Columbia line could interpose an American foothold on the Pacific slope, south of the competing Russian and British claims on the Northwest Coast including the Alaska littoral. Gray had given the United States a credible start but another element of the Doctrine of Discovery—timely follow-up to an initial assertion—was essential to perfecting a claim. This is the role Lewis and Clark were to play in establishing American sovereignty, a role enhanced by the fact that unlike Gray, who was a mere trader, the captains were explicitly imperial agents having, as Lewis phrased it, "the sanction of the government." [28]

In this sense, then, Lewis and Clark had far more at stake while in the Columbia's watershed than in the Missouri's, certainly in terms of national sovereignty interests if not exploratory glory. Yes, their work with the Missouri River tribes, aligning them to the American perspective on national prerogatives relative to trade, was important. So, too, were fundamental facets of exploration like finding the Great Falls and the headwaters near the divide. Still, Lewis and Clark encountered any number of traders and their own countrymen on the Missouri; they saw nary a white man on the Columbia. Thus, while the United States had a nascent and contingent claim to the Columbia River based on Gray's work, there was still very much a race between Great Britain and the Americans to turn imperfect claims into indisputable possession.[29]

This is why, Miller argues, Jefferson instructed Lewis upon reaching the Pacific to determine whether "any port within your reach [was] frequented by the sea-vessels of any nation." In sum, when Lewis and Clark ventured over the Continental Divide at Lemhi, "ownership of the Pacific Northwest and the Oregon Country was still very much in question," quoting Miller. Gray's discovery did not dispose of the question; it merely gave the United States a plausible footing on which to make a claim. The strategic promise of the Lewis and Clark Expedition, then, was that it would serve as the decisive agency for an American empire on the Pacific via one specific incremental objective. By establishing a primary headwaters line the captains would simultaneously buttress Gray and serve as an antidote to Mackenzie.[30]

Two could play this game, as demonstrated by the British response to Lewis and Clark. In December 1810 David Thompson, a fur trader/explorer for the North West Company, expressed concerns about the Americans who "were as usual... determined to be beforehand with us in the Columbia in ship navigation." By this time Simon Fraser had proved Mackenzie's Tacoutche Tesse to be a separate river, so Thompson's plan was to enter the Columbia at a far northerly point of access and, combined with his earlier explorations west of the divide, systematize the river's major tributaries. This work would be completed by the summer of 1811, when Thompson would paddle down the Columbia to the river's mouth and meet the Astorians, an American fur-trading outfit hoping to capitalize on the mercantilist vision first strategically enunciated by Mackenzie in 1801.[31]

Thompson had first apprenticed in the fur trade with the Hudson's Bay Company, but he left their employ for the North West Company in 1797. As noted in an earlier chapter, he was at the Mandan villages several years before Lewis and Clark arrived there but then later moved to outposts in the Canadian north. By 1800 he was determined to follow Mackenzie's lead west of the Continental Divide. In the summer of 1807 Thompson finally crossed into the Kootenay country, on waters tributary to the Columbia, and wintered there. The Kootenay River, fellow trader Alexander Henry later wrote sharply, "empties into the Columbia, far above the place which Captains Lewis and Clark proceeded on their way to the Pacific." For his part, Thompson was of the belief in 1807 that Vancouver's more extensive exploration of the Columbia via Broughton, as opposed to Gray's foraging in the saltwater estuary, gave Great Britain a superior foundational claim to the country drained by the great river.[32]

Thompson learned about fellow Nor'Wester Simon Fraser's 1808 voyage down Mackenzie's Tacoutche Tesse by June of 1809. That trip had been Fraser's turn for disappointment. He discovered that the river that would eventually bear his name (an honor bestowed by Thompson) emptied into the Pacific Ocean above the 49th parallel and, more to the point, appreciably north of the Columbia's mouth. Only now, sixteen years after Mackenzie's voyage to the Pacific and four years after Lewis and Clark toured the Great River of the West, was it clear that Mackenzie had been wrong about the northern fork of the Columbia. Thompson resolved to unravel this puzzle once and for all and commenced his final assay of the Columbia River system in the fall of 1810.[33]

On 9 July 1811 Thompson reached the confluence of the Snake and Columbia Rivers. Denoting the enduring strategic import of the great forks that Lewis and Clark had grappled with six years earlier, Thompson planted a pole in the ground on which he posted the following note:

> Know hereby that this Country is claimed by Great Britain as part of it's Territories and that the NW Company of Merchants from Canada... do hereby intend to erect a Factory in this Place for the Commerce of the Country around. D. Thompson.

When Thompson made his return to the forks on August 5th (after a brief sojourn with the Americans at Fort Astoria), he planted a flag at the Indian village there, and he also importuned the Natives to his British imperial outlook.[34]

Meriwether Lewis was dead by this time, the farseeing geopolitician Thomas Jefferson was out of office, and a full account of the American expedition to the Pacific had not yet been published. It was precisely the circumstance symbolized by Thompson's note and flag that the western-most extent of Lewis and Clark's expedition had been intended to pre-empt. Unlike the lands in the Louisiana Purchase drained by the Missouri River, over which the United States had an undisputed international title, the Columbia country was subject to competing claims, and the forks of the Great River of the West was a geographic pivot point of the first magnitude. East of the divide the geopolitical framework set for the captains was the more limited objective of transferring tribal allegiances from British hegemony to American. West of the continental crest the imperial objective was far more contingent and fundamental: establishing American legitimacy.

Such were the consequences of Lewis and Clark not having found the true headwaters of the main Columbia. Thus it should not surprise us that Clark said so little about reaching the main stem, and that later he and Lewis would tout the importance of "Clark's River." They might have imagined that they could tactically aid their patron, Thomas Jefferson, by obscuring things or providing alternative geographic solutions, buying time while the president and his successors secured by diplomacy an outcome that could not be grounded in exploration. In short, the strategies of silence and a new round of promising speculation postponed the day of reckoning about sovereignty over the Columbia River to some other time and place. Indeed, prefiguring the inherent weakness of his expedition's findings, Lewis told guests at a Washington dinner party held in his honor after returning from the Pacific that the establishment of a fur-trading post on the Columbia was required to validate his and Clark's explorations, a point Jefferson would later emphasize as well.[35]

The first American to encounter Thompson's effrontery at the forks was Alexander Ross of John Jacob Astor's Pacific Fur Company. Ross came upon the scene a month after Thompson's visit and he was predictably indignant. The chiefs from the Indian village at the confluence took their cue from Thompson's handbill and told Ross he could not pass farther north up the main Columbia. Instead, they pointed to the "south branch [the Snake River] as if to intimate," Ross reported, "that we might trade there." As Jack Nisbet observes, Thompson was directing the Americans to trade "in the territory Lewis and Clark had explored, while leaving the country he had charted to the North West Company." Ross viewed Thompson's broadside not merely in strict mercantile terms but also as an important racial corollary: a British attempt to incite the Indians in that district against the Americans.[36]

For his part, Thompson firmly believed that his exploits superseded those of Lewis and Clark and the Astorians. Thompson had read the first published letters of Lewis and Clark touting their voyage, but it was he who had discovered the true headwaters of the Columbia and definitively discerned the tributary patterns. Thompson biographer D'Arcy Jenish has observed, "Lewis and Clark had explored the final three-hundred-mile stretch known as the lower Columbia, whereas [Thompson] had traveled from the source of the river to its mouth, a full twelve hundred miles."[37]

By 1818 Thompson became concerned about American attempts to convince Great Britain that the 49th parallel boundary east of the Continental Divide should be extended westward to the Pacific. Three years later he wrote to a member of the Royal Geographic Society in London proposing what he believed to be a more equitable division. Thompson's logic was firmly rooted in the sequence of exploratory events starting in 1792–1793, through 1805, to 1811, conducted severally by Gray, Vancouver, Mackenzie, Lewis and Clark, and himself. As Jack Nisbet succinctly states, "the lands along the Snake River, which had been first visited by Lewis and Clark, would go to the United States, while the territory that Thompson had explored to the north would belong to Great Britain. Navigation of the lower river claimed by both Robert Gray and George Vancouver would be shared." In this manner Thompson succeeded Mackenzie as the British claimant to the northern, or main, fork of the Columbia.[38]

A Congressional report in 1821, on the sustainability of a pre-emptive American declaration of title to the Oregon country, concluded that a perfect claim under the principles of international law entitled the United States to "the whole extent of soil watered by the springs of the principal river or watercourse passing through it." Regrettably for the Americans, Lewis and Clark did nothing to assist in this regard. Indeed, as it would play out, during the final series of negotiations with the United States during the 1840s, the British claim to Oregon was heavily buttressed by Thompson's discovery of the true Columbian headwaters, replacing Mackenzie's premature claim. Correspondingly, the American negotiators never based their rights to Oregon on Lewis and Clark but only on Gray and the Astorians. This line of argument had been anticipated by no less a figure than Thomas Jefferson who said in 1816 that the American title to the Pacific Northwest "if we claim that country at all… must be [based] on Astor's settlement near the mouth of the Columbia River."[39]

Despite having a far less than perfect claim, by the time the Oregon boundary was settled in 1846 the geopolitical axis had turned entirely in favor of the Americans. The fur trade was now much diminished in importance. Visions of steam-powered railroad engines crossing the continent were in the air. Within these emerging contexts, the blow that Lewis and Clark absorbed in October 1805 at the forks of the Columbia related to river-based cross-continental links was softened if not rendered inconsequential. History, or rather demography, rescued the captains. In the mid-1840s, with the onset of extensive American settlement into the Northwest via the Oregon Trail and South Pass, the Snake River watershed, the booby prize in the fall of 1805, now took on a strategically advantageous prospect. American control of the Oregon country would be secured, but it owed not a whit to the efforts of Lewis and Clark.

At the forks of the Columbia in October 1805, William Clark was puzzled by the origin, direction, and imperial implications to be deduced from the rivers before him. The adjoining terrain, on the other hand, was knowable. There was still, Clark reported from their campsite on the Columbia, "no wood to be Seen in any direction." Clark was curious about how far the Indians had to "raft their timber" to make their fish-drying scaffolds near the forks. He had barely seen a stick of timber for a hundred miles to the east. As a scientific voyager, Clark was unrelenting in his gaze to discern some limit to this treeless topography, and his undeviating powers of observation provided one of the more salient instances of geographic knowledge produced by the expedition. Clark attributed the ubiquity of visual afflictions among the Native people living near the Snake-Columbia confluence, ranging from sore eyes to blindness, to over exposure to the sun's rays reflecting from the water and the wide-open country where "the eye has no rest." Clark may well have been describing his own sense of the stark, unromantic reality of this place.[40]

On October 18th, the third and last day at the "Forks of the Columbia," the weather broke cool. William Clark took a quick measurement of the sun just a little past 8 a.m., whereupon several canoes full of Indians from above visited the encampment. A brief parley was conducted, including an exchange of medals and wampum. Clark secured from the Indians one last map of the river system and villages upstream, evidence that he was still grappling with geographic problems. This being the end of the fishing season, the party laid in provisions for the downstream voyage, notably forty dogs, which they paid for with "articles of little value, Such as bells, thimbles, knitting pins, brass wire & a few beeds." Lewis used the occasion to enhance his vocabulary of the Wanapum, Yakama, and Nez Perce languages.[41]

Clark resumed his solar and lunar measurements at 9:37 a.m. He then unpacked his surveying equipment for the first time since the Great Falls of the Missouri, further evidence that he understood the importance of this place despite the minimalist style of his exploratory discourse. He first established a landmark on the opposite bank of the Columbia and then created a base line running north of the camp at the fork 148 poles (2,442 feet, or nearly half a mile) long. The siting of a second benchmark across the river, followed by some mathematical triangulations, resulted in a precise measurement of the width of the Columbia River at 960 ¾ yards. Employing the same methods with a different landmark on the opposite side of the Snake River, Clark measured the "Ki-moo-e nim" at 575 yards in width. Then fixing the latitude for this point of interest, ("especially at the mouths of rivers" as directed in President Jefferson's instructions to Lewis at the commencement of the venture), Clark's and the expedition's work here was done. That afternoon, the party "Set out down the Great Columbia."[42]

CHAPTER 7   William Clark:
            Scientific Geographer

THE SHARED COMMAND OF LEWIS AND CLARK HAS NATURALLY
invited comparisons between the two. In these, William Clark has traditionally—
and undeservedly, in my view—come out on the short end. Clark has chronically
been classified as both the non-scientist and the non-literary man of the two.
The expedition's traverse of the Columbia from its Snake River fork to tidewater
provides a welcome opportunity to re-evaluate Clark's contributions to the
venture, and to address both the misclassification of him as an inferior scientist,
and the underestimation of his prose.

   Most comparisons between the captains quickly turn to their differing though
complementary personalities and leadership styles, a topic we shall return to in
due course. Scholarly consensus and expedition lore hold that the captains each
had an equal share of the martial command. However, because most of the botanical and faunal descriptions found in the journals initially flowed from the pen
of Lewis, the two have not been perceived as equals when it comes to scientific
matters. While it's true that Clark wasn't the naturalist Lewis was, a more nuanced and fully contextualized analysis shows that Clark had his own distinct and
essential scientific specialty.[1]

   The very first observation Gary Moulton makes in his modern edition of the
journals is that the expedition "was preeminently a geographic endeavor, and
mapping the unknown lands was a principal objective." The goal of establishing a route across the continent for the purposes of commerce was necessarily
predicated on someone in the party being able to develop scientifically reliable
maps, derived in part from mathematical and astronomical calculations—like
those produced by Captains Cook and Vancouver. For the Expedition for
Northwestern Discovery, that person was William Clark who, as Paul Cutright
once noted, had "native talent as a maker of maps." As noted in two previous
chapters, William Clark was the principal geographic problem-solver when the
expedition faced uncertainty about how to proceed through the mountainous
terrain west of Lemhi Pass and on the Lolo Trail. Elliott Coues went so far as

to assert that Clark was "one of the greatest geographical geniuses this country ever produced." [2]

As so often proves true in the study of most any aspect of the expedition, the issue of Clark's scientific competency is obscured by Lewis's felicity for wordsmithing. As Silvio Bedini observed, Clark made "more significant contributions than are generally realized," but "Lewis may have been given more credit because his journal entries reflected superior qualities of writing and expression." Clark did not have the literary flair Lewis had, but he was committed to making a contribution to science. Since Lewis had long since stopped keeping his daily journal on Columbian waters, Clark's field notes and maps, and the more reflective notebook entries he completed after the fact, form the entirety of the expedition's scientific record of the voyage downstream. Clark did far more than a merely serviceable job on this leg. He was, instead, an exemplar of what Alexander Mackenzie called the methodology of the "scientific geographer." [3]

On the afternoon of 18 October 1805—supplied, rested, and still accompanied by the Nez Perce Chiefs Tetoharsky and Twisted Hair—the expedition "proceeded on down the great Columbia river." They knew this would be the final segment of their voyage west, but may have been surprised how eventful this first day on the main Columbia would be. The expedition was about to see, for the first time since they left the Mandan villages the previous April, a feature charted by European travelers.[4]

Clark's third course-and-distance entry for the 18th reads: "S.E. 1 ½ miles to mo. of a river 40 yds wide under a high Clift. in the Lard. Bend." This reference to the appearance of the Walla Walla River was followed by an observation that "here the river enters the high countrey rising abt. 200 feet above the Water." Now about sixteen miles downstream from the Snake/Columbia River confluence, Clark was observing the upstream opening into the Wallula Gap, a short but spectacular gorge through which the great river passes via a big sweeping bend to the southwest. The heights above the river were "bordered with black rugid rocks." At this juncture in the expeditionary record Clark next wrote in his notebook: "Saw a mountain bearing S. W. Conocal form Covered with Snow." Coming a few days after having reached the main stem of the Columbia, this first sighting of what would later be confirmed to be Mount Hood was the expedition's second great geographic marker that week. As noted earlier, Lewis and Clark were schooled in the contributions of Captain George Vancouver's 1792 maritime survey of the Pacific coast, including a series of snow-peaked mountains he named after now-obscure British dignitaries (Baker, Rainier, St. Helens, and Hood). With the sighting of a peak on Vancouver's charts, the Expedition for Northwestern Discovery was "back on the map," having left the world of known geography a thousand miles to the east. Lewis and Clark could now estimate how close they were to the ocean, their ultimate destination. [5]

Since Mount Hood is not visible at or near the water level from within Wallula Gap itself, just when or how did Clark sight it? Students of the expedition have questioned whether it's even possible to see Mount Hood from the bluffs *above* the gap and speculate about a corollary proposition, that Clark had somehow made a mistake by inserting the observation in the wrong place in the expedition's chronology. If the party made landfall near the confluence of the Walla Walla with the Columbia, Clark's description of their being "under a high Clift" is suggestive of a viewing opportunity. The hills there provide a gentle approach to elevated heights from the north. Perhaps Clark climbed the ramparts to the uplands behind the Two Sisters rock formation that is famous in Walla Walla Indian lore. Discernable amidst the smudges in Clark's field map for this area is the notation "rocks" precisely at the location of the Two Sisters. From the journals we know that Clark and Lewis liked to climb high promontories to view the terrain. Sometimes they did this alone and occasionally with companions. Only the week before, Lewis had climbed out of the Snake River canyon to see what lay ahead.[6]

Mathematical modeling and personal inspection on unusually clear days proves that it is possible to view Mount Hood from the bluffs above the gap. Furthermore, the preponderance of evidence found in the balance of the documentary record suggests that Clark did *not* make a mistake in the chronology of events since he had many opportunities to correct himself. The most telling indicator in this regard can be found in Clark's course and distance catalogue in his field notes from three days later, 21 October 1805. By that date the party was progressing toward a campsite near the Deschutes River's confluence with the Columbia. There, Clark wrote, "a round toped mountain imediately in front and is the one we have been going towards & which bore S.W. from the 2d course below the Forks." In the expedition's practice a "course" was a singular or a small subset of bearing and distance notations, and not a whole day's travel. Consequently, this confirms that the mountain was seen on the first day out from the "Forks," a segment of travel that terminated in the depths of Wallula Gap near Port Kelley, Washington.[7]

After making camp on the 18th, Twisted Hair and Tetoharsky informed the captains that one of the large Native villages the expedition had passed toward the end of the day's travel was the home "of the 1st Chief of all the *tribes* in this quarter." Apparently, this chief had called out to the Nez Perce guides so that the party might "land and Stay all night with him, that he had plenty of wood for us." Clark explained he would have been agreeable to this plan "if it had... been understood" at the time. However, once learning of this hospitable offer, Twisted Hair and Tetoharsky were asked to walk back upriver to invite "the Chief to come down and Stay with us all night which they did." Late that evening the distinguished visitor arrived, accompanied by twenty men, in possession of a large basket of mashed berries as a gift. He formed his own camp near that of the expedition.[8]

The great chief was Yelleppit, the head man of the Walla Walla band of Indians. The next day Yelleppit and the captains held a smoke for the stated purpose, Clark recorded, "that his people might Come down and See us." This vague expression of intent was probably a euphemism for a trading session. The word "Yah-lept" in Sahaptian means "trading partner." Clark probably ascribed the chief's intent to be his name. A peace medal exchange then followed. Yelleppit asked that the explorers might stay until midday. Pressed for time, Clark said "we excused our Selves and promised to Stay with him one or 2 days on our return which appeared to Satisfy him." [9]

Of all the great chiefs the captains encountered, Yelleppit languishes in relative obscurity, even though years later Clark told Nicholas Biddle that Yelleppit was "the greatest we met with." In part this is a function of the fact that he figured more prominently during the return trip the following spring, where all Lewis and Clark stories, with one or two exceptions, are relegated to the nether world of the anti-climactic. The re-engagement with Yelleppit in April 1806 is noteworthy for several reasons. First, he reconfirmed his desire to be friends with the Americans and to establishing a trading relationship with them. Second, it was at Yelleppit's village near the mouth of the Walla Walla River that Lewis and Clark learned about the overland shortcut they would take back to the Nez Perce villages where the party's horses had wintered. Most importantly, Yelleppit's comportment with the captains provides a valuable lesson about the vitality of Native agency on the Columbia Plateau early in the nineteenth century. [10]

By the spring of 1806 Lewis was as anxious to get on with the eastbound trip as Clark had been going west. But whereas, as noted above, Clark was able to fend off Yelleppit's fall 1805 pleading for an extended stay, Lewis had no such luck because he needed Native canoes to ferry the expedition's horses and gear across the Columbia. Using his leverage, Yelleppit simply refused to provide the craft unless the Americans stayed over for a night. Yelleppit subtly pressured the captains when he informed them that word had already been sent to the neighboring village of Yakama Indians to come down for an evening of dancing. A night of great festivity ensued. The next day, true to his word, Yelleppit furnished the canoes necessary to transport men and baggage across the river and on their way home. A humbled Lewis reported that the detachment "took leave of these friendly honest people the Wollahwallas." [11]

Once back underway westbound from Wallula Gap, the first benchmark noted on the distance table from the previous camp was "a rock... resembling a hat" fourteen miles downstream on the southern bank of the Columbia in the present state of Oregon. To come abreast of Hat Rock, the party had to pass several islands, including one where Indians drying their fish on scaffolds "hid themselves" until the voyageurs floated by. Four miles below "this fritened Island," Clark reported, "we arrived at the head of a verry bad rapid." At this place Clark landed on the Oregon side of the river "to view the rapid before we would venter to run it." He continued walking to the west on the south bank for the two miles it took to pass the now sunken and nearly forgotten Umatilla rapids, located where McNary Dam is today. [12]

Here, seven miles downstream from Hat Rock, Clark again espied a mountain to the west. Clark denominated it Mount Hood at first but crossed out that entry in his log and substituted it with "St. Helens." In its "corrected" form his extended leather-bound notebook entry stated:

> I assended a high clift about 200 feet above the water from the top of which is a leavel plain extending up the river and off for a great extent, at this place the Countrey becoms low on each Side of the river, and affords [a view] of the river and countrey below for great extent both to the right and left; from this place I descovered a high mountain of emence hight covered with Snow, this must be one of the mountains laid down by Vancouver, as Seen from the mouth of the Columbia River, from the Course which it bears which is *West* I take it be Mt. St. Helens.

Clark, having first determined this mountain was Hood, then St. Helens, had actually taken his first view of what would later be named Mount Adams.[13]

After discerning this new mountain, Clark quickly took sight of "a range of mountains in the Derection crossing, a conacal mountain S. W. toped with Snow." This last phrase is quite similar to the usage Clark employed at Wallula Gap the previous day to describe Mount Hood. Now properly seeing Hood to the southwest prompted the deduction that the "new" mountain must have been St. Helens. Clark then proceeded to describe the rapids with their "banks of Muscle Shells," where he stayed for two hours while watching the party's canoes pass the chutes and "Sholes" near the north (Washington) bank under the guidance of Meriwether Lewis. This set the stage for the incident involving William Clark, Sacagawea and the "Fritened Indians" recounted in an earlier chapter.[14]

Missing from this record is *any* evidence that Hat Rock was the locale from which Mount Hood or other Cascade Mountain volcanoes were first sighted, as the lore of LEWIS & CLARK in Oregon has it. The origin of this mythology is a notation in the corner of Clark's field map for this stretch of the river where he writes, in apparent juxtaposition to the location of Hat Rock, "From this rock a mountain Covered with Snow may be seen [.] Supposed to be the one Vancouvers Lieut calls Mount Hood." Clark never meant this observation to be taken literally, as some have done. As noted above, Clark did not disembark until he got to the Umatilla rapids, well beyond Hat Rock. Besides, from the top of Hat Rock it's impossible to see over the top of the wide and higher butte that lies to the west of it, thereby blocking any conceivable view of Mount Hood. At any rate, based on personal observation it appears physically impossible to climb to the top of Hat Rock. Nor, given the accelerated schedule of the expedition, would they have bothered with the labor such a climb would have entailed.[15]

The ascription of view potential from the country bounding Hat Rock may have been a later addition to Clark's field notes and not contemporaneous to his original log when traveling west. Clark made many additions to his 1805 Columbia River field maps during the return trip in 1806 in order to record the locations of campsites and other features. Indeed, Clark may have intended the famous notation for another "rock" just upstream. The Two Sisters, from certain angles, look like one rock and remarkably similar to Hat Rock in profile. The artist-explorer Paul Kane, traveling through this same country forty years after Lewis and Clark, wrote that where the Walla Walla River enters the Columbia, "we came in sight of two extraordinary rocks projecting from a high steep cone or mount about 700 feet above the level of the river. They are called by the voyageurs the Chimney Rocks and from their being visible from a great distance, they are very serviceable as landmarks." Kane observed further that "owing to the position in which I stood while taking the sketch, the other rock or chimney is not visible, being immediately in rear of the one represented." [16]

Any residual uncertainty in Clark's mind at the Umatilla rapids about which mountain was Hood was removed two weeks later. On 3 November 1805, in the vicinity of the mouth of the Sandy River at the western end of the Columbia River Gorge, Clark's course notes refer to "a high peaked mountain Suppose to be Mt. Hood." At that point the expedition had reached the upstream limit of Lieutenant William Broughton's voyage in the fall of 1792. Now able to match his bearings of the snow-capped eminence with that of the British explorer, Clark concluded: "the mountain we Saw from near the forks proves to be Mount *Hood*." This phrasing is suggestive of the speculation above that Clark's note on the map near the mark for Hat Rock was written after the fact since he was only now coming to a hard conclusion about the peak's identity. In language clearly reminiscent of his remark about the mountain first written near Wallula Gap, he again described Hood as "a Conical form but rugid." [17]

The pace of exploration now quickened. On October 20th Clark measured out forty-two miles of travel by dead reckoning, ending at a camp near present-day Roosevelt, Washington. This was the greatest distance covered in one day since the expedition left St. Louis. There was still "no timber of any kind on the river," Clark noted, adding with a hint of hopefulness relative to the prospect of wooded terrain ahead, that he saw "acorns of the white oake" which the resident "Met-cow-wes" told him they procured below. The next day, from the mouth of the John Day River, at long last, Clark perceived a "fiew Small Pine on the tops of the high hills." Native garments made from the furs of squirrels and raccoons—tree-dwelling species—reinforced this positive sign. Nevertheless, at camp that night the expedition bought from the neighboring "Wah-how pum" Indians what little wood they had (at a "high rate" Clark complained) so that they might have fuel to cook their dog meat and fish. [18]

For eleven days, since the confluence of the Clearwater with the Snake River, Clark had patiently read the landscape, slowly gaining access to the true extent of the Great Plain of the Columbia's width, looking for its potential western terminus. Clark's course-and-distance table for 21 October 1805 is a masterpiece in the empirical method, reflecting an undeviating commitment to observing the placement of the Columbia's course, rapids, rocks, and residents. His un-romantic discernment of such phenomena as landslides and a river "Crouded with Islands of bad rocks" created a catalogue of environmental portents for a still more tumultuous section of the Columbia. Contrary to a recent interpretation that the farther the captains got from Philadelphia the harder it was for them to maintain their scientific focus, Clark, at least, was at his best on the Columbia River.[19]

On October 22nd, the captains reset their westerly course down the Columbia and soon encountered the Deschutes River of Oregon coming in from the south. The cursory investigation of this smaller river (they did not even deign to name it at the time) was rooted in the expected appearance of the second set of great falls in their journey, one which had been foretold back in Nez Perce country, a month and a day earlier. Indeed, six miles below the mouth of the Deschutes, Clark found the "comencement of the pitch of the Great falls" of the Columbia. Back on the Clearwater, Twisted Hair told Clark that these falls were ten "Sleeps" away. Owing to their spill at Fishhook Rapids on the Snake and an extra day at the "forks" of the Columbia, to say nothing of the navigational proficiency of the Indians, the Expedition for Northwestern Discovery, by comparison, took sixteen days of river travel to cover that distance.[20]

Landing on the north bank, Clark walked out on the rocks to see the several channels through which the water flowed. The view portended the obvious necessity of a portage. A two-man reconnaissance indicated that the Indians used a narrow channel hugging the south bank to conduct their canoes downstream. Lewis and Clark hired a few Indians with horses to help pack the expedition's heaviest freight along a 1,200-yard portage adjacent to the falls near the present town of Wishram, Washington. As for the balance of the equipage, as Pvt. Joseph Whitehouse phrased it, "we went to carrying the baggage by land on our backs."[21]

Along the way, Clark marveled at the extent and manner by which the Indians "neetly preserved" a great quantity of fish, much of it, he was told, sold to white people "who visit the mouth of this river as well as to the nativs below." The expedition was now in the center of the great inland trade mart of the Columbia—a phrase that Clark made immortal on the return voyage—where tribes exchanged horses, beads, buffalo robes, cloth, and knives. Clark also astutely noticed the absence of Indian lodges on what is now the Oregon side of the river. The Wishram Indians apprised him that their enemies (Clark termed them the "Snake Indians") lived further inland to the south, and thus the Columbia served as a moat.[22]

The portage of the canoes along the south bank waited till the morning of October 23rd. It was led by Clark, aided by many of the men who ferried the small fleet across the river. The operation was conducted in two stages with "much dificulty," the captain reported, the first of which involved man-hauling their craft 457 yards, as noted with precision in Clark's journal and maps. Since Clark does not cite the distance in poles, as he would have while conducting a formal survey, he must have paced it off. Setting back into the river, Clark led the canoes (manned only by the "best Swimmers," John Ordway reported) through a mile-long channel until they hit a "pitch" eight feet high. Here they let the canoes down between two rocks using ropes made of elk skin. The cordage holding one

Lewis and Clark's "Great Falls of the Columbia," better known as Celilo Falls, served as the great cultural and physiographic divide between the Sahaptian-speaking tribes of the dry interior plateau to the east, and the Chinookan tribes of the green forested lands of the downstream. (Benjamin A. Gifford photo, Oregon Historical Society, #OrHi 1944)

of the canoes broke. The craft drifted downstream but was safely caught by some Indians. By 3 p.m. the entire detachment was safely below Celilo Falls at the portage camp on the north bank. Some men were sick from the fatigue of the effort, poor diet, or water quality—a circumstance recorded by Pvt. Joseph Whitehouse but not Captain Clark. Meriwether Lewis established the latitude for this landmark location, which Whitehouse said was to be called "the grand falls of the Columbia River." [23]

Considering the travel narrative as a literary mode, the absence of Lewis's voice at Celilo begins to take on truly great significance. The 24th of October gave rise to "a fine morning." Clark wrote, "Capt Lewis and three men crossed the river and on the opposit Side to view the falls which he had not yet taken a full view of." Lewis had stayed at camp on the north side the day before while Clark, the better "river man," crossed over to guide the canoe portage. Lewis wasn't writing at this juncture, so all that resulted from these inspections of the Great Falls of the Columbia River of a lexical nature is from Clark alone. His terse geomorphic description of this eminently important place reads in its entirety as follows:

> The first pitch of this falls is 20 feet perpendicular, then passing thro' a narrow Chanel for 1 mile to a rapid of about 18 feet fall below which the water has no perceptable fall but verry rapid. *See Sketch* No. 1. It may be proper here to remark that from Some obstruction below, the cause of which we have not yet learned, the water in high fluds (which are in the Spring) rise below these falls nearly to a leavel with the water above the falls; the marks of which can be plainly trac'd around the falls." [24]

No greater contrast between the writing capabilities, styles, and exploratory predisposition of Meriwether Lewis and William Clark can be made than their turns at narrative description of the magnificent falls of the Missouri and the Columbia respectively. In the modern published edition of the journals, Lewis's Missourian hyperbole takes up five full pages of print for 13–14 June 1805. His text, widely admired for its eloquence, is replete with a picturesque phrasing that flows in such a torrent that it becomes a veritable cascade of prose in its own right. A few passages will suffice, to wit:

> "... the grandest sight I ever beheld..."
> "... the water in it's passage down... brakes... into a perfect white foam which assumes a thousand forms in a moment sometimes flying up in jets of sparkling foam..."
> "from the reflection of the sun on the spray or mist which arrises from these falls there is a beatifull rainbow produced which adds not a little to the beauty of this majestically grand senery"
> "I wished for the pencil of Salvator Rosa or the pen of Thompson, that I might be enabled to give to the enlightened world some just idea of this truly magnificent and sublimely grand object... ."

"...again presented by one of the most beatifull objects in nature, a cascade of about fifty feet perpendicular...."

"at length I determined between these two great rivals for glory that this [falls] was *pleasingly beautifull*, while the other was *sublimely grand*." [25]

These passages are florid, self-conscious, and in some respects overdone. It is my view, however, that the Great Falls of the Missouri, though diminished by modern development, remain discernible to this day as a direct result of Lewis's literary skill. The extended passage from which the excerpts above are taken provided a first and lasting imprint of the Great Falls of the Missouri upon the American imagination. In the estimation of James Ronda, Lewis's text molded and shaped the way succeeding generations have come to see and understand the falls and the river of which they are a part. Indeed, Ronda tells us, Lewis's words have themselves become a "cultural inheritance." One can only wonder if the same would be true of the modern Columbia if Celilo had benefited from Lewis's expository text. [26]

Meriwether Lewis gave extravagant praise to rivers with far less grandeur than the Columbia, or the Missouri for that matter. Take the Marias River for example. Named for his cousin, Maria Wood, the muddy color of the Marias compared poorly "with the pure celestial virtues and amiable qualifications of that lovely fair one," Lewis wrote,

> but on the other hand it is a noble river;... in adition to which it passes through a rich fertile and one of the most beatifully picteresque countries that I ever beheld, through the wide expance of which, innumerable herds of living anamals are seen, it's borders garnished with one continued garden of roses, while it's lofty and open forrests, are the habitation of miriads of the feathered tribes who salute the ear of the passing traveler with their wild and simple, yet s[w]eet and cheerfull melody.

We still await the creation of the Marias River National Scenic Area as a companion to that of the Columbia Gorge. [27]

William Clark did not have the time or the inclination to extol the aesthetic qualities of the Columbia. The man who eventually became the poet laureate of the Columbia, Woody Guthrie, wrote his songs memorializing the river's glory within a political economy that was reveling in the prospects for hydroelectric and navigational development. This is not to suggest that Clark was in any way insufficient as an explorer. A case can be made that he was *superior* to Lewis in his pragmatic and realistic assessment of landscapes, or in this case, "riverscapes." Most telling about Lewis at the Great Falls of the Missouri is his conscious effort to create a generalized mood and scenic texture with words bordering on the poetic, heightened when the absence of a "pencil" foils his intent at depiction. By invoking Rosa, a seventeenth-century landscape painter from Naples and a favorite of travelers who wrote in the picturesque mode, Lewis purposely chose a model whose works cast an ornamental grandeur upon the landscape. James Thomson, also cited by Lewis, was an eighteenth-century Scottish poet whose work prefigured the Romantic Movement and its heroic aspirations. Unlike Clark, whose prosaic manner emphasized the independent value of landscapes, Lewis's penchant was to mediate the meaning of a place through his own identity.[28]

This was Lewis's habitual pose at key points during the journey. On the Missouri River, Lewis stressed the lyrical qualities of the White Cliffs and their "romantic appearance." Later he described reaching "the most distant fountain of the waters of the mighty Missouri," where Lewis asked his prospective readers to judge "the pleasure I felt in allying my thirst with this pure and ice cold water." It was as if this feature had no history prior to the appearance of the explorer-hero and had been provided by nature for his private enjoyment. Lewis's methods of description during the course of the expedition alternated between two modes. When he described individualized items like a specific plant or animal, he used the idiom of natural history observation. When the narrative requirements of his story dictated that he pose as a knowledgeable or adventuresome explorer venturing into the exotic unknown, he resorted to the descriptors of the sublime, with its emphasis on scene and emotional response.[29]

Clark, by contrast, worked in a comparatively artless style and was rarely taken by such a mediated artifice as Lewis's "senery." Clark was instead very much an empiricist. He never dwelled on the poetic novelties that attracted Lewis, content to leave such metaphysics to his colleague. This is not to suggest that Clark's observations about these new lands were any less worthy than Lewis's. Like Jefferson, whom Pamela Regis describes as a "confirmed measurer," Clark was captivated by the "quantifying urge." He worked in a different medium of expression than Lewis did, as captured in the coded phrase cited above: "*See Sketch* No. 1." Clark's two maps of the "Great Falls of Columbia River" have an unedited purity about them that is captivating in their color, exactitude, and quantity of detail. They possessed a more immediate utility than Lewis's labored sublimities because the expedition was fundamentally a cartographic enterprise. Not mere sentiment, Clark's maps record and reflect a penetrating pursuit of the particular, and he "sees" the Celilo area exceptionally well in his preferred manner.[30]

Elliott Coues, when he "rediscovered" the journals of Lewis and Clark in the late nineteenth century, was stunned by Clark's Columbia River cartography. It was "a great pity," Coues said, that Clark's map of Celilo Falls and the adjoining narrows were never engraved or printed. The drawing "is beautifully executed," Coues said, "and would have been very useful, besides doing Captain Clark as much credit as his famous map of the Great Falls of the Missouri."[31]

The rigorous fidelity to nature exemplified by Clark's map work was facilitated by the routine demand of having to draw the environment empirically. As the eighteenth-century British voyager Richard Walter phrased it, "those who are habituated to delineating objects, perceive them more distinctly than those who are not similarly accustomed." Though not as formally well educated as Meriwether Lewis,

William Clark impressed those who met him with his quick grasp of scientific principles. English botanist John Bradbury visited Clark in St. Louis several years after the expedition and commented to a friend that Clark was "more intelligent in Natural History than from his few opportunities of intercourse might be expected." Of course, he had studied this subject for the better part of three years next to a master, Meriwether Lewis.[32]

Clark's intuitive sense of geography told him that another obstruction lay below Celilo Falls. High water marks stained the rocks below the rapids. The impediment became quickly discernible. Clark's course from camp below the falls took him two and a half miles to a "tremendious black rock [which] Presented itself high and Steep appearing to choke up the river." A basalt ledge created a "large bason," or backwater eddy, which emptied into a "narrow channel of about 45 yards" in width and about one-quarter mile in length. In these "Short Narrows," as Clark called the place, "the water was agitated in a most Shocking manner boils Swell & whorl pools." [33]

Lewis and Clark were coursing the Columbia during its low-water season, and there was no exit from the river's rock-bound eddy that hemmed them in. Characteristically, Clark's predicament can be seen better in his maps than in his text. Courage becoming a virtue born of necessity, Clark took one of the biggest gambles of the expedition. Eschewing any thought of a portage, he led the bulk of the party through the channel. This was unqualifiedly Clark's decision because at this same time Lewis was still behind him "viewing" Celilo Falls and would follow the main party downstream later in the day.[34]

As Clark described the sequence in his lengthier notebook entry, he pulled out above the river's choke point because he was unable to see "where the water passed further than the Current was drawn with great velocity." He landed at the lodges of Indians living on the north bank, and accompanied by some of these villagers he went to the top of the rock that thwarted the river's flow. From there he could not only see the immediate "risque" to the expedition at the Short Narrows but also "the dificuelties we had to pass for Several miles below." Here Clark was referencing what he would eventually term the "Long Narrows" where, once again, the river was "intersepted by rocks." As for the imminent passage through the Short Narrows, Clark recorded, with emphasis in the original text, that "at this place the water of this great river is compressed into a Chanel between two rocks not exceeding *forty five* yards wide." Clark connected the obstruction he stood upon with the evidence of backwater visible at Celilo Falls. In amazement he then attested, for the third time, to the stunning realization that the "whole of the Current of this great river must at all Stages pass thro' this narrow chanel of 45 yards wide." [35]

Clark was confident that one of his "principal watermen," Pierre Cruzatte, could lead them safely through the Short Narrows "by good Stearing." "[A]ccordingly," Clark wrote, "I deturmined to pass through this place notwithstanding the horrid appearance of this agitated gut Swelling, boiling & whorling in every direction (which from the top of the rock did not appear as bad as when I was

William Clark did some of his best cartographic work in the Columbia basin. The cover illustration of this book (Celilo Falls), and this map of the Short and Long Narrows are classics in the history of early American exploration. These maps not only exhibit Clark's capacity as a cartographer, but also his ability to read the face of the country. (Missouri History Museum, St. Louis)

in it)," he added jovially. This sentence is one of the most visceral and lexically earnest expressions to be found anywhere in the journals of Lewis, Clark, or any other member of the expedition. Clark was astonished by the landscape's tangible effect on so awesome a natural power as the Columbia. We can discern his awareness of the extraordinary good fortune in the party's successful passage through the turbulent water by his additional observation that they had "passed Safe to the astonishment of all the [Indians]... who viewed us from the top of the rock." [36]

Clark next led the party westward toward the aperture of the Long Narrows, three miles away. Before reaching this second channeling of the river, Clark said he "put all the men who Could not Swim on Shore" at the first sign of rough water. He directed that the nonswimmers proceed ahead by land to an Indian settlement on the north bank. They carried a collection of important "articles" including their arms and papers, the latter no doubt a reference to the journals and possibly the traveling library as well. Clark and the boatmen later joined them at the Wishram Indian village that is today the site of Columbia Hills State Park, a place strategically located on the edge of yet another "bason" (or eddy) created by the Columbia being "blocked up with emence rocks." [37]

Clark's "Long Narrows" was known to the Indians as "Coyote's Fishing Place," and in the days of river steamboat traffic it was called "Five Mile Rapids." Though Celilo Falls became more famous because of its photogenic setting and other dramatic qualities, the Long Narrows was actually a more important place in the Native world. Celilo was only fished in the late summer and early fall. According to tribal historian and storyteller George Aguilar, Celilo Falls has become romanticized and now oft-eulogized, but the narrows was "the ultimate fishery" because it was "more economically productive" in that it was fished year-round. [38]

The Natives of the village above the Long Narrows, site of the famous Wakemup Mound archaeological feature, treated Clark "verry kindly." One of them invited Clark into his house, which the captain "found to be large and comodious." The ever-observant Clark noted this was "the first wooden houses in which Indians have lived Since we left those in the vicinity of the Illinois." Whitehouse referred to them as "verry nice comfortable houses" abetted by many flag mats for reposing. But Clark quickly went back to work. Having developed a taste for this Columbia River and its ability to surprise, he took two men and "walked down and examined the pass," meaning the head gate of the Long Narrows. He found the second narrowing slightly wider than the channel through which he had passed earlier in the day, this one varying between fifty and one hundred yards in breadth. It had one particularly bad rapid of note, and, of course, was longer, thus the name he gave it. The turbulence created by the compression of the Columbia within these basalt walls "Swels and boils with a most Tremendeous manner" [39]

During his walk to gauge the risks for another harrowing white-water run, Clark had the perspicacity to count 107 scaffolds the Indians had constructed to dry fish. This speaks to the scientific exactitude that Clark displayed relative to any

Clark was amazed to find the entire flow of the Columbia confined within the defiles of the Short and Long Narrows. The head gate to the Long Narrows is shown here—looking north to the location of today's Columbia Hills State Park in Washington. (Carleton E. Watkins photo, Oregon Historical Society, #OrHi 21649)

particularity that he encountered. Such a fascination with quantification, Pamela Regis reminds us, was considered a "distillation of reality" for Enlightenment-era explorers—"a universal language (arithmetic)" that made new lands and peoples accessible to comprehension. Clark wanted to learn more about the river and rapids below, but with evening approaching, he returned to the Indian village where he found everyone gathered, including Lewis, who, at last, had floated downstream from his unrecorded visit to Celilo Falls.[40]

The next morning Lewis joined Clark for a continuation of the reconnaissance of the Long Narrows cut short by darkness the night before. A set of helpful Indians "pointed out... the worst place in passing through the gut." Clark and Lewis thought the passage could be conducted "without great danger" and "determined to attempt the Chanel." However, the captains managed the risk by deciding to make a land portage for the "most valuable articles and run the canoes thro" the narrows thus lightened by weight and importance. That afternoon Clark guided the canoes, one by one, through the Long Narrows. John Ordway estimated the passage at two miles in length within perpendicular basalt walls forty-eight feet high. As a precaution, Clark spotted men on the bluffs above the river and equipped them with ropes "to throw in in Case any acidence happened at the Whirl." When the last canoe "Came over well," Clark found the moment "truly gratifying." Like the previous day, the Indians were again on the rocks above viewing this white-water maneuver.[41]

William Clark's brief but descriptive tale of the experience with the Short and Long Narrows is virile prose, in contrast to the romantic sentimentalism the now-mute Lewis might have rendered had he written about this place. References to "the gut," "whorl & Suck," and "hard rough black rock" reflect what Barbara Maria Stafford has called an undecorated, masculine style of rhetoric common in travel narratives in the late eighteenth and early nineteenth centuries. Clark was crude but concise, befitting more the outlook of a laconic seafarer as opposed to the painterly language of the gentleman traveler that was often Lewis's preferred idiom. Lewis waxed lyrically about rainbows, glittery mists, and sprays that did much to preserve what is left of the Great Falls of the Missouri. Clark's account of stomach-churning danger gave an entirely different cast to a stretch of the Columbia River that was, in time, erased from view behind the dam at The Dalles.[42]

Below the Long Narrows the current of the Columbia turned gentle, and the expedition's campsite the night of 25 October 1805, and the two days thereafter, was a fort-like rock formation above the river where the modern city of The Dalles, Oregon, is today. The detachment being at some remove from the river, a guard was posted to watch canoes left at the water line. However, this site was chosen as much for the convenience it lent to hunting as it was for defense because, at last, Clark noted the existence of "timber of different kinds" to his west and southwest. One particularly noteworthy species was oak, which Clark's contemporaries regarded as an indicator of good soil and climate. As a woodsman, Clark knew trees would provide cover for deer, and George Drouillard promptly killed one.

This 1867 photo of the Long Narrows, indicates the appropriateness of Clark's descriptive terminology. The Narrows are now inundated by the reservoir behind the dam at The Dalles. Note the high water mark on the canyon walls. (Carleton E. Watkins photo, Washington State Historical Society)

Clark shot a "verry fat" goose and espied evidence of beaver, another noteworthy species in symbiosis with trees. Providing the backdrop to this scene, as it had for time immemorial, was the Mount Hood of Broughton and Vancouver that Clark reiterated having seen "a Short distance below the forks of this river." [43]

From nearby pine trees the men collected pitch rosin to apply to the re-shaved bottoms of their basalt-battered flotilla. Recall from an earlier chapter that Lewis and Clark were unsettled here by the threat of attack relayed by the Nez Perce chiefs, Twisted Hair and Tetoharsky. The captains handed out the ubiquitous peace medals and other small presents to local Indians, which they thought "necessary at this time to treat those people verry friendly & ingratiate our Selves with them, to insure us a kind & friendly reception on our return." Lewis and Clark went out of their way to acknowledge several Native leaders "as chiefs," including making a fire "for those people to Sit around in the middle of our Camp." Pierre Cruzatte also played his violin, "which pleased those nativs exceedingly." One of the guards down at the river speared a salmon and with a little bear's grease secured from the Indians, fried it up. Clark said, "this I thought one of the most delicious fish I have ever tasted." Earlier and upstream near the forks of the Columbia, salmon were viewed with revulsion, but those procured at The Dalles this late in the season would not yet have exhausted their rich store of oil in the ensuing quest to reach spawning grounds and therefore would have been far more palatable. [44]

One day at The Dalles fort Clark noticed an eight-inch tide-like rise in the river level. He discounted the possibility of an actual tide because Native sources told him that there were more falls below. His conjecture was that the strong winds which had "Set up the river for 24 hours past" had caused this phenomenon. These gales kept the expedition for an unplanned third day and night at The Dalles. This extra increment of time allowed Lewis to work on his Indian vocabularies, including that of the Wishram, the easternmost Chinookan-speaking tribe. These people lived between the two narrows, a district Clark perceptively called "the levels," referring to the river-scoured terraces still quite evident today. [45]

After their few days at the rock fort, the canoes were loaded up and set back into the Columbia River. A mere four miles of voyaging later, the party was "obliged to lie by" for the rest of the day because of wind resistance. They camped on the Oregon side at today's Crates Point, below the modern Columbia River Gorge Interpretive Center. The expedition had barely landed when three Indians from a village below came to in "verry nice Canoes of Pine," ornamented with carvings of animals and other figures. With not a little admiration, Clark wrote, "The wind which is the cause of our delay, does not retard the motions of those people at all, as their canoes are calculated to ride the highest waves... . Those people make great use of Canoes, both for transpotation and fishing." [46]

Contrary to intelligence Clark and Lewis had received as far to the east as the Nez Perce villages, there were no white traders living below the falls or narrows. However, Euro-American presence in the region was becoming more pronounced with every mile traveled westward. Below The Dalles, Clark recorded having seen Indians in possession of a musket, a sword, trade blankets, a jacket, and "Several Brass *Tea* kittles which they appear to be verry fond of." [47]

The timber of which the explorers saw hints at The Dalles became more common during the ensuing two days of travel. Clark noted that the country adjoining the Columbia was becoming "thinly timbered with Pine & low white oake," the south bank in particular. Joseph Whitehouse exclaimed, "The Country here abounds with Timber of Pine & Cotton wood." Finally, Clark had reached the western limit of the Great Plain of the Columbia—a region he and his compatriots had first entered three weeks earlier at the confluence of the Clearwater and Snake Rivers. The more promising prospect of the woodlands, which in Clark's mind and narrative was immediately translated to "good hunting Countrey," turned him to a contemplation of the requirements that the oncoming season would soon present. Clark declared the Oregon side of the Columbia immediately west of Memaloose Island by Hood River, Oregon, "a good Situation for winter quarters if game can be had." Prospecting for winter campsites became a habit of mind for Clark from this place to the Pacific Ocean. [48]

Barbara Maria Stafford has observed that the whole point of the factual travel narrative "was to spread graphically before the reader and viewer a great range of exact information about the world." William Clark's notebook entry for 29 October 1805 is thus the archetype for the American Expedition for Northwestern Discovery on the Columbia. In a wide-ranging and continuous act of observation, Clark charted the expedition's course, recorded ethnological customs and data in detail, and created a catalogue of natural phenomena ranging from waterfalls, swans, and the snow on top of Mount Hood. At that night's camp the emergent diversity and abundance of the lower Columbian environment became a cataract unto itself in Clark's text. [49]

Environmental changes, as related to both climate and landscape, began to quicken. As John Logan Allen phrased it, the "transition on the western margin of the Great Columbian Plain was nearly as abrupt as it had been on the eastern margin of that barren and arid land." "Some little rain all night" was the headline for Clark's field log on the morning of October 30th. It had not rained so hard since October 13th when the expedition was halfway down the Snake River. Coming after brief showers the previous two days, this was the beginning of a trend in the weather that would become pronounced within the week. On the geologic front, during the initial three-mile course for the 30th Clark reported rocks projecting into the river seemingly having "fallen from the highe hills." These "projected rocks" were common in the bays and "nitches" (one of Clark's favorite words) at the river's edge, as were the "Cascades or Small Streams falling from the mountains" on the south side of the gorge. There was even the "remarkable circumstance" of "the Stumps of pine trees" in profusion some distance out into the river." [50]

Clark tried to make sense of this last, odd phenomenon. He opined that the river here resembled "a pond partly dreaned leaving many Stumps bare both in &

out of the water" and estimated that the current was only one mile per hour. The thought occurred to him that the river had been "damed up below from Some cause which I am not at this time acquainted with." Two miles farther down, he made a connection stating "we can plainly hear the roreing of the grand Shutes below." At the end of this day's voyage the party landed at one of several islands at the head of the rapids. Clark noted here that rocky outcrops choked the river as they had at Celilo and the set of narrows before. The expedition had arrived at what has come to be known through history as the Cascades of the Columbia. The place name for these rapids is actually a perversion of Clark's naming intent. When Clark referred to "Cascades" in his course-and-distance table, notebook, and maps, he meant the waterfalls flowing over the precipice of the Columbia River Gorge on what is now the Oregon side. (The best known of these is Multnomah Falls.) In his text and cartography, Clark referred to the watery impediment in the river as "The Great Shute" or "Great Rapids of the Columbia." [51]

In general terms Clark scientifically deduced the cause of the river's constriction—the legendary Bridge of the Gods firmly embedded in the region's Native American mythology. In his notebook Clark observed that the large numbers of rocks "projected into the river [had] the appearance of haveing Seperated from the mountains and fallen promiscuisly into the river." In response to Nicholas Biddle's later inquiries about this phenomenon, Clark said that the mountain on the north side of the Columbia "seems to have been undermined & fallen in" and thrown "large rocks into the current." [52]

Clark described what modern geologists refer to as the Bonneville Landslide. Indeed, Clark's observations touched off a scientific debate that rages to this day over the date of the landslide and its causation. On the return trip Lewis surmised that the slide was perhaps only twenty years distant, and in geologic terms we know now it was certainly a recent event. Tribal oral histories were so convincing on the matter of a land bridge temporarily damming the river that early anthropologists concluded the avalanche had been observed by Native people. Some scholars using radiocarbon dating posit that the landslide happened in 1562, while others place the event within the constraints of 1400 to 1450. An estimate favored by Gary Moulton holds that the event occurred between 1000—1100 A. D., whereas studies using lichen as a dating tool suggest that the Bonneville Landslide took place sometime between 1670 and 1760, a period provocatively bracketing the potentially causative Cascadia zone subduction earthquake of 1700 A.D. In any event, the impoundment created by the avalanche was of sufficient duration so as to "agree well with Indian oral history," state Robert L. Schuster and Patrick Pringle. Indeed, hundreds of stumps were still visible in the 1930s before the backwater created by Bonneville Dam drowned them. In sum, Clark's idea about the origin of the Sunken Forest of the Cascades has proved correct. Lewis's timing estimate seems to be off the mark, though closer than might have been once granted. [53]

On the night of October 30th—what Clark had termed a "Day dark and disagreeable"—the expedition camped on an island in the middle of the river just above the

The Cascades were the last whitewater impediment to downstream navigation for the expedition. (Carleton E. Watkins photo, Oregon Historical Society, #OrHi 71175)

commencement of the Columbia's last great rapid. This site, upstream from where the modern Bridge of the Gods crosses the river, is now inundated by the waters behind Bonneville Dam. Clark walked down a riverside path to view the rapids, his custom when meeting an obstacle to navigation in the river. He concluded that a 2½-mile portage of the expedition's stores would be required, though he held out the hope that the emptied canoes could be guided through the rock-strewn water from the shore. Looking at his surroundings Clark noted that the high country above the river was now "thickly Covered with timber." [54]

The next day, yet another "rainey disagreeable morning," Clark, now "more at leasure" than the previous evening, strolled the river's north bank an estimated ten miles, accompanied by Joseph Field and Pierre Cruzatte. The latter, referred to once again by Clark as his "principal waterman," inspected the rapids, of which there were three sets in descending order of risk, to determine the "practibility of the Canoes passing." For one-half mile the water of the uppermost "Great Shute" was confined within limits 150 yards wide, one-third greater than the Long Narrows and three times the width of the channel at the Short Narrows. But to Clark's eye the river still looked compressed. The water passed by large rocks interspersed in the stream "with Tremendious force," creating waves that the captain considered "remarkably high." On this trek Clark noted many Indian burial vaults ("the burrying place for maney ages") and abandoned village sites, and he also was fortunate to find a path "where the Indians make a portage." Near the end of this course Clark was presented with a long view down the river where it widened and, he said, "had everry appearance of being effected by the tide." [55]

The western terminus for this sojourn was a "very high" and "large black rock" on the north bank. Clark paced off the distance around the base of this "remarkable high detached rock" and estimated its height at 800 feet, a remarkably close approximation of its actual 840-foot elevation—further evidence of Clark's physiographic perspicacity. Clark called it "the *Beaten rock.*" Nicholas Biddle, the first editor of the journals, changed the entry to read "*Beacon*" rock, and it is by that name this landmark is known. Biddle's interlineation offered an explanation, of sorts. He wrote, "*beaten before—but really beacon.*" [56]

Biddle's cryptic comment creates a slightly antiquarian mystery, but one nevertheless grounded in Clark's ability to describe and comprehend topography. Stephen Beckham ascribes the "Beaten" terminology to "Clark's inimitable spelling." Clark *was* a notoriously bad speller, but his map composed later at Fort Clatsop continued to call it "Beatin" rock. Nor did Clark make an effort to change the nomenclature on this map when back in the field the following spring. If Clark or Lewis changed their minds about what to call this monolith, it was on the return trip when it was re-sighted. [57]

The more substantial issue is why something like Beacon Rock was noteworthy to begin with. Spying idiosyncratic monoliths was one of the favored interests of Enlightenment-era science. This cultural tradition endures to this day in the form of many national parks and monuments—like Devils Tower in Wyoming.

The freestanding singularity, heroic in its isolation, was a noteworthy finding to the nascent earth science community, which included Jefferson, Lewis, and Clark. As a purely aesthetic principle, the singular rock or mountain, as we saw earlier with Mount Hood, was a self-productive drama, an "event" in its own right demanding a response from the observer. Such tangible, massive phenomena did not go unnoticed in the travel narrative.[58]

The first day of November 1805 broke cold with a hard wind from the northeast. The party warmed itself with the labor associated with packing the expedition's gear over the 940 yards worth of hard rock shoreline and slippery hillsides. After watching Indians portage the upper Cascades, Lewis and Clark determined to haul their canoes out of the river proper and move them along the bank. They did this by creating a latticework of poles over which the craft slid from rock to rock as if on rollers.[59]

The phased portage concluded on November 2nd. Clark accompanied the nonswimmers who hauled the payload an additional mile and half below the last rapid. The once-raging Columbia River was here a smooth "gentle Stream," Clark wrote, widening to over two miles in breadth. A pastoral scene beckoned. "[T]he mountains leave the river on each Side," Clark observed, while the bottom land made visible by the receding bluffs was "extensive and thickly Covered with wood." Clark's journal and maps recorded the promising "Commencement of tide water" which, he said, had its effects "as high as the Beaten rock or the Last rapids." The Expedition for Northwestern Discovery's final passage to the Pacific was at hand.[60]

In the late nineteenth century, Elliott Coues, the second of the four editors of the journals of Lewis and Clark, founded the tradition of calling attention to the differences in the captains' literary styles. "Where Clark's syntax is exiguous," Coues wrote, "Lewis' is redundant, often with singularly intricate construction." Using a discerning architectural analogy, Coues said, "Clark is Doric, Lewis is Corinthian." More recently, Clay Jenkinson observed that Lewis used "a large, at times a pretentious vocabulary." In contrast to Clark's simple straightforward journal entries, Jenkinson writes, "Lewis strains after allusions, ideas… and— often enough—profundity." There was a purpose to Lewis's reach for literary flair, and though not intended to cast his partner into the narrative shadow (about which more later), this may have been the result nonetheless. What might be termed the "Lewis Mystique" permeates scholarly and popular understanding of the expedition because his self-conscious prose is alluring, especially in contrast to Clark's workmanlike approach to exploring. All the best-known stories about the expedition are those scripted by Lewis, dealing primarily with episodes on the Missouri River and in the vicinity of the Continental Divide.[61]

That Lewis's literary style has been favored among historians over Clark's scientific substance is unfortunate. This is especially true in regard to Columbia River studies because nowhere in the journey were Clark's strengths as a scientist and writer more evident. Even more generally, as Clay Jenkinson observes, the "narrative thread we have for the Lewis and Clark Expedition is essentially the work of William Clark." He composed the maps and a continuous chronology of the expedition, both fundamental elements to creating a history of the venture. Given the vagaries of Lewis's record keeping, the journals, Jenkinson says, "might justly be called a narrative by William Clark with occasional field notes and reveries by Captain Meriwether Lewis." If, then, William Clark was the expedition's primary reporter generally, per force his best work in particular was the voyage down the Columbia from the forks to the tidewater—a stretch of the river previously unexplored. His empirical record of the Columbia River Gorge, unburdened of comparisons to Lewis's frothiness, did not entitle him to the "literary fame" his colleague lusted after, but it was, in the phrasing of Alexander Mackenzie, worthy of the attention of the "scientific geographer." [62]

CHAPTER 8   Commerce and Pestilence
in Indian Country

ON 3 NOVEMBER 1805 THE LEWIS AND CLARK EXPEDITION
exited the western gate of the Columbia River Gorge. "The Countrey has a
handsom appearance," Clark wrote, "no mountains extensive bottoms." This
soothing prospect was also reflected in the journal of Joseph Whitehouse who
said the formerly turbulent Columbia was now "more handsome the current verry
gentle." Near the mouth of Oregon's Sandy River, Clark once again sighted Mount
Hood, ending weeks of speculation. He was now convinced that the first conical
peak espied below the forks of the Columbia on October 18th amidst Wallula Gap
was indeed this same snowy eminence, catalogued in Vancouver's explorations
more than a decade earlier. The American expedition was in fully charted territory
for the first time since the previous April at the Mandan villages in North Dakota.
Correspondingly, a sense of great expectation infused the outlook of the party,
reflected by Whitehouse, who stated that it was "agreeable to all calculations it
cannot be more than two hundred miles from this to the ocean." [1]

Before settling into camp on what came to be called Government Island,
Clark made two other observations that would loom large in the expedition's
future deliberations. First, he concluded the lower Columbia would be a "*good
wintering Place,*" a consideration that had occupied his attention from the time
he entered wooded terrain below the Long Narrows. Still more intriguing was
the news gleaned via sign language from the residents of a Watlala Indian village (Upper Chinookans linguistically) that they had seen "3 Vestles 2 days
below us." Clark did not elaborate on this disclosure, but it must have been
exciting to think that the Columbia was concurrently being visited by other
seafaring traders or explorers. [2]

On November 4th the expedition encountered an Indian village stocked with
what Clark said was "more Cloth and uriopian trinkents than any above[.] I
Saw Some Guns, a Sword, maney Powder flasks, Salers Jackets, overalls, hats &
Shirts." Patrick Gass remarked that the merchandise seemed "new." At a Cowlitz
Indian village, Clark the quantifier admired the fifty-two canoes he found there.

However, interactions with Native people soon began taking on another quality altogether. During the midday dinner a tomahawk pipe was stolen. All the day long Indian canoes paced the expedition with such persistence, Clark wrote, that "we proceeded on untill one hour after dark with a view to get clear of the nativs." Describing them as "constantly about us" and "troublesom" and wanting respite from their company "for one night," the party was finally able to make camp near the mouth of Salmon Creek in today's Clark County, Washington.[3]

The relief from Native company that William Clark was hoping to achieve was confounded that night by the "horrid" noise from the "emensely numerous" waterfowl that kept him awake. Clark noted, with phrasing soon to become a litany, that rain was making everyone "Cold and disagreeable." The next day the party made thirty-two more miles downstream, including passage by a "bold and rockey" shore, referring to the basalt narrows in the vicinity of Kalama, Washington. Clark closed out his observations for November 5th with a vintage topographic deduction. He noted that after emerging from the gorge of the Columbia the party had traveled sixty river miles through a "fertill and a handsom valley." Clark was referencing what geographers call the Willamette-Columbia lowlands running from Crown Point, Oregon to Longview, Washington. This "handsom" valley of the Columbia, Clark continued, was "at this time Crouded with Indians;" curious phrasing open to interpretation. He concluded the entry: "This is the first night which we have been entirely clear of Indians Since our arrival on the waters of the Columbia River." These two observations were foundational to what some of Clark's contemporaries considered the expedition's most noteworthy finding: the density of Native inhabitation of Columbia River country.[4]

To put Clark's comments in contemporary context we need to momentarily leave the specific chronology of events to consider, first, one of the earliest accounts of the expedition's intentions as reported in the *Columbian Repository* of Hudson, New York. In the fashion that was a common for spreading news before the development of press services, the newspaper's edition of 4 October 1803 related an account of the incipient Lewis and Clark Expedition that had originally appeared in a Louisville paper nine days earlier.

> The particular objects of this undertaking are at present matters of conjecture only; but we have good reason to believe that our government intend [sic] to encourage settlements and establish sea ports on the coast of the Pacific Ocean, which would not only facilitate our whaling and sealing voyages, but enable our enterprising merchants to carry on a more direct and rapid trade with China and the East Indies.[5]

The mercantilist and sovereignty goals expressed in this report were altogether true and could easily have been written by Jefferson's Secretary of the Treasury, Albert Gallatin. Consider next the Federalist *Columbian Centinel* of Boston, Massachusetts, for 5 November 1806 (after the return of the expedition), which reported an item that had appeared in a Baltimore newspaper the previous week. It read, in part:

A letter from *St. Louis*... dated *Sept. 23, 1806*, announces the arrival of Captains LEWIS and CLARK.... They went to the *Pacific Ocean*; have brought some of the natives and curiosities of the countries through which they passed, and only lost one man. They left the *Pacific Ocean* 23ᵈ March, 1806, where they arrived in November 1805; — and where some American vessels had been just before. They state the Indians to be as numerous on the *Columbia* river, which empties into the *Pacific*, as the whites in any part of the U. S.[6]

Noteworthy in these reports are, respectively, the prominence of American commercial ambitions for the Great River of the West and concern about Indians. When one reflects on the latter item and all that *could have* been considered newsworthy about the expedition as contained in Lewis's first published report after returning to St. Louis—the "great falls" of the Missouri, "tremendious mountains... covered with eternal snows," rivers that "abound more in beaver and Common Otter, than any other streams on earth"—this contemporary of the captains ascribed the greatest significance to the multitude of Indians living on the Columbia. The expedition's views on this matter seem to have been crystallized during the first week of November in 1805.[7]

Now returning to the course of the expedition on the lower Columbia, we note that on November 7ᵗʰ some members of the Wahkiakum band of Chinook Indians signed "that there were vessells lying at the Mouth of this River." These recurring reports mattered a great deal to Lewis and Clark. A fur trader's ship or that of an explorer could be the means by which the return trip was to be financed or conducted. With a replenished supply of trinkets secured from seafarers, the captains could easily purchase provisions necessary for their eastbound homeward journey to be used in trade with Indians. Beads and other items would have been secured via recourse to a letter of credit President Jefferson provided Lewis on the eve of his departure from Washington. This instrument enabled its carrier to draw money or supplies on the president's authority from any American officer around the world or any other nation's agents or merchants who would be repaid "on demand." [8]

From the very beginning of the expedition there was always the theoretical possibility that some or all of the party might actually return to the United States by ship and not by backtracking over land. Louis Pichon, secretary to the French legation at the American capital, on the basis of his conversation with Jefferson shortly after Congress authorized the expedition, was under the distinct impression that Lewis and his associates *were* going to return by sea. In addition, Lewis's letter of invitation to William Clark told his prospective co-commander that the mission was to reach the "Western Ocean" by means of the "Columbia or Origan River," the mouth of which he asserted was 140 miles south of Nootka Sound. At this latter place, Lewis told Clark, "a considerable European Tradeing establishment" could be found, and he continued blithely, "it will be *easy* to obtain a passage to the United States by way of the East-Indies in some of the trading vessels that visit Nootka Sound annually, provided it

The Columbia-Willamette lowlands were the most densely populated region by Native Americans of any visited by Lewis and Clark. ("Densely Populated Region" by Roger Cooke, Washington State Historical Society)

should be thought more expedient to do so, than to return by the rout I had pursued in *my* outward bound journey" (emphasis added).[9]

This sentence is interesting for three reasons. First, it conveys a highly developed sense of Northwest coastal geography and recent commercial history. It also suggests that Lewis may have been attempting to cajole Clark on the practicability of this voyage by minimizing the risk, if it could be assumed that a return voyage by sea augured less danger than crossing the continent a second time. Finally, note that when Lewis invited Clark aboard he was assuredly still thinking of the expedition as a "sole proprietorship," about which more will be said in a later chapter.

Lewis's views on the return-trip strategy were heavily informed by his instructions from Jefferson, formally issued the day after Lewis's invitation to Clark but the contents of which Lewis would have been long privy to. Jefferson told Lewis that should it appear workable, he was to send back "two of your trusty people" by sea, along with copies of the expeditionary journals if vessels of any imperial nation were encountered. On the other hand, Jefferson continued, "should you be of opinion that the return of your party by the way they went will be eminently dangerous, then ship the whole [party], & return by sea, by the way either of cape Horn, or the cape of good Hope, as you shall be able." The specific scenario that Jefferson thought would precipitate the use of the letter of credit was Lewis finding it "imprudent to hazard a return the same way." In this sense, then, the much anticipated encounter with ships from Atlantic America or Europe at the mouth of the great western river represented the prospect of a quick ride home as much as it did a triumphant arrival at mission's end.[10]

We shall continue with the expedition's westward progress in the ensuing chapter, but here, to more fully contextualize the significance of Lewis and Clark's encounter with Native culture, we will remain within the Willamette-Columbia lowlands and jump ahead in time to the following spring. After wintering on the coast the Lewis and Clark Expedition returned to this same "Crouded" Indian country of the Columbia Valley on 27 March 1806 and made camp. After departing Fort Clatsop on March 23rd all of their encampments had been on the south bank of the Columbia; this one was opposite the Kalama bluffs. Westbound the expedition routinely called on the north bank in this district, but the eastbound pattern was driven less by geographical inquisitiveness than the fact that the hunters sent ahead daily routinely found game on what is now the Oregon side of the river. The Cowlitz Indians, at their camp opposite the mouth of the river named for them near today's Kelso, Washington, confirmed as much to Lewis. These "extreemly hospitable" Natives implored the captain to remain "all day with them hunting the Elk and deer... in their neighborhood" but their "friendly invitation" was declined and the voyage resumed.[11]

The density of Native population on the Columbia at the time of Lewis and Clark is amply demonstrated by the expedition's experience on 30 March 1806. No fewer than eight distinct encounters took place during that day's voyage adjacent to today's Clark County, Washington. Lewis remarked that the various groups simply put into the river "apparently waiting our arrival." Lewis joked about how "they joined the fleet and continued with us some miles." The number of Native craft combined with their close accompaniment over a considerable distance prompted a compliment from Patrick Gass. He wrote, "The natives of this country ought to have the credit of making the finest canoes, perhaps in the world, both as to service and beauty; and are no less expert in working them when made." Lewis opined that the Indians' "principal object" was to "indulge their curiossity in looking at us." This appeared innocent enough, though he reported "most had taken the precaution to bring with them their warlike instruments." [12]

The size of the Native population in this region, combined with Lewis's assessment of the soil, which he characterized as "generally fertile of a dark rich loam and tolerably free of stones," prompted a prescient speculation on his part. He concluded "this valley would be co[m]petent to the maintainance of 40 or 50 thousand souls if properly cultivated and is indeed the only desireable situation for a settlement which I have seen on the West side of the Rocky mountains." The imagined settlers, of course, would be the yeoman farmers idealized by the patron of the expedition, Thomas Jefferson. The salutary attributes of the Willamette-Columbia lowlands sustained a large Native population, and even today one must travel east on the Lewis and Clark trail as far as Kansas City, Missouri to find as large a population as inhabits the Portland, Oregon metropolitan area. [13]

Lewis's comment about the habitability of the Willamette-Columbia lowlands is significant because it represents a departure from the orientation of British exploratory narratives in the Northwest, especially that of fur trader Alexander Mackenzie. The North West Company operative never imagined a peopling of an exotic district like the lower Columbia by Euro-Americans. For Mackenzie, the Indian way of life was presumed to be durable, though admittedly enhanced in his view by the mercantile arrangements surrounding the exchange of peltries for trade goods of European origin. As Bruce Greenfield explains, to someone like Mackenzie the distant western wilderness was "not very susceptible of being thought of as home," or as a potential one. Rather, as Mackenzie's own strategic plan made clear, the Columbia country was merely a passage to the Orient. [14]

In the early colonial period, Mackenzie's outlook reflects the way Atlantic America also thought of the West. But around the time of Lewis and Clark—with the Louisiana Purchase serving as the emblematic moment—the West was decreasingly perceived as "Indian country" and increasingly thought of as a bank of free land bereft of indigenous entitlement. American "land hunger" was the lens refracting Lewis's observation about the suitability of the Willamette-Columbia lowlands for settlement. Thus, where Mackenzie's narrative envisioned the West staying exotic, Lewis and Clark saw the glimmer of a new direction altogether—one where the West was occupied by their countrymen in advance of incorporation into the American nation-state. [15]

The Indian inhabitants of the lower Columbia could move a large number of people by canoe with ease. One day in early April 1806 the expedition was stationed opposite the Sandy River near today's Washougal, Washington to secure provisions for the next leg of the journey. Lewis saw ten canoes filled with Indian families call on the expedition's camp. These Indians were similarly intent on securing food, confirming reports that had come to the attention of the captains about resource scarcity upstream. With women and children aboard, these were obviously not war parties. Nevertheless, as a precaution in the face of a large Native presence, Lewis resorted to one of his favorite military tactics—a demonstration of the air rifle with which, he reported, the Indians "were much astonished." One large Indian family stayed with Lewis while Clark was away on an exploration of the Willamette River. They "conducted themselves in a very orderly manner," Lewis said.[16]

Clark was accompanied by a handful of men on the side-voyage to the river called *Mult no mah* by the Natives. On their course they passed by, but did not stop at, the home of their Indian pilot. This was in the vicinity of today's Portland International Airport. The young guide informed Clark that the name of this one-lodge village was "Ne-cha-co-lee." (It appeared on Clark's map "Nech-e-co kee" and later in Biddle's notes from his interview with Clark as "Neckokee.") Clark considered this lodge a small colony of the Shah-ha-la nation, later known as the Watlala Indians, a subgroup of Upper Chinookans whose domain extended as far as the Cascade Rapids to the east. This tribe had its largest village farther downstream on the Columbia, near today's I-5 Bridge between Portland and Vancouver. Coming ashore at the larger settlement, Clark marveled at the number (approaching one hundred) and nimbleness of the Native canoes. Here he failed in his attempts to barter for some wapato. Given the scarcity of food supplies at that time of the year, it is easily imagined that Clark's request put a strain on this community's subsistence. What was likely a reserved manner on their part, one grounded in vulnerability, Clark saw as "Sulkey" behavior. So he resorted to manipulative tactics to get his way.[17]

Clark threw portfire (an easily combustible twine-like substance used as fuses on cannons or, in the expedition's practicum, lighting campfires) into the Native household's hearth. He reported that it "burned vehemently" and "changed the Colour of the fire." Clark followed that trick by using a magnet to make his compass needle fluctuate wildly. This combination of scare tactics "astonished and alarmed these nativs and they laid Several parsles of Wappato at my feet, & begged... me to take out the bad fire" he noted triumphantly. In this episode we find William Clark at his worst moment around Indian people during the entire voyage. He gloried in the fact that he scared the women and children and that he had provoked an old blind man to speak with "great vehemunce, appearently imploreing his [God]." For whatever reason—perhaps a reflection back on Jefferson's directives about how to interact with Indians—Clark reformed his behavior. Lighting his pipe and offering the "Smoke" to the Indians, he gave back roots the women had placed before him. Having "Somewhat passified" them, Clark proceeded farther on down the Columbia on his way to a cursory inspection of the lower Willamette River.[18]

Clark knew from Alexander Mackenzie's experience that playing tricks on Indians by employing seemingly mystical powers could yield otherwise elusive favor. In his account of the voyage to the Pacific in 1793, Mackenzie described an incident wherein one of his men "lighted a bit of touch wood with a burning-glass, in the cover of his tobacco-box, which so surprised the natives, that they exchanged the best of their otter skins for it." Whether Clark yielded to the temptations found in Mackenzie's story or came to the tactic on his own, his comportment was an exception to what Thomas Slaughter refers to as Clark's tendency to be "more spiritually attuned to the cultures of the Indians" than Lewis.[19]

After traveling up the Willamette about ten miles, Clark and his party stopped again at this same village on the trip back to the provisioning camp on the Columbia. The tricks of the previous day had not been forgotten. Entering the house of the people he had tormented, Clark found that his mere presence "alarmed them So much that the children hid themselves, womin got behind their men, and the men hung their heads." He stayed "but a fiew minits and returned on board the canoe." That Clark was feeling some regret from the previous day is suggested by his stated desire "to Smoke with those people." But the damage was done. Anthropologist Greg Dening has pointed out that strangers are never fully aware of the offenses they have made—securing food when they have no right to, as noted above, or going where they have no right to go (as described in a later chapter in regard to burial sites), or even simply being seen if it happened to be a taboo time requiring the hiding of women. "[W]hat seasons of remembrance or festival," Dening asks, were disrupted when an explorer appeared?[20]

Clark's last cultural encounter during his side trip to the Willamette and back to Lewis and the main party opposite the Sandy River was one laden with great historical significance. Prior to returning to the provisioning camp, Clark's canoe called at the house of his Chinookan pilot. Recall they had floated by it the day before but did not stop. Behind the pilot's lodge Clark observed the ruins of a "very large Village." His curiosity aroused, Clark inquired of "the Situation of their nation, if scattered or what had become of the nativs who must have peopled this great town." What happened next evokes more empathy—both on the part of modern readers of the journals and, arguably, on the part of Clark himself—than any other event chronicled by the explorers during the three years of the expedition's mission. Clark writes: "an old man who appeared of Some note among them and father to my guide brought forward a woman who was badly marked with the Small Pox and made Signs that they all died with the disorder which marked her face, and which She was verry near dieing with when a Girl." Clark concluded from her apparent age that this outbreak must have occurred "28 or 30 years past, and about the time the Clatsops inform us that this disorder raged in their towns and distroyed their nation."[21]

Clark quickly turned away from this story to record some thoughts on Native dress, language, and the "great attention [paid] to their aged." One of these elders drew a map of the Willamette Valley that Clark had barely penetrated, with references to numerous tribes, the falls at today's Oregon City, and above that a country that was "an open plain of great extent." With this perfect description of the famed valley inscribed on his map, Clark "left the Village and proceeded on to Camp where I joind Capt. Lewis." It had been an eventful trip for Clark, one offering insights into both his character and the grand sweep of the Native encounter with Euro-Americans—including its pathogenic nadir. Clark's visit to the smallpox-decimated village, viewed with a wider lens, shows how his expedition with Lewis was part of a movement that resulted in the most important event in the human history of the Western Hemisphere—the displacement of indigenous populations by people of European, African, and Asian ancestry. Although the Lewis and Clark Expedition does not appear to have had significant pathogenic consequences itself, in the northern West it nonetheless played an important role in laying the groundwork for the eventual demographic transposition.[22]

Clark's generation was very familiar with the ravages of smallpox and the recent development of a vaccine to prevent the disease. In 1798 the Englishman Edward Jenner discovered that a benign cowpox would inoculate against human smallpox. Thomas Jefferson was one of the first Americans to experiment with the technique. Jefferson's attorney general, Levi Lincoln, advised the president that Lewis should take smallpox vaccine with him. In Jefferson's final instructions to Lewis, he was ordered to take some vaccine west, and he was told to inform the Indians he met of this medicine's "efficacy as a preservative from the smallpox; & instruct & encourage them in the use of it." However, in October 1803, while on the Ohio River, Lewis wrote the president asking for a re-supply of the "Vaxcine matter, as I have reason to believe from several experiments made with what I have, that it has lost it's virtue." [23]

Lewis and Clark never witnessed the horror of a smallpox plague firsthand, but they had studied the work of a previous explorer who had—Alexander Mackenzie. The Scotsman's geographical memoir contained a harrowing description of an outbreak of smallpox. This disease, Mackenzie said, was "the greatest calamity that could have befallen the natives." Smallpox, he wrote,

> spread its destructive and desolating power, as the fire consumes the dry grass of the field. The fatal infection spread around with a baneful rapidity which no flight could escape, and with a fatal effect that nothing could resist. It destroyed with its pestilential breath whole families and tribes; and the horrid scene presented to those who had the melancholy and afflicting opportunity of beholding it, a combination of the dead, the dying, and such as to avoid the horrid fate of their friends around them, prepared to disappoint the plague of its prey, by terminating their own existence.... Nought was left them but to submit in agony and despair.... Nor was it uncommon for the father of a family, whom the infection had not reached, to call them around him, to represent the cruel sufferings and horrid fate of their relations, from the influence of some evil spirit who was preparing to extirpate their race; and to incite them to baffle death, with all its horrors, by their own

poniards. At the same time, if their hearts failed them in this necessary act, he was himself ready to perform the deed of mercy with his own hand, as the last act of affection, and instantly to follow them to the common place of rest and refuge from human evil.[24]

The estimated Native death rate due to a variety of pandemics including small-pox approached 90 percent in the lower Willamette and Columbia River valleys during the period of the first encounters with Euro-Americans. A river William Clark had once described as "Crouded with Indians" became, appallingly, almost devoid of them. Robert Boyd calls the rate of loss "shocking," its impacts "devastating and revolutionary." Boyd's seminal study on the decline of Native people in the Northwest due to pathogenic causes concludes with this sentence: "What happened to Northwest Coast Native peoples must not be forgotten, needs to be told, and should be a lesson to us all who live during an era when epidemic diseases are largely a thing of the past." [25]

CHAPTER 9   The Illusion of
             Cape Disappointment

THE LEWIS AND CLARK EXPEDITION'S FIRST OBSERVATION OF
the influence of oceanic tides on the lower Columbia must have inspired a sense of
hopeful expectation within the party. After all, by late October of 1805 twenty-six
months had passed since Meriwether Lewis left Atlantic tidewater, and William
Clark, along with the majority of the other men, had been traveling for nearly as
long. Memories of the laborious ascent of the Missouri, the more recent crossing
of the Bitterroot Mountains, and the white-water dash down the Columbia River
receded with the heightened realization that the long-awaited goal of the Pacific
Ocean was almost at hand.[1]

For much of the preceding quarter-century, culminating in Robert Gray's discovery in May of 1792, maritime explorers from several European nations and the
United States had sought the grand confluence of the Great River of the West and
the Pacific Ocean, or truly any opening eastward into the continent. In the mid-
1770s the great Captain James Cook of Great Britain and Bruno de Hezeta, sailing
separately for Spain off the shore of the present states of Oregon and Washington,
missed the Columbia's outfall. Maritime fur trader John Meares, representing
British commercial interests, flirted with fame in 1788 and nearly beat Gray to the
great find. Meares ultimately concluded, however, that the headland he sighted
at the 46th parallel guarded a mere oceanic inlet, not the fabled gateway into
the heart of North America. For that reason he named it Cape Disappointment.
William Clark, as most accounts have it, mistook the river's mouth for the ocean,
in effect mirroring Meares' error. In this chapter we will examine the circumstances in which Clark found himself that help assess whether he was wrong too,
and if so why he came to his controversial conclusion.[2]

While Meriwether Lewis is usually cited as the great voice of their expedition,
one presumed shout by William Clark has come down through history as the
most famous declaration found in the record of their joint command: *"Ocian in
view! O! the joy!"* However, for more than one hundred years historians have been
dousing Clark's jubilation with water as cold as the Columbia's, claiming that

what he actually saw was not the true Pacific Ocean but merely the river's lower estuary. It's time for another look at this axiom of LEWIS & CLARK lore and scholarship.[3]

When the party set out from their camp east of today's Cathlamet, Washington on 7 November, the morning fog was thick, necessitating the services of an Indian pilot. This man wore a "Salors" garb and guided the expedition through the intricacies of the many islands and sloughs that frequent that stretch of the Columbia. One canoe became separated from the flotilla for most of the day but reunited with the party that evening. Near the end of his course-and-distance notes for this day, Clark included the following observation in his elkskin-bound daybook: "we are in view of the opening of the Ocian, which Creates great joy." [4]

This was the first—therefore the most immediate and, importantly, the most understated—version of three statements made by Clark about the oceanic sighting. This day's travel terminated near Pillar Rock, and in his original log Clark focused his attention on the rock itself, not the legendary westward view. He called this specimen of columnar basalt a "remarkable rock of about 50 feet high and about 20 feet Diameter… opposit our Camp [i.e., rising out of the water] about ½ a mile from Shore." Of the other journalists, only Joseph Whitehouse referenced the rock's characteristic form by noting that it "had very much the resemlance of a Tower." Notwithstanding Clark's joyful expression, Whitehouse, John Ordway, and Patrick Gass all fail to mention any particular excitement in camp that night, which is odd given Clark's original construction and later amplifications. [5]

The limited "opening of the Ocian" first described by William Clark in his field log was later expanded in his reflective notebook journal into the more frequently cited: "Great joy in camp we are in *View* of the *Ocian,* this great Pacific Octean which we [have] been So long anxious to See. and the roreing or noise made by the waves brakeing on the rockey Shores (as I Suppose) may be heard distictly." Note here that Clark specifies the sentiment to include the whole party, which is believable but again raises the question as to why none of the other journalists makes mention of this supposedly momentous occasion. Clark's third, shortest and best known version of the sighting pronouncement, found in his final recapitulation of courses and distances for the trip down the Columbia, has become one of the most famous exclamations in the history of exploration: "*Ocian in view*! O! the joy." Clark almost certainly wrote these last two passages months later.[6]

The meaning and accuracy of these statements have been much disputed by historians of the expedition. Almost all scholars have followed Reuben Gold Thwaites's 1905 assertion that from the vantage of Pillar Rock the explorers were looking at the Columbia estuary, not the ocean. Clark, in other words, had gotten ahead of himself. Stephen Ambrose mused about what Meriwether Lewis might have written at this "moment of triumph" and in his judgment deemed that Clark was "a bit premature" with his exclamation.[7]

But caution should be taken before asserting Clark was irredeemably mistaken or somehow irresponsible, especially when such a conclusion is based on the

Point Ellice looms in the background (to the right and behind the low lying island that did not exist in 1805) in this modern photo of Pillar Rock, now adorned with navigational equipment. Clark's misreading of Vancouver's map and the vista shown here led him to conclude that the ocean was in view from this vantage point. (Washington State Historical Society)

modern configuration of the Columbia and other circumstances that mitigate Clark's perception of the lower river and the adjoining landscape. To begin with, in this debate too much attention has been directed to what Clark *saw* and not enough to what Clark *heard*, since he records impressions from both senses in his second statement on the matter. A century ago Thwaites, though the first to cast doubt on the question of what Clark saw, nevertheless acknowledged that from Pillar Rock a storm surge of breakers could have been heard. In our noise-polluted modern world it is easy to forget how far sound once traveled. Five months earlier, when Clark was approaching the Great Falls of the Missouri, he could hear their rumble twenty miles away.[8]

So if Clark really was mistaken about what he saw, what would have deceived this otherwise astute observer of the physical world? To a significant degree the debate revolves around the definition of terms for certain bodies of water and the transition zones between them. For example, the Englishman William Broughton, for one, would have heartily agreed with Clark's conclusion. Working in service of George Vancouver and putatively in contest with Robert Gray, Broughton had an obvious imperial motive to recast the nature of the American's discovery. If, as Broughton believed, Gray had merely visited an oceanic inlet whereas he (Broughton) had traversed a stretch of the actual River of the West, then the initial American discovery claim to the watershed would have been weakened. Perhaps influenced by these implications Broughton determined that the *true* entrance to the Columbia River was not at the bar between Cape Disappointment and Point Adams, nor Baker Bay or Grays Bay where the inlet widens. In Broughton's estimation the estuary was three to seven miles wide and "intricate to navigate on account of the shoals that extend from nearly side to side [and] ought rather to be considered as a sound, than as constituting a part of the river." In Broughton's assessment a host of smaller streams near the ocean (most notably today's Grays River and the Lewis and Clark River entering from today's Washington and Oregon respectively), indeed the great Columbia River itself, all emptied into an inlet of the Pacific. "Broughton's Sound," if we might call it that fancifully, stretched as far to the east as today's Skamokawa, Washington, six miles *upstream* from Pillar Rock.[9]

Broughton's judgment was sustained, in a roundabout way, by one of the enlisted men of the Lewis and Clark Expedition, Pvt. Robert Frazer. In the prospectus to his never-published account of the journey, Frazer referred to "the Columbia river and the Bay [Broughton's "Sound" here] it forms on the Pacific Ocean." It must be noted that in many other instances Lewis and Clark corrected geographic findings based upon later observation or experience, even when it came at the expense of their reputation as discoverers. We saw this earlier with the renaming of what the explorers had initially called the Columbia (the Lemhi/Salmon/Snake system) into "Lewis's River." However, on the question of when he first saw the Pacific Ocean, Clark never wavered. On 1 December 1805, having by then traversed Cape Disappointment and a portion of the Long Beach Peninsula,

Clark wrote that it had been "24 days Since we arrived in Sight of the Great Western... Ocian." Counting backwards, the calendar takes us to 7 November and the camp at Pillar Rock. Furthermore, Clark's composite map of the lower Columbia, completed at Fort Clatsop later that winter, contains the note "Ocean in View" adjacent to the Pillar Rock camp.[10]

Clark's most definitive reassertion about his belief on this point can be found in the now most underutilized source of information about the expedition—the paraphrased account of the journals prepared for publication by Nicholas Biddle. Currently perceived as a lesser-grade evidentiary record in the face of the seemingly more authoritative reckoning found in the original manuscript journals, the Biddle narrative should never be neglected. We know that Biddle consulted with Clark at length (and to a lesser extent Pvt. George Shannon) while preparing his draft narrative for publication, the notes from which, annotated by Donald Jackson, are another often overlooked but immensely valuable source of documentation.[11]

Biddle's account for November 7th posits that just past a Wahkiakum Indian village of seven houses at today's Skamokawa, the river widened into "a kind of bay." This, of course, is a simple restatement of Broughton's more considered conclusion, and for that matter, John Meares' too. Thus, in quick succession three experienced explorers had views recorded in published accounts that employed the geographic conception of a bay to define this watery zone, which term, then as now, is more properly thought of as an adjunct to the sea than as an extension of a river. The Biddle narrative continues: "We had not gone far from the village when the fog cleared off, and we enjoyed the delightful prospect of the ocean—that ocean, the object of all of our labors, the reward of all our anxieties." Notwithstanding the interposition of Biddle's florid prose, this version suggests that the ocean came into view well *upstream* from the oft-disputed and more westerly vantage of Pillar Rock! "This cheering view," the Biddle version continues, "exhilarated the spirits of all the party, who were still *more delighted on hearing* the distant roar of the breakers" (emphasis added). Biddle tells us that from this locale the voyagers traveled many more miles further west until reaching a camp opposite Pillar Rock.[12]

A consecutive reading of the sources—Clark's log, journal, course and distance table, and Biddle's narrative—shows that with each retelling of sighting the ocean on the approach to Pillar Rock the story became strengthened, not diluted. More radically, the actual vantage for seeing (or hearing) the ocean has moved farther to the east to a point near Skamokawa. How might this be reconciled to the modern observer's sense of geographic reality?

The man-made jetties at the mouth of the Columbia River are one key to understanding the reasonableness of Clark's assertion. Their function is to regularize a channel to and from the sea, which they accomplish, effectively, by moving the point of the ocean's collision with the river appreciably farther to the west. Before the jetties were built, ocean storms surged much farther inland (i.e., upriver) than they do today, which the subsequent experiences of Lewis and Clark would prove. Old-timers recall seeing the surf line (a definitional characteristic of oceans) at the approximate location of the present Astoria-Megler Bridge. And it is instructive to note that Megler, a mile upriver from the bridge landing, was established as the north-bank terminus for the old ferry service from Astoria precisely because it was easterly enough to avoid the worst (but not all) that the Columbia's bar had to offer. There were many days when "oceanic" conditions at Megler kept ferries from being able to dock.[13]

The second and perhaps more compelling explanation to this puzzle is reapplication of the principle of normative geographic expectations, introduced earlier in this book. Modern understanding of standard geographic information and long-settled disputes prejudices us to the contingent world as the explorers saw it in real time. What many see as Clark's all too obvious mistake at or near Pillar Rock has to be appreciated from the river level view of 7 November 1805 and his cartographic understanding of the terrain in front of him. If we add to that mix problematic and subjective notions about the definition of river/bay/oceanic boundaries, we see that the orthodox interpretation that Clark was simply mistaken is itself a simplistic explanation that ignores the circumstances that led to his controversial determination. The issue cannot be resolved by simply drawing lines between the various headlands forming Baker Bay and Grays Bay on the Washington side, or Tongue Point and Point Adams in Oregon, and determining that the river is on one side of this putative boundary and the ocean on the other.

The answer to this mystery is what I would call the illusion of Cape Disappointment. We know Lewis made a copy of Vancouver's chart of the lower Columbia when preparing for the expedition in Philadelphia. We know too that the captains had this copy with them on their voyage and that it confused them. Indeed, Clark was emphatic in his dismissal of Vancouver's work in both his journals and in dialogue with Biddle. The imperial contest and implications associated with priority of Discovery rights in furtherance of a sovereignty claim probably contributed to Clark's outlook.[14]

Vancouver's map of the estuary clearly conveyed Cape Disappointment's hook-like protuberance extending southward from the mainland—a feature that Clark later depicted from his vantage at Station Camp. However, in this instance, the view of the world provided by a map in a library in Philadelphia had to be refracted through the lens of Clark's observations on the river in a dugout canoe. As the great nineteenth-century American historian Francis Parkman once stated, the historian "must study events in their bearings near and remote; in the character, habits and manners of those who took part in them. He must himself be, as it were, a sharer or spectator of the action he describes."[15]

What Vancouver's map did *not* adequately convey was the prominence of Point Ellice (where the bridge from Astoria lands on the Washington side) as a landmark if viewed from an *upriver* location such as Clark's at Skamokawa and Pillar Rock. Soon to be known to the party as "Point Distress," Point Ellice was a far more

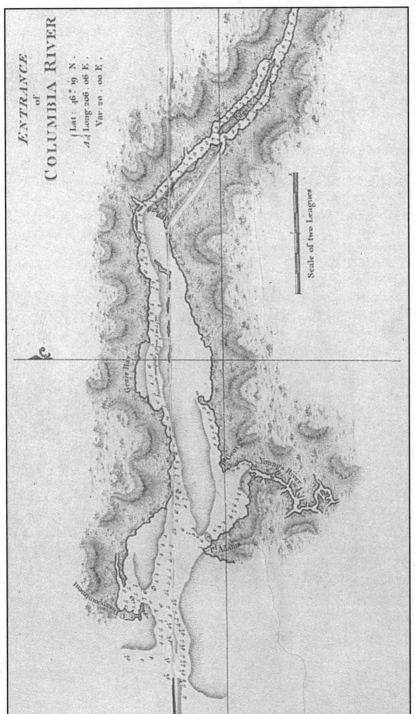

ENTRANCE
of
COLUMBIA RIVER

A. { Lat: 46° 19' N.
Long: 206 . 06' E.
Var: 20 . 00 E.

Scale of two Leagues

Gray's Bay

Young's River

Pt Adams

Hancock's River

This somewhat crudely drawn inset map from the atlas to George Vancouver's *Voyage of Discovery* (1798), showing the lower Columbia River as it disembogues into the Pacific Ocean, underplays the prominence of Point Ellice as viewed by William Clark from his vantage point upstream. (Washington State Historical Society) imposing landform when seen from Clark's river level vantage of November 7–8 than one would ever conclude by looking at it from today's common land-based points of observation or the direct approach on the bridge from Astoria (or, for that matter, from the direction Broughton originally mapped it: west to east). However, in the captain's log found in his elkskin-bound journal for November 8th on the course west from Pillar Rock, Clark was clearly operating on the assumption that the farthest landform he could see to the west on the north bank of the river was Cape Disappointment, an entry he later crossed out. Accordingly, once we account for his misreading of the topography, we see that Clark plausibly concluded that the horizon beyond this *faux* Cape Disappointment (i.e., Point Ellice) could only hold the waters of the Pacific Ocean. In actuality, from where Clark was first viewing the terrain, Point Ellice obscures the *real* Cape Disappointment. Only subsequent expeditionary experience would make this evident.[16]

Further substantiation of the notion that the party was taking in a view toward if not into the ocean can be discerned in the balance of the documentary record for November 8th. Whitehouse reported that shortly after departing Pillar Rock the view "continued as far as our Eyes could descern; & we expect that the River continues its width to the Mouth of it." This is significant reinforcement of what might be called the "Point Ellice effect." John Ordway commented, "we can See along distance a head" to the mouth of the river, and thus he also thought, the ocean. A nearly anticlimactic push to the Pacific appeared to be at hand. Such, however, hardly proved to be the case.[17]

To summarize: William Clark as an observant explorer at first discerned a view open to the ocean or like effect and tentatively ascribed this value in his daybook. As a good geographer he was relying on Vancouver's (imperfect) charts in forming his conclusions. The Columbia River was certainly beginning to look less a river and more like a bay or inlet. Lewis was bound to Clark in the same canoe and thus could not jump ahead. Nor was Lewis keeping his own journal. Clark had prepared himself for this moment, much as Lewis had prepared his thoughts in anticipation of heading west from Fort Mandan. Having made the first somewhat muted declaration of discovery, Clark adhered to it even in light of subsequent geographic revelation, indeed even trumpeted his initial burst of insight and enthusiasm. The subsequent debate, first propagated by Thwaites and now long-standing, draws strength from the uncritical foundation of LEWIS & CLARK lore with its supposedly unerring captains, compounded by a lack of appreciation for the contingent nature of real exploration, to say nothing of the emotions of a man who, at last, was no longer second fiddle but rather at the center of the expedition's story.

CHAPTER 10 Marooned

WITH THE OPENING TO THE OCEAN AHEAD, THE EXPEDITION for Northwestern Discovery proceeded gingerly along the north bank of the Columbia River. The estuary widened appreciably and with telling effect because suddenly "the Swells [became] too high to proceed," wrote William Clark. This was a portent of what would prove a physically and emotionally challenging week. Were those the swells of a river or an ocean? In this hybrid environment, canoes barely capable of negotiating a river were now in "Seas" and rolled about in such a manner that a number of the party got motion sickness, including hardy types like Reubin Field and Sacagawea. Maybe Broughton was right after all. It was at least as much a maritime environment as riverine because Clark noted they were soon forced to draw up their canoes on the bank "So as to let the tide leave them." Initially thinking this was a temporary delay, Clark recorded that "the Swells Continued high all the evening & we are Compelled to form an Encampment on a Point Scercely room Sufficent for us to all lie Clear of the tide water," and so they held over.[1]

Clark called the location of this campsite near today's Knappton Cove "Cape Swells." The situation only worsened the next day. "[H]igh Sees... broke against the Shore imediately where we lay," wrote Clark. The waves and tide combined to loosen the drift trees that were thick upon the shore and "tossed them about in Such a manner, as to endanger our Canoes very much." Only with the greatest of exertion, Clark wrote, were the men able to defend the canoes "from being Crushed to pieces between those emensely large trees maney of them 200 feet long and 4 feet through." Despite this "disagreeable time," Clark said the party was "Chearfull and full of anxiety to See further into the ocian." This last phrase echoed Clark's field note two days previous on the approach to the camp at Pillar Rock and confirms the notion that the explorers thought they had a view toward, if not into, the ocean. So, "at this dismal point we must Spend another night as the wind & waves are too high to proceed," Clark wrote.[2]

From the last rapids on the Columbia the detachment had traveled, by Clark's estimation, the following daily distances in miles: 13, 29, 32, 29, 34, and then the last 8 to Grays Bay. Here the expedition's rapid race to the Pacific came nearly to a halt. The already wet and windy weather was about to become far more tumultuous. Here it's worth reflecting that the most comfortable of days for Lewis and Clark anywhere on their travels would be rigorous for most people today. But within the context of their experience as explorers, how do we measure the degree of difficulty they faced? The Great Falls and Lolo Trail segments are truly of storied proportion and are generally regarded in LEWIS & CLARK lore to be the most difficult or harrowing episodes the expedition experienced. However, William Clark's direct, candid, and visceral reckoning of the circumstances at the mouth of the Columbia shows the second week of November 1805 to be the most dangerous time the entire party faced together.[3]

To place the travails of Lewis and Clark at the Columbia's junction with Pacific into context, let us briefly revisit the expedition's legendary encounters with the landscapes of Montana and Idaho. Rather than risk or danger, the operative descriptor for the Great Falls story should be fatigue. It appears from the captains' accounts that the condition of the men's feet predominated in their physical concerns. About the portage, Lewis wrote:

the men repaired their mockersons, and put on double souls to protect their feet from the prickley pears.[D]uring the late rains the buffaloe have troden up the prairie very much, while having now become dry the sharp points of earth as hard as frozen ground stand up in such abundance that there is no avoiding them. [T]his is particulary severe on the feet of the men who have not only their own wight to bear... but have also the addition of the burthen which they draw.

In a particularly poignant passage, Lewis states that during halts in the march "these poor fellows tumble down and are so much fortiegued that many of them are asleep in an instant; in short their fatiegues are incredible." Many of the men were limping, others fainted from exertion and heat, and yet, Lewis concluded, "no one complains, all go with cheerfullness." [4]

In a classic example of the division of responsibilities for which these captains are famous, they worked from opposite ends of a portage 18 ¼ miles long (Clark below the falls and Lewis above). Respectively, they commanded the departure or arrival of the work parties as they trudged across the plains. Clark, describing a group leaving the lower camp, said the men "haul with all their Strength wate & art, maney times every man... catching the grass & knobes & Stones with their hands to give them more force in drawing on the Canoes & Loads, and... every halt, those not employed in reparing the Couse; are asleep in a moment." He concluded that "to State the fatigues of this party would take up more of the journal than other notes which I find Scercely time to Set down." [5]

Lewis was situated amidst a "pretty little grove." This picturesque phrase is in keeping with his distinct taste for the word "cheerfulness" when describing the portage sequence. Notwithstanding the pronounced rigors faced by the expedition as a whole at the Great Falls, Lewis, at least, was having a grand time of it. He took pleasure in serving as cook, awaiting the arrival each day of the portage party from the lower camp. The occasional encounters with grizzlies, or "White bear," seem to have provided a modest brush with danger, if not entertainment. Though these bears were described as "troublesome," seeing two of them on an island in the river in front of him, Lewis wrote, "we… will make a frolick of it when the party return and drive them from these islands." [6]

Without a doubt the single most dramatic incident at the Great Falls took place on 28 June 1805. Clark and the portage squad were unable to make the full distance between the lower and upper stations, so a temporary camp was made on the plains. A thunderstorm blew in, and Clark and the Charbonneaus found shelter in a depression in the earth. As Lewis rendered the story, the first shower was moderate, but then "a most violent torrent of rain decended accompanyed with hail; the rain appeared to decend in a body and instantly collected in the rivene and came down in a roling torrent with irrisistable force driving rocks mud and everything before… it reached them." [7]

Toussaint Charbonneau was frozen with fright and failed to pull his wife and child up out of this cut bank, so Clark performed this duty heroically. According to Lewis, "but for Capt. C. both [Charbonneau] and his [wo]man and child must have perished." As it was, Clark was barely able to save himself, as the torrent rose to the depth of fifteen feet. The current was "tremendious to behold." Lewis closed, "one moment longer & it would have swept them into the river… where they must have inevitably perished." [8]

After the storm Clark pulled the scattered party back together up on the plain. Like Clark and the Charbonneaus, the rest of the men had all attempted to find cover. When the storm hit, "great Confusion" reigned. The men ran "leaveing their loads in the Plain, the hail & wind being So large and violent… and them naked, they were much brused, and Some nearly killed," Clark claimed, perhaps with some exaggeration. One man was "knocked down three times, and others," without any headgear, were "bloodey & Complained verry much." Ever the good captain, Clark "refreshed them with a little grog." [9]

That was the last of the excitement at the Great Falls. With snowcapped mountains facing them from several directions, Lewis concluded on the 4th of July that the detachment was "about to enter on the most perilous and difficult part of our voyage, yet I see no one repining; all appear ready to meet those difficulties which wait us with resolution and becoming fortitude." Celebrating the holiday and enjoying the last of the "sperits," the dancing and "mirth with songs and festive jokes" continued "untill late at night." [10]

A time-consuming but not particularly difficult crossing of the Rockies ensued. However, the subsequent encounter with the Bitterroot Mountains is the other great rival to the travails the party would experience on their final approach to the Pacific. Merely one day up the Lolo Trail, Clark's early and favorable report about this road's carrying capacity changed. It became a "most intolerable road," and the party and pack animals became "much fatigued." The difficulty of the "Steep & Stoney" path worsened to such an extent that the trail, Clark claimed, was "as bad as it can possibly be to pass." The expedition's horses started giving out. On 16 September 1805 Clark had "great dificulty in finding the road in the evining as the Snow had fallen from 6 to 8 Inches deep." Joseph Whitehouse said the men without socks were "forced to wrap Rags round their feet to keep out the cold." In a passage that would prefigure Clark's descriptions of conditions on the lower Columbia when facing oceanic storm fronts two months later, he described himself being "wet and as cold in every part as I ever was in my life." Another of his observations that night oddly foreshadowed what would prove to be chronic circumstances at the coast. In the mountains that night there was room "Scercely large enough for us to lie leavil, men all wet cold and hungary." [11]

On September 19th, to Lewis's "inexpressable joy," his platoon sighted Camas and Nez Perce prairies in the distance. Their Indian guide informed them "the Columbia river, in which we were in surch" would soon be found. However, before reaching this promising land, the narrow rocky road along the creek they followed became "excessively dangerous." The trail adjoined a "steep precipice, from which in many places if ether man or horse were precipitated they would inevitably be dashed in pieces." This passage is the apex of Lewis's concern about the physical safety of the expedition crossing the mountains. After Robert Frazer's "wonderfull escape" (when his horse fell and rolled into the creek one hundred yards below), the risk evaporated. Patrick Gass summed up the day's events, likening the "joy and rejoicing" among the men to that of seafaring voyagers who "first discover land on the long looked for coast," an interesting analogy for a terrestrial explorer 350 miles from the ocean. The party "retired to rest much fatiegued," Lewis wrote, but safe. [12]

Describing his mood after descending into the Nez Perce camp at Weippe Prairie, Lewis penned the pregnant passage about "having tryumphed over the rocky Mountains and... the flattering prospect of the final success of the expedition." Surely Lewis considered this mountainous divide to be not merely a physical passage but a metaphorical one as well—a test of will that he passed, both literally and figuratively. He conceded to himself, mistakenly as it should turn out, an ineluctably safe and uneventful passage to the Pacific. [13]

At the mouth of the Columbia River, however, things were neither safe nor uneventful. After two days' delay the swells at Grays Bay subsided. Clark ordered the canoes loaded, and the expedition voyaged ten miles to the west to what's now called Point Ellice—the northern terminus of the Astoria-Megler Bridge. There, however, around noon, the wind rose and "the waves became So high that we were compelled to return about 2 miles to a place we Could unload our Canoes, which we did in a Small nitch at the mouth of a Small run." After making a fire they dried their clothes, which were soggy from the continuous rain. They decamped on what little room availed itself at the base of "Purpendicular rocks or Steep assents to the hight of 4 or 500 feet." They waited a few hours, reloaded the canoes, and then "Set out in hopes to turn the Point below and get into a better harber." [14]

This second attempt at rounding Point Ellice also proved fruitless. Finding the *"waves & Swells"* (original emphasis; Clark had a penchant for accentuating extreme weather conditions in his journal) continuing to "rage with great fury below," the party was "obliged to return." Clark said the men "again unloaded the Canoes, and Stoed the loading on a rock above the tide water, and formed a camp on the Drift Logs which appeared to be the only Situation we could find to lie." In Whitehouse's version of the story, towards evening "we loaded our Canoes again, and proceedd on up the River in hopes to find a safer harbour." Traveling a "small distance" they "came to a large Spring run" in a bend in the river and encamped at the east end of what's known today as Clark's Dismal Nitch—site of a modern highway rest area. Clark closed out his entry citing the scarcity of provisions—"dried fish pounded which we brought from the falls." [15]

The rather understated manner in which William Clark described the party's failings—being "obliged to return" (twice)—stands in contrast to Meriwether Lewis's trumpeting of the first and unsuccessful attempt at recrossing the Bitterroot Mountains in the late spring of 1806. Ignoring Nez Perce advice, the expedition initially charged ahead on their eastbound trek but eventually had to return to the Indian village to secure a guide when they encountered deep snow and feared getting lost. Lewis reckoned at the time that this was the expedition's first "retreat" or "retragrade march." This may have been literally true as relates to a trek overland, but there is no denying the two failed attempts at rounding Point Ellice on the Columbia River on 10 November 1805 were backward movements. [16]

The lack of westward progress was yielding considerable frustration. In a passage from November 11th Clark stated, "we are truly unfortunate to be Compelled to lie 4 days nearly in the Same place at a time that our day[s] are precious to us." His concern was ratcheted upwards when some of the neighboring Cathlamet Indians stopped by. They were on their way downstream, intending to trade some fish "with white people which they make Signs live below round a point." The garb these Indians were wearing, including a sailor's jacket and trousers, only substantiated the apparent reality of this commerce. It gnawed at Clark that the Indians were able to get places the expedition could not. He looked on their capability with envy: "those people left us and Crossed the river (which is about 5 miles wide at this place) through the highest waves I ever Saw a Small vestles ride. Those Indians are Certainly the best Canoe navigaters I ever Saw." [17]

The physical elements were becoming horrific. Clark recounted:

tremendious waves brakeing with great violence against the Shores, rain falling in torrents, we are all wet as usial and our Situation is truly a disagreeable one; the great quantities of rain which has loosened the Stones on the hill Sides, and the Small Stones fall down upon us, our canoes at one place at the mercy of the waves, our baggage in another and our Selves and party Scattered on floating logs and Such dry Spots as can be found on the hill Sides, and Crivices of the rocks.

And so, while the Expedition for Northwestern Discovery had every form of evidence around them that they were near or indeed at the Pacific Coast, including high saline content in the Columbia River and "great numbers of Sea guls, flying in every derection," rather than enjoying a triumphant conclusion to their voyage, they were huddling in the nooks and crannies of the north bank of the Columbia while Native residents of the neighborhood blithely proceeded on with their business.[18]

The late fall Columbia estuarine environment had still more tribulation in store. On November 12th a thunderstorm struck early in the morning, bringing hail. The skies briefly cleared, but then "the heavens became darkined by a black Cloud from the S, W, & a hard rain Suckceeded" until noon. Clark said that the "Seas" were "braking with great force and fury against the rocks & trees on which we lie." As if to underscore a sense of dread not expressed at *any* point along the journey Clark wrote, with characteristic understatement, "our Situation is dangerous." Clark sprang into action. Seizing on the occasion of an ebbing tide, the expedition stored their canoes (weighing them down with stones to keep them from drifting off or being dashed to pieces by the waves) and gathered together what little of their possessions the men could carry. Then, toward evening, Clark said they marched "around a point to a Small wet bottom at the mouth of a Brook, which we had not observed when we Came to this cove; from it being verry thick and obscured by drift trees and thick bushes." Patrick Gass estimated the length of this trek to be about an eighth of a mile; Whitehouse refers only to a "short distance." The destination described by Clark is the mouth of Megler Creek at the western end of today's rest area—a place he later called "dismal nitich." [19]

Clark's Dismal Nitch, now a unit of the Lewis and Clark National Historical Park, unexpectedly served as one of the most dramatic locales along the entire trail. For the first time since the approach to the Yellowstone River in April 1805, the explorers were being held stationary for an extended time against their will. Even during the travails associated with the Great Falls of the Missouri and the Bitterroot Mountain passage, they had been able to proceed onward. At Dismal Nitch the detachment was effectively marooned. Clark's map shows the location of the campsite with a one-word description next to the date (10–15 November 1805): "Distressed." Nicholas Biddle, in his paraphrase of Clark's journal, described the situation as "now much more dangerous," among other reasons because the canoes—"our only means of escape from this place"—were at some remove from their scrutiny and at the mercy of wave action. Clark was not prone to a casual use of the term "dangerous." He employed it only twice before on the Missouri to describe situations when drifting logs threatened the keelboat.[20]

After Clark got the detachment into this "nitch," the first order was to find food. He sent out some men to hunt, but "they found the woods So thick with Pine & timber and under groth that they could not get through." Seeing some elk tracks, Clark started up Megler creek and "giged 3 Salmon trout." When added to the thirteen salmon other men secured, the party's exclusive diet of fresh fish is indicative of the straits the expedition was in. Joseph Whitehouse groused about eating "fresh fish, & pounded Salmon; which is by no means nourishing." [21]

With the failure of hunting parties on successive days, Clark next dispatched three men, Privates Gibson, Bratton, and Willard, in the most seaworthy craft at their disposal—"a Canoe built in the Indian fashion," acquired by Lewis above Celilo in exchange for one of the clunky dugouts, a hatchet, and a few trinkets. This third attempt to round the point only a mile away from Dismal Nitch was also thwarted. The men were forced to return, Clark recounted, because the waves tossed them about "at will." Summing up these dire circumstances, reflecting the physical and emotional nadir of the expedition, William Clark wrote this: "It would be distressing to a feeling person to See our Situation at this time all wet and cold with our bedding & c. also wet, in a Cove Scercely large nough to Contain us, our Baggage in a Small holler about ½ a mile from us, and Canoes at the mercy of the waves & drift wood." The expedition did not even have the small comfort of their oilcloth tents or other protective gear, stored upriver around the bend. As a consequence the "robes & leather Clothes are rotten from being Continually wet, and they are not in a Situation to get others… to restore them," Clark wrote. Whitehouse observed, "We have a very disagreeable time of it, the most part of our Men having slept in the rain, ever since the storm began, & are continually wet." [22]

It has been suggested by historians that William Clark was melodramatic in his descriptions at Dismal Nitch or simply self-pitying. Stephen Ambrose has more than hinted that Lewis was the more stoic of the two and would have put on a braver front. There is no basis for comparing the two captains at this juncture because, like the balance of the expedition's history in Columbia country, the end-of-voyage sequence suffers from the absence of Lewis's "voice." Nevertheless, an objective assessment of Clark's notes suggests that the tempest, gloom and sense of danger were real and pervasive. As Dayton Duncan writes, the circumstances of November 1805 "brought out the best in William Clark's journal writing." As demonstrated earlier with the sighting of the opening to the ocean, now that Clark was the principal witness, Duncan asserts, his entries were "more descriptive than usual, and filled with empathy for the plight of his men." [23]

With his unit hemmed in by natural forces, Clark sought a height of land behind the camp early on November 13th in order to survey the situation. Climbing to the top of the hill north of his riverside position, Clark covered three fatiguing miles over a slope so steep he was "obliged to drawing my Self up in many places by the bowers." By virtue of his elevated "ramble," Clark could see high waves below at "Point Distress," as it was termed in the formal tabulation of courses and distances and on one of his maps. Later that afternoon Lewis and Clark again dispatched three men, this time Privates Colter, Willard, and Shannon, in another vanguard movement west, the fourth attempt to turn the point. This group, at last, successfully separated from Dismal Nitch in the Indian canoe. Their goal, Clark stated, was to see if "they can find the Bay at the mouth & good harbers below for us to proceed to Safty." Patrick Gass observed, perhaps more candidly, that the

The Lewis and Clark Expedition was effectively marooned at "Dismal Nitch" for a week in November 1805, just three tantalizing miles from their terminal westward camp and the end of their transcontinental journey. ("Clark's Dismal Nitch" by Roger Cooke, Washington State Historical Society)

object of the Colter mission was "to ascertain whether there were any white people there, or if they were gone." A comment by Whitehouse that the threesome went "down to the Mouth of the Columbia River to make discoveries" could be read as supporting either Clark's or Gass's assessment and indicated an unusual role for enlisted men besides, a point we shall return to in the next chapter. To Clark, though, the safety of the expedition was paramount. In an ensuing passage, he speculated, "if we were to have cold weather to accompany the rain which we have had for this 6 or 8 days passed we must eneviatilbly Suffer verry much as Clothes are Scerce with us." [24]

Euro-American explorers had been visiting the Columbia estuary for only a little more than a decade, so Lewis and Clark, as relative newcomers, would have had limited knowledge about the climatic patterns of the region. What they *did* know is that the mouth of the Columbia was approximately the same latitude as Nova Scotia on the Atlantic seaboard and merely 1 degree of latitude south of Fort Mandan, both severe winter districts. With the passage of time the temperate nature of winters in the Pacific Northwest would be established. As late as 1857 when James Swan published his pioneering account, he took pains to allay concerns along these lines by pointing out that the climate "was never so cold as in the same parallel of latitude on the Atlantic coast." Nevertheless, the Lewis and Clark Expedition operated on the presumption that severe winter weather might arrive soon and persist for a considerable time, as evidenced in Joseph Whitehouse's entry of 23 November 1805, wherein he states that during winter it "is generally cold at this place." [25]

The rain continued all night on November 13th and into the 14th, their fifth day at Clark's Dismal Nitch. For food the expedition was still relying solely on fish. John Ordway bemoaned having "to Stay in this disagreeable harbour with nothing but pounded Sammon to Eat." Clark was wondering about the fate of the three men who had set out on the successful attempt at rounding distressful Point Ellice the day before. What significance was to be read into the fact that for the first time the voyagers did not return? That question was answered favorably at 10 a.m. the next day when five Indians from the Wahkiakum band arrived at Dismal Nitch and informed Clark "they Saw the 3 men we Sent down yesterday, at Some distance below." This might veritably have been the first good news in a week, that is, since the ephemeral sighting of the "Ocian" on November 7th. Shortly after the appearance of the Wahkiakum, Colter returned to the base camp by land. He did so as much to track down the Indians who had broken the lock on his gun and taken his knife and the "gig & basket" (by which he caught fish) as to report on geographic findings below. Clark had been suspicious of the situation when the Indians first sailed in because two Wahkiakum women "played off in the waves" as if to shield something from view.[26]

After Colter "forcably" took back his fishing gear, he reported on what he saw around the point, no doubt to a highly attentive audience. In his journal Clark quoted Colter as saying that "it was but a Short distance from where we lay around the point to a butifull Sand beech, which continued for a long ways" to the west. He had not seen any "white people." Willard and Shannon, Colter's erstwhile companions, had "proceeded on down" while he returned to the main party. This was all Meriwether Lewis could stand. Little had been heard from Lewis for a while, but now he asserted himself out of restlessness, frustration, or to preserve his reputation as an explorer. Unable to abide the situation at Dismal Nitch for whatever reason, in a late afternoon maneuver Lewis left, taking Drouillard, Frazer, and the Field brothers with him.[27]

The journal accounts of Lewis's departure from Dismal Nitch conflict with one another and are ambiguous to the point of confusion, a sure sign that something interesting in the expedition's dynamic was afoot. Clark first described Lewis as setting out "on the Shore" but alternately suggests that Lewis's group were put "around the Point" by canoe. Gass and Whitehouse said Lewis's squad set out "by land." Clark later reported that Lewis and his party were safely "on the Sand beech," and he made it clear that this news was delivered by one of Lewis's boat crew, who returned via canoe at dusk. When this craft arrived back at camp it was "half full of water, from the waves which dashed over in passing the point." Reconciliation of these accounts is only possible via recourse to Biddle's paraphrase. In that narrative we learn Lewis "was landed at the point whence he proceeded by land with four men and the canoe returned nearly filled with water." [28]

As intimated earlier, the reasons for Lewis's departure from Dismal Nitch are an even more complex story (which shall be expanded upon in the next chapter). Suffice it for now to say that by dint of pure willpower some members of the party had finally made it around "Point Distress." After a week of terrible weather November 15th broke "Calm & fair," and with now two successful roundings of the point below (first Colter, then Lewis), Clark was prepared to try his own hand at the passage. He "ordered the Canoes Repared and loaded" but damnably "the wind Sudenly Sprung up from the S. E. and blew with Such violence, that we could not proceed in Safty with the loading." The swells and waves made it "unsafe to proceed" with a movement en masse, so Clark went to the point by himself in a canoe unburdened with gear. He concluded from this experiment "it would be dangerous to proceed even in an empty *Canoe.*" Returning to camp Clark took advantage of a rare period of sunshine lasting until 1 p.m., directing that the men dry out the baggage, the bulk of which was soaked, put their firearms "in order," to keep them from rusting, and have the "ammunition examined" for potency. In addition to practical effect, Clark here seems intent on keeping the men busy to distract them from their predicament.[29]

Clark's recorded thoughts about this moment are filled with frustration, negating the transitory joy of the previous week. He called his time here on the north bank of the Columbia "the most disagreeable time I have experienced." With the difficulties of the Great Falls portage and Bitterroot Mountains traverse now fast diminishing in their relative significance, he described his field position as follows: "Confined on a tempiest Coast wet, where I can neither get out to hunt, return to a better Situation, or proceed on: in this Situation have we been for Six days past." [30]

At this gloomiest of junctures, however, fortune smiled. At 3 p.m. "the wind luled, and the river became calm," Clark wrote. Everything and person was loaded "in great haste and Set out, from this dismal nitich where we have been confined for 6 days passed." Heading down the river with the aid of an ebbing tide, the expedition finally passed "the blustering point," below which Clark found the "butifull Sand beech" described by Colter. Meeting an incoming tide and the "emence Swells from the main Ocean (imedeately in front of us) raised to Such a hite... I concluded to form a Camp on the highest Spot I could find," Clark reported. In his notebook entry Clark later recorded: "this I could plainly See would be the extent of our journey by water, as the waves were too high at any Stage for our Canoes to proceed any further down." Marooned no longer, the expedition had finally conquered Point Distress. [31]

CHAPTER II   The Solitary Hero

WILLIAM CLARK'S EXPLANATION OF MERIWETHER LEWIS'S
decision to leave Dismal Nitch deserves expanded scrutiny. Doing so sheds
considerable light upon the actual working relationship between the two men, in
contrast to the bromides frequently offered about their harmonious co-captaincy.
Consider first that Lewis's "object" in this undertaking, according to Clark, was to
"examine if any white men were below within our reach." This explanation strains
credulity. John Colter had just returned from the bay around "Point Distress"
and said that no traders or explorers were to be found. Colter would hardly have
missed sighting ships around Point Distress if there had been any. Pvt. Joseph
Whitehouse says Lewis ventured off to visit the Indian village Colter saw at the
mouth of the river—abandoned at the time—an even less credible scenario.[1]

There is a more plausible explanation for Lewis's evacuation from Dismal Nitch.
The broad pattern of Lewis's behavior over the course of the journey suggests his
motivation was narrow and purely personal. Colter's report upon his return to
Dismal Nitch that Alexander Willard and George Shannon were proceeding west
along that "sandy beech" makes plain the risk that someone other than Lewis
might be credited with the ultimate moment of discovery—reaching the Pacific
and that first dramatic and completely open view of the ocean. Lewis had nearly
all the other epochal moments of discovery to himself. He'd been the first to see
the Great Falls of the Missouri, and he had taken that legendary first glimpse
into the Columbia country from the crest of the Continental Divide. Would he
allow an enlisted man to beat him to the western edge of the continent? Lewis
developed a case of what mountaineers call "summit fever."

Several clues substantiate this thesis. First, there is the curious phrasing Clark
used to describe Lewis leading an advance party out of Dismal Nitch. Contrary
to the usual practice of characterizing all major decisions through the use of the
semantically inclusive "we," Clark states forthrightly that "Capt Lewis concluded"
on this course of action. Then there is the note Lewis posted at Fort Clatsop just
prior to its abandonment in March of 1806, hoping that some "civilized person"

might stumble upon the fort with his note still attached to its walls. Thereby the "informed world" would learn of the expedition, "sent out by the government of the U' States," that had penetrated the continent by way of the Missouri and Columbia Rivers "to the discharge of the latter into the Pacific Ocean, where they arrived on the *14th* November, 1805" (emphasis added). This date was purposively misleading on two counts. The great preponderance of the party on 14 November was still marooned east of Point Distress. William Clark and the bulk of the detachment would not successfully depart Dismal Nitch for another day. Secondly, the Colter party, as previously described, rounded Point Distress, the last impediment to westward travel, on the 13th.[2]

Lewis had made a habit of abandoning Clark, as he did again at Dismal Nitch, in quests for exploratory triumph. It was no coincidence that Lewis was the first to see the Great Falls or the Continental Divide; he engineered those moments. As Stephen Beckham phrases it, Lewis "was quick to 'jump ship' and dash for the prizes of discovery." Clay Jenkinson was the first scholar to note this tendency, observing that "Lewis took command at critical moments in the Expedition. He seems to have wanted to make the great discoveries of the Expedition alone." Lewis, Jenkinson writes, was a man "who struck poses." He had studied the role of explorer well, notably as enacted by Alexander Mackenzie, as detailed at length in a subsequent chapter.[3]

For most explorers this egotism would not have presented much of a problem. Lewis, however, had a co-commander. As noted in the earlier discussion about the expedition's Rocky Mountain "geography lesson," the lore of LEWIS & CLARK holds that the captains always saw eye to eye. There were, in truth, no overt disturbances in what Gary Moulton terms "their remarkably harmonious relationship," and from this he concluded "Lewis apparently treated Clark as... a partner whose abilities were complementary to his own." But appearances can be deceiving. A deconstruction of the journals proves that Clark was occasionally disappointed by Lewis's behavior and possibly annoyed to the point of resentment.[4]

From the beginning of the venture Clark was disadvantaged by his relationship to Lewis. Clark shared in the command of the expedition, Clay Jenkinson writes, "by virtue of Meriwether Lewis's magnanimity rather than in actual rank." Lewis had failed to deliver on Clark's promised promotion from lieutenant to captain. This gaffe resulted in both men having to pretend Clark was equal to Lewis in actual rank. Consequently, it should not surprise us that Clark, co-commander only because of an invitation from the (younger) man holding the original commission from the president, had been, as James Holmberg states, "very conscious of titles, rank, and his pride." Clark later reminded Nicholas Biddle that in rank and command he was *equal in every point of view* (emphasis in the original). When considered in conjunction with the larger body of Clark's crafty edits, demurrals, and disavowals in his own record plus those he later edited into Lewis's journals, his post-expeditionary comment to Biddle was tantamount to a protest. Clark was insistent that posterity not see his work in the field as that of a second in command or a junior officer even if in reality his rank was lower than Lewis's, as those in power in the nation's capital would have known too well.[5]

It was only through the fateful turns in Lewis's life that Clark had access to his associate's expeditionary record. Tellingly, Clark's first expressed concern after learning of Lewis's death was to ask rhetorically, "what will become of *my* papers" (later corrected to "*his* papers") (emphasis added). Clark had his own sense of ownership about the expedition, and he knew the journals Lewis was carrying when he died were essential to history's appreciation of their joint venture.[6]

As we saw in an earlier chapter and shall again later in this one, Clark was able to partially correct or otherwise recalibrate the record so as to more accurately reflect his contributions to the expedition. Clark never had access to certain documents (e.g., manuscripts other than the journals), and when Lewis went unbraked there is no doubt about whose expedition it was. Lewis's letter to his friend James Findley, sent downstream when the expedition was halfway up the Missouri in 1804, refers to "my party... of twenty six healthy, robust, active young men, accustomed to fatiegue and danger." Presumably William Clark, not mentioned as being on the voyage let alone being co-commander, was to be considered among that number. Then, in a private letter to his mother written shortly before the expedition left Fort Mandan in the spring of 1805, Lewis described having "arrived at this place... with the party under *my* command" (emphasis added). Excluding Clark may have been understandable if not excusable while writing to a friend or a close family member. However, Lewis later *published* a prospectus for the forthcoming account of travels and took credit not only for the prospective narrative but also the master map, which work had always been Clark's specialty. This map was to be compiled "from the collective information of the best informed travellers through the various portions of that region, and corrected by a series of several hundred celestial observations, made by Captain Lewis during *his* late tour" (emphasis added). This was double diminution of Clark's role: Lewis deigned to correct Clark while at the same time minimizing his primary contribution. It was precisely this hauteur that David McKeehan skewered in defense of his right to publish Sgt. Patrick Gass's journal in the face of Lewis's opposition to unauthorized accounts of the expedition.[7]

Though the expedition's journals have the surface appearance of being an empirical chronology of events, they are, often as not, autobiography. In her explication of the exploratory genre, Barbara Belyea distinguishes between the narrative form of "the 'I' who writes and the 'me' who is written about." Inevitably, Belyea states, the explorer as writer becomes "the main textual subject." Though this literary phenomenon was the norm for explorers, Lewis took it to extremes. Consider, for example, Lewis's famous description of the scene when the expedition left Fort Mandan. First, Lewis explicitly refers to Columbus and Cook (and inadvertently or otherwise to Mackenzie as well via his expropriation of the term "darling project," as described at length in the chapter after next). He then introduces the excitement associated with entering "a country at least two thousand miles in width, on which the foot of civillized man had never trodden." Next, Lewis wrote, "I could but esteem this moment of *my* departure as among the most happy of my life" (emphasis added). Framing this sentence Lewis consciously struck over the word "our" before "departure," so the solitary construction was no accident. As Clay Jenkinson says, here "Lewis's self-absorption is nearly complete." Lewis reduced a moment of common endeavor to what Thomas Slaughter calls a "singular and possessive accomplishment" that had the effect of reducing poor Clark "to the status of crew." Slaughter maintains that the ethos of exploration required of Lewis that he pose as the "singular hero." Indeed, departing from Fort Mandan, Lewis effectively edited Clark out of the narrative. This is the inversion of an episode occurring a year earlier when the expedition left the Wood River wintering-over campsite of 1803–1804 on the Mississippi. On that occasion Lewis wrote himself *into* a story when in fact he wasn't with the party on the first leg up the Missouri, joining it by going overland from St. Louis.[8]

As Clay Jenkinson avers, "at the critical moments of the Expedition, Lewis pushes the rest of the company out of his consciousness." Lewis's jumping ahead of Clark and leaving him at Dismal Nitch was a calculated stratagem in keeping with a tendency visible from the very beginning of the "collaboration" with Clark, aimed at putting himself in the historical spotlight should circumstances lend themselves to that eventuality. Consider, then, Clark's plight. During the course of the expedition, he had to regularly bear the indignity of reading how Lewis constructed this posed narrative when making a copy of Lewis's reflective journal entries.[9]

The first notable instance of Lewis's questing for glory west of Fort Mandan occurred during the approach to the Yellowstone River's confluence with the Missouri—what Lewis termed a "long wished for spot"—on the present border between North Dakota and Montana. Unfavorable winds had been retarding the progress of the watercraft for several days in late April 1805. Knowing from the reports of the hunters out ahead that the Yellowstone was not far away, Lewis determined to avoid any further "detention." He proceeded ahead by land with a few men "to the entrance of that river" to make the astronomical observations that would fix its position, "which I hoped to effect by the time that Capt. Clark could arrive with the party." When Clark finally caught up they quibbled a bit over the best location for the emplacement of a future trading post.[10]

Several weeks later, past the Milk River confluence in present-day eastern Montana, Lewis began to fret about reaching the source of the Missouri. He was "extreemly anxious to get in view of the rocky mountains." Clark's journal for this segment of the journey is largely a verbatim reiteration of Lewis's reflective notes, which makes differentiating Clark's activities and thoughts from those of his co-commander unusually difficult. Clark's rare deviations from Lewis's text, and a few clues left by Lewis, help to discern the sequence of events leading up to the first sighting of the Rockies and who was to claim credit for doing so.[11]

Clark's copy does not reiterate Lewis's anxiety about seeing the mountains, for reasons that will become clear in our explication of the journals' narrative of the ensuing fortnight. As chance would have it, a little more than a week later, on 19 May 1805, Clark ventured off on a solo ramble to the top of "the highest hill I could See." From that vantage he viewed a "high mountain" to the west. After Clark's return to the main party, Lewis reported this sighting in his journal, but the object therein was now more elaborately described as a "range of Mountains" with added detail gleaned from Clark about their extent and direction. Clark had seen the so-called Little Rocky Mountains of north central Montana. Five days later, Clark was again walking "on the high country" off the north bank of the Missouri. From that elevated vantage Clark saw what he termed the "North Mountns" and another chain to the south, the Judith Range, or in Clark's terminology, the "South Mountains." Lewis absorbed this intelligence and offered some speculations about the western mountains in his journal, but he did not venture to the heights himself.[12]

Six days later, May 25th, during his "walk of this day," Clark again viewed the mountains to the north and south but added, "I also think I saw a range of high mounts. at a great distance to the SSW. but am not certain as the horozon was not clear enough to view it with Certainty." These were the Highwood Mountains near Great Falls, Montana. Lewis's journal makes no mention of this sighting, which conveniently preserves the prospect of his discovering them, as we shall see. The next morning, 26 May 1805, Clark again "ascended the high countrey to view the mountains which I thought I Saw yesterday." From his new perch "much higher than where I first viewed the above mountains [yesterday]… I beheld the Rocky Mountains for the first time with Certainty." This line in Clark's journal for that day marks the commencement of what is more generally his copy of Lewis's remarks, deleting what would have been odd references back to himself in the third person, but of particular note here adding the phrase "with Certainty." The point or value of this edit in Clark's version is discernible when we see Lewis's original record for the same day, a document that was recorded before Clark's.[13]

Lewis's journal for May 26th first reports that "Capt. Clark walked on shore this morning" and in a rather pedestrian fashion recounts that his co-commander "had seen mountains," a perspective vested with no particular significance for a reason soon made clear. Then, in "the after part of the day," Lewis "also walked out and ascended the river hills," following Clark's lead and assuredly in response to his colleague's findings. Once at the heights Lewis considered himself "well repaid" for his labors "as from this point I beheld the Rocky Mountains for the first time." Again, Clark's copy of this entry from Lewis's transcript reads: "from this point I beheld the Rocky Mountains for the first time *with Certainty*" (emphasis added). What Clark had done here is to take Lewis's narrative baseline and massage it to reinforce his own prior sighting on the day before. Lewis's version proceeds to references of the "range of broken mountains seen this morning by Capt. C." However this gesture is quickly followed by Lewis's reversion to the form of the singular hero. Lewis recorded, "while I viewed these mountains I felt a secret pleasure in finding myself so near

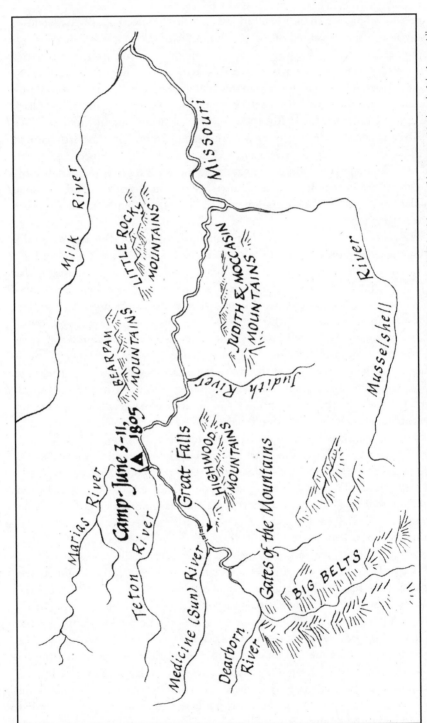

Contrary to geographical lore, the Rocky Mountains were many ranges deep in central and western Montana. (from *Lewis and Clark and the Image of the American Northwest* by John Logan Allen, courtesy Dover Publications, Inc.)

the head of the heretofore conceived boundless Missouri; but when I reflected on the difficulties which this snowey barrier would most probably throw *my* way to the Pacific, and the sufferings and hardships of *myself* and party in them, it in some measure counterballanced the joy I had felt in the first moments in which I gazed on them" (emphasis added). Clark dutifully copied all this Rocky Mountain Romance, but by subtly adding the words "with Certainty" at the outset of Lewis's textual soliloquy, he quietly asserts his proper place in the story of the authoritative first sighting of the Rocky Mountains.[14]

Next, consider Lewis's most famous discovery, the Great Falls of the Missouri. The Hidatsa told the captains that reaching this feature was the sure sign that they were on the correct route to the Columbia. This point was so axiomatic in the expedition's understanding of western geography that it served as the solution to the quandary faced by the party at the surprising appearance of the Marias River. Then and there Pierre Cruzatte and the other men in the detachment forced the captains' hands on the question of which branch of the river was the route to the headwaters of the river. Lewis complained that, contrary to his and Clark's opinion, Cruzatte, "an old Missouri navigator... had acquired the confidence of every individual of the party... that the N. fork [the Marias] was the true genuine Missouri." Indeed, the men were "so determined in this beleif, and wishing that if we were in error to be able to detect it and rectify it as soon as possible it was agreed between Capt. C. and myself that one of us should set out with a small party by land up the South fork [the Missouri] and continue our rout up it untill we found the falls." [15]

Tensions now emerged within the joint command because of what Thomas Slaughter calls the conventions of exploration as a "solitary event." As Lewis phrased it in his approximately 1,400-word account about the decision at the Marias, "this expedition [in search of the falls and thus the true Missouri] I prefered undertaking as Capt. C [is the] best waterman & c." William Clark's corresponding report numbers less than 200 words. Of Lewis's decision to jump ahead, he writes tersely about effecting a cache of one pirogue, tools, powder and lead, and as soon as "accomplished to assend the South fork." The absence of any nouns or pronouns in this last phrasing may be telling. His only mention of Lewis by name is to report that his co-commander was "a little unwell to day" and that he had to take "Salts & c." This would be the start of another pattern—Lewis becoming ill on those occasions when the fate of the expedition seemed to hang in the balance, an equivalence in Lewis's mind to his prospective reputation as a solitary and heroic explorer. Lewis described his illness as "disentary." [16]

In Thomas Slaughter's view, "companions create narrative problems for the explorer," as we saw earlier with John Ordway's and Joseph Whitehouse's candid expressions upon reaching the forks of the Columbia. In this case, when Lewis "jumped ship" on his quest for the Great Falls and exploratory glory, George Drouillard, Joseph Field, George Gibson, and Silas Goodrich accompanied him. However, a few days later, when Lewis encounters the "sublimely grand specticle" these men virtually disappear from the narrative. The experience with nature's wonder is Lewis's alone.[17]

Then later that summer, once the expedition reached the Three Forks of the Missouri, another great moment of discovery loomed—"seeing the head of the missouri yet unknown to the civilized world," as Lewis phrased it, and the Continental Divide from which it sprang. During this segment of the trip Clark had been proceeding ahead of the flotilla on land with the hunters, and he relished being in the vanguard. We know this from Lewis himself who noted that "Capt C. was much fatiegued[,] his feet yet blistered and soar," yet he *insisted* on pursuing his rout in the morning *nor weould he consent willingly* to my releiving him at that time by taking a tour of the same kind" (emphasis added). This remarkably insightful entry becomes even more interesting when posed with Lewis's next comment: "finding [Clark] anxious I readily consented to remain with the canoes." Something more than Clark just toughing it out is clearly at play here. Even Nicholas Biddle sensed the tension and attempted to sanitize the account by substituting the more neutral "*deturmined*" for the vexatious "insisted" found in Lewis's original text.[18]

Clark's intention was "to proceed on in pursute of the Snake Indians," the gatekeepers to the Rocky Mountain passage. An encounter with the Shoshone would have ensured Clark a central moment in the master narrative of the expedition's glories. Lewis, two days behind Clark, knew that his co-commander had "pursued the Indian road," had found an abandoned horse, and "saw much indian sign." Meanwhile, Lewis and the balance of the expedition labored in poling and hauling the canoes over the riffles in the riverbed.[19]

On July 25th Clark and his advance guard reached the Three Forks and then headed up what he termed the "main North fork" (later to be called the Jefferson River). This fork, Clark wrote expectantly, "affords a great Deel of water and appears to head in the Snow mountains." Here was Clark's main chance. Lewis himself observed that on the basis of a note left for him at the Three Forks, Clark was on a course "in the direction we were anxious to pursue." Unfortunately for Clark, his continued exertions in defiance of blistered and bruised feet (the result of repeated exposure to prickly pear cactus) and a somewhat straitened diet (not so much from supply but opportunity to eat), combined with oppressive midsummer heat, made him sick. Suffering from a high fever and chills, constipated, and losing his appetite altogether because of the fatigue brought on by his vigorous march ahead of Lewis and the canoes, Clark turned back to the Three Forks, exhausted. There he met with Lewis and the flotilla heading up the Missouri.[20]

For two days, 28–29 July 1805, Lewis doctored Clark at the Three Forks. Lewis had "a small bower or booth erected" for Clark's comfort because the "leather lodge when exposed to the sun is excessively hot." Clark's fever dissipated slowly, and though the recovery had begun he complained "of a general soarness in all his limbs." Lewis, however, was anxious to get going. On the 30th the detachment broke camp, but now it was Lewis on foot in that pivotal vanguard of hunters

The strained sublimity of Meriwether Lewis's description of the Great Falls of the Missouri inspired this engraving in a second generation edition of the expedition's journals. The falls today are compromised by a dam and power plant. (Courtesy of the Lewis & Clark College Special Collections)

while Clark and the voyagers brought up the rear. After only one day with this arrangement, Lewis admitted having "waited at my camp very impatiently for the arrival of Capt. Clark and party." Becoming by his own admission "uneasy" with this pattern, Lewis determined on the next day "to go in quest of the Snake Indians." Packing away a sheaf of papers with which to record notes that might be adapted into a narrative worthy of posterity's reading, Lewis took Drouillard, Charbonneau, and Sgt. Patrick Gass on this mission. Once again the excitement of becoming the exploratory hero brought on "a slight desentary," as had happened to Lewis when he jumped ahead of Clark in pursuit of the Great Falls.[21]

The day Lewis leapt ahead, August 1st, happened to be Clark's birthday. Clark reported tersely and with a tinge of hurt, "Capt. Lewis left me at 8 oClock." Left behind to slog up the gravelly bed of the Jefferson River with the canoes, Clark's physical problems mounted when his ankle swelled. One day ahead of the main party, Lewis reached the forks of the Jefferson and determined that the affluent known today as the Beaverhead River, with its warmer water and gentler flow, was the more navigable route. Lewis deduced that the Beaverhead "had it's source at a greater distance in the mountains and passed through an opener country than the other." Lewis left a note for Clark on a pole at the Jefferson forks instructing him on the recommended route for the canoes in case he did not return to this spot before the main party got there.[22]

Once a few miles up the Beaverhead fork of the Jefferson, Lewis could now see that it headed in a "gap formed by it in the mountains." With that promising prospect in front of him Lewis wrote, "I did not hesitate in beleiving the [Beaverhead] the most proper for us to ascend." Better yet, "an old indian road very large and plain leads up this fork." This was the path to the Shoshone, the Continental Divide, waters that drained to the Pacific, and to glory.[23]

Down below, Clark was barely able to walk. The "poleing men" and those hauling the canoes were "much fatigued from their excessive labours... verry weak being in the water all day." After his initial reconnaissance of the Beaverhead, Lewis returned to the forks of the Jefferson River expecting to find "Capt. C. and the party... on their way up." Lewis was dismayed because upon reaching the forks, he discerned that Clark had not taken the recommended route up the Beaverhead, but one to the northwest known today as the Big Hole River. Lewis sent Drouillard after him and later "learnt from Capt. Clark that he had not found the note which I had left for him at that place and the reasons which had induced him to ascend" the more rapid northwesterly branch. In a comic twist, a beaver had gnawed down the post holding Lewis's directions with near-disastrous consequences for poor Clark, who had simply followed the stream with the greatest flow—a fundamental hydrological principle that had always guided the expedition.[24]

Lewis reported that Clark pursued the "rapid fork" for nine miles, but after one of the canoes was "overset and all the baggage wet, the medecine box among other articles... lost," including a shot pouch, powder horn, and a rifle, he decided to return to the forks of the Jefferson. By the time this retrograde movement was completed, two other canoes filled with water, dampening "a great part of our most valuable stores" including the all-valuable Indian presents. Pvt. Joseph Whitehouse had nearly been killed on this excursion when he was thrown out of one of the canoes which "pressed him to the bottom as she passed over him." Had the water been two inches shallower, Lewis opined, the canoe "must inevitably have crushed him to death." Fortunately, none of the lead canisters containing gun powder had been breached even "tho' some of them had remained upwards of an hour under water." (Any significant amount of moisture would have ruined this vital supply with potentially disastrous consequences for the sustainability or defense of the expedition.) After recounting this story, Lewis then credited himself for having conjured the system of storing powder in lead containers rather than wooden vessels.[25]

What Lewis referred to rather pointedly as Clark's "mistake in the rivers" almost resulted in the loss of yet another man. Clark had sent George Shannon ahead to hunt before the decision to reverse course was made. Shannon, Lewis recounted, had the previous misfortune of being lost for fifteen days going up the Missouri the year before. Shannon found his way back to the party a few days later, and Whitehouse was alive if "in much pain," but Clark's spirits were as dampened as the baggage that had been under his care. Lewis, on the other hand, was reveling this day in his narrative on the naming of the affluents of the Jefferson River: the "*Wisdom*" and the "*Philanthropy*, in commemoration of two of those cardinal virtues" of the president who dispatched them. Clark recounts nary a word about this fanciful stuff in his journal's reckoning of that dismal day. He rather sparingly reported instead about Drouillard catching up with him with the news that the route he was on "was impractiabl" and that "all the Indian roades" led up the fork that Lewis had scouted. Clark "accordingly Droped down to the forks where I met Capt Lewis & party," he wrote with a hint of resignation. Clark's sore ankle was "much wors than it has been," the physical pain compounding the embarrassment of having taken the wrong turn.[26]

The captains traveled together for two days up the Beaverhead fork of the Jefferson, but by the end of the second day, 8 August 1805, Lewis had had enough. He decided to "leave the charge of the party, and the care of the lunar observations to Capt. Clark" while he would on the next day proceed ahead "with a small party to the source of the principal stream of this river and pass the mountains to the Columbia." The boil or cyst on Clark's ankle had "discharged a considerable quantity of matter," but it was still swollen and left him in "considerable pain," Lewis reported. The morning Lewis forged ahead "to examine the river above, find a portage if possible, also the Snake Indians," Clark recorded a poignant observation tinged with resentment: "I Should have taken this trip had I have been able to march." [27]

Clark's expression is one of the most suggestive of any to be found in the millions of words in the journals of the expedition. It exudes chagrin about not being able to make contact with the Shoshone and more particularly the Columbia River. Furthermore, one can intuit from it that after Lewis's previous forays in pursuit of the Yellowstone and the Great Falls, Clark for certain, and maybe both captains, had concluded it was his turn for glory. Elliott Coues was the first to observe that "Captain Clark was sadly disappointed at not being able to take the lead in the trip." More recently Stephen Ambrose said, "Clark wanted to lead" this reconnaissance, but that in the end it would prove Lewis's "most important mission." This, of course, gets to the heart of what was bothering Clark.[28]

These circumstances put the aforementioned corrections Clark made in Lewis's continental "geography lesson" into very sharp relief (see chapter 2). Fate, in the form of an ulcerous sore, may have denied Clark the opportunity to be the first over the Continental Divide. But he was determined that Biddle should know that the true comprehension of the complex Rocky Mountain district was his work, not Lewis's, demolishing the pretentious edifice Lewis had constructed in his journal. At the moment Lewis left Clark on the headwaters of the Missouri, Clark's rendezvous with destiny dissipated. Everyone in the party saw the consequences. As John Ordway put it, Captain Lewis had gone on ahead "to make discoveries." [29]

Three weeks later, when the expedition was about to leave the company of the Lemhi Shoshone, Lewis let slip his characteristic conceit when he referred, once again, to resuming what he called "my voyage." Such egotism has been an easy target from as early as 1807 in the form of David McKeehan's broadside defending the desire of his client, Patrick Gass, to publish an unofficial account of the voyage. Nevertheless, Lewis was not completely oblivious to his obligations to his friend and co-commander. Lewis later named the Clark Fork of the Columbia after him, in partial reciprocation for Clark having named the Lewis (Snake) River. But whereas Lewis had, in fact, been the first to the Columbia's waters, Clark's honor was a mere gratuity. As Elliott Coues observed, Clark had not been the proverbial "first white man" on the waters named for him, or at least, no more so than any other man in the expedition since the entire party crossed into the Bitterroot/Clark Fork watershed en masse.[30]

Throughout his joint venture with Lewis, William Clark's modesty shone through, a virtue not easily credited to his partner. As we have seen, though, Clark was not averse to correcting the worst of Lewis's self-indulgences by emphasizing his own contributions. In another telling instance, this one from the June 1806 return trip over the Lolo Trail, Clark's "verbatim" copy of Lewis's journal, in which Lewis had recounted the expedition's first contact with the Nez Perce at Weippe Prairie, Clark corrected Lewis's "we" (by which Lewis had included himself in Clark's vanguard contact with the Nez Perce, though Lewis was in fact trailing well behind) to "I," thus reinstating himself as the first to reach Weippe Prairie. (We can safely surmise that if the roles had been reversed and Lewis had been the first to Weippe, a singular "I" would have appeared in his original transcript.) However, Clark's presence as a companion in exploration was merely the most obvious narrative problem for Lewis as the solitary discoverer. Also on the same return crossing of the Lolo Trail, Lewis wrote with his unlimited sense of self-importance, "I met with a plant the root of which the shoshones eat." Clark the copyist balanced the record by noting that it was Sacagawea who "Collected a parcel of roots of which the Shoshones Eat," in reference to the western spring beauty, a white flower.[31]

Years after the expedition Clark privately criticized Lewis for the predicament his co-captain had put him in, referencing the "trouble and expence" of getting the journals into print. Lewis, like a cowbird, truly had laid his eggs in Clark's nest. But Clark, in the end, was up to this task, and possessing the advantage of having been the more diligent journal-keeper, he exercised the option of editing the expedition's documentary record in several key instances to create a more accurate account of events. In this respect, Clark was both the expedition's first historian and later the historian's friend, for the benefit of posterity. We are left, then, to wonder: had Lewis lived to write the official account of the expedition, how would Clark have fared in that narrative? Evidence left in the proto-manuscript as reflected in Lewis's notebook for the spring and summer of 1805 suggests he would have extolled Clark's virtues and assistance, but he, Lewis, would have been the sole hero of the story.[32]

CHAPTER 12   End of Voyage

MERIWETHER LEWIS'S FAUX HEROIC URGENCY OF 14 NOVEMBER 1805 had broken the Expedition for Northwestern Discovery into two distinct commands. Clark's primary concern with the trailing detachment was finding a place of comparative safety—something that had eluded him since November 8th. Rounding Point Ellice, though, he came upon the long sandy beach and stopped. He wrote, "this I could plainly See would be the extent of our journey by water." Given all the attributes of beauty that would be attached to it, this beach was like a tropical paradise in comparison to the world of Dismal Nitch with its drift-log encampment, crashing waves, and men sheltering themselves in the crevices of hillsides. This beach encampment, not Fort Clatsop, is more properly to be understood as the western terminus of the expedition.[1]

The modern disappearance of the sand beach west of Point Ellice is a noteworthy change in the environment of the lower Columbia since the days of Lewis and Clark. Today there is a hint of this beach only at the lowest of tides. Pioneer settler James Swan frequently walked from Chinook Point (upon which Fort Columbia State Park currently rests) to Point Ellice. Swan observed that the beach between these two headlands was from half a mile to a mile in width at its greatest extent, to several hundred feet at its narrowest. Indeed, "Chenook beach" extended so much farther south and out into where one finds the river channel today that looking east and past the promontory of Point Ellice Swan could see the "snowy head" of Mount St. Helens. There is no longer such a terrestrial vantage point.[2]

Nevertheless, Clark's attention was drawn west, to a "full view of the *Ocian*." Point Adams on the south bank of the Columbia and Cape Disappointment on the north formed an aperture approximating 45 degrees of perspective onto the river's confluence with the Pacific. After establishing some initial bearings and distance estimates toward each promontory, Clark attempted to reconcile his place within Vancouver's cartographic record. From Lewis's copy of the original engraving, he recognized the general shape of the bay that British mapmakers had derived from Vancouver's findings. Missing was an island that Clark believed the

British had recorded. In truth, Vancouver's charts had merely intended to record a shoal. Either Lewis's copy was faulty or Clark misunderstood the cartographic image, making a sandbar into an island. As would become distinctly clear to later observers in the settlement era, sandbars at the estuary move about constantly.[3]

The principal ethnographic finding made while Clark's command coasted westward past Point Ellice was a large but deserted village of the Chinook tribe, numbering thirty-six houses. This community was just west of the first creek that fell into the Columbia beyond Point Distress. This rivulet, Clark wrote, "waters the Country for a few miles back." Clark's undated but authoritative "Estimated Distances in Miles Ascending the Missouri, Crossing the Rockey Mountains & decending... the Columbia River" and other "remarkable places" prepared at Fort Clatsop locates the sand beach camp, therein named "Station Camp," near the old Chinook village and two miles west of "Point Distress," (Ellice today). John Ordway estimated the distance from Point Ellice to a "point open Slope" (the modern location of Fort Columbia, also known as Chinook Point), downstream from the Station Camp, at three miles. This measurement is consistent with Clark's, since Ordway was calculating distance to a more westerly point. Clark's ensuing survey of the Columbia's north bank (described later in this chapter) began at the creek immediately downriver of Point Ellice, fixing a location for Station Camp at 5,874 feet still farther west, or a little more than a mile. This camp (whose name will be discussed later in this chapter) was described by Clark as being located "between the hight of the tides, and the Slashers in a Small bottom." (The term "Slashey" in the vernacular of Lewis and Clark's Virginia and Kentucky homelands referred to a wet, low swampy place, grown over with cattails. The "bottom" Clark mentions here probably referred to the foot of the hill behind Station Camp.) Of the other journal keepers, only Pvt. Joseph Whitehouse provides additional topographic detail of the scene. He said, "The Country appeared to lay lower than it had been," and the sand beach camp was "at the head, or upper part of a large bay." [4]

After settling into this safe harbor, Clark was met by George Shannon who, with Alexander Willard, had been with Colter in the first vanguard movement two days earlier. Shannon informed Clark that Lewis was intent on proceeding still farther west to the ocean shore, taking Willard and the four others who, with Lewis, had been sent around Point Distress via canoe from Dismal Nitch. Lewis had ordered Shannon to wait on the beach for Clark's eventual arrival from Dismal Nitch. Whitehouse referred to this situation as Lewis having "gone on, to another Bay," meaning beyond Chinook Point. Shannon had dutifully returned to the sandy beach from an "Indian Hut" ten miles farther west (in the vicinity of today's Ilwaco), which is where Lewis found him and Willard after the captain hurried around Point Distress the day before.[5]

Shannon also conveyed a warning from Lewis for Clark's benefit to be careful of the "thievish" Indians who, Shannon sheepishly admitted, had stolen his and Willard's rifles "from under their heads" while sleeping on the night of the 13th. He and Willard believed they had secured their safety by hinting to the Chinook Indians that they were members of a larger party, news that was probably common information to the Natives anyway. Nevertheless, having lost their armaments, Shannon and Willard were trudging eastward when they met Captain Lewis "& party." The appearance of five more explorers, per Shannon, "alarmed the Indians" so they returned his and Willard's guns. Left unstated is how much farther to the west Shannon and Willard had gotten. Lewis ran into them at the foot of Cape Disappointment, the top of which offered an untrammeled view to the western horizon.[6]

Some of these Indians were still in Shannon's company when he met up with Clark and the even larger party now having since arrived on the beach at Station Camp. Clark immediately put the Chinook on notice, stating that if anyone from their tribe stole something, "I would have him Shot." This bit of contentiousness shows, once again, how often the experiences of the Lewis and Clark Expedition mirrored those of Alexander Mackenzie. Indeed, in this case, Mackenzie's outlook may have informed the expectations of the Americans. Upon his arrival at Pacific tidewater twelve years earlier, Mackenzie apprehended "that some hostile design was meditated against us." The Scotsman told his men "to be very much upon their guard, and to be prepared if any violence was offered to defend themselves to the last." After just one day on tidewater, Mackenzie reported that his men "were very anxious to get out of the reach of the inhabitants of this coast." Mackenzie reached salt water in July and had the luxury of being able to commence a return journey immediately, an option not available to Clark and Lewis. Clark surely hoped to avoid violence in such a vulnerable position, so his recourse was to "Chastise" the Chinooks and treat them "with great distance."[7]

Even so, this was the most intense intercultural encounter since the confrontation with the Teton Sioux in late September of 1804. Not coincidentally, both the Teton Sioux and the Chinook were hardened by exposure to the globalized fur trade and prized the privileges of geography that allowed them to control commerce in their respective quarters by acting as gatekeepers, if not monopolists. For the Chinook, repeated encounters with fur traders had clearly changed them, both in regard to commercial etiquette—they had evolved from friendly negotiators to great hagglers—as well as their physical well-being. (John Boit, who sailed with Robert Gray across the bar in 1792, had described the Chinooks as "fine looking fellows and the women are very pretty." Clark later agreed that "maney of the women are handsom," though a mere thirteen years later "Pocks & Venerial" were common, further evidence of the pathogenic aspect of globalization.)[8]

After what had been a very trying week, Clark and the party settled into their new camp on "Haleys bay," named for what was later deduced to be the Indians' "favourate Trader." (Today this body of water is known as Baker Bay.) The evening of November 15th was "fare & pleasent." Better still, the men were "all Comfortable in the Camps they have made of the boards they found at the Town above," that is, the abandoned Chinook Indian village. Here the Americans felt sovereign enough to expropriate its material for their huts with none of the misgivings expressed when they earlier took boards from Native communities along the Snake River and used them for firewood.⁹

When William Clark had been at Camp River Dubois opposite St. Louis in January 1804, he had estimated that the party would reach the Pacific Ocean sometime between May and July of 1805. They had run about five months late, which, under the circumstances, was not bad "time." Clark had also then forecasted that the expedition would stay at the Pacific Coast around two weeks before turning homeward. This would prove reasonably accurate as well (depending on the definition of "turning homeward," as discussed later). On November 16ᵗʰ Clark caught his breath and began the process of geographic recapitulation and conformation. He first conjoined Shannon's more westerly reconnaissance with his own assessment of the topography west of the "Stormey point." (This was the third name Clark gave this feature in addition to the previous designations of "Distress" and "Blustering." Surely it loomed large in Clark's sense of story and place.) For the first time in weeks the hunters, including the slave York, were able to get out, bagging some deer, geese, and ducks. The now relatively clear weather also allowed Clark to direct that the stowed baggage be put out to dry on what he called "our beech." At noon Clark established the camp's latitude with his sextant. Cloudy skies that night prevented any lunar observations. With the party now finally in safe harbor, the Pacific Ocean in view, and game to eat, Clark could once again resume his role as a scientific geographer.¹⁰

The most memorable journal passages from this day, however, come not from Clark but three enlisted men, Pvt. Joseph Whitehouse and Sgts. Patrick Gass and John Ordway. Whitehouse, in his journal for 16 November 1805, re-states the developing consensus that the expedition was in "plain view of the *Pacific Ocean*," with its "waves rolling & the surf roaring very loud." Emulating Clark's earlier comment, Whitehouse wrote, "We are now of opinion that we cannot go any further with our Canoes." He then explicates the meaning of this passage, stating, "we are at an end of our Voyage to the Pacific Ocean, and as soon as discoveries necessary are made, that we shall return a short distance up the River & provide our Selves with Winter Quarters." This interpretive expansion of Clark's act of calling a halt at the sandy beach has three values. First, Whitehouse clearly intended to communicate, more definitively than Clark did in the excitement of the moment on the 15ᵗʰ, that the westward journey of the Expedition for Northwestern Discovery was over. His comment about "discoveries necessary" also prefigures some side trips that members of the party were about to undertake to fulfill the mission's cartographic imperative. Finally, Whitehouse unmistakably implies that the party at its arrival at the ocean had every intention of returning well upstream for the winter.¹¹

Patrick Gass expands upon the Whitehouse insights, first by extolling the "full view of ocean, at this time more raging than pacific." Then he boldly declares, "We are now at the end of our voyage, which has been completely accomplished according to the intention of the expedition, the object of which was to discover a passage by the way of the Missouri and Columbia rivers to the Pacific ocean; notwithstanding the difficulties, privations and dangers, which we had to encounter, endure and surmount." Like his earlier account of the "romantick grandeur" of the Snake River canyon, Gass's language here seems heavily influenced by the rhetoric of Meriwether Lewis.[12]

Finally, we must consider John Ordway's undated computation of mileage traversed by the party starting from their canoe deposit on the Missouri's tributaries east of the Continental Divide. This instrument was probably composed at Fort Clatsop (which makes its content all the more salient), and in it Ordway referred to Chinook Point ("point open Slope") as being "below [the] perminent Encampment of the party of N. W. Discoveries in 1805." Along with Gass and Whitehouse, Ordway's phrasing is a remarkable summing up of the expedition's charter, main courses, and especially the sense of the mission having been accomplished. The combined effect of these passages runs contrary to the long-held view in the lore of LEWIS & CLARK that the western "end of the trail" was Fort Clatsop. The cumulative evidence derived from these journal entries is that the terminal westward camp for the "party of N. W. Discoveries" was on the north bank of the Columbia at Station Camp.[13]

All of this may matter little to those who think the true "end" of the trip must be calculated to mean the successful return to St. Louis the following year. (Donald Jackson stated that Charlottesville, Virginia, should be considered the trail's terminus. Lewis returned there in December 1806.) Nevertheless, the pride imbued in Sgt. Gass's end-of-the mission journal note is analogous to that of the mountain climber. Mountaineers surely think they have reached the pinnacle of their trip when they achieve the summit, not upon their return to the base of the mountain. Unmistakably, the "summit" for the voyage of the Expedition for Northwestern Discovery was Clark's establishment of Station Camp.[14]

That "Station Camp 1805" (as it was officially denominated later) was trail's end can be gleaned from a comment Clark made on November 21st. That day, many weeks before Fort Clatsop was built, Clark stated the expedition's "homeward bound journey" was delayed by another bout of stormy weather. Patrick Gass seconded this view with his companion entry that "the waves ran so high, that we could not set out on our return, which it is our intention to do as soon as the weather and water will permit." Fort Clatsop deserves to be thought of as a very important place in the study of Lewis and Clark, but it is *not* the expedition's westward terminus. It is best considered the first significant stop on the eastward, return trip.[15]

While the foregoing addresses the debate as to "where" Lewis and Clark's trail ends, still unresolved is the sticky contest of wills between Clark and Lewis as to "when" this mission was accomplished. This question turns on Lewis's exploratory ego, as seen in his feverish desire to get out of Dismal Nitch and beyond Point Distress in order to achieve a full view of the ocean and maybe make contact with a ship's captain. This topic will be addressed at length in a later chapter. Suffice it for now to say that Clark, in his field maps and finished cartography, marks the beach camp he established with the main party as the official location of the expedition from the 15th to the 25th of November.[16]

At about 1:30 p.m. on November 17th, Clark noted that Meriwether Lewis had finally returned from a trip around Cape Disappointment and "Some distance on the main Ocian." Whitehouse once again pointed out what Clark either neglected or chose not to record—that Lewis "had seen no white people or Vessells." This substantiates the interpretation outlined in the preceding chapter. Lewis was *not* content with Colter's initial reconnaissance west of Point Distress and was eager for a gloried encounter with a ship captain. Notwithstanding tantalizing rumors that white men were to be found downriver, first heard from the Nez Perce and many times thereafter, there were no ships at the coast when the expedition reached that destination.[17]

The pioneer resident James Swan determined that fifty-six vessels, starting with Robert Gray's *Columbia Rediviva*, had visited the estuary by 1805. Usually with the onset of the tumultuous fall weather (like that which Lewis and Clark had just seen firsthand), ship captains headed for more salubrious climes. Guidance provided with the publication of George Vancouver's *Voyage* in 1798 had been quite persuasive in this regard. William Broughton's widely disseminated narrative of his entrance into and exit from the Columbia was extraordinarily instructive. Edward Bell, a clerk aboard Broughton's *Chatham*, wrote that in crossing the shifting bar of the Columbia he had "never felt more alarmed & frightened in his life, never having been before in a situation where I conceived there was so much danger." Vancouver himself was foiled in his attempt to take the *Discovery* in after Broughton had already done so with the *Chatham*. After his arduous reconnaissance up the Columbia in two smaller craft, it took Broughton a week to discern the right conditions—circumscribed by tides, shifting winds and shoals, and constant squalls—to get beyond Cape Disappointment and back out into the ocean. Even as late as 1841, the British trader Edward Belcher told Charles Wilkes that the only salutary time for mariners to visit the Northwest coast was in the summer.[18]

Broughton shared his predicament with British shipmaster James Baker (for whom the bay is named) of the trading vessel *Jenny,* which was lying at anchor just inside Cape Disappointment. Baker reported to Broughton that "a constant succession of bad weather had prevented his putting to sea; that he had made several attempts, but from the violence of the surf and its breaking intirely across the entrance, he had not been able to effect that purpose." Not coincidentally, Broughton and Baker were made captive to coastal conditions from 4–11 November 1792, thirteen years to the week before Lewis and Clark were similarly marooned at Dismal Nitch. Edward Bell of the *Chatham* offered a summative assessment: north of the 40th parallel along the Pacific Coast in the fall and winter "the very worst of weather is always experienced." [19]

One wonders what Lewis might have written about his trip to and beyond Cape Disappointment, which venture would have included an unobstructed view of the earth's widest ocean. As the most accomplished of all the journal writers, would Lewis have been inspired to write passages that could compete with the literary grandeur of his exploits on the Missouri River or at the Continental Divide? Sadly, we have no text from Lewis equal to his incantations of the legacy of Columbus or Cook upon leaving Fort Mandan; no evocations of "visionary inchantment" or "sublimely grand specticle" of the Great Falls or the "most distant fountain of the waters of the mighty Missouri." Whatever Meriwether Lewis said or thought when he walked that sandy stretch of the Long Beach peninsula is lost to the mists of time. If Lewis were writing, one could only speculate about how differently the popular understanding of the expedition's conclusive westward phase would have come down through history. We can assume that with regard to the popular perception of the expedition, Columbia River stories and the end of voyage drama would be far better known, many not having been "discovered" until this century as a function of scholarly data mining in the modern edition of the journals. We can also infer from his silence that the Columbia was a far more difficult stream for Lewis to assimilate. Alas, what should have proved the culminating moment of an American epic, without Lewis, becomes, in Clark's hand, a hard and depressing camping trip.[20]

However, as noted in an earlier chapter, whatever William Clark's limitations as a litterateur, he was an accomplished geographer. In a startlingly understated passage given its relevance to the geographic scope of the expedition, William Clark noted on 17 November that he "Surveyed a little" on the sandy beach before him and "made Some observns [observations]". Clark's "little" survey would prove to be an emblematic moment for the entire enterprise because it facilitated creation of a noteworthy map and also suggested to Clark the most fitting name for the camp that marked the end of the voyage. In short, acting as he so often did as the expedition's historian, Clark brought out his surveying equipment to cartographically fix the summit of their great western voyage.[21]

The specifics of Clark's survey are found in their published form in the most recent edition of the journals amidst the larger body of Fort Clatsop documentation. As Gary Moulton points out, the survey data were oriented upsides-down in relation to the accompanying narrative text of 7 December 1805, suggesting that on November 17th Clark simply leafed ahead to some empty pages in his elkskin-bound journal and recorded his Station Camp measurements there. By December 7th he had filled up the intervening spaces in the log. In any event, from these notes Clark would later be able to compose his detailed map of the pivotal north bank of the Columbia River's mouth, including his signature ideogram pointing directly to the location of Station Camp.[22]

Topographic surveys are conducted, then as now, by means of geometric triangulation. By creating base lines of established length (through the use of "chains," an early version of measuring tapes) and then "turning angles" on fixed points of observation, it is possible to determine the length of the other two sides of the triangle. Thus Clark could calculate the distance from the "observatory" to the

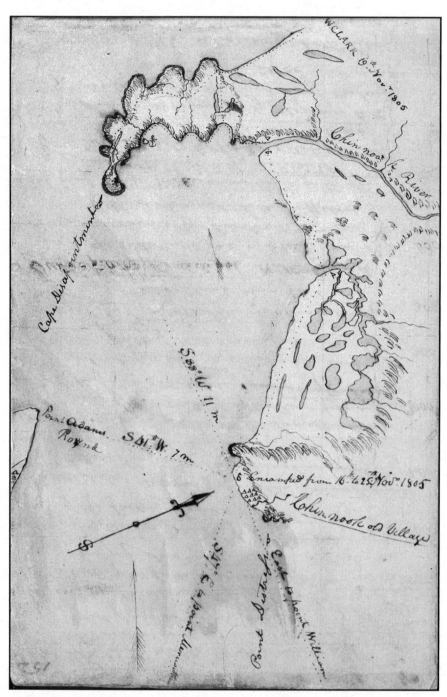

William Clark's map of the north bank of the Columbia at its junction with the Pacific, complete with his characteristic ideogram pointing to Station Camp, documents the importance of this place as "trail's end." (American Philosophical Society)

"point of observation." In practical terms, this is how Clark was able to measure the width of the Columbia River's estuary.[23]

The term "observatory" looms large in the history of exploration. All great explorers, from the greatest of the age, James Cook, who preceded Lewis and Clark, to those like Charles Wilkes who succeeded them, established observatories so that they might scientifically establish the precise location of significant places on the planet. Their maps specifically inscribed the location of "observatories." This mathematically based model of exploration was essentially created by Cook and practiced during his three great voyages to the Pacific during the third quarter of the eighteenth century. Cook's efforts, historian William Goetzmann notes, made him a great national hero in Great Britain, including a membership in the Royal Society and formal audiences with King George III. The several Pacific Ocean voyages of Cook, with their contingents of artists and scientists, created an entire curriculum of exploratory techniques—keeping a journal, sketching headlands and other landmarks, cataloging plants and animals, and especially creating maps using scientific methods of cartography. Combining the attributes of both the explorer and the storyteller (think of an imaginary hybrid figure of Neil Armstrong and Walter Cronkite), Cook became the best-known man in the Western world. At the time of his death, one of Cook's contemporaries referred to his tragic demise in Hawaii as "a great loss to the Universe." In emulation of Cook, all the other great empires of Europe—France, Spain, and Russia—dispatched their own worldwide voyages of exploration, also focusing on the Pacific.[24]

William Goetzmann has referred to this wave of scientific exploration as the "Second Great Age of Discovery," and Cook was its exemplar, much as Columbus was the prototypical figure of the first age. (Lewis would refer to both on the day the expedition ventured into terra incognita.) Thomas Jefferson, as a man of the Enlightenment whose larger ethos presumed it was possible to rationally understand and typify the world, was versed in the great intellectual excitement created by Cook and his successors—notably George Vancouver and Alexander Mackenzie. Indeed, in his confidential message to Congress of 18 January 1803 requesting an authorizing appropriation for the venture that became the Expedition for Northwestern Discovery, Jefferson played upon the honor of the young United States relative to this international context. The president wrote:

> While other civilized nations have encountered great expense to enlarge the boundaries of knowledge, by undertaking voyages of discovery, & for other literary purposes, in various parts and directions, our nation seems to owe to the same object, as well as its own interest, to explore this, the only line of easy communication across the continent, and so directly traversing our own part of it.

In effect, Lewis's extended training in Philadelphia before the start of the voyage was an attempt to school him in the methodology that Cook and his mentor from the Royal Society, Sir Joseph Banks, had created. However, the effective division of labor resulted in Clark becoming the expedition's cartographer. It was in keeping with Cook's still then new model of exploration that Clark set about creating a scientific record for the location of the expedition's terminal westward camp.[25]

Clark had previously conducted a host of such surveys during the voyage. The one establishing the location of Station Camp was merely the last in a series of them; none was conducted on the return trip. The first survey employing the chain and compass assayed the confluence of the Ohio and Mississippi Rivers in November 1803. During the spring and summer of exploration in 1804, Clark got his instruments out with some regularity, measuring the widths of the Gasconade, Osage, and Kansas Rivers at their confluences with the Missouri. (He also used his chain to help compute the time it took for a stick to float a certain distance, yielding a calculation on flow velocity.) Clark also surveyed what he termed an "antient fortification," a feature in Nebraska since determined to have been a natural sandstone formation. On the more westerly end of the trip, Clark measured the width of the Missouri at Fort Mandan, the Yellowstone and Missouri Rivers at their confluence, plus those of the Musselshell and Marias. Clark's most extensive survey was that of the portage route around the Great Falls of the Missouri and of the falls themselves. The latter effort took three full days and was the only one more complicated than his work at Station Camp. The Three Forks of the Missouri was a likely candidate for triangulation, but Clark was laid up at that juncture with an ulcerous ankle and related maladies. As noted in an earlier chapter, Clark also used his chain and protractor to measure the width of the Columbia and its junction with the Snake.[26]

Clark's survey at the coast commenced at the mouth of the first creek he noted when rounding Point Distress. To set out his lines of sight he used the open expanses of that beautiful sandy beach so often mentioned in the journals. (The alternative was to clear a path through brush, which was both unnecessary and would have taken a lot of time.) The first high tide at Station Camp on November 17th occurred at approximately 10:15 a.m. The ordering of his day indicates that Clark conducted astronomical observations at noon, which scientific protocol would have dictated. Lewis arrived from Cape Disappointment at 1:30 p.m., and it was after his fellow commander's arrival that Clark makes mention of his survey. With the tide at full ebb by 5:00 p.m., Clark would have used the remaining daylight (sunset is 4:46 p.m. at that latitude on said date) for his mapping exercise upon the now-widening beach.[27]

Moving on a westerly path across the sand, Clark, with the assistance of at least two men, measured out incremental distances in "poles" (using a two- pole chain Lewis had secured in Philadelphia, thirty-three feet in length), where several "Stakes" were driven into the ground. From these stakes, or "stations" in surveying parlance, Clark swept east to west with his gaze and established directional bearings on all the major landmarks, or benchmarks, on the lower Columbia. (The term benchmark relates to verticality and is more conventionally understood and used colloquially than the corresponding term for movement across a horizontal plane: stations.) In succession, Clark went through a series of sightings of present Tongue Point ("Point William"); Smith Point ("Point Meriwether") in present day Astoria, Oregon; Saddle Mountain behind it; Point Adams; and lastly Cape Disappointment, almost due west on the north bank of the river but across the expanse of Baker Bay.[28]

Because the principles of geometry are unchangeable, it's possible to reconstruct Clark's survey. Since Clark planted a stake "at Camp" one can determine, with reasonable exactitude, the location of where the voyage had come to an end. A modern surveyor merely has to measure westward (in "poles" converted to feet) from the first "Stake." Obviously inspired by one of the most detailed of his few terrestrial surveys, Clark named the expedition's western terminus "Station Camp" when compiling the final record of the distances covered from Fort Mandan to Cape Disappointment.[29]

Starting from the first and largest creek west of Point Distress, Clark placed two stakes, the second of which was at the abandoned Chinook village. From this town Clark measured out yet another stake South 84 degrees west to a distance of sixty-eight poles. *Journals* editor Moulton in his transcription was unable to make out the next word. Having viewed Clark's original notes at the Missouri Historical Society (MHS), and with the aide of a magnifying glass, an MHS archivist and I determined that the word appears to be "creek." From this small stream (which appears on Clark's draft field map) he bore "N 89° West 94 Poles." Here he placed the "Stake at Camp." Adding the two increments (68 + 94) yields a distance of 162 poles. A pole equals 5.029 meters. Thus we know the village that the explorers raided for wood was 814.7 meters or 2,673 feet (or almost exactly the half a mile Clark estimated by dead reckoning beforehand) east of Station Camp. When converted to the modern landscape, Station Camp is found to land a hundred yards east of St. Mary's Catholic Church in the roadside town of McGowan, Washington. Once a nondescript wayside, Station Camp is now arguably one of the most important sites on the Lewis and Clark trail, having been made a unit of the Lewis and Clark National Historical Park in 2004. Its elevated status is one of the principal outcomes of the recently completed bicentennial of the expedition.[30]

The detail and consistency of Clark's record, however arcane at first glance, are of immense importance. The one essential aspect of the Lewis and Clark Expedition was its geographic scope. Clark's survey at Station Camp was highly symbolic, as it typified the expedition's practice of following the new procedures of scientific exploration. Lewis had advised Clark, in the letter inviting him to join the venture, that the scientific aspects of the mission would be of interest to not merely the United States but "the world generally." Thomas Jefferson, who had the first word on this expedition, uttered what was nearly his last on the subject in 1816. The most important justification "due to the public," Jefferson wrote, "depends on these astronomical observations, as from them alone can be obtained the correct geography of the country, which was the main object of the expedition."[31]

Americans today, having been born or matured in a country that has been the most prosperous and powerful in the history of the world, do not have a sense of the contingent nature of history. As historical amnesiacs, we look back into the past through the lens of the intervening successes and national accomplishment. We think, all too cavalierly, that because of our contemporary prowess it was always thus for America. It is worth remembering that the nation that commissioned these captains was merely in its twentieth year of recognized independence from Great Britain when Meriwether Lewis received his instructions from Thomas Jefferson. And the country's future was by no means certain or guaranteed. Indeed, a few short years after Lewis and Clark's return, the nation's capital was sacked by British troops, and Jefferson's successor's wife (Dolley Madison) would cut a portrait of George Washington out of its frame in the White House to preserve it for posterity. The informed opinion of much of the Western world was that Americans were rustic rabble-rousers, with no literature or artistic tradition to speak of—an impression these early Americans were extremely self-conscious about, including Jefferson.[32]

Though no small amount of lore has grown up around Lewis and Clark, certain of their accomplishments within the context of their own time are perhaps *under*appreciated. A singular example is Clark's contributions to geographic comprehension, work that he reveled in. In his correspondence back to the United States, written a few days before the expedition took leave of Fort Mandan heading west, Clark rendered what might be termed the return address for that establishment—its latitude and longitude plus its distance in river miles from St. Louis. Similarly, then, Clark named the terminal westward camp using the nomenclature of mathematics and scientific observation.[33]

Lewis and Clark had successfully competed in the great intellectual contest of their era—scientific exploration—with the likes of Cook, Vancouver, La Pérouse, Malaspina, and Alexander Mackenzie. Theirs was a magnificent achievement, and one not lost on those of their countrymen who were attentive to such things. In a letter to his friends at the American Philosophical Society, Jefferson later gloried in the expedition's additions to "our knolege of the geography & natural history of our country, from the Missisipi to the Pacific." The common citizens of Fincastle, Virginia, in their toast to Lewis and Clark upon their safe return, touted the captains' explorations of "bold & unknown rivers." "You have the further satisfaction," this salutation continued, "to reflect that, you have extended the knowledge of the Geography of your country [and] in other respects enriched Science." In reply, Clark acknowledged that "the expedition has been productive of those advantages to our country, Geography, and science that you are willing to imagine." [34]

CHAPTER 13   Following Mackenzie,
the Protocols of
Exploration, and the
Conventions of the
Travel Narrative

ON THE EVENING OF 17 NOVEMBER 1805, FOLLOWING AN
afternoon of surveying, William Clark asked his mates at Station Camp if there
was anyone "who wished to See *more* of the Ocean" (emphasis added), indicating
Clark thought he was on the Pacific despite being ten miles inland. (The same
view today is deceiving because the jetty from Oregon's Point Adams protrudes in
a northwesterly direction into the ocean proper nearly six miles, creating a sense
of enclosure at the bar of the Columbia that was not present 200 years ago.) Clark
reported that two-thirds of the expedition was "Contented with what part of the
Ocean & its curiosities which Could be Seen from the vicinity of our Camp." This
contentment also suggests that a distinct majority of the party was worn out, with
little appetite for exploring.[1]

Ten men accompanied Clark on the sojourn to the "main Ocian" the next day,
including Sgts. John Ordway and Nathaniel Pryor, the Field brothers, George
Shannon, John Colter, Toussaint Charbonneau, and York. Proceeding west along
the north bank Clark continued taking course and distance notes, including an
eastward back sighting of "Camp Point," to facilitate mapping. Reaching the area
between "a bluff of yellow Clay" (still visible from the Port of Ilwaco) and the
foot of Cape Disappointment, Clark noted this was the area "in which the nativs
inform us the Ships anchor, and from whence they receive their goods in return
for their peltries." Clark's maps of this vicinity depict symbols of anchors or ships
in the deep arm of Baker Bay.[2]

At this harbor Clark "found Capt Lewis name on a tree," his partner having
preceded him to this spot by four days. Whether he had foreknowledge of Lewis's
mark or was surprised to stumble upon it, we don't know, but Clark was at any

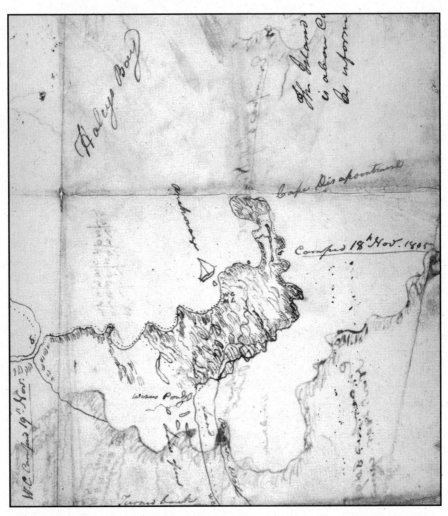

William Clark's field sketch of Cape Disappointment shows the location of where both captains inscribed their names on trees, according to exploratory convention and in emulation of Mackenzie's behavior. See initials "WC" and "ML" in the center of the image, near the ship in the "anchorage." (Yale Collection of Western Americana, Beinecke Rare Book and Manuscript Library)

rate quick to follow Lewis's lead by engraving his "name & by land the day of the month and year, as also Several of the men." Lewis had probably chosen this tree initially because of its proximity to the preferred anchorage of the intermittent coastal traders. We know from other sources that similar inscriptions had been left by mariners from New England at this anchorage. Lewis could have been inspired by such marks, but as much if not more likely, his intention was wrapped up in the imperial nexus that was always the subtext of the western third of the voyage. Carving his name into a tree would nominally prove the success of his and Clark's voyage across the continent to any subsequent passerby, plus serve as a sign of incipient American sovereignty. We don't know the specific nature of Lewis's mark other than his name, but Clark consciously modeled his inscription after the notation left by a Scotsman on a rock at Bella Coola on the British Columbia coast which read: "Alexander Mackenzie, from Canada, by land, the twenty-second of July, one thousand seven hundred and nintey-three." [3]

The figure of Alexander Mackenzie, a fur trader for the Canadian-based North West Company, is regularly invoked by historians in relation to the origins of the Expedition for Northwestern Discovery. Less appreciated is how his geographical memoir, *Voyages from Montreal*, intersects with the story line of the Lewis and Clark Expedition once the Americans were in the field. In many respects it appears that *Voyages* served as a veritable trail guide and forecast of events to come. The American explorers emulated a number of Mackenzie's tactics, as any frontiersman may have been expected to deploy, but in addition the captains often echoed, and, as we saw earlier in regard to William Clark at the forks of the Columbia, even plagiarized many textual passages. Marking trees was merely the most obvious example of Mackenzie's influence. [4]

Mackenzie's report of his successive voyages to the Arctic in 1789 and the Pacific in 1793 first appeared in print in London in October 1801. Thomas Jefferson read Mackenzie's narrative in 1802. By all accounts the president was prompted into the venture that became the Lewis and Clark Expedition by reading Mackenzie's strategic flourish in the volume's concluding paragraphs. Drawing on his own, James Cook's, and George Vancouver's surveys, Mackenzie described an imperial vision based on the determination that the Columbia River was the key "line of communication… pointed out by nature" between the Atlantic and Pacific Oceans. Furthermore, "its banks also form… the most Northern situation fit for colonization, and suitable to the residence of a civilized people. By opening this intercourse between the Atlantic and Pacific Oceans, and forming regular establishments through the interior, and at both extremes… the entire command of the fur trade of North America might be obtained." [5]

The fur trade now seems merely a quaint relic of a more colorful age. In Jefferson's time Mackenzie's vision was a grave threat to American commercial aspirations because the Scotsman painted his imperial picture in starkly competitive terms. The fur trade, he said, was a "field for commercial enterprise, and incalculable would be the produce of it, when supported by the operations of that credit and capital which Great Britain so pre-eminently possesses." This strategic plan would preempt the "American adventurers," Mackenzie sneered, "who without regularity or capital, or the desire of conciliatory future confidence, look altogether to the interest of the moment." [6]

As we have noted in earlier chapters, Lewis and Clark had a copy of Mackenzie's *Voyages* with them and referred to it often, especially at times when they were doing geographic problem-solving. Lewis and Clark refer to tribes that they did not encounter but Mackenzie did and cite technical information about the fur trade they also secured from the Nor' Wester's account. Indeed, on a somewhat routine basis, Mackenzie's narrative either informed or appears to have anticipated some of the more interesting passages found in the journals of Lewis and Clark, always without acknowledgment. [7]

For example, William Clark, in his journal for the first full day of travel after leaving Fort Clatsop in the spring of 1806, mysteriously refers to Captain Cook's conclusion that Native canoes on the Northwest coast had human teeth embedded in their surface for decorative purposes. Clark proceeded to criticize Cook for not paying close attention to detail because two canoes he and Lewis saw were festooned with shells, not teeth. This is a puzzle because it seems unlikely that Clark had read Cook's narrative. Copies of Cook's journals would have been extremely rare in the frontier culture Clark grew up and matured in. Lewis may have scanned Cook's account during his studies in Philadelphia or at Jefferson's home on Monticello. It's possible Lewis lent this insight to Clark in the field, though this, too, is doubtful because Lewis, who more readily associated himself with great explorers and was writing again by this time, would have been likelier to mention this first in his own journal. Instead, he is silent on the subject. However, it was not Cook directly but rather Mackenzie who provided the insight that was the source of Clark's observation. Mackenzie noted in *Voyages from Montreal* that Cook reported "the people of the sea-coast adorned their canoes with human teeth." Mackenzie then added that Cook "was mistaken: but his mistake arose from the great resemblance there is between human teeth and those of the sea-otter." Thus, Clark slyly appropriated Mackenzie's corrective insight about Cook but kept Mackenzie's origination of this information hidden. [8]

The presence in the Lewis and Clark account of many narrative conventions and literary tropes common to the history of discovery reveals that the captains, while not always directly imitating Mackenzie, were as apt students of exploratory protocol as the Scotsman himself was. Consider Lewis's acquisition of a dog to accompany him on the voyage, a staple in juvenile literature about the expedition. Like Lewis's "Seaman" of the Newfoundland breed, Mackenzie's pet appears in the narrative hunting, patrolling, acting playful, and, rather melodramatically, getting lost. To be sure, this canine-companion-to-the-explorer tradition actually preceded Mackenzie and lasted many more decades after Lewis. The mascot phenomenon was an affectation of Enlightenment-era exploration that may have been a vestige of the chivalric tradition of the medieval manor. John Meares also had a Newfoundland dog named "Towser", and Charles Wilkes, during his circumnavigation of the globe for the United States starting in the late 1830s, had a Newfoundland named "Sydney". Thus, the lovable "Seaman" was a sentimentally endearing but hardly unusual aspect of exploration that the lore of LEWIS & CLARK promotes. Lewis, like Mackenzie, probably thought of having a dog along for the trip as a necessary accessory for the fashionable explorer.[9]

One author speculates that Lewis and Clark changed their wardrobe on 8 November 1805 at Pillar Rock in anticipation of a ceremonial arrival at the end of their voyage or an encounter with the captain of a fur-trading vessel. This is conceivable, and if true, may have been inspired by *Voyages*, wherein Mackenzie described preparations for a "becoming appearance" at a post. Composing an impressive arrival scene was very much a tradition in the fur trade, one adapted from Native practice. Shortly before his arrival at the Pacific, Mackenzie shaved and changed his "linen," his mates following this "humanising example." The explorer David Thompson, several years after Lewis and Clark, reported that his party "Staid 'till 6:25 Am shaving & arranging ourselves" the day they expected to reach Fort Astoria. This custom, like the obligatory canine companion, lasted well into the nineteenth century as well. John C. Frémont and his men, prior to their return to Fort Laramie in 1842, shaved and put on their finest clothes, in Frémont's case his dress blue uniform. On a subsequent expedition to the Oregon Country, Frémont shaved prior to his arrival at Fort Vancouver. Lewis and Clark may have had similar intentions. Alternatively, in the Biddle narrative Clark asserts the change of clothes at Pillar Rock was the function of a more quotidian concern: their garments were simply wet. [10]

Though Meriwether Lewis was always more intent on living up to the role and expectations of an explorer in the tradition of a Columbus or Cook, it was Clark who was particularly bent on emulating Mackenzie's inscription. Whereas Lewis appears to have marked his name on trees only twice that we know of, Clark did so more than a dozen times during the course of the expedition, one of which is still extant on Pompeys Pillar. (For this last inscription on the Yellowstone, Clark actually used the same type of red paint that Mackenzie employed at Bella Coola.) Stephen Ambrose has argued that Lewis took Mackenzie's signature on a rock at the Pacific as "a direct, open, irresistible challenge." While there is no documentary evidence to support this assertion, it was at any rate William Clark who more intently subscribed to this protocol, probably as much to join Lewis in making exploratory claims as to counter Mackenzie.[11]

Historians have always been more intrigued by Meriwether Lewis's idiosyncrasies, but this one of Clark's merits some extended attention. Thomas Slaughter theorized that Lewis and Clark repeatedly inscribed their names at the coast for self-assurance in light of the supposedly "devastating news" that other explorers had reached the mouth of the Columbia River before they did. Slaughter conjoins this implausible notion with the equally dubious assertion that Lewis and Clark hid their knowledge of Vancouver from prospective readers of their account.

In truth, as far to the east as Wallula Gap, Clark made references to the cartography of the Vancouver expedition and did so regularly thereafter. Furthermore, Meriwether Lewis made copies of Vancouver's charts when he was preparing for the expedition in Philadelphia. He could hardly have been surprised that English-speaking people had beaten him to the Columbia estuary.[12]

Far more credible than Slaughter's explanation is a straightforward imperial theory. John Logan Allen observed that the acquisition of Mackenzie's *Voyages* for the expedition's library was more meaningful for Clark than for Lewis. The reason, Allen argued, is that Lewis had been a student of continental geography long before the expedition, while to Clark much of Mackenzie's account would have been revelatory. Even more directly, William Goetzmann, the eminent scholar of American exploration history, writes, "Despite Clark's scientific dedication, imperial rivalries were not far from his mind." As a westerner growing up on a rabidly anti-British frontier, this would have been a common outlook.[13]

Whatever else might be said about it, Clark's scrawling rejoinder to Mackenzie at the Pacific Ocean was intentionally transparent to anyone versed in the practice of exploration and the literature of discovery. Such may not be said for Lewis's use of Mackenzie. Stephen Beckham notes that a "faint echo" of Mackenzie can be found in Lewis's miscellaneous reports dispatched from Fort Mandan. Indeed, Lewis regularly borrowed from Mackenzie in both the structure of his narrative and the style of his prose. Although the scientific ethos of the Enlightenment was the emergent cultural fashion of the late eighteenth century of Cook, Vancouver, Mackenzie, and Jefferson, there were other, still vibrant, intellectual currents. Meriwether Lewis came to maturity in an era Percy Adams once characterized as "an age of plagiarism," a period in history when extensive borrowing from the works of others was not the offense it is considered today. This is an oft-overlooked tradition, one mostly ignored by historians of Lewis and Clark, resulting in a naïve understanding of the literary construction of the Lewis's journals. [14]

Meriwether Lewis is now well known for his spotty journal keeping and, subsequent to the completion of the voyage, writer's block. That someone who struggled with his writing should have secretly sought the aid of another author should hardly seem surprising. If a colorful narrative was part of what an explorer was expected to deliver to his waiting audience, what, really, was such a struggling writer like Lewis to do? Even so gifted and prolific an author as Thomas Jefferson structured his natural history of Virginia on the model created by Major Robert Rogers' *A Concise Account of North America*. Jefferson merely organized his narrative sections after Rogers, demonstrating what Pamela Regis terms "a continuity of tradition" forming the literary style of early North American natural histories. Lewis borrowed structure from Mackenzie, too, and occasionally substance.[15]

Consider first one of Lewis's most romantic passages, the oft-quoted paragraphs written on the occasion of the expedition's departure from Fort Mandan in April 1805. Comparing his venture with those of Columbus and Cook, Lewis admitted to giving vent to his imagination, which wandered "into futurity."

The picture in his mind "was a most pleasing one.[E]ntertaining as I do, the most confident hope of succeeding in a voyage which had formed a *da[r]ling project* of mine for the last ten years, I could but esteem this moment of my departure as among the most happy of my life" (emphasis added).[16]

With a whole winter to prepare for the construction of this entry, Lewis carefully contemplated its composition. After all, he had not written a daily note since the previous February and even then only because Clark went downriver with half the men on a hunting expedition and somebody had to keep the Fort Mandan chronology. With Alexander Mackenzie's *Voyages* on hand, he would have read the Scotsman's thoughtful reflection on an equally propitious moment—the abandonment of what was thought the Columbia River for an alternate overland route to the Pacific Ocean in June 1793. On that occasion Mackenzie wrote of "contriving means to bring about a reconciliation with the natives, which alone would enable me to procure guides, without whose assistance it would be impossible for me to proceed, when my *darling project* would end in disappointment" (emphasis added).[17]

In the succession of key events on the voyage west from Fort Mandan, the echo of Mackenzie's voice and the modeling of his behavior continues to be heard and seen again and again. Now, to be sure, in the course of consecutive crossings of the continent in corridors separated in some places by only several hundred miles, English-speaking explorers would inevitably have similar experiences and express them in conventional literary terms common to their culture. Still, it is clear from a careful reading of their journals the two captains were consulting *Voyages* frequently. They felt such anxiety about this dependency on a rival (Mackenzie) that they could not and did not acknowledge him.

Consider first the dramatic assessment at the confluence of the Marias River with the Missouri. Lewis and Clark insisted, against the opinion of every other member of the party, that what the captains referred to as the "South" fork of the Missouri was the main stem of the river. Clark and Lewis each made an initial reconnaissance—Clark of the Missouri and Lewis of the Marias—to analyze the situation. In the end, the men swallowed their reservations and fell into line behind the captains. In his memorable description of this moment, Lewis wrote that the men of the detachment "said very cheerfully that they were ready to follow us any wher[e] we thought proper to direct but that they still thought that the other was the river." [18]

In several instances Mackenzie used nearly identical tactics and language to describe the same group dynamic. For example, at the Arctic in the summer of 1789, when doubt crept into the minds of his men about whether they would ever reach the sea, circumstances dictated that Mackenzie try to boost morale. He assured them that the expedition would soon reach the ocean. In response, the men, Mackenzie wrote, "declare themselves now and at any time ready to go with me wherever I choose to lead them." Years later, after Mackenzie crossed the Continental Divide on the voyage to the Pacific, discretion required abandoning

Alexander Mackenzie, painted here by Thomas Lawrence ca. 1800. Mackenzie's *Voyages from Montreal* served as the comparative backdrop to the Lewis and Clark Expedition. (Thomas Lawrence, "Sir Alexander Mackenzie", c. 1800, National Gallery of Canada, Ottawa)

the idea of a southerly voyage down the Columbia (really the Fraser) in favor of an overland trail to the west. Once again, after a verbal appeal to "their fortitude, patience, and perseverance," Mackenzie's men "unanimously assured me, that they were as willing now as they had ever been, to abide by my resolutions, whatever they might be, and to follow me wherever I should go." [19]

Arguably, the most storied passage in the entirety of Meriwether Lewis's oeuvre is his nearly poetic description of the Great Falls of the Missouri. Attempting to paint a picture with words, Lewis wrote some of his most memorable lines. A few shall suffice. The first set of falls Lewis happened upon were, he said, "the grandest sight I ever beheld,... the water in it's passage down... assumes a thousand forms in a moment sometimes flying up in jets of sparkling foam." Adjoining the falls there was "a handsom little bottom of about three acres which is deversified and agreeably shaded with some cottonwood trees;" plus "a few small cedar grow near the ledge of rocks where I rest." Lewis marveled at "the reflection of the sun on the spray or mist which arrises from these falls" and the "beatiful rainbow produced which adds not a little to the beauty of this majestically grand senery." The next day, as Lewis continued his solo tour of the falls, he came to another cascade which he billed "one of the most beatifull objects in nature." Comparing the two, Lewis concluded that this second of "two great rivals for glory... was *pleasingly beautifull*, while the other was *sublimely grand*." [20]

Working in the genre of the international travel narrative, Lewis knew he was expected to see and describe wonders of nature. Not knowing upon reaching the Great Falls that he would see more spectacular sights, he strained to apply every colorful phrase his mind could compose. Mackenzie had similar encounters with the sublime. His history of the fur trade that introduced the personal accounts of travels to the Arctic and Pacific Oceans in *Voyages* contained a comparably exotic scene: the Methy Portage near the present northern border between Saskatchewan and Alberta. At this divide between the Hudson Bay and Mackenzie River drainages, the Scotsman reflected on the view presented by the Clearwater River where it flows into the Athabasca. The final precipice of the portage, Mackenzie wrote, "rises upwards of a thousand feet above the plain beneath it, commands a most extensive, romantic and ravishing prospect." This valley, he continued, "at once refreshed and adorned by [the river], is about three miles in breadth,... displaying a most delightful intermixture of wood and lawn, and stretching on till the blue mist obscures the prospect." "Nor," Mackenzie concluded, "when I beheld this wonderful display of uncultivated nature, was the moving scenery of human occupation wanting to complete the picture." [21]

In his famous coda to the romantic grandeur of the falls, Lewis wrote that on reviewing his text he became so "disgusted with the imperfect idea which it conveyed of the scene that I determined to draw my pen across it and begin agin." Lewis wished that he "might be enabled to give to the enlightened world some just idea of this truly magnificent and sublimely grand object." Lewis's putative limitations regarding the inexpressibility of natural wonders, a literary tactic intended to create a sense of drama, were not unique; indeed, as a rhetorical device it was so standard in travel literature as to become cliché. In the spring of 1793, shortly after starting on his ascent of the Peace River, Mackenzie had his own epiphany in nature, a few days east of the present British Columbia-Alberta border. The river "displayed a succession of the most beautiful scenery I had ever beheld... . This magnificent theatre of nature has all the decorations which the trees and animals of the country can afford it....The whole country displayed an exuberant verdure; the trees that bear a blossom were advancing fast to that delightful appearance, and the velvet rind of their branches reflecting the oblique rays of a rising or setting sun, added a splendid gaeity to the scene, which no expressions of mine are qualified to describe." [22]

An inadequacy of language struck Mackenzie again on the return from the Pacific. Reflecting on their "homeward journey," Mackenzie and his companions gazed out on the scene before them. He wrote, "Such was the depth of the precipices below, and the height of the mountains above, with the rude and wild magnificence of the scenery around, that I shall not attempt to describe such an astonishing and awful combination of objects; of which, indeed, no description can convey an adequate idea." [23]

Alexander Mackenzie revisited this theme at the conclusion of his account. Returning to the fort from which he had commenced his voyage, he observed, "Here my voyages of discovery terminate. Their toils and their dangers, their solicitudes and sufferings, have not been exaggerated in my description. On the contrary, in many instances, language has failed me in the attempt to describe them." Thus, Meriwether Lewis's conceptualization of his encounter with the sublime, or perceived limitations related thereto, drew on a literary tradition that Mackenzie, among others, also employed routinely. [24]

Similarly, there are experiences in Mackenzie's *Voyages* that prefigure several aspects of the now-mythic story of Lewis at Lemhi Pass. Reporting on the geographical information provided by Cameahwait about the country west of the divide, Lewis said the "information fell far short of my expectation or wishes." The Salmon River to the west "was obstructed by sharp pointed rocks and the rapidity of the stream such that the whole surface of the river was beat into a perfect foam as far as the eye could reach." Likewise, when Mackenzie reached the Continental Divide at a more northerly intersection twelve years earlier, he also heard reports that "could not be more unfavourable or discouraging." Mackenzie, like Lewis and Clark years later, was eventually convinced by Indian informants of the advisability of abandoning the dream of a quick river descent to the ocean and proceeding overland instead. [25]

Nor is the beloved LEWIS & CLARK story of Lewis's "fraturnal" or "national hug" with the Shoshone unique. Mackenzie experienced a remarkably similar gesture. On his final push to the Pacific, Mackenzie came to what he called the "Great Village." He started his greeting by shaking hands but soon a succession of villagers took him serially in their arms. "These embraces," Mackenzie related, "which at first rather surprised me, I soon found to be marks of regard and friendship." At this village, Mackenzie's flattering reception was capped by the chief presenting "a very handsome robe of a sea-otter skin, which he had on, and covered me with." This scene, of course, is echoed in the popular episode within the Lemhi epic when Cameahwait adorned Lewis with his tippet, an object the captain prized so much he had his portrait drawn wearing it. This is not to suggest that Lewis extrapolated this incident from Mackenzie's account or invented it. Rather, it is offered to show that what at first glance or in isolation appears to be an exceptional incident is, within a comparative context of continental exploration, anything but. Both stories are strongly suggestive of what might be termed the deeply internalized structure of first encounters as composed through time by Western civilization.[26]

Lewis also appears to have studied Mackenzie's stratagem of securing Indian support of the expedition in the short term with promises of trade in the long run. Mackenzie once told a group of Native people that if he secured help at that moment, he would return himself "or send others to them, with such articles as they appeared to want: particularly arms and ammunition, with which they would be able to prevent their enemies from invading them." Correspondingly, Lewis told Cameahwait "that after our finally returning to our homes towards the rising sun whitemen would come to them with an abundance of guns and every other article necessary to their defence and comfort, and that they would be enabled to supply themselves with these articles on reasonable terms." The Shoshone, Lewis stated, "expressed great pleasure at this information and said they had been long anxious to see the whitemen that traded guns; and that we might rest assured of their friendship." [27]

Lewis's Lemhi script echoes parallel moments in Mackenzie's discourse with remarkable fidelity. When Lewis returned to the Missouri side of the divide with Cameahwait and a band of Shoshone to meet Clark and the rest of the party, he reported that "every article about us appeared to excite astonishment in their minds." This phrase is reminiscent of the episode when Mackenzie crossed the divide and found himself on the upper reaches of what would later be named the Fraser River, recording that the resident Indians observed "every thing about us, with a mixture of admiration and astonishment." Lewis remarked that the Shoshone even admired the "segacity" of "Seaman", using the same favored descriptor Mackenzie often employed for his canine companion.[28]

Because Lewis ceased writing on the westbound voyage at the Nez Perce villages, Clark's account provides the principal voice of the expedition to its terminus at the ocean. As we saw in an earlier chapter, Clark indisputably plagiarized *Voyages from Montreal* and Mackenzie for content associated with his description of Native people when he reached the forks of the Columbia. Also noted earlier, Lewis made no known record of his motivations or findings when he left Clark at Dismal Nitch, but we can guess that Mackenzie was part of the equation. In a post-expeditionary letter the artist Charles Willson Peale wrote to a friend after painting Lewis's portrait (which would have availed much conversation), Peale seems to have been impressed upon with one salient fact: whereas "McKinsey only went to a River which ran into the South Sea," Lewis and Clark actually visited the ocean.[29]

After his literary lapse during the westbound third of the journey, Lewis resumed his journal-keeping on the eastbound voyage, and there we find yet another instance where the experience, if not the voice, of Mackenzie resonates in the journals. In June of 1806 Lewis concluded that it would be "madnes" to proceed through the snow-choked Bitterroots without a guide. Accordingly, the detachment returned to the prairie at Weippe, which, Lewis determined, was the first retreat or "retrograde march" the expedition had been compelled to make. In describing the mood in camp that night, Lewis said, "the party were a good deel dejected tho' not as I had apprehended they would have been." Comparably, thirteen years earlier Mackenzie had reluctantly concluded that his voyage down what he believed to be the Columbia could not proceed any farther. Worse, he and his men had to retrace a considerable distance in order to hit the jumping-off point for the trail that would eventually lead them to the ocean at Bella Coola. Mackenzie was distressed at this turn of events because, as he wrote, "in a voyage of this kind, a retrograde motion could not fail to cool the ardour, slacken the zeal, and weaken the confidence" of the party.[30]

Students of the Expedition for Northwestern Discovery know that the stories of Mackenzie and Lewis crossed again in David McKeehan's acid critique of the latter's ego and accomplishments. Defending the right of his client, Sgt. Patrick Gass, to publish what Lewis considered an unauthorized account of the expedition, McKeehan asserted that many facets of Lewis's "darling project" had been exaggerated. McKeehan published his complaint as an open letter to Lewis in a Pittsburgh newspaper dated 14 April 1807, occupying an entire page of print. Of the several streams of McKeehan's thinking, what most interests us here is his observation on the one point that was touted with the greatest fanfare in the bicentennial era's most popular accounts—"the hazardous nature of the enterprize and the courage necessary for undertaking it." [31]

McKeehan stated, "Mr. M'Kenzie, with a party consisting of about one fourth part of the number under your command, with means which will not bear a comparison with those furnished you, and without the *authority*, the *flags*, or *medals* of his government, crossed the Rocky mountains several degrees north of your rout, and for the *first time* penetrated to the Pacific Ocean." The mocking continued; indeed, it dug deeper. McKeehan observed, "You had the advantage of the information contained in his journal, and could in some degree estimate and guard against the dangers and difficulties you were to meet." In contrast to the thirty-three-member Lewis and Clark Expedition, Mackenzie's 1793 entourage consisted of ten men, six French-Canadian voyageurs (two of whom had been on the voyage to the Arctic four years before), two Native guide-interpreters, and a second in command, Alexander McKay. Not as formidable a figure as

William Clark, McKay was an able assistant who later figured in another famous episode in Northwest history, going down with the *Tonquin* at Clayoquot Sound on the west coast of Vancouver Island in 1811.[32]

The most important aspect of McKeehan's commentary is the insight about the value Lewis placed on Mackenzie's account—it could only have come from Patrick Gass, Lewis's former colleague. Another, perhaps stronger, clue to the ubiquity of Mackenzie's *Voyages* as handbook is found in the journal created by Joseph Whitehouse. In the preface to the copy of Whitehouse's original field notes, the former enlisted man observed that during the voyage he "furnished" himself "with books, and also got from Captains Lewis and Clark, every information that lay in their power, in order to compleat and make [his] Journal correct." This revealing passage gives us a rare insight into one of the most important aspects of the expedition's operations—the composition of the journals. The inferences to be drawn from Whitehouse are that the traveling library was frequently referred to, and when we add Gass's hint (via McKeehan) we must conclude one of the most frequented volumes was Mackenzie's *Voyages*.[33]

In one notable instance, Whitehouse (or someone on his behalf) outdid his commander's penchant for Mackenzian phrasing. At the conclusion of prefatory comments, the copyist who prepared the polished version of Whitehouse's journal stole a whole paragraph from Mackenzie's narrative. The Scotsman, in the preface to his book, wrote:

> I am not a candidate for literary fame: at the same time, I cannot but indulge the hope that this volume, with all its imperfections, will not be thought unworthy the attention of the scientific geographer; and that, by unfolding countries hitherto unexplored, and which, I presume, may now be considered as part of the British dominions, it will be received as a faithful tribute to the prosperity of my country.

The fair copy of Whitehouse's journal reemployed this precise text except for substituting "United States" for "British dominions." This was indeed the age of plagiarism.[34]

In March of 1808, provoked by press reports about the return of Lewis and Clark and probably in response to Lewis's letter warning the public about unauthorized accounts (the same instrument that riled McKeehan), Mackenzie issued his only known comment about the American expedition. In a letter to Viscount Castlereagh, the British Secretary of State for War and the Colonies, Mackenzie took his own turn at belittling the American accomplishment. Advising Castlereagh on the imperial consequences of Lewis and Clark's venture, Mackenzie wrote:

> [I]t being evident from the exertions of the American Government, that it is their intention to claim under the right of Discoveries of Captains Lewis and Clark, who, it is said, have traversed the Country by Land and Water from the Missisipi

to the Pacific Ocean exclusive Privileges to the intermediate Country, as well as to the Coast Northward from the Spanish Boundary to the Latitude of 50, but these Pretensions may be resisted on the following grounds; that if they found their Claims on Discovery, it is notoriously groundless in the first Place—as to the North West Coast, because the whole of it had been visited by Great Britain, and other nations, and settlements made in some Parts, long before the United States of America existed as a Nation and lately by this Country [Great Britain] at Nootka, being before they acquired Louisiana, or fitted out the expedition of Discovery under Captains Lewis and Clark; and, in the second Place, as to the intermediate Territory: because I myself, known to have been the first, who crossed thro' it to the Columbia, and from the Columbia to the Pacific Ocean in the year 1793.[35]

It is frequently averred that Meriwether Lewis never prepared a line of copy intended to form the published narrative of his expedition. This is mistaken on two counts. First, consider the polished nature of much of what appears in Lewis's notebooks. As observed earlier, most if not all of Lewis's account of the voyage up the Missouri from Fort Mandan to Lemhi Pass was unquestionably a first draft of text intended for publication and not a record of proceedings made in the field. In that sense, it serves as a proto-narrative for what Lewis intended to publish. Second, there is the matter of Lewis's "Essay on an Indian Policy" that appeared in an inconclusive and truncated form as an appendix to the edition of the Lewis and Clark journals paraphrased by Nicholas Biddle and published in 1814. To the modern eye the attachment of Lewis's "Essay" seems oddly intrusive because it has no apparent tie to the course of events just described by Biddle. However, the mere fact that Biddle included it suggests that William Clark or Thomas Jefferson may have encouraged him to do so because they knew of their deceased friend's intention for this narrative: an intention that only makes sense within the Mackenzian paradigm that was Lewis's narrative milieu.[36]

As a draft policy statement, Lewis's "Essay" is an obvious rejoinder to the concluding few paragraphs of Mackenzie's *Voyages from Montreal* and could well have been intended as the preface to the larger narrative Lewis was supposed to write. In this document, Lewis issued a challenge to his government every bit as vehement as the fur merchant did to his British superiors in the concluding paragraphs of *Voyages*. Lewis's serial recommendations constituted a strategy specifically aimed at thwarting the British on the upper Missouri. Lewis asked, "can we begin the work of exclusion too soon?" If not, Lewis predicted, "no such attempts will ever be made, and, consequently... we shall for several generations be taxed with the defence of a country which to us would be no more than a barren waste." By this Lewis meant to imply that the British would have trapped out the country.[37]

The North West Company undersold their American competition on the upper Missouri, rankling Lewis. In addition to the active exclusion of the British, Lewis advocated such countermeasures as the formation of a series of posts on the Missouri from which Indian agents for the American government and other guards could enforce licensing regulations such as the prohibition of alcohol and the distribution of sovereignty tokens. In short, Lewis argued, the United States needed a more forthright commercial policy "in order to contravene the machinations by the Northwest company for practice in that quarter." Turning Mackenzie's epithet "adventurers" in *Voyages* into a virtue, Lewis stated, "If the American merchant does not adventure, the field is at once abandoned to the Northwest company." [38]

In this manner, Meriwether Lewis, in his last major pronouncement about the West before his death, concludes his own story by taking it back precisely to the origins of the expedition. In Mackenzie's very last paragraph in *Voyages,* he spoke of the "many political reasons" guiding his mind on the matter of expanding Great Britain's commercial prospects. Surely Lewis in his "Essay" was working in the same mercantilist idiom. Lewis, through secret observation, closely trailed Alexander Mackenzie, both literally and figuratively. Seemingly, the Scotsman was nearly as constant a companion to Lewis before, during, and after his "darling project" as William Clark had been. [39]

CHAPTER 14 The "Vote" at Station Camp

DURING HIS SOJOURN TO AND AROUND CAPE DISAPPOINTMENT, William Clark and his squad "crossed the neck of Land low" to the "foot of a high open hill projecting into the ocian." Clark and the others climbed this headland and then "deceded to the N. of it and camped." From the heights of what came to be called McKenzie Head, Clark observed waves that "brake with tremendious force in every direction." Settling in that night after a supper of brant and fish, Clark, speaking as much for himself as the men, said they appeared "much Satisfied with their trip beholding with estonishment the high waves dashing against the rocks & this emence ocian." This distant shore brought other reckonings to mind. The men were "Chearfull" but what next? Clark said they "express a Desire to winter near the falls." [1]

On 19 November 1805 Clark and his men traveled north from McKenzie Head approximately nine miles, the last four on a "large Sand bar." At a spot within the southern limits of Long Beach, Washington, Clark "Turned back." This short phrase was a note on his draft map next to his initials, "WC." In his journal Clark says he again marked his name on a tree with the "Day of the month & year &c. and returned." The combination of inscriptions, on paper and on wood, was a symbolic summing up for the captain. This was Clark's last mile west and the most northwesterly destination of the Expedition for Northwestern Discovery. Contrary to the assertions of others, Clark's turnaround at Long Beach and not the whale site at Cannon Beach, Oregon, represents geographically "the farthest reach of the party outward from St. Louis." [2]

Clark's squad then turned south toward the base of the headlands at Cape Disappointment and struck straight across the low isthmus to a camp that night at the mouth of the Wallacut River northeast of today's Ilwaco. In this vicinity they found one of the expedition's canoes, "which had been left by the first party that Came down," meaning Colter's team that turned Point Distress on November 13th. From the Wallacut River, Clark "proceeded on to [Station] Camp" east of Chinook Point. The outbound trip from Station Camp to the "main Ocian" had required

Clark and the men to climb up over the "Steep assent" of the slopes of Chinook Point, but for the return on the 20th they found the tide out. Using a meaningful expression to conclude that day's entry, Clark said: "we walked home on the beech." His wording here hints at an early sentimental attachment to Station Camp, substantiating that site's status as the terminus of the westward voyage.[3]

All was well at Station Camp upon the conclusion of what Patrick Gass called "Capt. Clarke's tour N. W. along [the] coast." Several delegations of Chinook Indians had visited, and their principal chiefs, Comcomly and Shelathwell, had been given the customary peace medals and a flag. One of the Indians Clark found upon his return to Station Camp "had on a roab made of 2 Sea Otter Skins the fur of them were more butifull than any fur I had ever Seen," he wrote. The owner refused "many things," including blankets and a coat, wanting only the much prized blue beads in exchange. A trade was enabled because Sacagawea had many such beads on her belt. (She was later to be compensated by Clark with a blue cloth coat.) This anecdote proves how Sacagawea, if not the heroine of legend, was still integral to the daily life of the expedition. The truth of this was to be reinforced before the week at Station Camp was over.[4]

Now that Captains Lewis and Clark had satisfied themselves with separate walks on the sands north of Cape Disappointment, the perspective of the party turned toward the east and the first segment of the voyage home. The seasonal weather figured prominently in this refocusing of interest. Only a week earlier Clark feared the party might suffer terribly if a wintry freeze settled in, but now with some local experience he was beginning to discern the surprisingly mild climate of the Pacific Coast. Yes, the rain was as "Disagreeable" as ever, but, he reported, "We have not had One cold day Since we passed below the last falls or great Shute," meaning the Cascades of the Columbia. On balance, Clark concluded that the climate was "temperate, and the only change we have experienced is from fair weather to rainey windey weather." Indeed, Clark reported that the waves accompanying yet another rainstorm prevented the "homeward bound journey" back up the Columbia.[5]

Clark soon regretted not having successfully broken camp. "O! how horrible is the day," Clark recorded on Friday, November 22nd. The storm that blew in caused "waves & brakers" to fly over Station Camp. One canoe was split by being tossed around on the shore by the surf. Wet and confined to camp and therefore unable to hunt, the party had only a few roots to eat. Patrick Gass said, "we were not yet able to set out," referencing the incipient return voyage. Joseph Whitehouse clarified this point, stating that the weather had "detain'd us, at our Camp from going up the River again, to look out for Winter Quarters." He went on to observe that the captains intended to leave "as soon as the Weather would permit, and the Season of the Year advancing made it absolutely necessary that it should be the case." [6]

The 23rd was a fair day, allowing the hunters to procure three deer and some fowl for a meaty repast. For the third time Clark inscribed his name on a nearby tree. Lewis used his branding iron (now in the possession of the Oregon Historical Society) to mark his association with the end of the voyage for a second time. But unlike at the anchorage near the cape, or Clark's solo inscription on the sands of Long Beach, here all "the men all marked their nams on trees about the Camp." (In his more reflective journal Clark states that "the party all Cut the first letters of their names" on the trees, raising the interesting question as to whether Sacagawea and York did too.) Each person to a different alder tree initialed his name as if attempting to shout to posterity, "I made it here." This was the moment when everyone in the expedition, great and small, made their claim on history. As a collective affirmation of mission accomplishment, this vignette offers still more proof regarding the importance the expedition granted to Station Camp. As a commemorative gesture it also signaled their imminent departure.[7]

On the evening of the 23rd, a common event occurred, but one with great consequence as revealed in several of the journal entries for the ensuing day. That night, Clark said "7 Indians of the *Clatt Sopp* nation" came over from the opposite side of the river. The visitors' intention was to barter, but this proved frustrating to both sides because, as Clark told it, the Indians demanded too much in payment. Offering an insight into his short-term outlook, Clark said he was careful about expending any merchandise in trade at the coast because they had to depend on it for a portion of their subsistence on "our return home." [8]

A clearing of the weather at midday on November 24th facilitated a round of astronomical observations that continued into the early evening. Then, as Clark's elkskin-bound field notes show, a poll of nearly every member of the party was conducted. Only through a cross-reference to the journals of Patrick Gass and John Ordway is it clear just what Clark recorded. Gass said that night the captains "consulted" with the party on where they were to spend the winter. Ordway noted the captains sought "the oppinion of the party" as to the location of a "place for winters quarter." Clark's extended notebook entry refers to "the Solicitations of every individual." The lowest-ranking journalist, Pvt. Joseph Whitehouse, painted the best word picture of the scene: "In the Evening our Officers had the whole party assembled in order to consult which place would be the best, for us to take up our Winter Quarters at." [9]

The word "vote" never appears in the journals to describe this activity. Reuben Gold Thwaites, editor of the centennial edition of the journals over one hundred years ago, seems to have coined the usage. He referred to "a vote of the men, as to the location of winter quarters" and later "the vote taken on this occasion." The first historian in the modern era to reference this episode, and one disinclined to romanticize the history of Lewis and Clark, was James Ronda. In *Lewis and Clark among the Indians* Ronda referred, in passing, to the expedition "taking a vote." Gary Moulton, in his editing of the modern edition of the journals subsequent to the publication of Ronda's book, expanded on Clark's table of names and recommendations, stating in a footnote that it "represents the vote taken." He continued, "It is worth noting that York and Sacagawea voted." [10]

The Thwaites, Ronda, and Moulton references to "the vote" were cursory mentions. Dayton Duncan, coproducer of the Ken Burns documentary film about the expedition, which has done much to re-mythologize the Lewis and Clark story, was the first to invest the event with extraordinary meaning via a single sentence in his *Out West*, first published in 1987. He wrote that the issue as to where to camp for the winter "was put to a vote, and in a ceremony that would predate the exercise of democracy in the United States by sixty-five and one hundred and fifteen years, respectively, York (a black slave) and Sacagawea (a woman and an Indian) were allowed to participate." However, full amplification of the "vote" came in *Undaunted Courage* by Stephen Ambrose. After analyzing the meaning of the various locales referenced in Clark's polling data (as his entry might be characterized), Ambrose discussed the meaning of this episode in expansive terms: "This was the first vote ever held in the Pacific Northwest. It was the first time in American history that a black slave had voted, the first time a woman had voted." The first of these assertions is culture-bound to Anglo-American history and probably inaccurate. The second is dubious because there is no way of knowing. The third is simply wrong. Women, both black and white, voted in New Jersey from 1776 until 1807. The Duncan-Ambrose thesis about the great meaning of vote at Station Camp was then turbocharged in Ken Burns' nationally televised documentary about the expedition. Duncan later referred to the vote as "the most powerfully meaningful single moment of an expedition filled with powerful, meaningful moments. This moment was beyond meaningful. It was transcendent." [11]

Ambrose, Duncan, and Burns have been severely criticized for their interpretation of this episode. Thomas Slaughter says they made "too much of a shrewd leadership device" and that in no way was this tally evidence of the "democratizing influences of wilderness travel." Slaughter was particularly incensed at the imputation that York and Sacagawea's involvement in this episode warranted the idealization of Lewis and Clark as racial or gender liberals. Referring to York, Slaughter writes that "finding democracy within slavery is not history; it is racist romance." [12]

One need not relish the demolition of LEWIS & CLARK lore as much as Slaughter does to conclude that perhaps too much has been made of "the vote." First of all, *if* what transpired at Station Camp was an election, it was not even the first one to occur during the course of the expedition. After Sgt. Charles Floyd died in the summer of 1804 on the Missouri River, the captains "ordered a *Vote* of the men for a Sergeant" (emphasis added), noting here that this term had known utility within military protocol but was not applied at Station Camp. Later, at the famed decision point of the Marias/Missouri confluence, the expedition was so divided on the course to the headwaters that, as Joseph Whitehouse wrote, "a Council was held by our Officers, and the opinion of our Men were all taken." Nor in the broader pattern of continental exploration was the notion of trail democracy entirely foreign. We have already seen that Alexander Mackenzie conferred with his compatriots in decisionmaking. A few years after Lewis and

Clark, Robert Stuart, leader of the Astorians returning overland, conducted a vote on whether to proceed across the open plains of Nebraska in the winter or retreat to a spot with more trees for shelter, firewood, and habitat for game. The fur traders voted 5-2 in favor of turning back.[13]

According to Dayton Duncan what happened at Station Camp was remarkable because it was "a move that broke with all the rules of military command and protocol." Lewis and Clark could have simply ordered the expedition to the next camp, but they didn't, thereby opening up the issue for historians to assess what this moment in time truly meant. The "vote" became one of the most popular stories during the recent bicentennial because it tapped into the secular mythology of American culture. The resonance created by the fact that Thomas Jefferson authored both the highest expression of American civic idealism in the Declaration of Independence *and* the Expedition for Northwestern Discovery made for a powerful propellant.[14]

To gain some perspective on this episode, it's important to remember that universal white manhood suffrage was neither common in the United States of 1805, nor, for that matter, an essential aspect of Jeffersonian Republicanism. Indeed, Virginia was late among the states in surrendering property ownership as a prerequisite for the franchise. However, the first decade of the nineteenth century was, Peter Kastor reminds us, "a time when people throughout the United States were hard at work defining both citizenship and nationhood." Loyalty to federal officials and authority was a highly valued commodity in the recently acquired Louisiana Purchase. The political landscape in this new American territory was very slippery because of the novelty associated with incorporating a new jurisdiction into the nation's body politic from a foreign country, a large one at that, and complicated further by a concomitant immaturity of civic ties and controls. The Burr/Wilkinson conspiracy to separate Louisiana (or some subset of it) from the United States testifies to this and so does the appointment of Meriwether Lewis, a staunch Jeffersonian loyalist and nationalist, as governor of Louisiana after the expedition. It is only in retrospect that we see Jefferson's choice as an odd one because Lewis was as bad a politician as he was good at exploring.[15]

In 1805, while the Lewis and Clark Expedition was penetrating the far west, the United States Supreme Court ruled that the residents of territories, like Louisiana, to say nothing of an exploring party camped at the Pacific Ocean, existed outside the constitutional paradigm. Full civil rights (as constitutionally recognized at the time), the court ruled, adhered solely to residents of the states. It was not until 1820 that the Supreme Court expanded the notion of "the national community" to include citizens of states *and* territories, so long as they resided within the confines of the country as defined by international law. Nevertheless, concurrent with this expansion of sovereignty and scope of American citizenship, we must recall that one of the first things the United States government did when it took administrative control of Louisiana was to disenfranchise people of African origin. This great scandal in American history, and serious blot on Jefferson's legacy, involved previously free blacks who had served in the Spanish militia garrisoned in New Orleans. The Black Codes implemented soon after Louisiana came under American governance were an attempt at creating a nationalized solidarity among disparate communities of white people who had suddenly come under the suzerainty of the United States.[16]

All that said, Thomas Slaughter, in a coda to his generally critical view of Lewis and Clark, says the expedition "became our journey as a nation and a people, one that we cannot, and perhaps should not, let go." The "vote" at Station Camp would also thus seem to qualify in Slaughter's paradigm as a *found triumph*, that is, a story previously "lost in words never read." Only a few passing mentions about "the vote" occurred in print before the bicentennial, and the name Station Camp as the place where it occurred was completely unknown prior to the recent observance. The present always dictates what stories from the past are important, and any commemoration, especially, is more about the issues of its time than the past event being celebrated. The "vote" conducted by and for the expedition in November 1805 is a powerful one with self-evident appeal in modern times. Though a fugitive and ephemeral act, the "vote" on the Columbia struck a chord during the recent bicentennial telling because, as backward-glancing viewers, we are, per Slaughter, "prisms through which the journals' light is refracted time and again." [17]

James Ronda has called Lewis and Clark's voyage "the emblematic American journey." Indeed, "all of American history can be imagined as a journey," Ronda states, in reference to intercontinental migrations from prehistoric times to the present, or cross-continentally, in the form of trails such as Route 66, the Alaska Highway, or Interstate 80. However, the movement of the American people is not limited to a passage through space. Journeying through time can have a moral dimension where the objective is not the discovery of place but of the self and of others. Station Camp is an evocative place within the idiom of Lewis and Clark and American national mythology because of its dual nature—endpoint on a monumental physical journey across the continent as well as an imagined way station along the grand experiment of American self-governance.[18]

Nevertheless, it's worth remembering that the "vote" at Station Camp was not a formally constituted election. Lewis and Clark were always in command and could have decided the matter of where to overwinter themselves. Even Dayton Duncan suggests that the "vote" was a subtle manipulation of group psychology intended to countervail the groundswell of interest within the party to leave the coast and head back up the Columbia, just when the captains were coming to the conclusion they should stay in the vicinity of the coast. Recently, Stephenie Ambrose Tubbs observed, on the basis of her own camping experiences, "that when you have a say, or think you have a say, you don't complain, which is a motivating factor for consulting the crew." [19]

Furthermore, on the matter of Clark's supposed racial liberalism, James Holmberg's study of the captain's life and letters after the expedition offers a heartbreaking insight into the evil hold slavery could exert on a man, even an otherwise good one like William Clark. After his return from the west to Kentucky and later once in office in St. Louis, Clark whipped his slaves and was prepared to sell York to a more severe master if he did not perform "his duty as a Slave." In a reversal of their roles relative to Native people, Meriwether Lewis tried to temper Clark's passions about York's perceived ingratitude and misbehavior, to little effect. Clark wrote in 1809 that he had "trounced" most of his slaves, including York because of his "Sulky" attitude. Clark never followed through on his threat to sell York, instead renting out his services when doing so would expedite York's reunion with his family near Louisville. In another instance, however, Clark did free a slave, stating that the institution of "perpetual involuntary servitude to be contrary to the principles of natural justice." Such, states Holmberg, were the "seemingly contradictory attitudes" some slaveholders abided.[20]

Still, even with these concessions and discounts, at Station Camp we find a community of Americans, thousands of miles from their homeland, resorting to some elements of the "town meeting" to help determine their immediate fate. Wherever this event stands on the register of democratic practice, at a minimum it reveals, as Albert Furtwangler noted, that after many months of companionship "the captains observed new relations of interdependency with their men." In this vein, James Ronda once referred to the expedition as a "village on the move" and stated elsewhere that "we need to know much more about the life of that community." This much we do know. When the Expedition for Northwestern Discovery began in 1804, the convention of governance was strictly military in nature. Courts-martial and their attendant floggings were a somewhat ordinary occurrence. But west of Fort Mandan the dynamic changed. As Ronda writes, "over time and through adversity the company became a community." Meriwether Lewis said as much, when, in the spirit of good feelings ambient upon the party's reaching the Yellowstone River in the spring of 1805, he referred to the detachment as "our little community." Indeed, the bond created by common endeavor became a virtue unto itself, transcending mere civic or community values to an even higher order of interpersonal relationship. When Patrick Gass lost Lewis's tomahawk going up the Jefferson River in August 1805, Lewis expressed regret at this occurrence, but he quickly added, "accedents will happen in the best families." [21]

Dayton Duncan calls the site of Station Camp "hallowed ground" in deference to the national ethos of self-governance and related values. The practical issue at stake may have been unexceptional, even ordinary. Lewis and Clark established hundreds of camps. The scholarly debate is fired over whether or not this occasion at Station Camp was the embodiment of egalitarian idealism and other intimations of a pluralistic democratic society. Because critics relish pointing out that York remained a slave at the end of the expedition or that the captains always maintained martial command does not mean, Duncan says, that the "vote" at Station Camp wasn't "a significant moment for the people involved" or "resonant" history. This event, Duncan believes, can be important without being "a turning point in American history." In the end we must remember that early in the nineteenth century considering oneself an "American" was still a novelty. Many, if not most, citizens of the United States at that time, Peter Kastor explains, "had a localized outlook that emerged from shared experiences." How appropriate and quintessentially American then, that the intensely shared and transcontinental experience of the Expedition for Northwestern Discovery should terminate physically within sight of the Pacific Ocean—and ethically with some of the trappings of a community gathering.[22]

The popular antipodal views of Lewis and Clark during the bicentennial posed the captains either as heroes unalloyed or as destroyers of the Garden of Eden. Surely there is a temperate latitude between these poles at which to place the expedition. Doing so within the specific context of the expedition's decision-making at Station Camp, if posed against an extreme and imaginary alternative, such as an abusive command rife with dissension, can be seen as meaningful without being as fully redemptive as modern legend would have it.

The actual "vote" at Station Camp might not have happened but for the chance visit of the Clatsop Indians on November 23rd, referenced earlier. On 21 and 22 November, Clark, Gass, and Whitehouse all made references to an eagerness for a departure from the coast and commencement of the homeward voyage. There seemed to be little game where they were stationed, and the Chinooks were such hard bargainers they would soon run out of trade merchandise. Clark said this induced every member of the party to make "diligent enquiries of the nativs" as to where game animals were abundant. These investigations led to the conclusion that elk were plentiful on the south bank opposite them and deer equally so upstream "Some distance." Surely, the visit of the Clatsops on the 23rd was instrumental in its influence over the "vote," every bit as much as paid advertising effects elections in our own time.[23]

Clark analyzed the regional intelligence and their situation in the following manner. Elk were larger than deer, more easily killed, and offered more nutritious meat for food and superior skins for garments. This was an argument for staying put. Being near the sea facilitated the procurement of salt for seasoning and curing meat to be consumed during the winter and the return trip. The prospect of maritime fur traders or explorers returning to the mouth of the Columbia lingered. The Indians suggested that oceanic voyagers might appear as soon as March (which in fact proved to be the case unbeknownst to the captains). Clark divined that the expedition could secure goods (such as beads, a common form of exchange in Indian country) from the traders with which, in turn, they could "purchase provisions on our return home." Literally as an afterthought, Clark also cited the now-apparent temperate climate as an inducement to staying near the coast. He correctly gauged that the coastal weather was "much milder than that above the 1st range of Mountains," meaning the Cascades.[24]

Such were the issues as put to the expedition. Clark's tally of the "vote" has three columns because there were actually several "propositions" on the "ballot." In the left column he listed the name of every member of the expedition.

The middle column identified each "vote" on the immediate question, that is, whether to cross and examine what was to be found on the other side of the Columbia or simply head upstream without tarrying any more at the coast. The third column tallied where to go *if* circumstances on the opposite shore were not satisfactory.[25]

William Clark stated that "with the Solicitations of every individual, except one" the party concluded "to Cross the river and examine the opposit Side." The first to be polled, no doubt keeping with camp protocol, were Sergeants Ordway, Pryor, and Gass. Clark may have overstated the results when he said only one was against an immediate crossing. Sacagawea, or "Janey," as she is referred to endearingly in Clark's notes, was "in favour of a place where there is plenty of Potas," referring to wapato roots. Her preference for this edible, starchy tuber, which grows in the muck of ponds, marshes, and sloughs, no doubt reflected her Native womanly predilection for the gathering of an abundant carbohydrate and trade item. Besides, half-rotten elk meat would have been of little value to her child compared to, say, mashed "potas." Meriwether Lewis opined, "Proceed on to morrow & examine The other side," with hunting grounds and salt as an objective. Clark was voluble in stating his own view in conclusion. He favored "proceding on without delay to the opposit Shore & there examine... the disposition of the Indians, & probibilaty of precureing Subsistance." Clark went on to speculate about the prospective arrival of "Tradeing vestles." From the fur traders, Clark postulated, they could procure a sufficient supply of goods to more than compensate "for the bad liveing we Shall have... on Pore deer & Elk we may get in this neighbourhood." [26]

But what to do if, upon inspection, the absence of sufficient subsistence or a troublesome "disposition of the Indians" on the south bank argued for an immediate voyage back upstream—then where? This second tally was far more diverse. Ten votes were recorded for the vicinity of the Sandy River, including those of the sergeants, boatman Pierre Cruzatte, Captain Lewis, and John Shields, the last of whom wanted to go there forthwith on the first tally. "[N]ear the falls" (perhaps Celilo but more likely the Cascades or slightly above, on account of a supply of wood) was the preferred overwintering spot at the campfire discussion during Clark's ramble to Cape Disappointment. However, by the time of the "vote" at Station Camp this choice must have lost some strength because the notion now had only six adherents, including Reubin Field and the hunter George Drouillard. An otherwise unspecified "up the river" fielded the largest tally—fourteen votes—for a fallback position. Clark, alone, was in favor of the idea of heading to the "neighbourhood of the Frendly village near the long narrows" and to stay there until they could continue farther upstream in the spring. This would have put Lyle, Washington, on the map of LEWIS & CLARK lore, supplanting Astoria, Oregon. Clark's preference in this tally was the most easterly and may provide more definition as to what the choice of the "falls" cited above meant. That's thirty-one votes, in a thirty-three-person party. The male members of the Charbonneau family, *pere et fils,* did not and could not "vote", respectively.

Perhaps the Gallic Charbonneau the elder, a fur trader with a history of working for British commercial interests, was simply bored by all this American community building.[27]

Summing up the evening's discussion and tally, William Clark took pains to note Meriwether Lewis's strong inclination to winter at the coast. He cited Lewis's affinity for salt and faith that the arrival of a trading ship was "probable." John Ordway described the first of these reasons as being decisive. Lewis was also of the mind that heading upriver "would not inhance our journey in passing the Rockey mountains," which proved to be prescient given the expedition's experience the ensuing spring. Clark seems to have been inclined to vacate the coastal district altogether. He viewed saltwater "evil in as much as it is not helthy." He averred that "two or three weeks Exemination on the opposide if the propects are any wise favourable, would not be too long." In short, he would relent in favor of the majority view and that of his co-commander. But, he concluded, if the party could not "subsist on the above terms," he was of the view that they should proceed eastbound, making "Station Camps" until they got into the Columbia Gorge. It was here, the last night on their sandy beach home on the Columbia that Clark first phrased the term that would denominate the place for posterity. Not only that, it seems that he was projecting the desire to establish other extended camps that would facilitate the surveying and mapping of the Northwest.[28]

Properly, it seems now, on a Monday, 25 November 1805, Clark reported that it was "a fine day... we loaded and Set out up the river." The westering days of Lewis and Clark were over.[29]

CHAPTER 15 Winter's Delay

WIND AND WAVES MADE IT IMPOSSIBLE FOR THE EXPEDITION for Northwestern Discovery to cross to the opposite bank of the Columbia River from their position at Station Camp. So, on the day of departure, 25 November 1805, the party instead proceeded upstream to where the Columbia was relatively narrow and a passage to the south bank could be made in relative safety. This was near the Pillar Rock camp of November 7th, nominal site of the "ocean in view" exclamation.

On November 26th the expedition crossed the Columbia, and with a slight tail wind behind them began coasting the south side. Clark described the effort as "decending to see *if* a favourable place should offer on the So[uth] Side to winter & c" (emphasis added). The survey establishing the location of Station Camp endured in his thinking about the architecture of the lower river. In Clark's course and distance table for the 26th he referenced a trajectory—"Pt. No. 2 to Cape Disappointmt"—in one of his directional bearings. This was a line from Tongue Point to Cape Disappointment. The camp that night was in the "Deep bend" found east of Tongue Point on the outskirts of the modern city of Astoria, Oregon.[1]

The next day the expedition traversed this promontory. The customary encounter with swells in the estuary forced the voyagers to disembark at the narrow isthmus linking Tongue Point to the mainland. The water on the ocean side of the point was saline, Clark noted, while that upriver from them was "fresh and fine." Good water to drink was just about the only favorable attribute of this campsite.[2]

On November 28th, yet another storm blew in making their situation, in Clark's now trademark characterization for the lower Columbia, "truly disagreeable." The weather of that month, to say nothing of the cumulative effect of two year's worth of wear, had rendered the expedition's gear nearly useless. Clark said the "tents [were] So full of holes & rotten that they will not keep any thing dry." Pinned down again, the captains determined to find some of those deer and elk that had been so highly recommended by Natives when they were on the opposite shore. Several of the men were positioned at the neck of the peninsula while a larger number tried, without success, to "drive" some game from the point into the sights of the stationary hunters. The next recourse was the adjoining woods of the mainland, but that also yielded nil. In a passage reminiscent of his darkest day at Dismal Nitch, Clark rued that he could neither go "back or forward, and we have nothing to eate but a little Pounded fish" that had been purchased at Celilo. The wind blew with "Such violence that I expected every moment to See trees taken up by the roots," Clark said, and some were indeed blown down. It seemed as if the lower Columbia on the cusp of winter had an endless capability of stupefying William Clark—he called the conditions "Tremendious." Even this experienced frontiersman was made to tremble by the "dreadfull weather" that can be experienced where the Columbia collides with the Pacific.[3]

Meriwether Lewis's first journal entry on the Columbia River occurred 29 November 1805. Mute since September 22nd (a period of 67 days) and therefore silent during the eventful trip down the Snake and Columbia, he now began a fragmentary journal of three days duration. "*I determined...* to proceed down the river," Lewis wrote, "in surch of an eligible place for our winters residence and accordingly set out early this morning in the small canoe accompanyed by 5 men" (emphasis added). This statement does not have the quality of an investigative "cross and examine" character as expressed during the "vote" at Station Camp nor Clark's contingent expression of November 26th. Rather, it seems Lewis was reverting to his "solitary" mode.[4]

Separated from Clark and his continuous chronology of the expedition, Lewis chose to keep a record of this vanguard movement. Gary Moulton notes that his entries are found on five loose sheets of paper probably ripped out of one of the bound notebooks. The last time Lewis ventured off in this fashion was his foray around "Point Distress" on November 14th in an attempt to catch up with the squad, led by Colter, that had initially escaped from Dismal Nitch. One cannot resist wondering whether at that time Lewis also ripped a few pages loose from a notebook to record his experiences on the trip to Cape Disappointment. On nearly every other occasion like this—the decision at the Marias, the Great Falls of the Missouri portage, questing for the Continental Divide, the Bitterroot passage, to say nothing of the extended separation from Clark on the return trip—Lewis was conscious of the need, given the general command from Jefferson, to keep a record of his detached movements. The one notable exception is the excursion of 14–17 November to Cape Disappointment. This was such an anomaly as to suggest, though we cannot be certain, that Lewis kept an ephemeral record of some sort on that trek, but it was lost. On the other hand, the circumstances at Dismal Nitch were so distressful that access to the baggage where the notebooks would have been stored may not have been possible. There is a third scenario. The failure to link up with a fur trader or maritime explorer, or simply a lack of inspiration, deflated the prospect of a narrative crescendo, and so he destroyed those notes. This would have been akin to making real on his threat at the Great Falls of the Missouri to "draw my pen across" his description of that landmark.[5]

While Lewis was off with George Drouillard, Reubin Field, George Shannon, John Colter, and Francois Labiche to look for those elusive elk and a winter camp, Clark, ever the master of logistics, made the best of the situation, having the men dry out their leather garments, "before the fire, and prepareing it for use—they haveing but fiew other Species of Clothing to ware at this time." However, the smoke got in their eyes, which was "emecencly disagreeable." Off to the west Lewis was frustrated during his coursing of Youngs Bay. He recorded on November 30th that there was "no fresh appearance of Elk or deer in our rout so far." He was eager to meet up with the Clatsop Indians who had, he said, "tantilized us with there being much game in their neighbourhood." It is with that comment, and the ensuing one, that the tenor of the Native dialogue prior to the "vote" at Station Camp becomes more discernible. Lewis continued, "this information in fact was the cause of my present resurch, for where there is most game is for us the most eligible winter station." [6]

December turned with Clark's men mending their clothes and socks while their captain mused about the preternatural aspect of this environment. The roar and thunder of the Columbia's confluence with the Pacific, at once "tempestous and horiable," had worn on Clark for twenty-four days, counting back to the sighting from Pillar Rock. With a clever petulance, he refused to call it the Pacific Ocean (he wrote, "I have not Seen one pacific day Since my arrival in its vicinity") but rather "the Great Western... Ocian." His sour mood was compounded by the absence of his co-commander: "I have no account of Capt. Lewis Since he left me." Pvt. Joseph Whitehouse amplified what Clark merely implied when he wrote that the members of the party were "all anxiously waiting for the arrival of Captain Lewis." Clearly the nervous energy of the men, as well as their physical well-being, was being tested by the coastal turbulence. [7]

On December 2nd Clark's concern about Lewis's foray grew significantly. The specific question that pressed on him, as it did Lewis, was whether "Elk or deer Can be found Sufficent for us to winter on." If not, Clark confided to his journal, "I shall move from this place, to one of better prospects for game," that is, to a point upriver. Happily for Clark, one of the hunters soon returned to the Tongue Point camp with the marrowbones of an elk. Clark dispatched six men in one of the canoes to retrieve the carcass. With palpable relief Clark reported, "This is the first Elk we have killed on this Side [of] the rockey mounts." [8]

With the nutrition from a single elk in their stomachs the "Sperits of my men" were revived "verry much," Clark wrote. This phrasing about esprit de corps is reminiscent of the captains' characterizations of straitened and uncertain circumstances finding food in and a way out of the Bitterroot Mountains, testimony to the ubiquity of these experiences during the course of the expedition. But in another confounding twist to his Columbian travails, Clark was without an appetite because of gastric distress, yet another analogue to the Lolo Trail. "[P]lenty of meat and incaple of eateing any," he complained. In due course, he was able to digest some elk meat soup, stocked with wapato roots garnered from

Chinook Indians. By 3 December Clark was sufficiently recovered from his ailment—or was simply trying to lift his own spirits—to inscribe his name on a tree for a *fourth* time "imediately on the isthmus [—] William Clark December 4th 1805. By Land from the U. States in 1804 & 1805." The lack of a nod to Lewis is noticeable.[9]

Clark became increasingly anxious about Lewis's fate. "I fear Some accident has taken place in his craft or party," he wrote on December 4th. He went on to state that "Capt Lewis's long delay below has been the cause of no little uneasiness on my part for him, a 1000 conjectures has crouded into my mind respecting his probable Situation & Safty." Clark occupied himself by recording fluctuations in the tides. Late that day, Lewis finally returned to the isthmus, having found a "good Situation" for a winter camp. It was "on a Small river which falls into a Small bay a Short distance below" in a neighborhood with a sufficient supply of elk so as to address the issue of sustainability. Clark noted that Lewis's report was "verry Satisfactory information to all the party." This and adjacent verbiage in his journal suggests that the captains sought concurrence in the strategy confirmed in the "vote" at Station Camp a week and a half earlier. Putting their trust in Lewis's reconnaissance, Clark said, "we accordingly deturmined to proceed on to the Situation which Capt. Lewis had Viewed as Soon as the wind and weather Should permit and Comence building huts &c." [10]

The whole party set out from Tongue Point on the morning of December 7th for "the place Capt Lewis pitched on for winter quarters." After rounding Astoria's Smith Point, the expedition ascended a creek that was tributary to what Clark named "Meriwethers Bay," in his mistaken notion that Lewis was the first white man to survey it. Clark concluded the travelogue by stating, "at this place of Encampment We propose to build & pass the winter." Unlike the Clark, Gass, Ordway, and Whitehouse expressions upon reaching Station Camp the previous 15–16 November, there is not a hint here of exploratory accomplishment. Rather, the mundane predominates. What would be termed Fort Clatsop was simply, as Gass phrased it, "our intended wintering place." It had the perceived attribute in Clark's mind as being "the Center of... hunting Countrey." Clark's first act was to set out for the ocean, which he could hear roaring, to find a place to make salt. Given his distaste for the substance, the stated purpose was "for the Support of the Men." Upon his small party's return on December 10th, Clark found "Capt Lewis with all hands felling trees" for a fort.[11]

The explorers marveled at the felicity by which the grand fir split into beautifully straight and wide lumber. Patrick Gass said the wood "makes the finest puncheons I have ever seen." Clark reported, "the log works of our building" was framed up by 14 December 1805. The "Chinking, Dobbing Cutting out" openings for doors continued through the 21st. The flooring and bunks in several of the huts were completed on the 22nd and by Christmas Eve a majority of the party had settled into their accommodations—by Christmas night they all had. On Christmas Day their new abode was formally named Fort Clatsop, in honor of the local

Indians. After a touching exchange of meager presents, including Sacagawea's gift of weasel tails to Clark, the party suffered through a "bad Christmass diner" of spoiled elk meat, fish, and a few roots. Clark mused that they would have preferred spending "the nativity of Christ in feasting, had we any thing to either raise our Sperits or even gratify our appetites." In a passage that prefigured Clement Moore's (1822) classic Christmas tale, Clark could at least take satisfaction that the party was "Snugly fixed in their huts." [12]

With the completion of a stockade around their rude cabins on December 30th, it can be said that the Expedition for Northwestern Discovery's long mundane winter at Fort Clatsop commenced. Many of the men were sick or hurt on the eve of the new calendar year. Weathering the daily rain was a constant fatigue, as was hunting elk and hauling it back to camp before the meat spoiled in the damp but relatively warm climate. When the sun actually shone on 30 December, John Ordway was prompted to remark that occurrence was "verry uncommon at this place." There were notes to review; maps to draw; saltwater to boil; food to be prepared; latrines to be maintained; ethnological, botanical, or zoological observations to record; and geographical reports to write. This is how Lewis occupied much of his time over the winter, reflecting a return to action suspended after emerging from the Bitterroots. With an ample supply of deer and elk, it was finally possible for the party to make new garments and moccasins out of hides. But on the whole, the winter at Fort Clatsop often seemed bereft of direction and purpose. "The reasons for raising Fort Clatsop," James Ronda writes, "seemed less compelling than those that had brought Fort Mandan to life." Perhaps William Clark said as much in a line written at the time of the establishment of Fort Clatsop that their intention was, merely, to "pass the winter." [13]

There were occasional marvels and other interesting episodes that broke the monotony. The most famous of these was news that a whale foundered on the ocean shore. Lewis was intrigued by the prospect that whale oil rendered from the blubber might enhance their living conditions during the upcoming winter. When Clark's small squad set out to find the whale on 6 January 1806, Sacagawea insisted on going along. Lewis recorded her pleading: "she observed that she had traveled a long way with us to see the great waters, and that now that monstrous fish was also to be seen, she thought it very hard she could not be permitted to see either (she had never yet been to the Ocean)." This is probably as close as the journals come to relating a direct quote from her. [14]

One day the Clatsop Indians arrived at the fort with a man whom Clark termed "lighter Coloured than the nativs are generaly." He described this fellow as freckled, with red hair, about 25 years of age and "half white at least." Clark concluded that this man could understand but did not speak English and nonetheless "possessed all the habits of the indians." This individual was later known to the Astorians (who established their fur-trading fort a mere six years hence) as Jack Ramsay. His name was tattooed on his arm. Gary Moulton asserts that an Indian with red hair would have had to inherit that trait from both parents, so this descendant of early European coastal traders who shipwrecked or deserted must have had a complex genealogy.[15]

Undoubtedly the most significant development to occur at Fort Clatsop was the moment Meriwether Lewis picked up the pen and began a comprehensive set of journal entries commencing 1 January 1806. Moulton refers to this notebook, continuing through 20 March 1806 (and thus nearly to the end of the stay at Fort Clatsop), as "one of the richest in natural history and ethnographical data." The timing of Lewis's resumption of literary and scientific duty smacks of a New Year's Resolution. He offers no retrospective glance other than merely to Christmas the previous week. Of this, Lewis said, "our repast of this day [January 1] tho' better than that of Christmass, consisted principally in the anticipation of the 1st day of January 1807, when in the bosom of our friends we hope to participate in the mirth and hilarity of the day, and when with the zest given by the recollection of the present, we shall completely, both mentally and corporally, enjoy the repast which the hand of civilization has prepared for us." With this doleful flourish, reinforcing the general sentiment that the winter at Fort Clatsop was something to be endured, the "voice" of Meriwether Lewis returns to the narrative of the expedition.[16]

Correspondingly, William Clark, who had served as the primary chronicler since September, subsumed his perspective by resorting to merely copying the passages of Lewis. Clark subordinated himself in this way automatically every time Lewis resumed keeping his journal. (When Clark was not in Lewis's company at Fort Clatsop he kept a separate record, the best example being the trip across Tillamook Head to view the whale that had beached itself.) However, Clark did not stop writing original entries until January 3rd, perhaps waiting to see if Lewis's resolve for keeping a journal would be sustained. Or, Lewis did not really recommence writing until January 4th and he simply backdated a few days' worth of entries. In any event, the onset of a quiet period within the fort left Lewis bereft of any excuses. Perhaps even Clark encouraged him to refocus his efforts. Lewis was the first to express interest in visiting the whale site, but Clark ended up leading that little expedition. This was perhaps a function of the "Sacagawea dynamic" (if she was determined to venture out, assuredly it would only have happened on Clark's watch), or Lewis was finally in a writing groove and did not want to distract himself.[17]

As if to put a punctuation mark on his general views of the lower Columbia, William Clark's entry of 2 January 1806 tellingly refers to "our delay" at Fort Clatsop. By the end of January 1806 a sense of ennui had fully set in. "Nothing worthy of notice occurred today," wrote Lewis on the 29th and a similar inscription again on the 30th. Hunting, boiling seawater for salt at the manufactory near today's Seaside, Oregon, maintaining weather tables, and waiting out the rainy weather were the predominant camp activities. On January 9th Whitehouse first mentions that "the Men in the fort were employed mending their Clothes, airing the baggage, making moccasins dressing Skins" for clothing, an activity which he mentions at least once a week through March 16th. To break up the monotony of dressing skins, the captains directed the men to clean their firearms.[18]

Lewis and Clark had little passion for their ordinary life on the Northwest coast. This can be discerned, for example, in Meriwether Lewis's terse opening to his journal entry of 2 February 1806. "Not any occurrence today worthy of notice; but all are pleased, that one month of the time which binds us to Fort Clatsop and which seperates us from our friends has now elapsed," he wrote. Having completed the principal body of interpretive observations about the Native people, Lewis began to fill his time conducting botanical analyses. This included an attempt at creating a typology of the mixed species coastal forest. These and other observations would provide a fount of information for subsequent generations of naturalists.[19]

Another of the few significant developments at Fort Clatsop occurred on February 11th when Clark completed his map of "the country though which we have been passing from Fort Mandan to this place." Lewis wrote this line as if constraining himself from mentioning his current locale by name. The creation of this vitally important map had taken much of Clark's time in the preceding few weeks. Nevertheless, it was Lewis who wrote the first interpretation of what Clark's cartography revealed. The route they traveled west, Lewis stated, was "the most practicable and navigable passage across the Continent of North America" except for a shortcut from the Great Falls of the Missouri to "Traveler's rest" on the Bitterroot River of Montana. This latter discovery, Lewis averred, came "agreeably" from "the natives." He concluded that "the distance between those two points would be traveled more advantageously by land" than navigation. Still, little now remained of the legendary Northwest Passage as a geographical concept.[20]

Clark had not spoken of this map until Lewis brought the issue forward. He was prompted to expand on Lewis's comments by observing in his own notebook that the "large river which falls into the Columbia on its South Side at what point we could not lern; which [river] passes thro those extencive Columbian Plains from the South East." This was a reference to the near-mythical "Multnomah" River, what is known today as the Willamette River and whose opening into the Columbia they had missed the previous fall. Expanding on what he understood to be Indian conceptions of the geography of the three corners of present Oregon, Idaho, and Nevada, Clark mistakenly concluded that this "other or westerly fork" of the Columbia "may afford a practicable land Communication with New Mexico." Unlike his discernment of the workings of the tributaries to the Snake River the previous fall, Clark's deduction here was wrong. Having no working knowledge of the West's Great Basin, an anomalous feature which eluded conjecture and would not come into full geographic comprehension for several more decades, he established the imaginary headwaters of the "westerly fork" in the approximate vicinity of today's Winnemucca, Nevada. In any event, the ruminations of mid-February 1806 at Fort Clatsop set the stage for several mini-expeditions during the return voyage. Clark would make a trip up the Willamette in April, and Lewis would later conduct a reconnaissance of the shortcut from the Bitterroot Valley to the Great Falls of the Missouri while Clark proceeded down the Yellowstone River.[21]

In mid-February 1806 Lewis's scientific orientation turned to the zoological side of the biologic spectrum. The luxury of time and a stationary status facilitated descriptions of birds, fowl, fish, shellfish, reptiles, foxes, deer, wolves, sheep, antelope, sea otters, raccoons, and squirrels. Nearly every day Lewis picked a new genus or species to describe. A major objective of the "delay" at the coast was completed on February 21st with the return of the last of the men sent to make salt. Twelve of the twenty "gallons" of salt were placed in two kegs and reserved for the return voyage. The remainder was used for curing meat during the balance of their stay at Fort Clatsop. By late February at least six men, including Sergeant Ordway, were ill. Clark wrote that "we have not had as many Sick at one time Since we left the Settlements of the Illinois," now two winters past. "[T]he general Complaint appears to be bad colds and fevers, with a violent pain in the head, and back, something I believe of the influenza." If Clark's diagnosis was correct, the men could only have caught the flu from the neighboring Indians who would have gotten sick, in turn, from contact with visiting traders.[22]

The constant rain and damp, plus what Lewis rightly considered a poor diet combined with the general level of inactivity, had taken a toll on the men physically and mentally. After citing the limited supply of elk meat, some of which was tainted, Lewis reflected his sour outlook with the following sarcastic appraisal: *"a comfortable prospect for good living."* When Clark took his turn at copying Lewis's entry, he made the criticism more site-specific: *"what a prospect for good liveing at Fort Clatsop at present"* (emphases in the originals). On March 3rd Lewis complained that "every thing moves on in the old way and we are counting the days which separate us from the 1st of April and which bind us to fort Clatsop." This servitude had to continue, Lewis analyzed, because a departure before then would be "folly." He knew from his inspection the previous fall that on the plains of the Columbia there would be "no fuel except a few small dry shrubs." The plan was to stay in the vicinity of Fort Clatsop and the attendant proximity of the elk, unless the game was to leave for higher elevations with the arrival of spring. Were that to happen, Lewis wrote, "we have determined to ascend the river slowly and indeavor to procure subsistence on the way," preparatory to the final push into the foothills of the Rocky Mountains.[23]

The first inkling that the detachment was close to the decision to leave Fort Clatsop appeared a few days later. On March 6th Sgt. Patrick Gass said a few men were "employed in repairing the canoes." Elaborating on Lewis's timetable for departure, Gass said the strategy behind this work was to "be able to set out on our return [upriver] immediately, should our hunters be unsuccessful." On the 9th, erstwhile metal bender John Shields had been set to work making elkskin sacks to contain documents and other articles that needed to be kept dry. William Clark's journal entry of 12 March 1806, noted a supply on hand of 358 pair of moccasins, in addition to an inventory of dressed hides for shirts, overalls, and capotes, all readied "for the homeward journey." Surely, the "delay" on the coast, as Clark had once called it, was nearing its end. On the 12th Sergeant Ordway reported that the canoes were being "corked & pitched" in readiness. And on the same day Whitehouse added, "Two of our party were employed in making of Oars." As the departure became imminent, the logistical implications of resuming the voyage loomed more in Clark's mind than Lewis's. This can be discerned not merely from the inventory of supplies, but also Clark's supplement to Lewis's entry of March 13th. Therein he reported Indian intelligence that the first run of salmon up the Columbia would begin in early April. If that did not prove true, then he thought "it will be unfortunate for us" since salmon "must form our principal dependance for food… above the Falls and it's S. E. branch [i.e., the Snake River] to the Mountains." [24]

By the middle of March negotiations for purchasing canoes from the Clatsop Indians had begun, but they were not going well from Lewis's perspective. As he phrased it, they "would not dispose of their canoes at a price which it was in our power to give consistently with the state of our Stock of Merchandize." (In the end the explorers would simply steal one.) All that remained of the once-ample supply of small trade goods could be held, Lewis said, in two handkerchiefs. The balance of their stock for barter consisted of six blue robes and a scarlet one, an army coat and hat, five robes made from the remnants of an American flag, and a few pieces of cloth trimmed with ribbons. Upon this inventory, Lewis continued, "we have wholly to depend for the purchase of horses and such portion of our subsistence from the Indians as it will be in our powers to obtain." This, he concluded, was "a scant dependence indeed, for a tour of the distance of that before us." [25]

On Monday 17 March 1806, two weeks ahead of the predetermined schedule, the expedition's canoes were readied for departure. The deciding factor was the weather. As Lewis explained, if the party waited until April 1st to depart, they ran the risk of being delayed by a storm or, worse, a series of them. The particular challenge, Lewis penned, was the initial segment of their route from Fort Clatsop to the villages of the Cathlamet Indians where the ocean-like swells of wide Columbia finally dissipated in the relatively narrow passage of the river. Not wanting to countenance being marooned on the lower Columbia a second time, he and Clark determined to leave when the river was next "calm" and be done with it. The lessons of 8–15 November 1805 on the approach to and stay at Dismal Nitch had been well learned. [26]

There was now little left to do at Fort Clatsop, but for Meriwether Lewis there was a sovereignty obligation to attend to, one which also presented an opportunity that would discretely burnish his reputation at the expense of Clark's. As foreshadowed in an earlier chapter, on March 18th Lewis composed a short narrative, made in triplicate, giving two copies to Clatsop Indians plus another that was posted inside the fort. The intended recipient was any ship captain that might soon appear in the neighborhood. Lewis's one paragraph history of the expedition, all that might have been known of their fate without a successful return journey, said, in its operative part:

> the party consisting of the persons whose names are hereunto annexed, and who were sent out by the government of the U' States in May 1804 to explore the interior of the Continent of North America, did penetrate the same by way of the Missouri and Columbia Rivers, to the discharge of the latter into the Pacific Ocean, where they arrived on the *14th November 1805,* and from whence they departed the _____ day of March 1806 on their return to the United States by the same rout they had come out" (emphasis added).

On the reverse side of this transcript Lewis or Clark sketched out their understanding of the "connection of the upper branches of the Missouri with those of the Columbia… on which we also delienated the track we had come and that we meant to pursue on our return where the same happened to vary." [27]

This message-in-a-bottle-like text formed a Discovery claim within the regnant scheme of international law, since it can be read to assert an American title to the Columbia watershed. It has the additional value of allowing us, on close inspection, to see once again the compulsion of Meriwether Lewis to place himself at the center of the story, to the exclusion of Clark and the remainder of the expedition. This he does by attributing the accomplishment of reaching the Pacific Ocean to the entire party on *November 14th,* when, as we saw earlier, the Colter vanguard turned Point Distress on the 13th and the balance of the party was still marooned with poor Clark at Dismal Nitch. Clark let the assertion pass for the moment in his verbatim copy of Lewis's note. He wouldn't have contradicted the contents of what was likely to be a historic document. But this episode probably served as the foundation for an ensuing dialogue between him and Lewis over how to determine the date the expedition achieved the mission of reaching the Pacific.[28]

Evidence for such a discourse can be found by discerning how Lewis and Clark framed the first two letters they dispatched upon the expedition's return to St. Louis in September 1806. Donald Jackson determined that Lewis originated both his own letter to Thomas Jefferson and, more particularly, the text for Clark's famous letter to one of his brothers (probably Jonathan). The contents of the latter missive were expected to be shared with an eager frontier press, and thus it was the Clark family correspondence, not Lewis's official letter to Jefferson, that first informed the public's understanding of what happened during the expedition and when. Clark's final version of what Lewis had initially prepared for him, dated 23 September 1806, was first published in Frankfort, Kentucky on 9 October 1806 and widely republished by other newspapers. This is what the explorers expected to happen. To our point here, Lewis's *private* letter to Jefferson does not mention a date in association with reaching the Pacific Ocean. His *draft* of Clark's *public* letter stipulated "On the 14th of November we reached the ocean," replicating the account contained in the note left at Fort Clatsop. However, Jackson reports that

Lewis's draft inscription was struck over in Clark's handwriting with 17 November offered as a substitution. In the final version of the letter, the one Clark actually sent his brother, Clark retains the November 17th date, thereby consciously contradicting Lewis's message left at Fort Clatsop. This is a curious turn. When William Clark disagrees with Meriwether Lewis there is a story to tell.[29]

James Holmberg notes that a number of the dates in both Lewis's draft of Clark's letter of September 23rd and Clark's final version are wrong. He attributes this to a combination of faulty memories and the captains' not seeking the obvious recourse of their journals. Perhaps, looking at the record another way, there's a more intentional explanation. The note Lewis left at Fort Clatsop creates the unmistakable impression that Lewis considered 14 November 1805 as the key date, no doubt because he figures prominently in the story for that day, having jumped ahead and out of Dismal Nitch. On the other hand, Clark's journal and maps show that he attached greater significance to 15 November when he and the larger party reached the safety of Station Camp. Approaching St. Louis, with the exploits of the expedition about to become a matter of public knowledge, the captains' divergent perspectives had to be reconciled.[30]

There are two reasons Clark put forth neither November 14th nor 15th but instead chose November 17th as a compromise date for accomplishing the mission. First, his survey establishing the location of Station Camp was conducted that day—a landmark event in the cartographic history of the enterprise. The 17th was also the occasion of Lewis's return to Station Camp from his tour around Cape Disappointment and the coast. This would have been the first day Lewis *and* Clark were at Station Camp together.

Of the key dates in the history of the expedition recorded in both the draft and final versions of Clark's letter to his brother, only the date of departure from Fort Clatsop (March 23rd, 1806, not March 27th as written) seems an innocent mistake. *All* of the other variations in the letter intended for public consumption differ from the known sequence of events (as recorded in the journals). This was purposeful. The controlling intention here seems to have been primarily William Clark's. As an explorer occasionally troubled by Lewis's solitary pursuits and as chief cartographer with ready access to the maps containing the campsite chronology, Clark had the motive and means to balance the account of accomplishments. It was Clark who was, in effect, "the expedition's historian." Upon returning to St. Louis and the expected publicity attendant upon a successful expedition, Clark leveraged his command of the documentary record for strategic effect. In so doing he prefigured the steps he would take years later to correct Lewis's journal on the eve of Nicholas Biddle's publication, as recounted in an earlier chapter.[31]

Clark's September 1806 chronological reconstruction focused on five key events during the expedition, concluding with the aforementioned arrival at the Pacific. The first in this series was reaching "the foot of the rapids" at the Great Falls of the Missouri on 14 June 1805, which date Clark did not correct in Lewis's draft letter and was carried over in the final. However, Lewis's first encounter with the falls actually occurred on June 13th. Next in the sequence of important moments was the party's arrival at the Three Forks of the Missouri, putatively on 27 July 1805. However, William Clark actually reached the forks on July 25th, the sole instance when he was the first captain to a major object of discovery, granting Lewis a courtesy he would expect in return. As for the epochal Continental Divide story, Lewis drafted language referencing how he had reunited with Clark at Camp Fortunate at the expedition's head of navigation on the Missouri on 17 August 1805. However, Lewis does aver, for the benefit of Clark's letter, that he had "penitrated with a party of three men to the waters of the columbia," an event which took place on August 12th, but that date goes unmentioned in the end-of-voyage correspondence. Both Lewis's draft and Clark's final letter have the expedition emerging out of the Bitterroot Mountains wilderness on 22 September 1805, when in fact Clark came upon the Nez Perce villages on Weippe Prairie on September 20th. And, as noted at the outset, the final version of Clark's published letter states, "On the 17th of November [1805] we reached the Ocian." However, in this instance his text corrected Lewis's draft that had the event occurring on November 14th.[32]

Nigh upon St. Louis, and likely earlier, Clark contrived, with at least partial concurrence from Lewis, a compromise version of the "discovery calendar" suitable to an exploratory command structure led by two men who on the most noteworthy occasions during the voyage happened to be separated. This frequent separation created a particular problem for Clark that needed a solution. So, whether it was to his occasional personal advantage or not, in his letter and proto-press release Clark simply adopted a date when both captains were in each other's company on or near the occasion of their great discoveries or other momentous occasions. In the case of arriving at the foot of the Great Falls of the Missouri, Clark worked in the date by which both he and Lewis knew of the existence of the falls.[33]

What might be termed Clark's "common date of discovery" strategy was clearly settled upon after the departure from Fort Clatsop. Clark had seen the note Lewis posted at Fort Clatsop and at the time left the date uncorrected in his copy of Lewis's remarks. Clark would have thus known what this portended when it came to chronicling the expedition's history. He may have conceived this strategy to underscore posterity's understanding of his co-captaincy of the venture, giving privileged status to equality of command rather than first to the finish line. I believe Clark settled on this scheme by the time he returned to the confluence of the Yellowstone and Missouri Rivers in August 1806. Upon reaching these forks on the homeward journey, Clark referred to it as the locale where the westbound party "had *all* encamped the 26th of April—1805" (emphasis added). To use one of the captains' favorite phrases, it is worthy of remark that Lewis ventured ahead to reach the confluence on April 25th.[34]

James Holmberg suggests that the correspondence of 23 September 1806 was jointly authored, and this is certainly true to an extent. However, it is nonetheless true that William Clark was always contending his partnership modality versus

Lewis's lone hero propensity, even months and years after the voyage. In a letter written in January 1807 to Secretary of War Henry Dearborn, a man who surely knew of Clark's value and contributions, Lewis referred to "my late tour to the Pacific Ocean." Lewis used that exact phrasing two months later when he attempted to scare off "spurious publications" or otherwise unauthorized accounts of the expedition. David McKeehan, the publisher of Patrick Gass's journal, the first book-length account to appear in print, took Lewis to task for this presumptuousness. Calling Lewis "Your Excellency," McKeehan mocked him for daring to interfere "in this affair of the journals of what you very modestly call *your late tour*." In another fusillade, McKeehan chided Lewis for his callous attitude toward his companions, such as Gass. McKeehan wrote, "Perhaps I ought to beg pardon for using the word *companions*, as it has been thought proper at the seat of government to degrade them to mere '*Followers*.'" [35]

During the recent bicentennial much of the literature about the expedition seemed an exercise in retrospective hagiography. McKeehan's contemporary insights offer a healthy corrective vision. From the time he was eighteen years old, Meriwether Lewis wanted to be an explorer. He pleaded with Thomas Jefferson to join the American Philosophical Society subscription expedition of 1792, an assignment that went instead to the botanist André Michaux. Perhaps this was just as well for Lewis, since that venture was doomed to failure. But Lewis long remembered the disappointment. Leaving Fort Mandan for the far west more than a decade later, he described the impending voyage as "a da[r]ling project of mine for the last ten years." Then, as secretary to the president in 1803, upon first learning of Jefferson's interest in tracing the Missouri to its source, Lewis again "renewed his sollicitations," which this time resulted in the command. [36]

At the end of his tragically short life it seems to have occurred to Lewis that none of the trappings of glory that he had sought so assiduously mattered much. In a letter to a close friend a little more than a year after his return to St. Louis, he wrote of the anguish brought on by his troubled love life. Describing himself as a "*perfect widower with rispect to love*" with a "*void*" in his heart, "certain it is, that I never felt less like a heroe than at the present moment." Clearly this passage indicates that Lewis felt he was or should be regarded as a hero, and though telling in itself, this self-reflection opens a door to another intriguing hallway, the realm of Lewis's personal relationship with Jefferson, Clark, and women generally. One is hard pressed to imagine Clark writing this way. [37]

Before leaving Fort Clatsop, after completing the short note to be posted on the wall of the fort and given to the Indians, the captains briefly considered whether to compose a lengthier report that the Natives might deliver to coastal traders. On reflection, lacking confidence that the Indians could serve as a medium for such a report, Lewis said, "we declined making any." However, he did use the journal entry of March 18th as the occasion to expand and amplify on the track for the return, explaining where it "happened to vary" from the outbound voyage. Tempted to send several of the crew back by sea, Lewis thought the better of it.

Leaving any men behind to wait for a ship left both the overland return party and particularly the coastal remnant small and vulnerable to attack. The risk was compounded by Lewis's surmise that a coastal trader would spend the ensuing summer exchanging merchandise with the Indians and not immediately return to the eastern seaboard of North America. He concluded, no doubt correctly, that he and Clark could get back to the United States on a timelier basis. Besides, Lewis reasoned—and this was the definitive thought—he needed as large a party as possible to divide it three or four ways "to accomplish the objects we have in view," referencing the side explorations in the Missouri Basin. This was the first intimation of the captains' intention to split the party at Traveler's Rest in the Bitterroot Valley, which they did on 3 July 1806.[38]

Several days of rain prevented the last application of pitch to the canoes, but it did allow Lewis additional time to reflect on their coastal sojourn. On 20 March 1806, he wrote, "Altho' we have not fared sumptuously this winter and spring at Fort Clatsop, we have lived quite as comfortably as we had any reason to expect we should; and have accomplished every object which induced our remaining at this place except that of meeting with the traders who visit the entrance of this river." Lewis went on to explain that the primary benefit of such an occurrence would have been the acquisition of merchandise for trade with the Indians which "would have made our homeward bound journey much more comfortable." Lewis's prized salt supply was deemed "sufficient to last us to the Missouri." [39]

With many of the men complaining of being unwell, Lewis expressed confidence that if the party could just simply get "under way" they would become "more healthy." Lewis the physician turned psychologist noted that proceeding on "always had that effect on us heretofore." By March 21st, down to one day's provisions, the captains reluctantly sent out the hunters. Privates Shields and Collins soon returned to the fort from nearby environs without any game. George Drouillard and the Field brothers were therefore ordered to head up the river above Tongue Point to lay-in provisions for the shortly expected arrival of the larger party. On the 22nd, Lewis gave Fort Clatsop and its furnishings to Coboway, the Clatsop chief who was "much more kind an[d] hospitable to us than any other indian in this neighbourhood." Having made this testimonial will, the expedition was "determined to set out tomorrow at all events." The huckleberries were leafing, Lewis noted, which reminded the party of spring and, no doubt, easterly destinations.[40]

CHAPTER 16   The Return Voyage
and the Dissolution of
Meriwether Lewis

THE WINTER'S DELAY AT FORT CLATSOP ENDED 23 MARCH 1806, appropriately enough the second full day of spring. Yet another rainy morn presented itself, and there was some debate about whether to depart as scheduled. In one of the few instances where indecisiveness of command is even hinted at in the documentary record, Joseph Whitehouse opined, "Our Officers were undetermined, whether they would set out, on our homeward bound Voyage; or not." However, at noon the weather turned fair, and the captains ordered the canoes loaded. Lewis wrote, "at 1 P. M. we bid a final adieu to Fort Clatsop." The "homeward bound journey," as Clark had originally termed it both the previous November 21st and again this day, had resumed. Lewis kept an almost hour-by-hour account of the party as it inched away from the grasp of Fort Clatsop.[1]

Nothing of great consequence occurred until the expedition reached a point opposite the "Quicksand river" (now the Sandy) near today's Washougal, Washington. This would prove an unusually significant encampment. First, it served as the base for William Clark's investigation of the Willamette River, mentioned earlier. As Clark told Nicholas Biddle after the expedition, he simply had not believed the "Quicksand" was sufficient to drain the expansive country to the south of the Columbia. Clearly, some other feature had to explain the vast watershed before him, likely the long-rumored "Multnomah." Thus, a delay was ordered for "a day or two" to solve Clark's geographic puzzle. This pause also allowed the hunters to procure an ample supply of meat before the expedition passed the "Western mountains" (the Cascade Range). Experience had shown that the Columbia Gorge and plains to the east were short on game.[2]

While Clark and several others went voyaging about ten miles up the Willamette to do some dutiful geographic in-filling pursuant to completing his mapwork, Lewis managed the camp. He sent out several parties of hunters. Those remaining in camp were set to making rope out of elk skin, a tool necessary to guiding the expedition's canoes through the turbulent waters ahead. Later that day the wisdom of the decision to call a temporary halt to the eastward voyage was reinforced by a series of visits by Indian families descending the river. Lewis reported, "they informed us that they resided at the great rapids and that their relations at that place were much streightened at that place for the want of food; that they had consumed their winter store of dryed fish and that those of the present season had not yet arrived." The Indians communicated to the explorers that the tribes above them were in the same difficulty and that the spring runs of salmon would not commence for another month yet.[3]

Lewis continued, "This information gave us much uneasiness with rispect to our future means of subsistence." Lewis recounted that above Celilo Falls there were no big game animals, such as deer and elk, to depend on. Furthermore, he guessed that the tribal horse herds on the Columbian Plain ahead would be "very poor most probably at this season, and if they have no fish their dogs must be in the same situation." Despite this "gloomy prospect for subsistence on any terms" Lewis determined that it was "inexpedient to wait the arrival of the salmon[,]" as he was fearful that a month's delay would put a timely recrossing of the Bitterroot and/or Rocky Mountains in jeopardy. He did not want to risk getting to the waters of the Missouri so late that "the ice would close" it. From experience two years before, Lewis knew that he had to get below the Mandan villages on the Missouri by early November or he ran the chance of getting caught by a freeze on the northern plains.[4]

Lewis was also under the (mistaken) impression that the Nez Perce departed for the buffalo plains east of the Rockies around the beginning of May. As he saw it, if the Nez Perce left the Clearwater district "before our arrival we may probably find much difficulty in recovering our horses; without which there will be but little possibility of repassing the mountains." This, truly, was a dismaying prospect, recalling many of the emotions from the time when the expedition was trying to acquire horses from the Shoshone for the westbound trip. Only in this case, as Lewis painted the scene, the expedition might not merely be forced to return unsuccessfully; it could be temporarily or possibly permanently marooned west of the Rockies! Lewis concluded decisively, "we are therefore determined to loose as little time as possible in geting to the [Nez Perce]."[5]

On 4 April 1806 Lewis and Clark were apprised that the meat secured by the hunters would soon be dried. This was a signal that the voyage was about to resume. Several men were ordered upstream as a vanguard hunting party to wait upon and provision the larger detachment trailing behind. At first light on April 6th the meat was packed into the deerskin casings and the canoes loaded. After breakfast the return voyage recommenced.[6]

The seasonal variation in the Columbia River's flow was pronounced, and Lewis characterized the rapids at the Cascades as being "much worse" than they had been the previous fall. As he explained, during the descent "there were only three difficult points within seven miles, [while] at present the whole distance is extremely difficult of ascent." In Lewis's estimation the river here was twenty feet higher than it had been the previous fall. And the water was appreciably colder too.

Several decades later the Wilkes Expedition measured the temperature of the Columbia at different seasons and found the water to be sixty-eight degrees in September but only forty-two during the spring freshet.[7]

If the environment wasn't rigorous enough, the challenge of the return voyage was compounded by a pattern of difficulty with the Indians that lasted through a hundred miles of eastward travel. Meriwether Lewis was at the center of this story, in the handful of episodes that stand out during an otherwise anticlimactic homeward trip. Indeed, a recounting of the problematic relationship that unfolded in April 1806 between Lewis and the Natives of the Columbia River country offers new insight into a fundamental element of the Lewis legend—his dissolution after the expedition.

Few aspects of the Lewis and Clark Expedition elicit as much debate and discussion as the circumstances surrounding the death of Meriwether Lewis in October 1809, a little more than three years after the conclusion of his voyage to the Pacific. The principal point of contention traditionally has been whether Lewis was murdered or committed suicide. The modern scholarly consensus lands heavily on the latter proposition, grounded in the fact that Thomas Jefferson and William Clark, who knew Lewis well, never said or did anything that would lead to a conclusion that their friend and colleague had met with foul play. In fact, they were convinced the opposite was true. As Stephen Ambrose put it, "neither Jefferson nor Clark ever doubted that Lewis killed himself." Both men would have been in a position to either track down a murderer or commission an investigation into a crime. Neither did. Still, it is unlikely there will ever be any proof on the matter unless Lewis's remains are exhumed. Inevitably, the subject will be shaped by speculation and informed interpretation based on the existing evidence, much of which is problematic in itself.[8]

Thus, of late, the argument has shifted from "did Lewis commit suicide?" to the presumption that he did, precipitating in turn a scholarly quest for intimations of Lewis's mortality. A recent study by humanities scholar Clay Jenkinson is a formidable example of this new search for an understanding of Lewis's character, particularly in regard to how events internal to the expedition may have played a role in Lewis's decision to kill himself years later at Grinder's Stand. The reason for Lewis's suicide forms one of the principal subtexts of Stephen Ambrose's wildly popular *Undaunted Courage*. In Ambrose's estimation, Lewis was "a good man in a crisis," an able frontiersman, intellectually curious about the natural world, and a capable commander of men. At the same time, however, Ambrose said Lewis had a short temper and could be impetuous. Lewis also developed a "swelled head as a result of the adulation he had received," took drugs, and drank a lot of alcohol.[9]

Though Lewis's dissolution has become a somewhat fashionable topic in our own time, speculations about his psychological condition go back to the year of his death. One of the earliest press reports on the explorer's demise noted that Lewis was rumored to have incurred expenses for which no appropriations had been made. The federal government in Washington, DC, had rejected a voucher he had proffered for reimbursement. This loss, if multiplied by similar objections

Portrait of Meriwether Lewis by Charles Willson Peale, taken shortly after the expedition's return. (Meriwether Lewis by Charles Willson Peale, from life, 1807. Independence National Historical Park)

to other expenses Lewis had obligated, threatened to bankrupt him. "We can hardly suppose," stated the anonymous correspondent, that Lewis's financial travail "alone, could have produced such deplorable consequences," that is, killing himself. Postmodernist studies of Lewis and Clark, which deconstruct the texts associated with the expedition, have begun to create an interpretive theory substantiating the notion of "exploration as an interior voyage," in other words, exploration as a discovery of self as much as a discovery of new people or new lands. A survey of the journals and main currents of discourse surrounding Lewis's presumed suicide suggests that the first cracks in Lewis's psyche occurred on the return voyage up the Columbia River.[10]

From his first few days west of the Continental Divide in the summer of 1805 until he recrossed the Bitterroot Mountains in June 1806, the country drained by the Great River of the West confounded Meriwether Lewis. As recounted earlier in this book, on 12 August 1805 Lewis and a handful of men descended Lemhi Pass "to a handsome bold running Creek of cold Clear water.[H]ere I first tasted the water of the great Columbia river," Lewis said. His exhilaration was short-lived. The next day, he learned "unwelcome information" from Shoshone Chief Cameahwait about the difficulty of following the Columbian headwaters "to the great lake where the white men lived." Lewis inscribed in his journal for August 14th that the Shoshone account of lands and rivers west "fell far short of my expectation or wishes," language that could well serve as the epigraph for the western third of the trail traversed by the Expedition for Northwestern Discovery.[11]

The *physical* challenges and privations experienced by the Lewis and Clark Expedition as it crossed the Bitterroot Mountains, coursed through the numerous rapids of the Snake and Columbia Rivers, and absorbed the pummeling of oceanic storms and their near-constant rain have been chronicled herein and elsewhere. The *psychological* toll exacted by the harsh geographic extremes of the Columbia's country, however, has rarely been analyzed. William Lang, in his pathfinding essay, addresses the effects of the Columbian environment on William Clark during the trip down the river in the fall of 1805. Coping with stress, however, seems a more appropriate item for study in regard to Meriwether Lewis on the trip upriver in the spring of 1806.[12]

Lewis's most reflective moments typically occurred when the expedition paused for logistical reasons, such as staging portages, overwintering, or waiting out bad weather. Because we have little from Lewis's pen in the documentary record west of the divide in 1805, insights into his thinking about the once promising but ultimately troublesome geography of the Columbia country must emerge from the journal entries made during the expedition's extended stopovers during the winter and spring of 1806. Fort Clatsop, Rock Fort at The Dalles, and Camp Choppunish among the Nez Perce constitute a serial set of observation points—west, central, and east—from which Lewis rendered his reflections. Though the climate and topography of each place was markedly different from the other two, Lewis's outlook on the Columbian world was, taken as a whole, decidedly unfavorable.

The expedition's frame of reference for the Columbia was the Missouri River, which drained a vast open country that was a hunters' paradise. By contrast, after only nine days of managing the Lemhi Pass portage and the reconnaissance of the Salmon River, Clark recorded that the men were already concerned about "Starveing in a Countrey where no game of any kind except a fiew fish can be found." The salmon were "pleasent eateing" but did not have the caloric value of the large game inhabiting the Missouri plains. To Lewis, the Missouri watershed was a cornucopia of riches. His favored metaphor for the Columbia country was a prison.[13]

Lewis was quite explicit on this point on the way back up the river at The Dalles. On 17 April 1806, gazing out on the wide-open vista before him, Lewis mused that it stood in contrast to previously "having been so long imprisoned in mountains and those almost impenetrably thick forrests of the seacoast." John Logan Allen concludes that for Lewis the northern West as garden "stopped at the Rockies; beyond the mountains, themselves not much good for anything, were the treeless and barren plains of the Columbia." The heavily timbered Cascade Mountains were west of this desert and, though plentiful with game, not fit for agrarian pursuits. In Allen's estimation, Lewis's perception of the Columbia lowlands and coastal districts was that they were "dank and choked with timber and underbrush." To which there was a cultural corollary. The regnant theory of natural history during Lewis and Clark's time held that climate helped create national identity. As a principle applied to Native people we see how Lewis extrapolated a negative casting of the region's aboriginal inhabitants from the troublesome climate and topographies bounding the Columbia River.[14]

Lewis, contrary to the springtime 1806 reflection cited above, initially viewed leaving the Columbian Plain in the fall of 1805 with relief. The first published account of the journals edited by Nicholas Biddle phrased it thusly: "After being so long accustomed to the dreary nakedness of the country above, the change is as grateful to the eye as it is useful in supplying us with fuel." But in time even the lower Columbia region came to be regarded in a negative light. On 2 February 1806, a bored Meriwether Lewis reported that nothing of significance happened, "but all are pleased, that one month of time which binds us to Fort Clatsop and which separates us from our friends has now elapsed." The cumulative effect of the litany of complaints found in Biddle's tale about straitened diets and oppressive weather is that, according to John Logan Allen, the Columbia country is presented "least favorably of all western regions in the official reports of the expedition."[15]

The notion of confinement also informed Lewis's outlook during the return trip, when the journey home came to a temporary halt at the eastern end of the Columbia Plateau, in May 1806. The Bitterroot Mountains presented themselves, the captain wrote, as an "icy barier which seperates me from my friends and Country, from all which makes life esteemable." This lament evokes the same sentiment and psychological significance Lewis felt at Fort Clatsop a few months before. On the previous New Year's Day, Lewis had imagined being "in the bosom of our friends... when with the zest given by the recollection of the present, we shall completely, both *mentally* and corporally, enjoy the repast which the hand of civilization has prepared for us" (emphasis added).[16]

A sense of dread infused Lewis's perspective at this eastern exit from his western cell. On 21 May 1806, anticipating the return trek through the Bitterroots, he wrote of the need to lay in provisions "for that dreary wilderness" ahead. The delay with the Nez Perce gave ample time for Lewis to churn over the "wretched portion of our journy, the Rocky mountains." Once the Bitterroot traverse finally commenced on June 15th, Lewis, fearful of becoming "bewildered in these mountains," turned back because snow hindered progress and made the path very difficult to see. On the second attempt, starting June 24th, now guided by several helpful Nez Perce youths, the expedition made it over Lolo Pass, and Lewis was free of his Columbian captivity. He reflected on June 27th that "we were entirely surrounded by those mountains from which to one unacquainted with them it would have seemed impossible to have *escaped*" (emphasis added).[17]

While Lewis's captive mentality in Columbia country was unusual for the expedition—none of the other journalists evinced the sentiment in any pronounced manner—it was not unique in the annals of North American exploration. The most famous example involves Samuel Hearne, an Englishman who undertook a mission for the Hudson's Bay Company aimed at determining where Indians in the Canadian north secured the copper they exchanged with the fur traders. Hearne's journey in the early 1770's led to the discovery of the Coppermine River flowing into the Arctic Ocean, but, to our point, his account of the expedition published in 1795 had many of the trappings of a captivity narrative. For his part, Meriwether Lewis escaped Columbia country and in a virtual sigh of relief "bid adieu to the snow" on 29 June 1806. Having at last eluded the clutches of his northwestern prison, he now faced the pleasant prospect of returning to the Missouri River. By July 11th Lewis was back in the vicinity of the Great Falls in present-day Montana where the air "was pleasant and a vast assemblage of little birds which croud to the groves on the river sung most enchantingly." [18]

Enchantment is not a word associated with Lewis's discourse on the Columbia River. It is a term, however, that Lewis used with some regularity east of the Continental Divide, most famously to describe his encounter with the White Cliffs of the Missouri—"seens of visionary enchantment"—an expression that became emblematic of his Missouri River experience. Nevertheless, Lewis's fondness for Missouri River enchantment, juxtaposed with a Columbia River experience nearly devoid of such sentiment, begs for deeper analysis beyond the surface allusion to poetical delights and literary style. Doing so helps us understand the origins of his dissolution.[19]

Over a hundred years ago Elliott Coues was the first to hint at some preternatural force in the story of the expedition, a force that worked to a negative effect. In a provocative footnote to the original paraphrase of the journals prepared by Nicholas Biddle, Coues made the following observation about Meriwether Lewis's psychological difficulties on the return trip up the Columbia in the spring of 1806:

"It has always seemed to me there was some natural demoralizing agency at The Dalles and Cascades of the Columbia." The circumstances at The Dalles that led Lewis to commit "assault and battery," as Coues characterized Lewis's aggressiveness toward Indians there, are well worth investigating because they provide insight into the darkness that pervaded Lewis's view of the Columbian world.[20]

The April 1806 traverse that ran eastward from the Cascades past the Long and Short Narrows to above Celilo Falls was Meriwether Lewis's private hell. For several weeks, as the expedition moved upstream over difficult landscapes and watersheds, certain members of the Upper Chinookan and Sahaptian tribes hounded the slow-moving and therefore vulnerable explorers. In recognition of this potential travel hazard in Indian country, North West Company fur trader and explorer David Thompson later advised making friends with riverside Indian villagers going downstream even when circumstances did not dictate doing so. "[I]n descending the current of a large river," Thompson wrote, "we might pass on without much attention to them; but in returning against the current our progress will be slow and close along the shore, and consequently very much in their power." This was precisely the predicament Lewis and Clark faced.[21]

The tumult began when the expedition encountered the Cascades. The Great Rapids of the Columbia, as Clark called them, were far more turbulent than they had been during the portage of the previous fall because of the run-off from the mountains. During the portage around them several Indians pushed Pvt. John Shields off the trail and stole Lewis's dog and an axe. Provoked by this harassment, Lewis gave his men authority to shoot the Native villagers if the dog was not returned. Lewis fumed in his journal that if there were any more incidents or if the Indians "insulted our men we should put them to instant death." [22]

Explicit threats to Indians were rare for Lewis and Clark, and nothing quite this contentious had occurred since the expedition's test of wills with the Teton Sioux on the Missouri River nearly two years before. A little more than a week later, the expedition began the transition from a river voyage to an overland caravan. At The Dalles, Lewis supervised the portage around the narrows while Clark proceeded farther upstream to the Wishram village near Celilo Falls to negotiate for horses. Having Clark take on the hard negotiations associated with this duty was a wise division of labor. Clark could treat Indians with practical efficiency, while Lewis seemed to get wrapped up in an early version of cultural politics and nationalist prerogatives. More specific to the present circumstance, Lewis's nerves were becoming so frayed that by his own admission he became very agitated with one of his own men. Pvt. Alexander Willard had let wander some of the small herd of horses already secured. "I reprimanded him more severely for this peice of negligence than had been usual with me," Lewis confessed.[23]

While even-tempered Clark was conducting the tedious bargaining for horses upriver at Wishram, Lewis's journal for the concurrent period in April 1806 is replete with rants aimed at the Native inhabitants. On April 20th Lewis wrote of the Tenino villagers at the head of the Long Narrows that "they are poor, dirty, proud, haughty, inhospitable, parsimonious and faithless in every rispect, nothing but our numbers I beleive prevents their attempting to murder us at this moment." Among other incidents Lewis complained about "repeated acts of villainy" and expressed annoyance at getting "pased and repassed" by Natives who "behaved themselves with distant rispect towards us" on a trail that, it must be said, ran through their homeland not his.[24]

It might be asked what Clark thought of his co-captain's comportment. An axiom of LEWIS & CLARK lore holds that the captains always shared a mutual, cooperative outlook, and it would be wrong to conclude that William Clark ever held Meriwether Lewis in anything but a brotherly regard. (The familial analogy is no stretch of the imagination, since Clark named his first son after Lewis.) Still, we know from episodes recounted in earlier chapters that it would be naïve to believe that Clark always agreed with Lewis. Clark always chose discreet methods for expressing his divergent opinions, however, and never directly challenged Lewis in the field because doing so would constitute a breach in the command structure. Clark was too good a soldier for that.[25]

In his customary copy of Lewis's remarks, Clark chose not to include his colleague's acid characterization of those people as "inhospitable, parsimonious or faithless." Nor did he record Lewis's observation about the expedition's size staving off an imminent attack, a potential that apparently only Lewis saw. To the contrary, Clark said the Tenino who so irked Lewis "appear entirely harmless." (David Thompson reached this same conclusion in 1811. Having read a transcript of Lewis's summary letter about the expedition and Patrick Gass's published account, Thompson wrote, "Saw nothing of the reported bad Indians.") Lewis subsequently recorded that if he caught an Indian stealing "any article from us I would beat them severely." When a tomahawk was then stolen, Lewis ratcheted up the tension. Unable to find the pilfered item after searching the Indians, in a fit of pique Lewis "ordered all the spare poles, paddles and the ballance of our canoe put on the fire as the morning was cold and also that not a particle should be left for the benefit of the indians." It is not hard to discern from this scene, one of Lewis's own construction, which of these motives—warmth or spite—was primary.[26]

Native disregard for the sanctity of the expedition's possessions was a reciprocal expression in the face of Lewis and Clark's clumsiness in someone else's homeland. The Indians no doubt felt these newcomers had no business being there and disrupting life. The situation got worse when one Indian, seeing this wasteful destruction taking place, attempted to retrieve an oarlock from the bonfire, an act the obstreperous Lewis characterized as "stealing." Lewis gave this man "several severe blows and mad[e] the men kick him out of camp. I now informed the indians that I would shoot the first of them that attempted to steal an article from us." Lewis warned the Tenino "that I had it in my power at that moment to kill them all and set fire to their houses." Patrick Gass saw Lewis lose his composure by striking the Indian and noted that this "was the first act of the kind, that had happened during the expedition." [27]

Clay Jenkinson, a close student of Lewis's personality, suggests that it was not a coincidence the foregoing transpired in the absence of William Clark, who was at a village farther upstream. Later that summer the only fatal encounter with Indians during the expedition—Lewis's fracas with the Blackfeet—occurred when Clark was on the Yellowstone hundreds of miles away. In both of these encounters Lewis was without his emotional and diplomatic balance wheel.[28]

Lewis rejoined Clark above Celilo, but his troubles on the Columbia were far from over. Except for a few men transporting some camp cargo in canoes, the expedition had become an overland party. Progress was disrupted when Toussaint Charbonneau's horse bolted and returned to the village where it was purchased, a point opposite the mouth of the Deschutes River. Lewis assigned two men to accompany Charbonneau back to the village to secure the horse and riding gear— a saddle and a robe. When the squad returned with the horse and saddle but not the robe, Lewis exploded. Over this trivial matter he ordered Sacagawea (an interesting choice in itself, and perhaps evidence of frustration with that family) forward with a message to Clark with directions to halt the front of the column while he went back to the same village "being determined either to make the indians deliver the robe or birn their houses." Being disposed "to treat them with every severyty," Lewis galloped to the village accompanied by a few men. Just as Lewis arrived, Francois Labiche found the robe hidden in one of the lodges and the situation was defused.[29]

Consider the situation. The expedition had finally secured enough horses to convey gear and some of the men quickly across the semi-arid Columbia Plateau to the Nez Perce villages. Charbonneau, for whom Lewis later said he had the least regard among his men because of many missteps and gaffes, loses his horse blanket. Over this triviality Lewis conducts a partial retrograde movement, and worse, endangers the expedition by risking a violent exchange with the Natives. Lewis gives every evidence here of coming undone and was completely oblivious to Jefferson's code of conciliation with the tribes. Meanwhile, Clark productively occupied the time now on his hands "waiting for Cap Lewis" by climbing Haystack Butte to view the range of peaks in the Cascade chain.[30]

A few days later, Lewis's Columbia country troubles continued with an episode precipitated by the decision to abandon the last of the canoes still being used to transport some of the heavier articles upriver. The residents of the Wahowpum village four miles east and on the opposite side of the river from today's Blalock, Oregon, "tantalized" the men, Lewis reported, "with an exchange of horses for our canoes." However, once the Indians discerned "that we had made our arrangments to travel by land they would give us nothing for them [the canoes]," Lewis said, and so he "determined to cut them in peices sooner than leave them on those terms." [31]

What are we to make of this? Surely, Meriwether Lewis was not the first explorer to crack under the strain of command, nor would he be the last. After several voyages and many years of exploration in the Pacific Ocean, even the great Captain James Cook grew tired, impatient, and became more easily provoked.

Charles Wilkes, commander of the great United States Exploring Expedition, was once on the verge of a nervous breakdown too. Jenkinson, in his profile of Meriwether Lewis, writes that a "fatal disorganization" did not simply fall on the captain during the last year of his life. That is, Lewis's psychological difficulties and descent into suicide had a longer history than the threat of financial setbacks and a loss of political stature in 1809. "Did anything happen 'out there,'" Jenkinson asks, "to bring on Lewis's mental collapse?" I believe the answer to that question is yes, and Jenkinson's "out there" is, more particularly, along the banks of the once promising Columbia River.[32]

Surely Lewis's behavior on the Columbia in April 1806 indicates a man stressed to his limit and seemingly to a point just short of nervous collapse. It is here that we find the explicit onset of a troubled trajectory that terminated at Grinder's Stand three years later. Just two weeks after the foregoing incidents, Lewis flew into another temperamental rage when a Nez Perce Indian mocked Lewis's penchant for dog meat by throwing a live puppy on his plate. "I was so provoked at his insolence," Lewis reported on May 5th, "that I caught the puppy and threw it with great violence at him and... siezed my tomahawk and shewed him by signs if he repeated his insolence I would tommahawk him." Though using an element of the phrasing employed by William Clark at the village of the "Fritened Indians" below Wallula the previous October—"I could have tomahawked every Indian here"—in this instance, Lewis intended real violence, a sentiment Clark only feigned through a figure of speech. That the "puppy incident" was of a piece within a larger pattern is documented three days later when Lewis chided the expedition's hunters "severely for their indolence and inattention" to orders. Clark makes no mention of these infractions, yet another instance of his demurrals in the face of Lewis's ill-temper.[33]

LEWIS & CLARK lore celebrates the expedition's salutary relationship with the Nez Perce tribe, and so the incident with the puppy is a distinct anomaly. Both Stephen Beckham and Thomas Slaughter have suggested that the rigors of trail life and the scarcity of provisions contributed to the deterioration of Lewis's relationship with the Nez Perce. This may be true to an extent, but over the long course of the expedition there had been equal, if not far greater, challenges presented to Lewis that did not bring about this kind of reaction. In the specific locale of the "puppy incident," Lewis himself would shortly remark, "nobody seems much conserned about the state of provision." This was, after all, a place that Lewis himself said nature had dealt "a liberal hand." [34]

What, then, was the "demoralizing agency," as Coues phrased it so long ago, leading to Lewis's dissolution? It could simply have been the summative effects of physical and psychological fatigue after a long expedition, one that didn't realize all the geographic and commercial promise originally envisioned by President Jefferson. Lewis had identified himself with Jefferson's vision to such an extent that when it unraveled so did he. However, Coues was on the right track in suggesting that some unusual externality was at play on that stretch of the Columbia, one that

Portrait of William Clark by Charles Willson Peale, taken shortly after the expedition's return.
(William Clark by Charles Willson Peale, from life, 1807-1808. Independence National Historical Park)

at a minimum exacerbated some internal susceptibility of Lewis's. Complications arising from cultural circumstances that Lewis often found mystifying are one possibility. The Astorians, Lewis's close contemporaries in western travel, were always respectful of places Indians considered sacred. It might be asked whether Meriwether Lewis was sufficiently circumspect. Here we enter a realm that is admittedly speculative in nature, but, given the generally uncertain nature of what led to the dissolution of Meriwether Lewis, is well worth exploring.[35]

I believe the precipitating element for Lewis's difficulties on the return up the Columbia was his penchant for visiting Indian burial grounds. On 31 March 1806 at their provisioning camp on the approach to the Cascades, Lewis describes the farthest downstream occurrence of Indian burial vaults and related Native practices. Clark, interestingly, makes no mention of such matters, being more concerned with the geography of the region, specifically the location of what came to be known as the Willamette River.[36]

On April 11th, during the difficult portage of the Great Rapids, Lewis left the lower camp and walked downstream "to observe the manner in which these people inter their dead." Inspecting one of the eight sepulchers, each of which measured about eighty square feet, Lewis observed "that the human bones filled it perfectly to the hight of about three feet." This was the burial ground of the Watlala Chinookans who populated many villages between the provisioning camp and the Cascades. This was the same day Indians set upon John Shields on the trail, threw stones at other members of the portage party, and stole Lewis's dog. Lewis never made the connection between these "seenes of outradge" and his visit to the burial places of the Indians near the provisioning camp and another near Beacon Rock just below the Cascades.[37]

On April 15th Lewis called for a stop at Lower Memaloose Island near present-day Hood River, Oregon, so he could examine "the deposits of the ded at that place." The island was a burial ground for Indians who lived near The Dalles, the same people who would shortly provoke Lewis with great regularity. The burial vaults were similar to those he had seen below the rapids and, Lewis wrote, some were "more than half filled with dead bodies." That same day Lewis noted that none of the tribes would trade for horses. Two days later at Rock Fort, he complained that "few of the natives visited my camp today and those only remained a few hours." Becoming suspicious, Lewis speculated that a "hostile designh" had been formulated by the residents of what had been described the previous year as the "Friendly Village." Clark, who was trading for horses in a far more exposed position on the north bank of the river at the gate to the Long Narrows, did not express similar concerns.[38]

Based on observations made by Lewis's contemporaries, his visit to the burial island was viewed as a sacrilege by the tribes whose ancestors were interred there. A closer reading of Mackenzie's *Voyages* would have instructed Lewis that an unceremonious visit to an Indian graveyard was something done only to an enemy. David Thompson, who passed through the same area several years after Lewis, also wanted to visit the burial vaults on the Columbia, but his Indian guide "begged of me not to do it, as the relations of the dead would be very angry." Even Captain James Cook's demise was tied, in part, to a similar cross-cultural misunderstanding. In general terms, Cook's death can be attributed to his hot-headed response to the changed cultural dynamic brought about by his unplanned return to Hawaii. Cook had an emergency need for spar poles, but his men used poor judgment by felling timber on a burial ground and carrying off a fence protecting this spot and using it for firewood.[39]

In short, Lewis likely became a persona non grata among the Natives living near The Dalles. In their eyes he was someone who needed to be punished for his effrontery, as his subsequent torment shortly proved. In the same way, Lewis's most fractious time with the Nez Perce—the "puppy incident"—occurred near the time when he observed their burial sites. On 7 May 1806 Lewis describes Nez Perce funerary practices, although it isn't certain when he visited the graveyard. Preceding this was the May 5th episode with the dog and the additional circumstance, recorded by Lewis, of an elderly man who told other Nez Perce "that he thought we were bad men and had come most probably in order to kill them." With the help of Apash Wyakaikt, who paced them from the Clearwater River to the forks of the Columbia the previous fall, and a young Shoshone boy living amidst the Nez Perce, Lewis talked himself out of this accusation. Nevertheless, it fit the paradigm as explicated by the narratives of Mackenzie and Thompson and Cook's experience—only enemies visited gravesites.[40]

The fatalistic pall cast upon Lewis by his Columbian experience extended to his account of events once back across the Continental Divide. At the Great Falls of the Missouri, ruminating on the delay of one of his favored men, George Drouillard, Lewis had "settled it in my mind that a whitebear had killed him." When Lewis learned about Pvt. Hugh McNeal's encounter with the same species, he observed, "there seems to be a certain fatality attached to the neighbourhood of these falls." This perspective was no doubt informed by Lewis's own encounter with a grizzly in this vicinity the previous year and seems also to have formed a premonition of the difficulty about to arise on the trip up the Marias that began two days later. On July 25th, the day before Lewis shot and killed two Blackfeet Indians, Lewis was frustrated by cloudy weather, which made impossible the astronomical observations necessary to fix his latitude. This was compounded by the fact that his chronometer had stopped, making any attempt at establishing longitude fruitless. Lewis quipped, "the fates were against me." [41]

If Lewis was metamorphosed on his tour of the West, these episodes form merely the *exterior* facets of the devolved personality—an exhibition of nervous exhaustion all the more stark in contrast to the calmer and frequently more enlightened behavior of William Clark. By journey's end, Thomas Slaughter writes, "Lewis was already dead; only his body was still alive." Slaughter's morbid metaphor is a caricature of what many scholars sense, namely, that Lewis's later suicide was seeded before the voyage ended.[42]

As shown many times before, the experience of Alexander Mackenzie may prove instructive as to what the *interior* of Lewis's mentality looked like in 1806 and later. We have seen that Lewis emulated the Scotsman with great regularity, up to and including borrowing from Mackenzie's narrative idiom for inspiration. Though Lewis may not have deduced it, Mackenzie also suffered from writer's block at the end of his second voyage, taking eight years to get an account of his explorations into print. Scholars who have addressed Mackenzie's career refer to a Lewis-like post-expeditionary depression as a possible cause, but they ignore Mackenzie's benighted state or explain it away as the result of exhaustion or troubling business concerns.[43]

Mackenzie himself was more straightforward in explaining his mental condition. In a private letter to his cousin, Roderick McKenzie, written in the spring of 1794, Alexander Mackenzie laid out a scenario that Meriwether Lewis may have lived through as well. In the fall of 1793, following his return from the Pacific, Mackenzie had intended to start copying his journal,

> but the greatest part of my time was taken up in vain Speculations. I got into such a habit of thinking that I was often lost in thoughts nor could I ever write to the purpose. What I was thinking of, would often occur to me instead of that which I ought to do. I never passed so much of my time insignificantly, nor so uneasy. Although I am not superstitious, dreams amongst other things, caused me much annoyance. I could not close my eyes without finding myself in company with the Dead. I had some visions of late which almost convinced me that I had lost a near relation or a friend.[44]

Were these the types of dreams, visions, and morbid thoughts that Lewis had in the spring and summer of 1806 or, more intensely, in the fall of 1809? Might they have been prompted by comparable wilderness experiences? Did they lead to his suicide? There is, of course, no way to be sure, but there is one aspect of Lewis's death that is strongly, strangely reminiscent of yet another trail incident in Columbia country.

On 9 October 1805, during the expedition's westbound journey, the evening encampment on the Clearwater River was the scene of a riveting and mysterious incident. That night a woman among the many Nez Perce at the fire "began Singing Indian" and then proceeded to distribute camas root. She expected that each person to whom she made an offering would partake of it. As Pvt. Joseph Whitehouse reported, events took a dramatic turn when "One of our Men refused to take [the roots] from her, [and] she grew Angry, and hove them in the fire." Then she took a sharp flint from her husband and "cut her Arms in many places." Patrick Gass said the woman cut her arms from the wrists to the shoulders. With blood gushing out, the Nez Perce woman tore off her beads and copper necklace, giving some to the assembly, singing all the while, drinking her blood, and making a hissing noise. She then ran toward the river, only to be retrieved by relatives. She fell into a speechless, paralyzed state, revived at last by water thrown on her face. When she came to, the characteristically sympathetic William Clark presented her a few small items. The whole episode lasted thirty minutes.[45]

Of the several journalists who recorded the incident, Clark has the least to say about it, referring only to the "Singular acts of this woman" and that she scarified herself "in a horid manner." That Clark wrote so little may suggest that it was Meriwether Lewis who declined the offering and inadvertently precipitated the woman's response. Lewis was only beginning to recover from severe intestinal distress brought on in no small measure by an over-ingestion of the same food-stuff the woman was offering, the expedition having emerged from the Bitterroot mountain wilderness two and one half weeks earlier.[46]

What the various members of the expedition referred to as "madness" or a "fit" was likely an exercise in Native American spirituality, perhaps the shamanistic practices of what's known as the Feather Cult amongst Sahaptian people. This curative ritual commences with singing. Other defining characteristics are dancing with twists and spins and entering trance-like states of consciousness. In Native cosmology, illness could be caused by possession by evil spirits or abandonment by guardian allies. In either case, disease was viewed as a symptom of a deeper spiritual conflict. The disconcerting episode Lewis and Clark became a part of may have been an instance of the Columbia Plateau tradition of mutilating oneself if perceived to be haunted by roaming spirits. Nez Perce men also fasted and purged themselves before important undertakings such as hunting trips. This could be the reason Twisted Hair and Tetoharsky absented themselves from the Americans when they set out from Canoe Camp on 7 October 1805 even though, as Clark noted, the chiefs had "promised to accompany us." The Nez Perce men rejoined the expedition at the end of the following day.[47]

In this context, Lewis's physical condition after emerging from the Bitterroot Mountains takes on additional meaning. Sick to the point of prostrate debilitation ever since arriving at the Nez Perce villages on Weippe Prairie, Lewis had been forced to forsake virtually all responsibility for the expedition. Beginning 23 September 1805 and for most of the ensuing twelve days, Clark made note in his log about Lewis's weakened state. Lewis was so ill he could scarcely ride a horse and barely walk. On October 7th, the day of departure from Canoe Camp, Clark complained that he was still "obliged to attend every thing." Witnessing this, the Nez Perces may have interpreted Lewis's near continuous purging and food avoidance as a cleansing ritual similar to theirs, or a particularly good candidate for "Indian Medicine." In the Native world, plants were known to have curative powers, and the Nez Perce woman may have been trying to impart magical power to all those who ate the camas root she offered. Rejecting this food was a grave insult bordering on the sacrilegious.[48]

The Nez Perce woman's bloodletting, like her offering of roots, may also have been an attempt to cure the weakened Lewis. Slashing the body was also the means by which one could acquire spiritual strength. David Thompson witnessed several incidents reminiscent of the Clearwater episode. In 1801 Thompson's Indian guide, not feeling well, called his wife near and asked if she had a flint. When she responded in the negative, the guide made a lancet out of his own flint, opened a vein in her arm, and having drawn three-quarters of a pint of blood in a bowl and drank it. When Thompson and his men reacted with revulsion, the guide asked,

> have I done wrong? [W]hen I find my Stomach out of order, the warm Blood of my Wife in good Health refreshes the whole of my Body & puts me to rights; in return, when she is not well I draw Blood from my Arm, she drinks it, it invigorates & gives her Life. All our Nation do this, and all of us know it to be good Medicine.[49]

After setting out from Kettle Falls on another trip in 1811, Thompson stopped at a Native village at the mouth of the San Poil River in north central Washington where it flows into the Columbia. The Indians insisted on dancing, Thompson related, so "that we might be preserved in the strong Rapids we had to run down our way to the Sea." This ceremony was also frequented by the singular acts of one woman, "who always danced out of the Crowd & kept a line close along us, & always left the others far behind." This behavior was noticed by the chief who "called her to order" by directing that she dance with the other Indians or get a partner. She did both, Thompson wrote, "but still kept close to us." Two days later, at Thompson's next port of call on approach to the Okanogan River's outfall, yet another dance was conducted "for our good voyage & preservation to the Sea & back again, & that they might see us as well in every way as at present." All of Thompson's contemporaneous experiences—ceremonial departures, bloodletting, and the "singular" acts of a woman—seem to be the formative elements of Lewis and Clark's mysterious night on the Clearwater.[50]

Meriwether Lewis pulled into Grinder's Stand on the Natchez Trace four years and a day after the incident with the Nez Perce woman on the Clearwater. In one account of the story, when Mrs. Grinder and others entered Lewis's room they reportedly found him cutting his limbs with a razor, like the woman in the incident on the Clearwater. When Lewis asked, rather oddly, for water to "heal his wounds," was he envisioning a re-enactment of the revivification of the Nez Perce woman? There is no direct evidence to conclude decisively that Lewis was harkening back to that strange night in Idaho, but the coincidence is haunting, and no adequate explanation has been offered for that odd aspect of his death scene. Lewis would have known that you kill yourself by opening an artery, not by scarification. Self-mutilation, however, raises still more questions about the Grinder's Stand tableau. Carolyn Gilman argues, and congenially so, that Lewis occasionally lost himself in his Indian identity. Perhaps this theory should be extended to his death scene as well. There are no answers to these speculations. We only know that at his end Lewis was a tormented soul. As for why, each of us is free to choose what we find persuasive.[51]

A popular modern explanation for Lewis's demise comes in the form of what Clay Jenkinson derides as the "new orthodoxy": Lewis was manic-depressive, suffering from bipolar disorder as the condition is known diagnostically. This theory, popularized by Stephen Ambrose, apparently without foundation in scholarly literature, is the equivalent of the Warren Commission's "single bullet theory." The commission concluded that one of Lee Harvey Oswald's shots hit both President John Kennedy and Governor John Connally, making him the sole assassin. Correspondingly, the Ambrose paradigm has Lewis's manic-depression explaining the two great mysteries surrounding the career of Lewis—why he did not always keep a journal and why he committed suicide.[52]

That Lewis was suffering from significant psychological imbalances at the end of his life seems beyond dispute. In itself, however, that does not mean he was bipolar. Manic-depression is a trendy diagnosis in modern society, but little critical analysis has been applied to Lewis's behavior as correlated to the literature of mental illness. Manic-depression is a serious disorder that involves more than just occasionally feeling blue or more cheerful than usual. Those who suffer from the disease exhibit pronounced, nearly debilitating swings in mood, behavior, and energy. These alternate between expansive thinking and self-image and high energy levels in the manic phase, to lethargy, impaired mental acuity, and inability to find pleasure in what would normally be pleasure-inducing activities during the depressive phase. (The latter characteristics also define unipolar depression.) Ambrose himself notes that, except for his time with the Nez Perce in 1805 when he suffered from intense gastrointestinal distress, Lewis was always fully involved in facing the challenges of the venture. Absent the physical manifestations of recurring bipolarity, then, the burden of the reductive manic-depression thesis falls to Lewis's sporadic journal-keeping.[53]

Counter to the bipolar theory, the gaps in Lewis's journal come not at the most psychologically stressful times on the journey, but rather the least. Lewis's failure to keep a consistent journal the first year of travel on the Missouri was somewhat in keeping with travel literature's focus on "unknown regions." The Mackay/Evans venture in the 1790s proves that, as far west as the Mandan villages, the French voyageurs with the Expedition for Northwestern Discovery were, as Charles Hoffhaus has observed, "merely showing Lewis and Clark what had been their own backyard for over a century.... . The idea that [the American expedition] was 'exploring' country they and their fathers and grandfathers had traversed annually for decades would surely have struck them as a good joke."[54]

From April through September 1805, Lewis describes heading up the Missouri where no whites had been before, finding the Continental Divide, and crossing the Bitterroots. From January through April 1806, he writes extensively about waiting out a miserable winter at Fort Clatsop and traveling against the spring freshet on the Columbia River. Conversely, we have his silence during the long summer of exploration up the oft-traveled Missouri in 1804, and he is quiet again during the languid float in reverse down to St. Louis from the Mandan villages in the summer of 1806. Even this was mostly a function of having been shot in the buttock and not some ephemeral mental state. The only anomaly then, and a large one, is the final push to the Pacific from the Nez Perce homelands in the fall of 1805. However, in that case Lewis, in effect, prefaced the void in his journal by writing about "having tryumphed over the rocky Mountains and… the flattering prospect of the final success of the expedition." He may have seen the last phase of the westward voyage as anticlimactic, especially because, like the lower Missouri, the lower Columbia River had already been frequented by Euro-American explorers.[55]

There are other reasons to doubt the manic-depression theory. This condition is on the severe end of a range of mood disorders in which "significant interference with the normal functioning of life" occurs. Students of the expedition have been frustrated by the lack of diligence in Lewis's journal-keeping; but by itself or combined with Lewis's competency over the span of the voyage, there is not sufficient evidence to conclude that he was in the recurring debilitated state required to meet the clinical definition of manic-depression. People suffering from bipolar disorder also tend to be obsessively organized, which would not seem to apply to Lewis's comportment in regard to the journals. Furthermore, depressive phases are frequently seasonal in nature, and there is no correlation of this syndrome and the times when Lewis stopped writing. The more direct correlation between writing and not writing is his having been the first explorer to see a particular part of the expedition's route or not.[56]

Furthermore, suicide is more common in people suffering from unipolar depression than bipolar manic-depression. Morbid thoughts, fitful sleep, heavy drinking, constant pacing—all the behaviors exhibited by Lewis during his last days—are many of the classic symptoms found at the nadir of depression. Those who think alcohol will deaden the pain, like Lewis, only end up making their mental illness worse. It is also instructive that symbolism and the power of suggestion play a formidable role in the construction of suicidal tableaux, something worth noting given the Clearwater incident and the manner by which Lewis killed himself. A memory or the awareness of the suicidal attempts of others can establish a stylistic context—an aesthetic—for one's own suicide.[57]

Theories abound for the causes of Lewis's unbalanced state, including the most salacious—the onset of tertiary syphilis. Raymond Wood's study of John Evans, who ventured to the Mandan villages several years before Lewis and Clark, led him to the conclusion that chronic malaria may have led to Evans's eventual derangement. (A severe case of malaria can mimic mental illness or drunkenness, Wood states.) Lewis too may have suffered from an attack of malaria, but if we must resort to modern diagnoses for an eighteenth-century man I suggest Post-Traumatic Stress Disorder (PTSD) is the best explanation for the onset of Lewis's fatal depression. PTSD often occurs in conjunction with alcohol and drug abuse, affects a person's ability to function, and can precipitate depressive episodes. Occupational instability—work avoidance, interpersonal conflicts, and failure to perform duties—the hallmark of Lewis's post-expeditionary life, is a common outcome for those with PTSD. Lewis had at least two traumatic experiences, defined diagnostically as a real or perceived threat of physical injury or death or other similarly horrifying circumstances, during the course of the expedition. The first was when he stared down a grizzly that attacked him near the Great Falls of the Missouri westbound, and the second was the fatal skirmish with the Blackfeet on the return trip. In regard to the bears, Lewis once said, their "being so hard to die reather intimedates us all." On the night of his death, Lewis is reputed to have said to his servant who found him mortally wounded, "I am no coward; but I am so strong, [it is] so hard to die." [58]

My application of modern diagnoses to Lewis's breakdown is admittedly speculative, and my conclusions can only be categorized as possible explanations for Lewis's dissolution. A nineteenth-century understanding may or may not be less conjectural than forensic psychiatry, but it at least has the advantage of chronological propinquity. Francis Parkman, writing 150 years closer to Lewis than our current vantage wrote,

> To him who has once tasted the reckless independence,... the haughty self-reliance, the sense of irresponsible freedom, which the forest life engenders, civilization thenceforth seems flat and stale.... The wilderness, rough, harsh, and inexorable, has charms more potent in their seductive influence than all the lures of luxury and sloth. And often he on whom it has cast its magic finds no heart to dissolve the spell, and remain[s] a wanderer and an Ishmaelite to the hour of its death.[59]

If Meriwether Lewis killed himself, as was commonly believed in his time and our own, then his death, like others of this sort, was, as psychologist Kay Jamison phrases it, "a final gathering of unknown motives, complex psychologies, and uncertain circumstances." Troubling as it is that a capable person would take his own life, it is no less so for those who face the void created by the absence. As Jamison suggests, the suicide's death "insinuates itself far too corrosively" into the dreams, expectations, and fears of those left behind.[60]

Here we have an intimation of why Lewis's self-destruction draws scholarly interest and public fascination 200 years after his death. He was the protégé of Thomas Jefferson, who was arguably the most influential intellectual in American history. Lewis himself was an accomplished figure in one of the most highly regarded fields of human endeavor—exploration. He was widely admired and feted. As the poet Edwin Arlington Robinson once phrased it, he had "everything to make us wish that we were in his place," including the opportunity to see that most treasured part of the continent, the American West, in its near primal state. [61]

All of this may not have been enough for Lewis, and even if he did not kill himself, his life had become a shambles, having lost or squandered schooling, social standing, fame, honor, Jefferson's regard, and potential riches. Nevertheless, it is almost certain that the turning point in Lewis's life occurred during his "darling project"—the expedition to the Pacific—and that it became manifest in Columbia country on the return voyage.[62]

EPILOGUE The Fidelity of William Clark

ONE OF THE STATED PURPOSES OF THIS BOOK IS A REBALANCING of our understanding of the captains' respective contributions to the Expedition for Northwestern Discovery. It would be unfortunate, then, to end without one last emblematic story from the return featuring William Clark. This vignette is the kind of moral tale that makes the account of the expedition so compelling.

Starting a few miles above Celilo Falls on the north bank of the Columbia River, the expedition began the longest continuous overland segment of the entire journey. For the first few days the expedition still had two canoes acting as tenders for hauling cargo, but now the path taken by Lewis and Clark was truly what typically it was not: an actual trail. Somewhat chastened by the Charbonneau incident recounted in the previous chapter, the captains drew up a new "order of march." The men were divided into groups, alternating each day between those who marched and those who rode horseback. Lewis stated that "haveing divided the party agreeably to this arrangement, we proceeded on through an open plain country." John Ordway described the trail as "Smooth" and "back from the river." Washington Highway 14 follows such an alignment, to this day. The expedition had only thirteen horses to carry camp equipment and riders, thus having mounts for only about a third of the men at any one time. Most of the horses were stallions, a fact that led Clark to term their performance on the trail as "troublesom." On 22 April 1806, he said, the party made fourteen miles but only with the "greatest exirtion." Their camp that night was in the vicinity of the modern John Day Dam.[1]

The next "stage" on the road home also proved a long hard trek. The expedition conducted what Lewis termed a "march along a narrow rocky bottom on the N. side of the river" for twelve miles. Lewis said, "the sands made the march fatieguing." Propitiously, this day Lewis and Clark met yet another in a now-lengthening list of helpful Nez Perce people: a man and his family returning home with thirteen horses in tow, "most of them young and unbroken." The Nez Perce man, whom Clark had just seen at the Long Narrows and who had returned a bag of lost gunpowder, offered to hire out these horses. However, as Lewis maintained, he and Clark preferred to own rather than lease, so they initially rejected this offer. Lewis reported that they were wary of having to "mentain" the whole family. Proceeding a little farther to the mouth of Rock Creek in today's Klickitat County, Washington, the detachment made camp.[2]

The next day, overcoming their initial reservations, the captains rented three horses from the Nez Perce caravan, and bought three more from nearby Tenino villagers. Now for the first time since their emergence from the Bitterroot Mountains and departure from the canoe camp on the Clearwater River the previous fall, the expedition was entirely an overland venture. Notwithstanding the obvious and recurring challenges presented by river travel during the intervening half year, this stretch of trail in eastern Klickitat County, was quite rigorous in its own right. Clark said the course ran through an "open Countrey rugid & Sandy between Some high lands and the river." Lewis said the "road" was "rocky and sandy alternately" and accordingly "difficult and fatieguing." Lewis reported that "most of the party complain of the soarness of their feet and legs." He attributed this condition to "walking over the rough stones and deep sands" after a winter on the "soft soil" at Fort Clatsop had weakened their stamina. Lewis said his own left ankle gave him "much pain." For relief, he bathed his feet in the cool waters of the Columbia. Of the journalists, only Patrick Gass had a positive comment about reentering "the great and beautiful plains of [the] Columbia." [3]

April 25th began routinely. The expedition broke camp and traveled eleven miles to an unusually large Indian village of 700 souls. The now-usual attempts at trade for horses ensued (unsuccessfully), and the Nez Perce "fellow traveller" (as Lewis called him) pointed out the principal chiefs of the "Pish-quit-pahs" village (likely a band of the Walla Walla Indians) so that the captains could bestow two of their peace medals. Late in the afternoon the expedition departed the village accompanied by about eighteen young Indian men on horseback. It must have been quite a scene. Lewis was smitten by the quality of the Indians' horses. "I did not see a single horse which could be deemed poor and many of them were as fat as seals," Lewis recorded in his journal, using an interesting oceanic analogy. His astonishment was grounded in the knowledge that with the spring grass still low these horses had subsisted during the winter on the "dry grass of the plains." Nevertheless, they were ridden "with greater severity than is common among ourselves," by which Lewis meant the animals were more durable.[4]

Lewis described this particular stretch of terrain in terms consistent with the trail's character since leaving the Long Narrows: "the river hills are about 250 feet high and generally abrupt and craggey in many places faced with a perpendicular and solid rock." For emphasis Lewis added, "this rock is black and hard." Clark's eyes, meanwhile, were fixed elsewhere. While traversing this sere, difficult landscape just east of today's Klickitat-Benton county line, Clark, who was at the rear of this spectacular cavalcade, noticed that Pvt. Hugh Hall "had fallen behind out of my sight." Clark quietly stated in his journal that he directed Hall to ride.[5]

Sgt. Patrick Gass's journal fills out the picture of what transpired. He reported that the men "complain of their feet being sore" and then quietly added, "the officers have to go on foot to permit some of them to ride." Conjoining the Clark and Gass entries for this day, it seems clear that Captain Clark gave up his horse so that Private Hall could ride the balance of the day's march. The gesture was significant enough to capture Gass's attention, as it did most likely for every man in the party. To the frequently asked question of why the Lewis and Clark Expedition was a success, one need only know this story to see the answer.[6]

To fully appreciate the significance of Clark's gesture, it is essential to consider that Clark had *twice* court-martialed this same Hugh Hall during the shakedown phase of the voyage up the Missouri River in the spring of 1804. Hall's first offense was going AWOL (after attending a community ball held for the explorers in St. Charles, Missouri), and he was later charged with breaking into one of the expedition's whiskey kegs. In the first instance Hall pled guilty, and the court recommended leniency. Clark, as the commander officer of the court-martial detail, concurred with this judgment. For the second crime (ruled "Contrary to all order, rule, or regulation") Hall was sentenced to fifty lashes well laid on.[7]

Clark's giving up his horse to the man he had once ordered whipped illustrated both the evolving nature of the social bonds within this roving community of Americans and Clark's strong identification with the interests of the men under his command. It was not the first example of Clark's empathy. Going up the Beaverhead fork of the Jefferson River in August 1805, the voyagers found both their spirits and their stamina sapped by constant exposure to the gravelly bed of a cold mountain stream, so much so that the men began to plead with Clark that they might abandon the river and proceed thence to the Continental Divide by land. Clark confided to his journal, "I passify them." This remark is suggestive of an encouraging talk, not the *sturm* and *drang* of Lewis's discourse with the men at the Marias decision point. Later in this difficult ascent Clark joined in the laborious work by taking "to a pole" himself as the crew pushed their craft upstream.[8]

A final testimonial to Clark's well-deserved reputation as an empathetic commander can be found in the death of Sgt. Charles Floyd on the Missouri in 1804 and its aftermath. Floyd's demise is among the most fabled stories in the lore of LEWIS & CLARK and needs little recounting here. Less known is how much Floyd's family appreciated Clark's care at the time of Charles's death. The deceased man's brother, Nathaniel Floyd, later consoled his sister by telling her that Charles "was well cared for" at the time of his death because "Clark was there." Indeed Clark seems to have had a very strong sense of duty related to Floyd's memory. Meriwether Lewis later recounted, in the spring of 1806 when the expedition was among the Nez Perce, that William Clark "prized" recovering a tomahawk that had been stolen on the westbound segment—one that Clark "was desireous of returning... to [Floyd's] friends." [9]

William Clark's stewardship of relationships with men such as Hall and Floyd surely helped inspire Pvt. Joseph Whitehouse's great post-expeditionary testimonial. Near the conclusion of the preface to the fair copy of his journal, Whitehouse wrote: "I cannot in justice to myself omit saying, that the manly, and soldier-like behaviour; and enterprizing abilities; of both Captain Lewis, and Captain Clark, claim my utmost gratitude." Whitehouse also recognized

> the humanity shown at all times by them, to those under their command, on this perilous and important Voyage of discovery; I hope will fill the breasts of Men who were under their command with the same, and make their characters be esteem'd by the American people, and mankind in general; and convince the generous Public, that the President of the United States, did not misplace his judgment, when he appointed them to the command of this party on discovery; which is of so great a magnitude and utility, to the United States and mankind in general.[10]

Here, in this summing up, at last, William Clark gained what he had so fervently sought, parity with President Jefferson's protégé, emissary, and esteemed naturalist.

CONCLUSION   Final Reflections on Lewis, Clark, and the Promise of the Columbia River

THE RECENT CONCLUSION OF THE LEWIS AND CLARK bicentennial offers a fitting vantage point from which to reflect on the meaning of the expedition on its own terms, plus intervening and latter-day values that have been attached to it. With the publication of the modern edition of the journals, edited by Gary Moulton, the full array of expeditionary documentation is now accessible in one source, thus opening a window for researchers into the whole range of the explorers' experiences—physical, psychological, and intellectual.

Over the course of the twentieth century and now into the twenty-first, beginning with the centennial of the expedition and the first full flowering of public interest in Lewis and Clark since they returned from the Pacific, the scholarly and popular understanding of the explorers has evolved continuously. In general terms, the early paradigm, and the longest-lasting, had Lewis and Clark exploring an empty land. This might be called the heroic phase of "Lewis and Clarkiana," one that is not altogether vanquished, at least in the popular realm. During the height of the bicentennial the Eagle Bronze Foundry in Lander, Wyoming, promoted a limited edition Lewis and Clark sculpture "suitable for discriminating homes... and corporate board rooms," and a companion version in monumental scale "appropriate for city parks, corporate campuses, [and] exclusive residential enclaves." Titled "This is the Way!" the work was touted as "a heroic portrayal of Captains Lewis & Clark, depicting their unwavering courage, steadfast determination and masterful leadership of the Corps of Discovery." Continuing, the foundry's broadside says the scene depicted in the sculpture shows Lewis "who dismounts and climbs to the nearest high point, waving his hat and signaling back to the corps 'This is the Way!'" However, more than just hailing the men forward, the "story within the story" has Lewis "also calling the young, raw and irrepressible United States, bursting with energy and full of adventure and brawl, to pursue its destiny." Oddly, like the earlier centennial, the bicentennial coincided with a nettlesome period of American adventurism abroad, which this type of bombastic rhetoric reflects.[1]

James Ronda's antithetical model, viewing the course of the expedition from the Native American point of view as found in his *Lewis and Clark among the Indians* (1984), commenced a healthy corrective phase. The dominance of Native voices, projects, and events during the recently concluded commemoration was an extension of Ronda's pathbreaking work. One of the things I have attempted in these pages, to continue in the dialectical mode, is a synthesis—showing that the Lewis and Clark Expedition, particularly in Columbia River country, was truly an integrated phenomenon—a genuine joint venture between Anglo-Americans and Native Americans.

Indians, most notably Old Toby of the Shoshone tribe and Twisted Hair and Tetoharsky of the Nez Perce, among others, were in dynamic response to Lewis and Clark at all times of their mutual engagement. This might not be readily apparent with a cursory reading of the journals. What Pamela Regis calls the "manners-and-customs" approach for presenting Indians in narrative form, one which Lewis and Clark occasionally resorted to stylistically, was a part of the tradition of travel literature ever since global touring by Europeans became common in the fourteenth century. This rhetorical style, not fully supplanted until the late nineteenth century by the discipline of anthropology, was, Regis says, inherently unreliable because prejudicial outlooks "blinded its practitioners to the history of the people they were depicting." However, if mined for all their potential, the journals of Lewis and Clark are not merely an intermittent or somewhat skewed glance into the Native world. As presented and analyzed in this book, the journals, sometimes unwittingly, reveal many instances of Indians not merely interacting with the expedition but rather actively shaping its course and destiny.[2]

Within the totality of the Lewis and Clark experience, the Columbia country serves as the best platform for analysis in this regard. It held the highest density of Native population that the captains encountered, a circumstance they complained about from time to time. The sociological or, if you will, governmental integrity of the tribes in the Northwest was still quite strong at the time of Lewis and Clark's arrival. There has been a modern resurgence of tribal sovereignty, reflected in recent commemorative observances through such devices as the "Tent of Many Voices," featuring tribal political and cultural leaders. This renewal demonstrates the reintroduction of Native agency to the lives of the West's non-Indians to a degree not seen since the first half of the nineteenth century. In that sense, modern westerners have begun a return to the contingent world of those first American explorers in the region—Lewis, Clark, Frémont, and Isaac Stevens. What Native people say and do—invoking treaty rights, among other things— has transformed jurisdictional relationships by adding tribal government to the long standard federal/state paradigm.

This reminds us that, taken in the long view, the purpose of the movement Lewis and Clark inaugurated in parts of the West was cultural/racial/national displacement. As explorers they were, to borrow Roger Kennedy's phrase, "agents of cellular imperialism" in league with fur traders, some of whom—

notably Alexander Mackenzie and David Thompson—were their competitors, and others of whom were countrymen whose interests they were trying to advance. Lewis and Clark had a vague sense of their role in this epic demographic shift, at least to the extent that any of us truly sees where our lives fit into the broad pattern of history. If they and their peers during the Enlightenment era of exploration were troubled by this, they had a compensating, perhaps diversionary coping device. Bruce Greenfield suggests that the "rhetorical strategies" of science and discovery, which occupied our principals in different ways, mitigated their awareness of the consequences of their appearance in the Native world.[3]

Earlier in this book we saw Indians adopted as guides by Lewis and Clark, a strategy pioneered in the Northwest by Alexander Mackenzie. It is the duty of the historian to likewise conduct readers through a story, illuminating the foundational elements and structural framework that help tell it. In these pages I have attempted, using the Columbia country setting for the most part, to provide a deeper level of reporting so as to penetrate the surface of the commonly perceived Lewis and Clark master narrative. A fair reading of Nicholas Biddle's first published edition of the journals would have led any attentive reader to the conclusion that the far Northwest—the traverse of Columbia country—was the most difficult part of the trip. Over the years, in the works of such authors as John Logan Allen and William Lang, scholars have expanded and amplified Biddle's portrayal of a stressful Columbian experience. I've attempted in these pages, by examining serially those stresses, whether they arise from harsh climate, cultural misunderstandings, or geographic uncertainty, to reveal a different story of the expedition than the overly simplistic and formulaic one historians of the expedition, by and large, have created. As James Ronda phrases it, "not all the pieces fit to make a single complete picture." It must said that we still do not have all the pieces (hoping that more documentary evidence might yet turn up), nor have all the pieces we do have been fully analyzed, and so the work must continue.[4]

Meriwether Lewis, who periodically serves as the central figure in our story (as indeed he would have preferred it), wanted to be a man like Alexander Mackenzie: "always in control of himself, his men, and his movements," as Bruce Greenfield describes the great British fur trader and explorer. The numerous linkages to Mackenzie recounted herein demonstrate clearly that Mackenzie's life, his managerial and literary styles, and his book—*Voyages from Montreal*—were always at the top of Lewis's, and to some extent Clark's, mind. Because he bore the burden of constructing a continuous narrative about the expedition—a duty he did not fulfill—Lewis failed to meet the Mackenzie literary standard. During the westbound voyage in Columbia country in the fall of 1805, Lewis was either distracted by the physical and cultural environment or defeated by it. Like a fighter in a boxing match who has lost hope of victory, Lewis didn't answer the bell for the last, most important, round. His letter to Thomas Jefferson after returning safely to St. Louis in September 1806 was a game attempt at arguing he had matched Mackenzie's accomplishment, but the journals, including their gaps and silences, tell a different and largely disappointing story. This disappointment undoubtedly contributed to Lewis's lack of resolve in writing them up into a final publishable form.[5]

Much was asked of Meriwether Lewis, the first official explorer of a new nation. His young country needed the strategic advantage of a Northwest Passage that interfaced with the Missouri. The reputation of the great Captain James Cook, whom Lewis admired, was largely founded on "negative discovery;" that is, Cook disproved the existence of the great southern continent that was the putative counterpart to Eurasia or an oceanic route to Europe via the Bering Strait. Lewis, who asked much of himself, probably could not abide the fact that he had not discovered a truly practicable transcontinental trade route that a Missouri River to Columbia River link had promised and saw that "negative discovery" as a distinct failure.

There is a certain irony here. Mackenzie's own difficult northerly traverse and encounters with hostile Indians did not offer a practicable trade route either. In a way, Mackenzie bluffed his way through. Jefferson took the bait found in *Voyages*, and Lewis ended up feeling disappointed about his route when in truth his exploits and findings were not materially inferior to Mackenzie's. To extend the boxing metaphor, when the captains returned to St. Louis the Mackenzie/Lewis fight was a draw in all but literary terms.

In deconstructing the journals of Lewis and Clark and comparing them to those of explorers who came both before and after, we find that, on closer inspection, many of the presumably exceptional and therefore storied elements of the Lewis and Clark experience are not so unusual after all. Elements ranging from endearing stylistic expressions to more practical matters such as running short of food were prefigured in the voyages of Cook, Vancouver, and Mackenzie. In turn, the captains' experiences anticipated those of Thompson, Frémont, and Wilkes.

Providing a corrective in the form of comparative history does not make the Lewis and Clark saga less interesting. Stereo sound (Indian voices and agency) and binocular vision (seeing Mackenzie in the background at all key intersections in the journey) combine to offer a richer, more faithful rendering of reality. Native people like Cameahwait, Old Toby, Twisted Hair, and Yelleppit were not nameless accessories or bit players in the story of Lewis and Clark. At times, they dominated the scene. Tribes like the Chinook at the coast or the Tenino at The Dalles displayed considerable autonomy.

The Lewis and Clark experience on the upper Missouri—with its scenes of visionary enchantment inflated by latter-day mythmakers into emblematic expressions for the entirety of the voyage—was a more pleasant period for the explorers than their time in Columbia country. This is reflected in the privileged status for Missouri stories in the lore of LEWIS & CLARK. However, at the time of the expedition's initial appearance on the upper Missouri, neither the fertility of the soil, profusion of game, nor the romantic grandeur of the landscape was complicated (at that moment) by encounters with Indians. The Columbia country—its mountains, gorges, thick forests, and equally fertile plains—had comparable (perhaps superior) aesthetic and natural attributes to those of the Missouri country. We need no other evidence of its riches than the extensive modern population the Columbia sustains plus its ample supply of national parks & forests, scenic areas, and volcanic monuments. These features were mentioned but not emphasized and rarely touted by Lewis and Clark because the natural abundance and wonder they represented were compromised by the sizable Native population competing for the bounty.[6]

In other words, Lewis's grandiose and attractive rhetoric of discovery on the Missouri, from Fort Mandan to the Continental Divide, was allowed its full flowering by the absence of other balancing influences—principally the presence of autonomous Native people—that competed for his attention west of the Continental Divide. Lewis's emphasis on his aesthetic response to the landscape from April to August of 1805 on the upper Missouri also overwhelmed the scientific mode of botanical and faunal description which could otherwise only be conducted when the party was stationary and Lewis had access to his traveling library. In that sense, Lewis's formidable work analyzing the plants and animals in the environs of Fort Clatsop, for example, was accidental, or at least coincidental.

As for the aboriginal people, Lewis could safely strut among them on the Missouri, knowing he was the latest imperial "boss," with all the national authority of the United States behind him, itself sustained by international sanction. However, once across the Continental Divide, where the terrain was more difficult and at times alien, and the Indians both numerous and autonomous, Lewis, now lacking the luxury of imperial authority over the tribes, not to mention the time, good health, and inclination to overlay this part of the journey with a painterly discourse, fell silent. Thus was the rhetoric of the American exploring party transformed. The westbound story found in Clark's Columbia River account reflects a more compact relationship with Native people and the landscape. It is no coincidence that the construction of a culturally distancing form—Fort Clatsop—gave the notoriously stand-offish Meriwether Lewis the "space" he needed to feel comfortable writing again.[7]

The expedition's—or at a minimum Lewis's—interactions with the tribes in Columbia country were either intensely friendly or distinctly hostile. They seem never to have been merely neutral in tone. Without access to big game except during their stay at Fort Clatsop, the expedition was routinely dependant upon Indians for food. The explorers' need for heightened geographic clarity once they had deviated from the relative simplicity of merely heading up the main stem of the Missouri River also forced them into closer ties with the Columbia's Indian people and, along with it, awareness of local customs. We saw this particularly in the strategy employed by Twisted Hair and Tetoharsky of calling attention to Sacagawea's presence in a party of strangers as proof of peaceful intentions. Not surprisingly, Lewis and Clark had the highest opinion of tribes that proved most helpful to them—notably the Walla Walla and the Nez Perce.[8]

Thus, what Bruce Greenfield calls the rhetoric of local knowledge formed the principal strain of exploratory discourse for Clark and Lewis in Columbia country.

This is evident in, among other ways, the particularized nature of William Clark's maps and narrative description of the party's dramatic run down the Columbia. Clark's exactitude in detailing the course of the great western river stands in distinct contrast to Lewis's airy aesthetics on the upper Missouri. In sum, the Columbia country was shared terrain for Lewis and Clark, not only internationally, with Vancouver and Mackenzie and soon Thompson, but with autonomous and assertive Indians. The Columbia watershed, Greenfield relates, was "a mosaic of inhabited lands whose peoples [had] their own senses of history and destiny independent of that of the United States." [9]

In a fashion, the recently completed bicentennial observance recreated some of the same conflicts in narrative modes found in the original journals. The publication of Stephen Ambrose's *Undaunted Courage* unofficially kicked off the era, emphasizing Lewis as a soldierly and imperial paragon. The Ken Burns and Dayton Duncan documentary film gave full expression to the romantic grandeur of the expedition's Missouri phase. The prominence of tribal perspectives in such bicentennial forums as the so-called "Signature Events" and "Corps II" traveling Chautauqua substantiate the continued vitality of indigenous or localized knowledge.

All in all, the complex intercultural relationships attendant upon the Lewis and Clark Expedition's time in Columbia country teaches us more about events to come in the West than do the explorers' celebrated Missouri stories. The ninety years that followed the captains' trek was a continuous contest over terrain in the West. The northern plains, effectively "unpopulated" west of the Mandan villages in Lewis and Clark's world view, turned out to be the part of Indian country most difficult to incorporate under American hegemony. The seeming certainty of American dominion that facilitated Lewis's flighty aesthetics on the Missouri in 1805 dissipated into decade after decade of Indian wars and related tribulations. Nonetheless, Lewis and Clark's narrative made a lasting imprint, and the dominant perception of the West in nineteenth-century art and literature privileged the visual appeal of the northern plains. [10]

The type of individuation of tribal people seen in the captains' Columbia country narratives—the dynamic agency found in the stories of Cameahwait, Old Toby, Twisted Hair, and Yelleppit—did not long endure in the accounts of subsequent explorers visiting the "lands of Lewis and Clark." In the accounts of Pike, Long, Frémont, and Stevens we see instead what Bruce Greenfield calls the "trope of aesthetic appropriation" reigning supreme. Meriwether Lewis's transcendent claim to lands via the presumption that he was the first civilized man to see and describe a particular landscape became the dominant mode of perception and description for those who followed him. This style was prefigured and best modeled by Lewis with his first sip of Columbian water—an "Adamic moment" in the West if ever there was one. With his ritualistic identification with the Columbia River, Lewis imagined that he was also the heroic inheritor of that country. His subsequent experiences did not meet those expectations or wishes, nor perhaps, given modern-day issues of environmental sustainability in the Northwest, have his figurative descendants. [11]

Meriwether Lewis was far from perfect and he succeeded to the extent he did largely because of the compensating qualities of William Clark. Still, the trail they forged together is a monument to their perseverance in the face of near constant struggle, occasioned by an assortment of triumphs and disappointments. Their mission held great promise, and if that promise was not entirely fulfilled, the effort was no less worthy.

Acknowledgments

This book has been inspired, encouraged, supported, and the writing
of it endured by many people.

First, I would like to thank all of the authors whose works I have used and cited.
I stand in their debt, whether or not I happen to agree with them on matters of
interpretation; or they with me for that matter.

I owe a special expression of gratitude to Clay Jenkinson, not only because of
his influential publications and the Foreword to this book, but for years
of helpful criticism. When others lost confidence he remained constant with
his encouragement.

Two generations of trustees of my long-time employer, the Washington State
Historical Society, have offered support in many forms, including the gift of a
full set of the modern journals of Lewis and Clark to support my research.
I would like to especially mention, in a form of chronological order, those
trustees who took an unusual interest in this project and the ten years it took to
complete it: David Lamb, Beth Willis, Chuck Twining, Robert Clark,
David Edwards, Charlotte Chalker, Denny Heck, Larry Kopp, Dan Grimm,
Alex McGregor, and Mike Allen.

I will always be thankful to all those associated with my publisher,
The Dakota Institute, for their commitment to seeing this book into print.
Foremost among them is David Borlaug, President of the Institute's parent
organization, the Lewis & Clark Fort Mandan Foundation. David, along with
Clay, literally adopted this book when it was orphaned. Steve and Yvette Finney
whipped many problematic passages into shape with their savvy copy editing.
Sarah Trandahl, Kevin Kirkey and Wendy Spencer were indispensable in
moving things along.

Lastly, I'd like to thank my family for their endurance. My wife, Chris,
displayed a decade's worth of patience while I absented myself to work the
keyboard, spread note cards and type-written pages all over the house, and
she calmed my nerves many times when the computer acted up. And, my son
Dominic, to whom I dedicated this book, for sharing the joys of many a
road trip, from El Paso in the south to Fort Liard in the north.

BIBLIOGRAPHY

Adams, Percy G. *Travelers and Travel Liars, 1660–1880*. Berkeley: University of California Press, 1962.

Aguilar, George W. Sr. *When the River Ran Wild: Indian Traditions on the Mid-Columbia and the Warm Springs Reservation*. Portland: Oregon Historical Society Press, 2005.

Allen, John Logan. *Lewis and Clark and the Image of the American Northwest*. Mineola, New York: Dover Publications, 1991. (Reprint edition.)

_____. "Geographical Knowledge and American Images of the Louisiana Territory." In *Voyages of Discovery: Essays on the Lewis and Clark Expedition*, James P. Ronda, editor. Helena: Montana Historical Society Press, 1998.

Ambrose, Stephen. *Undaunted Courage: Meriwether Lewis, Thomas Jefferson, and the Opening of the American West*. New York: Simon & Schuster, 1996.

Barry, J. Neilson. "Columbia River Exploration, 1792." *Oregon Historical Quarterly*, 33:1–2 (March, June 1932).

Beckham, Stephen Dow. *Lewis & Clark: From the Rockies to the Pacific*. Portland: Graphics Arts Center Publishing, 2002.

Beckham, Stephen Dow, et al. *The Literature of the Lewis and Clark Expedition: A Bibliography and Essays*. Portland: Lewis and Clark College, 2003.

Bedini, Silvio A. "The Scientific Instruments of the Lewis and Clark Expedition." In *Voyages of Discovery: Essays on the Lewis and Clark Expedition*, James P. Ronda, editor. Helena: Montana Historical Society Press, 1998.

Belyea, Barbara, editor. *Columbia Journals: David Thompson*. Seattle: University of Washington Press, 1998. (Reprint edition.)

_____. "The Silent Past is Made to Speak." In *A Confluence of Cultures: Native Americans and the Expedition of Lewis and Clark*, Linda Juneau and David Purviance, editors. Missoula: University of Montana, 2003.

_____. "Heroes and Hero Worship." *Oregon Humanities* (Spring 2004).

Boyd, Robert. *The Coming of the Spirit of Pestilence: Introduced Infectious Diseases and Population Decline among Northwest Coast Indians, 1774–1874*. Seattle: University of Washington Press, 1999.

Burns, Ken, producer and director. *Lewis & Clark: The Journey of the Corps of Discovery*. Burbank, CA: PBS Home Video, 1997.

Chaffin, Tom. *Pathfinder: John Charles Frémont and the Course of American Empire*. New York: Hill and Wang, 2004.

Chuinard, Eldon G. "How Did Meriwether Lewis Die? It Was Murder." *We Proceeded On*, 17:3 (August 1991); 17:4 (November 1991); 18:1 (January 1992).

Conner, Roberta. "Our People Have Always Been Here." In *Lewis and Clark Through Indian Eyes*, Alvin Josephy Jr., editor. New York: Alfred A. Knopf, 2006.

Cooney, Robert P. J. Jr. *Winning the Vote: The Triumph of the American Woman Suffrage Movement*. Santa Cruz: American Graphic Press, 2005.

Coues, Elliott, editor. *History of the Expedition Under the Command of Lewis and Clark*. 4 volumes. New York: Francis P. Harper, 1893.

Cutright, Paul Russell. *A History of the Lewis and Clark Journals*. Norman: University of Oklahoma Press, 1976.

_____. "Rest, Rest, Perturbed Spirit." *We Proceeded On*, 12:1 (March 1986).

Dening, Greg. *Beach Crossings: Voyaging Across Times, Cultures, and Self*. Philadelphia: University of Pennsylvania Press, 2004.

DeVoto, Bernard, editor. *The Journals of the Lewis and Clark Expedition*. New York: Houghton Mifflin, 1973.

_____. "'Passage to India': From Christmas to Christmas with Lewis and Clark." In *Voyages of Discovery: Essays on the Lewis and Clark Expedition*, James P. Ronda, editor. Helena: Montana Historical Society Press, 1998.

Duncan, Dayton. *Out West: A Journey Through Lewis and Clark's America*. Lincoln: University of Nebraska Press, 2000. (Reprint edition)

_____. *Scenes of Visionary Enchantment: Reflections on Lewis and Clark*. Lincoln: University of Nebraska Press, 2004.

Ewers, John C. "Plains Indian Reactions to the Lewis and Clark Expedition." In *Voyages of Discovery: Essays on the Lewis and Clark Expedition*. James P. Ronda, editor. Helena: Montana Historical Society Press, 1998.

Fausz, J. Frederick, and Michael A. Gavin. "The Death of Meriwether Lewis: An Unsolved Mystery." *Gateway Heritage*, 24:2–3 (Fall 2003/Winter 2004).

Feltskog, E. N., editor. *Parkman: The Oregon Trail*. Madison: University of Wisconsin Press, 1969.

Fisher, Vardis. *Suicide or Murder? The Strange Death of Governor Meriwether Lewis*. Chicago: A. Swallow, 1962.

Fritz, Harry. "Native Voice: The New Lewis and Clark." In *A Confluence of Cultures: Native Americans and the Expedition of Lewis and Clark*, Linda Juneau and David Purviance, editors. Missoula: The University of Montana, 2003.

Furtwangler, Albert. *Acts of Discovery: Visions of America in the Lewis and Clark Journals*. Urbana: University of Illinois Press, 1993.

_____. "Captain Lewis in a Crossfire of Wit: John Quincy Adams v. Joel Barlow." In *Voyages of Discovery: Essays on the Lewis and Clark Expedition,* James P. Ronda, editor. Helena: Montana State Historical Society Press, 1998.

Gibbons, Loren M. "All Them Horses and One Poor Mule: A Numerical Accounting of the Corps of Discovery's Livestock." *We Proceeded On*, 28:3 (August 2002).

Gilman, Carolyn. *Lewis and Clark: Across the Divide.* Washington, DC: Smithsonian Books, 2003.

Goetzmann, William H. *New Lands, New Men: America and the Second Great Age of Discovery.* New York: Viking, 1986.

Gough, Barry. *First Across the Continent: Sir Alexander Mackenzie.* Norman: University of Oklahoma Press, 1997.

Greenfield, Bruce. *Narrating Discovery: The Romantic Explorer in American Literature, 1790-1855.* New York: Columbia University Press, 1992.

Hall, Brian. *I Should Be Extremely Happy in Your Company: A Novel of Lewis and Clark.* New York: Viking, 2003.

Harper, J. Russell, ed. *Paul Kane's Frontier.* Austin: University of Texas Press, 1971.

Harrison, Brian. "Wapato: *Sagittaria Lotifolia.*" *Northwest Coast* (Spring 2009).

Hauser-Schäublin, Brigitta. "Witnesses of Encounters and Interactions" In *Life in the Pacific of the 1700's: The Cook/Forster Collection*, Stephen Little and Peter Ruthenberg, editors. 2 volumes. Honolulu: Honolulu Academy of the Arts, 2006.

Hayes, Derek. *First Crossing: Alexander Mackenzie, His Expedition across North America, and the Opening of the Continent.* Seattle: Sasquatch Books, 2001.

Holmberg, James J., editor. *Dear Brother: Letters of William Clark to Jonathan Clark.* New Haven: Yale University Press, 2002.

_____. "Fairly Launched on My Voyage of Discovery." *We Proceeded On*, 35:3 (August 2009).

Howay, Frederic W., editor. *Voyages of the Columbia to the Northwest Coast, 1787–1790 and 1790–1793.* Portland: Oregon Historical Society Press, 1990.

Hunsaker, Joyce Badgley. *Sacagawea Speaks: Beyond the Shining Mountains with Lewis and Clark.* Helena: Two Dot Books, 2001.

Jackson, Darin, et al. "Posttraumatic Stress Disorder and Depression Symptomatology in a Sample of Gulf War Veterans: A Prospective Analysis." *Journal of Consulting and Clinical Psychology*, 69:1 (2001).

Jackson, Donald, editor. *Letters of the Lewis and Clark Expedition, with Related Documents: 1783–1854.* 2d ed. 2 volumes. Urbana, University of Illinois Press, 1978.

_____. "Jefferson, Meriwether Lewis, and the Reduction of the United States Army." In *Voyages of Discovery: Essays on the Lewis and Clark Expedition*, James P. Ronda, editor. Helena: Montana Historical Society Press, 1998.

————. *Thomas Jefferson and the Rocky Mountains: Exploring the West from Monticello.* Norman: University of Oklahoma Press, 2002.

Jamison, Kay Redfield. *Touched with Fire: Manic-Depressive Illness and the Artistic Temperament.* New York: Free Press, 1993.

————. *Night Falls Fast: Understanding Suicide.* New York: Alfred A. Knopf, 1999.

Jefferson, Thomas. *Notes on the State of Virginia.* William Peden, editor. Chapel Hill: University of North Carolina Press, 1955.

Jenish, D'Arcy. *Epic Wanderer: David Thompson and the Mapping of the Canadian West.* Toronto: Doubleday Canada, 2003.

Jenkinson, Clay S. *The Character of Meriwether Lewis: 'Completely Metamorphosed' in the American West.* Reno: Marmath Press, 2000.

————. *A Vast and Open Plain: The Writings of the Lewis and Clark Expedition in North Dakota, 1804–1806.* Bismarck: State Historical Society of North Dakota, 2003.

————. "Thomas Slaughter's Expedition: Exploring (and Deploring) Lewis and Clark." *Oregon Historical Quarterly*, 105:4 (Winter 2004).

Josephy, Alvin Jr., editor. *Lewis and Clark Through Indian Eyes.* New York: Alfred A. Knopf, 2006.

Kastor, Peter J. *The Nation's Crucible: The Louisiana Purchase and the Creation of America.* New Haven: Yale University Press, 2004.

Kennedy, Roger G. *Mr. Jefferson's Lost Cause: Land, Farmers, Slavery and the Louisiana Purchase.* London: Oxford University Press, 2003.

Kingston, C. S. "Sacajawea as Guide: The Evaluation of a Legend." *Pacific Northwest Quarterly*, 35:1 (January 1944).

Kukla, Jon. *A Wilderness So Immense: The Louisiana Purchase and the Destiny of America.* New York: Alfred A. Knopf, 2003.

Lamb, W. Kaye, editor. *The Journals and Letters of Sir Alexander Mackenzie.* London: Cambridge University Press, 1970.

————. *The Voyage of George Vancouver, 1791–1794.* 4 volumes. London: Hakluyt Society, 1984.

Lang, William L. "Lewis and Clark on the Columbia River: The Power of Landscape in the Exploration Experience." *Pacific Northwest Quarterly*, 87:3 (Summer 1996).

————. "Describing a New Environment: Lewis and Clark and Enlightenment Science in the Columbia River Basin." *Oregon Historical Quarterly*, 105:3 (Fall 2004).

Lawrence, Donald B. and Elizabeth G. Lawrence. "Bridge of the Gods Legend, Its Origin, History and Dating." *Mazama*, 40:13 (December 1958).

Layman, William. "Hawkbells: David Thompson in North Central Washington." *Columbia*, 5:4 (Winter 1991).

McCartney, Laton. *Across the Great Divide: Robert Stuart and the Discovery of the Oregon Trail.* New York: Free Press, 2003.

Merritt, J. I. "Cameahwait's Geography Lesson." *We Proceeded On*, 29:4 (November 2003).

Miller, Robert J. *Native America, Discovered and Conquered: Thomas Jefferson, Lewis & Clark, and Manifest Destiny.* Westport, CT: Praeger, 2006.

Moorehead, Alan. *Fatal Impact: Captain Cook's Exploration of the South Pacific— Its High Adventure and Disastrous Effects.* New York: Barnes & Noble, 2000. (Reprint edition.)

Moulton, Gary E., editor. *The Journals of the Lewis & Clark Expedition.* 13 volumes. Lincoln: University of Nebraska Press, 1983–2001.

National Geographic. "Lewis & Clark: Great Journey West." Washington, DC: National Geographic Video, 2002.

Nelson, W. Dale. *Interpreters with Lewis and Clark: The Story of Sacagawea and Toussaint Charbonneau.* Denton: University of North Texas Press, 2003.

Nisbet, Jack. *Sources of the River: Tracking David Thompson Across Western North America.* Seattle: Sasquatch Books, 1994.

_____. *The Mapmaker's Eye: David Thompson on the Columbia Plateau.* Pullman: Washington State University Press, 2005.

Nokes, J. Richard. *Columbia's River: The Voyages of Robert Gray, 1787–1793.* Tacoma: Washington State Historical Society, 1991.

_____. *Almost a Hero: The Voyages of John Meares, R.N., to China, Hawaii, and the Northwest Coast.* Pullman: Washington State University Press, 1998.

O'Connor, Jim E. "The Evolving Landscape of the Columbia River Gorge: Lewis and Clark and Cataclysms on the Columbia." *Oregon Historical Quarterly*, 105:3 (Fall 2004).

Phelps, Dawson A. "The tragic death of Meriwether Lewis." *William and Mary Quarterly*, 3:13 (July 1956).

Philbrick, Nathaniel. *Sea of Glory: America's Voyage of Discovery; the U. S. Exploring Expedition, 1838–1842.* New York: Viking, 2003.

Plamondon II, Martin. *Lewis and Clark Trail Maps: A Cartographic Reconstruction.* 3 volumes. Pullman: Washington State University Press, 2000–2004.

Portelli, Allesandro. *The Death of Luigi Trastulli and Other Stories: Form and Meaning in Oral History.* Albany: State University of New York Press, 1991.

Posner, Gerald. *Case Closed: Lee Harvey Oswald and the Assassination of JFK.* New York: Random House, 1993.

Regis, Pamela. *Describing Early America: Bartram, Jefferson, Crevecouer, and the Influence of Natural History.* Philadelphia: University of Pennsylvania Press, 1999. (Paperback edition.)

Report on the Columbia River and Minor Tributaries. (House Doc. 103, 73rd Congress, 1st session).

Report on the Snake River and Tributaries. (House Doc. 190, 73rd Congress, 2nd session).

Reynolds, Nathaniel D. "Dating the Bonneville Landslide with Lichenometry."

Washington Geology 29:3-4 (December 2001).

Ronda, James P. *Lewis and Clark among the Indians.* Lincoln: University of Nebraska Press, 1984.

_____. " 'A Darling Project of Mine': The Appeal of the Lewis and Clark Story." In *Voyages of Discovery: Essays on the Lewis and Clark Expedition*, James P. Ronda, editor. Helena: Montana Historical Society Press, 1998.

_____. " 'So Vast an Enterprise': Thoughts on the Lewis and Clark Expedition." In *Voyages of Discovery: Essays on the Lewis and Clark Expedition,* James P. Ronda, editor. Helena: Montana Historical Society Press, 1998.

_____. " 'The Writingest Explorers:' The Lewis and Clark Expedition in American Historical Literature." In *Voyages of Discovery: Essays on the Lewis and Clark Expedition*, James P. Ronda, editor. Helena: Montana Historical Society Press, 1998.

_____. *Finding the West: Explorations with Lewis and Clark.* Albuquerque: University of New Mexico Press, 2001.

_____. "Counting Cats in Zanzibar, or, Lewis and Clark Reconsidered." *Western Historical Quarterly*, 33:1 (Spring 2002).

_____. "Troubled Passages: The Uncertain Journeys of Lewis and Clark." *Oregon Historical Quarterly*, 106:4 (Winter 2005).

Ruby, Robert H., and John A. Brown. *The Chinook Indians: Traders of the Lower Columbia River.* Norman: University of Oklahoma Press, 1976.

Schuster, Robert L., and Patrick T. Pringle. "Engineering history and impacts of the Bonneville Landslide, Columbia River Gorge, Washington-Oregon, USA." In *Proceedings of the First European Conference on Landslides*, Jan Rybard, Josef Stemberk, Peter Wagner, editors. Exton, PA: A. A. Balkema Publishers, 2002.

Slaughter, Thomas P. *Exploring Lewis and Clark: Reflections on Men and Wilderness.* New York: Alfred A. Knopf, 2003.

Spence, Mark. "Let's Play Lewis & Clark! Strange Visions of Nature and History at the Bicentennial." In *Lewis & Clark: Legacies, Memories, and New Perspectives*, Kris Fresonke and Mark Spence, editors. Berkeley: University of California Press, 2004.

_____. "*Sayaapo* and the Remaking of Lewis and Clark." *Oregon Historical Quarterly*, 105:3 (Fall 2004).

Stafford, Barbara Maria. *Voyage into Substance: Art, Science, Nature, and the Illustrated Travel Account, 1760–1840.* Cambridge: MIT Press, 1984.

Swan, James G. *The Northwest Coast; or, Three Years Residence in Washington Territory*. 1957. Reprint edition, Fairfield, WA: Ye Galleon Press, 1966.

Taber, Ronald W. "Sacagawea and the Suffragettes." *Pacific Northwest Quarterly*, 58:1 (January 1967).

Thompson, Sally. "Misnomers Along the Lewis and Clark Trail." In *Confluence of Cultures: Native Americans and the Expedition of Lewis and Clark*, Linda Juneau and David Purviance, editors. Missoula: The University of Montana, 2003.

Thwaites, Reuben Gold, editor. *Original Journals of the Lewis and Clark Expedition, 1804–1806*. 8 volumes. New York: Dodd, Mead & Company, 1904–05.

Tubbs, Stephenie Ambrose. *Why Sacagawea Deserves the Day Off and Other Lessons from the Lewis & Clark Trail*. Lincoln: University of Nebraska Press, 2008.

Wilkes, Charles. *Narrative of the United States Exploring Expedition*. 5 volumes. Philadelphia: C. Sherman, 1844.

Wilson, Douglas C., et al. *Historical Archaeology at the Middle Village: Station Camp/McGowan Site (45PC106), Station Camp Unit, Lewis & Clark National Park, Pacific County, Washington*. Vancouver, WA: Northwest Cultural Resources Institute, Report No. 1, Fort Vancouver National Historic Site, 2008.

Wood, W. Raymond. *Prologue to Lewis and Clark: the Mackay and Evans Expedition*. Norman: University of Oklahoma Press, 2003.

Wood, W. Raymond, and Thomas D. Thiessen. *Early Fur Trade on the Northern Plains: Canadian Traders Among the Mandan and Hidatsa Indians, 1738–1818*. Norman: University of Oklahoma Press, 1985.

Ziak, Rex. *In Full View*. Astoria: Moffitt House Press, 2002.

NOTES

PROLOGUE

[1] Gary E. Moulton, ed., *The Journals of the Lewis & Clark Expedition*, 13 vols. (Lincoln, 1983–2001), 5:74, 81, 88. Hereafter cited as *JLCE*. The term "Corps of Discovery," per se, never appears in the primary documentary record associated with Lewis and Clark. The phrasing was a portion of the subtitle to Patrick Gass's early and unauthorized account of the expedition, from whence it took its currency. See Stephen Dow Beckham et al., *The Literature of the Lewis and Clark Expedition: A Bibliography and Essays* (Portland, 2003), p. 105. Hereafter cited as Beckham, *Literature*. Though the term "Expedition for Northwestern Discovery" (or its variants including "Corps of Volunteers for Northwestern Discovery") is hardly ubiquitous, it has the merit of authenticity and will be used herein accordingly. See Donald Jackson, ed., *Letters of the Lewis and Clark Expedition, with Related Documents: 1783–1854*, 2nd ed. (Urbana, 1978), 1:113, 210; 2:549. Hereafter cited as Jackson, *Letters*. *JLCE*, 3:14, 153, 170, 172 n. 10; 9:231-232.

Furthermore, the military term typically employed in the journals relative to the command structure was "detachment," not "corps." The prime example is the "Orderly Book" containing the rules of military comportment and discipline. Instructively, the first *"Detachment Order"* at Camp River Dubois on 1 April 1804 records the names of men selected for the "Perminent Detachment." A subsequent order at Wood River stated "No man of the Detachment Shall leave Camp without permission from the Commanding officer present." Meriwether Lewis retrospectively wrote of 14 May 1804 as the day "the detachment left the mouth of the River Dubois." After his court martial, Private Moses Reed ran the gauntlet through the "Detachment." Ibid., 2:187, 212, 412, 488.

The ubiquity of the generic term "Corps of Discovery" seems to have its roots and draws its popularity from John Logan Allen, who was the first scholar to extensively use the phrase as an alternative moniker for the Lewis and Clark Expedition. John Logan Allen, *Lewis and Clark and the Image of the American Northwest* (New York, 1991), p. xix, passim. Hereafter cited as Allen, *Lewis and Clark*.

[2] *JLCE*, 5:228-229.

[3] *JLCE*, 5:229.

[4] *JLCE*, 5:232-236; 243; 245-246.

[5] *JLCE*, 5:248-249.

[6] *JLCE*, 5:232; Stephen E. Ambrose, *Undaunted Courage: Meriwether Lewis, Thomas Jefferson, and the Opening of the American West* (New York, 1996), p. 295. Hereafter cited as Ambrose, *Undaunted Courage*. Jackson, *Letters*, 1:117 n. 137.

[7] Ambrose, *Undaunted Courage*, pp. 295, 307, 431, 461-465. Some tangible evidence of this supposition can be gleaned by a quick count of the number of pages Stephen Ambrose devotes to what could be called the "Missourian" phases of the expedition, versus the "Columbian." Ibid., pp. 133-267 and pp. 297-312 respectively. This was compounded by an even more egregious imbalance in the film documentary about the expedition created by Ken Burns and written by Dayton Duncan, a production heavily influenced by Ambrose's perspective. See Dayton Duncan and Ken Burns, producers, *Lewis & Clark: The Journey of the Corps of Discovery* (PBS, 1997).

[8] Ambrose, *Undaunted Courage*, p. 297.

[9] *JLCE*, 4:9; Ambrose, *Undaunted Courage*, p. 307. Lewis's lyrical phrase describing the

White Cliffs of the Missouri—"seens of visionary inchantment"—became the tagline for the state of Montana's underwriting announcement appended at the conclusion of the aforementioned Ken Burns documentary. *JLCE*, 4:229.

[10] *JLCE*, 2:4.

[11] *JLCE*, 4:284-285. The best source on the journals as literature and the contrasting styles of the captains is Albert Furtwangler, *Acts of Discovery: Visions of America in the Lewis and Clark Journals* (Urbana, 1993). Hereafter cited as Furtwangler, *Discovery*.

[12] James P. Ronda, "Troubled Passages: The Uncertain Journeys of Lewis and Clark," *Oregon Historical Quarterly*, 106:4 (Winter 2005), p. 539. Hereafter cited as Ronda, "Passages."

[13] Ronda, "Passages," p. 526.

[14] In coming to the conclusion that not enough critical thought has been brought to analysis of the texts of Lewis and Clark, I have been influenced by the provocative, though often flawed, work of Thomas P. Slaughter, *Exploring Lewis and Clark: Reflections on Men and Wilderness* (New York, 2003). Hereafter cited as Slaughter, *Exploring Lewis and Clark*. See especially pp. xiv, 32, 48-51. Regarding the proposition that the journals have no more to offer, see Harry Fritz, "Native Voices: The New Lewis and Clark," in *A Confluence of Cultures: Native Americans and the Expedition of Lewis and Clark*, ed. Linda Juneau and David Purviance (Missoula, 2003), p. 62 (qtn.), 63. Hereafter cited as Juneau and Purviance, *Confluence of Cultures*. James P. Ronda, "'The Writingest Explorers:' The Lewis and Clark Expedition in American Historical Literature," in *Voyages of Discovery: Essays on the Lewis and Clark Expedition*, ed. James P. Ronda (Helena, 1998), p. 322. Hereafter cited as Ronda, "The Writingest Explorers," Ronda, ed., *Voyages*. Clay S. Jenkinson, "Thomas Slaughter's Expedition: Exploring (and Deploring) Lewis and Clark," *Oregon Historical Quarterly*, 105:4 (Winter 2004), p. 631. Hereafter cited as Jenkinson, "Slaughter's Expedition."

[15] Jenkinson, "Slaughter's Expedition," pp. 626 (qtn.), 631. I shall use herein Jenkinson's denomination LEWIS & CLARK, literally writ large, to denote facets of the Lewis and Clark story that help constitute the "mythic... master narrative," cited above. Mark Spence, "Let's Play Lewis & Clark! Strange Visions of Nature and History at the Bicentennial," in *Lewis & Clark: Legacies, Memories, and New Perspectives*, ed. Kris Fresonke and Mark Spence (Berkeley, 2004), p. 229. A representative example of Spence's insight can be gleaned from a recent promotional piece that encouraged retracing the journey of Lewis and Clark so as to "walk where they walked, see what they saw and feel what they felt." Found in "Lewis and Clark Trail: The South Dakota Adventure," an ephemeral publication of South Dakota Department of Tourism and State Development (n.d.), p. 1; Ronda, "Passages," p. 541.

[16] Ronda, "The Writingest Explorers," Ronda, ed., *Voyages*, p. 322. John L. Allen, "Geographical Knowledge and American Images of the Louisiana Territory," Ibid., pp. 54-55 n. 16.

CHAPTER I

[1] *JLCE*, 5:74.

[2] Allen, *Lewis and Clark*, pp. 8, 19, 23-24.

[3] Ibid., pp. 30, 38, 44; W. Kaye Lamb, ed., *The Journals and Letters of Sir Alexander Mackenzie* (London, 1970), p. 321. Hereafter cited as Lamb, *Mackenzie Journals*.

As described at length later in this chapter, the Native term for the stream that Mackenzie encountered near the 54th parallel was "Tacoutche Tesse," by which name it was generally referred to in his journals. Mackenzie's western explorations were conducted during the summer of 1793, therefore without the knowledge of Gray's place name or Vancouver's cartography fixing the exact location of the river's mouth. It was only at the conclusion of his narrative, published in 1801, that Mackenzie linked his "Tacoutche" with the "Columbia river" by name, and presumed thereby that he had discovered the headwaters of the Great River of the West. Ibid., p. 417.

4 Lamb, *Mackenzie Journals*, pp. 15, 21; Jackson, *Letters*, 1:12-13.

5 Jackson, *Letters*, 1:16, 17, 18, 21, 61. Jefferson reiterated the prime instruction to Lewis in a letter dated 16 November 1803 which found Lewis at that winter's campsite on the Mississippi. Jefferson began, "The object of your mission is single," adding the last two words for emphasis upon the original, "the direct water communication from sea to sea formed by the bed of the Missouri & perhaps the Oregon." This was one of the earliest appearances of the term "Oregon" in what would become the standard form. Ibid., 1:137. The first mention of the river "Ouragon" is attributed to Robert Rogers, an English adventurer from the French and Indian War era, who published an account of North American geography in 1765. Jonathan Carver, another veteran of the French and Indian War from Connecticut, published his *Travels Through the Interior Parts of North America* in 1778 and therein perpetuated Rogers' term, though now abridged to "Oregan." Donald Jackson, *Thomas Jefferson and the Rocky Mountains: Exploring the West from Monticello* (Norman, 2002), pp. 91, 93. Hereafter cited as Jackson, *Jefferson*.

6 Jon Kukla, *A Wilderness So Immense: The Louisiana Purchase and the Destiny of America* (New York, 2003), pp. 260-261. Hereafter cited as Kukla, *Wilderness So Immense*. To solve his constitutional problem, Jefferson emphasized the commercial advantages that might accrue from the Lewis and Clark Expedition. The president's letter to Congress stated: "The *interests of commerce* place the principal object within the constitutional powers and care of *Congress*, and that it should incidentally advance the geographical knowledge of our own continent can not but be *an additional gratification* (emphasis added). Jackson, *Letters*, 1:13. See J. Neilson Barry, "Columbia River Exploration, 1792," *Oregon Historical Quarterly*, 33:1 (March, 1932), pp. 31, 36, 40; 33:2 (June, 1932), p. 145, 154. Hereafter cited as Barry, "Columbia River Exploration." Jackson, *Letters*, 1:46, 47 n. 1, 48 n. 2; 53; *JLCE*, 1:5, map 2; 5:198 n. 2.

7 *JLCE*, 1:map 2. For a capsule biography of Mackenzie, see William H. Goetzmann, *New Lands, New Men: America and the Second Great Age of Discovery* (New York, 1986), pp. 101-103. Hereafter cited as Goetzmann, *New Lands*; Frederic W. Howay, ed., *Voyages of the Columbia to the Northwest Coast, 1787-1790 and 1790-1793* (Portland, 1990), p. x. Hereafter cited as Howay, *Voyages of the Columbia*. W. Kaye Lamb, ed., *The Voyage of George Vancouver, 1791-1794* (London, 1984), 1:117, 188. Hereafter cited as Lamb, *Vancouver*. Broughton left Vancouver's squadron in California after the 1792 season of exploration and found his way to Great Britain via land passage across Mexico to the Atlantic. Ibid., p. 117; Robert Ruby and John Brown, *The Chinook Indians: Traders of the Lower Columbia* (Norman, 1976), p. 52. Hereafter cited as Ruby and Brown, *Chinook Indians*.

8 Lamb, *Vancouver*, 1:201, 206, 242; Robert J. Miller, *Native America, Discovered and Conquered: Thomas Jefferson, Lewis & Clark, and Manifest Destiny* (Westport, CT, 2006), p. 3. Hereafter cited as Miller, *Native America*.

9 Lamb, *Mackenzie Journals*, pp. 455-456, 455 n. 6; Allen, *Lewis and Clark*, pp. 70, 74-83; Barry Gough, *First Across the Continent: Sir Alexander Mackenzie* (Norman, 1997), pp. 134-138. Hereafter cited as Gough, *Mackenzie*. Jefferson ordered his own copy of *Voyages* in June 1802 and probably read it that summer. See Donald Jackson, "Jefferson, Meriwether Lewis,

and the Reduction of the United States Army," in Ronda, ed., *Voyages*, pp. 64, 70 n. 9. Hereafter cited as Jackson, "United States Army." Jackson also surmises that Jefferson might have purchased a copy of Mackenzie's *Voyages* for Lewis's use in the field. Jackson, *Letters*, 1:56 n. Although Mackenzie denominated his southward flowing river "Tacoutche Tesse" or Columbia in his narrative, neither Arrowsmith's map of North America in 1802 (the last map of his published before Lewis and Clark ventured off), nor King in 1803 used the term "Columbia" on their maps. Arrowsmith, with King later emulating him, used "River Oregan" but only in juxtaposition to the lowest extent mapped with certainty by Broughton. Mackenzie would have had a compelling imperial reason to conclude his Tacoutche Tesse was the Columbia, because it countered Gray. King, working for the United States, had an equal and opposite reason for emphasizing the term "Columbia." Inexplicably, he let the British terms stand. Furthermore, Arrowsmith very subtly in his 1802 map hedged his bets by prominently placing the words "Great Fork" and "Principal Branch" at the headwaters of the Tacoutche Tesse, something Mackenzie did not do on his prototype manuscript and published maps. In so doing, Arrowsmith had British commercial objectives in mind. Through cartographic suggestion, he could help stay Robert Gray's hand and the imputed American claim to the great river, should Gray's "Columbia" and Mackenzie's "Tacoutche Tesse" prove to be the same stream. See maps relevant to this discussion in Derek Hayes, *First Crossing: Alexander Mackenzie, His Expedition across North America, and the Opening of the Continent* (Seattle, 2001), pp. 198, 234, 250, 264, 279. Hereafter cited as Hayes, *First Crossing*. King's map is at *JLCE*, 1:map 2. Also see Beckham, *Literature*, pp. 56-57 on the Mackenzie-Arrowsmith-King connection.

[10]   Allen, *Lewis and Clark*, pp. 102-103; Jackson, *Letters*, 1:27-28, 33.

[11]   Lamb, *Vancouver*, 1:112; 2:759-761; for Bell see Ibid., p. 760, nn. 4, 5.

[12]   Jackson, *Jefferson*, p. 94; Jackson, *Letters*, 1:16 n., 47 n., 246-247.

[13]   Jackson, *Letters*, 1:109, 111.

[14]   Lamb, *Vancouver*, 1:112; 2:758, 758 n. 2; Allen, *Lewis and Clark*, pp. 133, 176.

[15]   James J. Holmberg, "Fairly Launched on My Voyage of Discovery," *We Proceeded On*, 35:3 (August 2009), p. 22. Hereafter cited as Holmberg, "Fairly Launched."

[16]   W. Raymond Wood, *Prologue to Lewis and Clark: The Mackay and Evans Expedition* (Norman, 2003), pp. 34, 132. Hereafter cited as Wood, *Prologue*.

[17]   Wood, *Prologue*, p. 114; Jackson, *Letters*, 1:12.

[18]   Wood, *Prologue*, p. 149.

[19]   Wood, *Prologue*, pp. 182-183.

[20]   An edited version of Biddle is constituted as Elliott Coues, editor, *History of the Expedition Under the Command of Lewis and Clark* (New York, 1893), 1:226. Hereafter cited as Coues, *History*. *JLCE*, 3:310, 362; Jackson, *Letters*, 1:230.

[21]   *JLCE*, 3:368; Wood, *Prologue*, p. 182.

[22]   *JLCE*, 3:368; Wood, *Prologue*, p. 150; Allen, *Lewis and Clark*, pp. 247-248.

[23]   In the proto-historic period, the Shoshone ranged over much of Montana and Wyoming, almost to Mandan country. When trade guns fell into the hands of the Blackfeet and other tribes via British traders, the Shoshone were relegated by their neighbors to the foothills on either side of the Continental Divide because of superior firepower. Native scholar Amy

Mossett has recently offered the revisionist idea that it was the Crow Indians who initially captured Sacagawea, not the Hidatsa as commonly believed. She posits that through an exchange, Sacagawea ended up with the Hidatsa and eventually Charbonneau and through him to Lewis and Clark's company. In partial substantiation of this idea, Clark's map of the Yellowstone River, prepared at Fort Mandan and informed by Sheheke, a Mandan chief, shows the Crow Indians living on the upper Yellowstone. The Three Forks of the Missouri, where Sacagawea was captured, form the watershed immediately to the west of the Yellowstone's headwaters. Wood, *Prologue*, pp. 96, 114; personal communication with Amy Mossett, 3 June 2006. Also see John C. Ewers, "Plains Indian Reactions to the Lewis and Clark Expedition," in Ronda, ed., *Voyages*, pp. 175-176, 189. For William Clark's interpretation of Sacagawea's perspective on how the Shoshone were forced into the mountains by raiders from the eastern plains, see *JLCE*, 8:182. A fictional account of the Lewis and Clark Expedition postulates that the Hidatsa were purposefully treacherous in the travel advice they gave. More likely, the Hidatsa were simply doing the captains a favor by sending them in a safer direction than the Medicine River route. After all, when Lewis and Clark returned to the Hidatsa homelands in the summer of 1806, Chiefs Black Moccasin and White Buffalo Robe Unfolded were "extreamly pleased to See us," William Clark reported. Brian Hall, *I Should Be Extremely Happy in Your Company: A Novel of Lewis and Clark* (New York 2003), p. 237. Hereafter cited as Hall, *Extremely Happy. JLCE*, 8:298, 300 nn. 3, 4. Charles McKenzie, a British trader that Lewis and Clark met at Fort Mandan, later confided in correspondence that the Indians had trouble understanding the captains' intentions. See W. Raymond Wood and Thomas D. Thiessen, *Early Fur Trade on the Northern Plains: Canadian Traders Among the Mandan and Hidatsa Indians, 1738-1818* (Norman, 1985), pp. 238-239; *JLCE*, 3:241. Gary Moulton has written that the Medicine River route "was the route that the Hidatsas had told them of at Fort Mandan," which Lewis and Clark missed on their westward journey, with the implication that this was the corridor that had been advised. Ibid., 8:96 n. 7. However, given McKenzie's insight that the Indians had trouble understanding the captains' intentions, for Moulton's view to be sustained requires the Hidatsa to have fully absorbed Lewis and Clark's strict purposes as defined by Jefferson's instructions—"the most direct & practicable water communication across this continent for the purposes of commerce"—a questionable proposition. Jackson, *Letters*, 1:61.

[24] *JLCE*, 3:368; 7:242.

[25] *JLCE*, 3:368; 4:13 n. 11. For similar references to the Nez Perce, see Ibid., 5:220, 242.

[26] *JLCE*, 3:368; Allen, *Lewis and Clark*, p. 223.

[27] *JLCE*, 3:368-369; 5:192.

[28] *JLCE*, 3:258, 265, 268-269 (qtn.), 276, 298, 303, 308, 369, 374; Coues, *History*, 1:221 n. Raymond Wood points out that the only part of Sheheke's map drawn in the chief's "way" that Clark deigned to recapitulate was the eastern part of Montana emphasizing the Yellowstone system, not the Missouri proper. Wood, *Prologue*, p. 114.

[29] Jackson, *Letters*, 1:225.

[30] *JLCE*, 3:374. Clark's Fort Mandan map was sent to Jefferson along with a host of plant and animal specimens that had been collected on the trip up the Missouri in 1804. Lewis prefaced its arrival by saying it "will give you the idea we entertain of the connection of these rivers, which has been formed from the corresponding testimony of a number of Indians who have visited the country, and... we therefore think it entitled to some degree of confidence." Several versions of this map were copied from the Clark manuscript by Nicholas King over the ensuing few years, but the original is no longer extant. On Clark's map from Fort Mandan, as adapted serially by King, the "Oregan" of King's 1803 map has

now become the Columbia, and its previous east/southeasterly branch, became one that ran strictly south to north, as per Lewis's letter to his mother from Fort Mandan. The name of the northerly fork was foreshortened to "Tacoutche River," and King seems to have given its course a second line of engraving, indicating greater width than the southern branch, both having been designated by dotted lines in the 1803 version. King's design choice may reflect the priority of designation via Mackenzie for the Tacoutche Tesse or it was a function of Arrowsmith's manipulative notation about "Principal Branch." In any event, King's cartography on the size of the northern branch was in the end correct but at the time conjectural, as Lewis and Clark's informants had no information beyond the base of the mountains footing the southern branch. *JLCE*, 1:89, maps 2, 32a, 32b, 32c; Jackson, *Letters*, 1:233, 237 n. 8, 252.

[31] Jackson, *Letters*, 1:233.

[32] *JLCE*, 4:71; Allen, *Lewis and Clark*, pp. 262-263.

[33] *JLCE*, 4:198.

[34] *JLCE*, 4:246, 271. The men had good reason to fear the south fork of the Missouri River, and that maybe their party as well would "termineate in the mountains." As prescient as Clark and Lewis were, from the bluffs above the Marias-Missouri confluence the Rocky Mountains present themselves as a backdrop on the apparent trajectory of the Missouri, while the Marias tends in the direction of gentle plains.

[35] *JLCE*, 11:190.

[36] *JLCE*, 4:299 (qtn.), 437; 9:190; 11:243. Moulton's annotation that Ordway "uses the term 'Columbian River' very broadly in the next few weeks" exemplifies one of the pitfalls of documentary editing wherein normative understandings brought about by subsequent experience and knowledge subtly vitiate our understanding of what these explorers believed to be the case in "real time." Ibid., 9:191 n. 3.

[37] *JLCE*, 5:59, 65.

[38] Allen, *Lewis and Clark*, p. 291 n. 15; Wood, *Prologue*, p. 178.

CHAPTER 2

[1] Jenkinson, "Slaughter's Expedition," p. 626. Jenkinson's larger argument is that the body of popular lore conformed into "LEWIS & CLARK" gave rise to the debunking leitmotif of Thomas Slaughter's post-modernist critique of the expedition, cited earlier as Slaughter, *Exploring Lewis and Clark*, passim. Lewis's quote at Lemhi is found at *JLCE*, 5:74.

[2] For the scholarly consensus about the Lemhi Disappointment see, for example, William L. Lang, "Describing a New Environment: Lewis and Clark and Enlightenment Science in the Columbia River Basin," *Oregon Historical Quarterly*, 105:3 (Fall 2004) p. 360; Ambrose, *Undaunted Courage*, pp. 266-267; Dayton Duncan, *Scenes of Visionary Enchantment: Reflections on Lewis and Clark* (Lincoln, 2004), p. 99. Hereafter cited as Duncan, *Scenes*. Also see Carolyn Gilman, *Lewis and Clark: Across the Divide* (Washington, DC, 2003), pp. 185-211, the companion volume to the national bicentennial exhibition, and the interpretive film about Lewis on Lemhi Pass that is a part of the exhibit, both of which are characteristic in this regard. Hereafter cited as Gilman, *Across the Divide*. For other treatments of the "Lemhi Disappointment" see: Ken Burns, *Lewis & Clark: The Journey of the Corps of Discovery* (PBS, 1997); the Imax film *Lewis & Clark: Great Journey West* (National Geographic, 2002); Hall, *Extremely Happy*, pp. 228-237.

[3]   For Lewis's first glimpse of a complex Rocky Mountain chain see *JLCE*, 4:280.

[4]   Allen, *Lewis and Clark*, pp. 291-292.

[5]   Ambrose, *Undaunted Courage*, pp. 266-267; Duncan, *Scenes*, p. 99.

[6]   Jackson, *Letters*, 1:233.

[7]   *JLCE*, 3:333-334, 336, 367-368, 383 n. 1; Wood, *Prologue*, pp. 114, 132. For information on the Hidatsa as western geographers, see Clay S. Jenkinson, *A Vast and Open Plain: The Writings of the Lewis and Clark Expedition in North Dakota, 1804–1806* (Bismarck, 2003), pp. 260 n. 17, 282 n. 345. The Mandan and Hidatsa also gave David Thompson, a British trader and surveyor, a tutorial on western geography in 1798. Thompson was dispatched to the Mandan and Hidatsa in response to Evans's ephemeral foray in furtherance of Spanish attempts to re-establish hegemony over the Missouri uplands. While with the Mandan, Thompson encountered some "Mountain Indians" (probably Shoshone or Crow). They told him that upstream the Missouri had a "high fall" and traversed three ranges of mountains beyond. Furthermore, Thompson learned that "another river not so large [as the Missouri] goes off the other side" of the Continental Divide. This was almost certainly a reference to the Lemhi/Salmon/Snake River system, tributary to the Columbia. Jack Nisbet, *The Mapmaker's Eye: David Thompson on the Columbia Plateau* (Pullman, WA, 2005), p. 24. Hereafter cited as Nisbet, *Mapmaker's Eye*.

[8]   As Roger Kennedy colorfully observes, the Appalachians "lie in range after range like the spines of great lizards asleep amid the cranberry bogs and early frosts." Roger G. Kennedy, *Mr. Jefferson's Lost Cause: Land, Farmers, Slavery and the Louisiana Purchase* (London, 2003), p. 55. Hereafter cited as Kennedy, *Lost Cause*.

[9]   *JLCE*, 4:280.

[10]   J. I. Merritt, "Cameahwait's Geography Lesson," *We Proceeded On* (November, 2003), pp. 36-37. Hereafter cited as Merritt, "Geography Lesson."

[11]   *JLCE*, 5:77, 81; Allen, *Lewis and Clark*, p. 292.

[12]   *JLCE*, 5:74, 79; Mackay's instruction to Evans reads as follows: "When you will see some [Indian] nations, raise your flag a long way off as a sign of peace, and never approach without speaking to them from a distance." Before encountering Cameahwait's band, Lewis had seen several Shoshone women and a single man and once he got within half a mile of them, he unfurled his flag and advanced toward them alone. He failed in his first attempt at engineering a parley with this smaller group, but then succeeded with Cameahwait. Wood, *Prologue*, p. 177; Ambrose, *Undaunted Courage*, pp. 268-269.

[13]   *JLCE*, 5:81; Allen, *Lewis and Clark*, p. 295.

[14]   *JLCE*, 5:83. Though Lewis does not say so, Gary Moulton has suggested that in the absence of Sacagawea and Charbonneau, both of whom were still with Clark on the Missouri side of the ridge, all geographic communications were facilitated by George Drouillard, a half-Shawnee mixed blood proficient in sign language. Ibid., 5:85 n. 6.

[15]   *JLCE*, 5:88-89.

[16]   *JLCE*, 5:89-90.

[17]   *JLCE*, 5:90-91.

[18]   *JLCE*, 5:94 n. 2, 95 n. 16.

19 *JLCE*, 5:88.

20 *JLCE*, 2:85; 3:16-17, 41, 112 (qtn.), 205 nn. 1, 312 and 327; 5:88, 94 n. 1; 8:298 (qtn.); 9:99; Gilman, *Across the Divide*, p. 194.

21 Sally Thompson, "Misnomers Along the Lewis and Clark Trail," in Juneau and Purviance, eds., *Confluence of Cultures*, pp. 151-152. Hereafter cited as Thompson, "Misnomers." Also, Gilman, *Across the Divide*, p. 194.

22 *JLCE*, 5:106, 111; Thompson, "Misnomers," p. 152.

23 *JLCE*, 5:142.

24 *JLCE*, 5:61-109, passim. Likewise, after Clark set out to inspect the Columbia River on August 18th, during which time Lewis managed the portage over the divide, the latter's notebook journal includes information about Clark's activities through August 26. Ibid., pp. 117-173, passim. Lewis's scientific entries are at Ibid., 5:77-80. See Barbara Belyea, ed., *Columbia Journals: David Thompson* (Seattle, 1998), pp. ix, xvi, xvii, xxi, for analysis of the distinctions between "campfire journals" and texts that filter the accounts of exploration for narrative effect. Hereafter cited as Belyea, *Columbia Journals*.

25 See Merritt, "Geography Lesson," pp. 36-37.

26 Coues, *History*, 2:495, 521-525. Moulton's edition of the journals has placed the "geography lesson" in the body of the narrative where Lewis inscribed it. However, Reuben Gold Thwaites, in his edition from a century ago, moved Clark's early information about the Columbia River country to August 20th, when Clark says he secured it, noting that the contents had been copied or rewritten by Lewis. Thwaites' editorial decision was faithful to the actual sequence of events, but it obfuscated Lewis's subterfuge by which he purported to have secured the information. Reuben Gold Thwaites, *Original Journals of the Lewis and Clark Expedition, 1804-1806* (New York, 1904–05), 2:379 n. 2. Hereafter cited as Thwaites, *Original Journals*. Clark visited with Biddle for three weeks in April 1810 in Fincastle, Virginia, and again in Philadelphia in the spring of 1813. Jackson, *Letters*, 2:497, 546, 595.

27 Jenkinson, "Slaughter's Expedition," p. 626.

28 Belyea, *Columbia Journals*, pp. ix, xvii; Clay S. Jenkinson, *The Character of Meriwether Lewis: 'Completely Metamorphosed' in the American West* (Reno, 2000), p. 52. Hereafter cited as Jenkinson, *Lewis*.

29 Percy G. Adams, *Travelers and Travel Liars, 1660-1880* (Berkeley, 1962), pp. 10, 16, 223. Hereafter cited as Adams, *Travel Liars*.

30 Slaughter, *Exploring Lewis and Clark*, p. 48; *JLCE*, 2:8-35; Belyea, *Columbia Journals*, pp. v, xxi. Paul Cutright holds the view that Lewis did not keep a journal prior to Fort Mandan. In so doing, Lewis may have been operating on the same principle Alexander Mackenzie used in the formulation of his accounts of travel in 1789 and 1793. That is, Lewis deigned to pick up the narrative thread from a western base camp (like Mackenzie had in the form of Fort Chipewyan on Lake Athabasca) from which the exploration of *terra incognita* began in earnest. Paul Russell Cutright, *A History of the Lewis and Clark Journals* (Norman, 1976), p. 171. Hereafter cited as Cutright, *Journals*. Lamb, *Mackenzie Journals*, pp. 163, 237.

31 Belyea, *Columbia Journals*, p. xvi; *JLCE*, 2:23-24.

[32] *JLCE*, 2:21-22, 25; Coues, *History*, 1:xiii. Of special interest relative to William Clark's voluminous field notes is his elkskin-bound journal covering the period from 11 September 1805 through December 31st of that year. These notes serve as the primary record for the expedition's traverse of country from the Bitterroot Valley in Montana to the Pacific Ocean.

[33] Belyea, *Columbia Journals*, p. xvii; Slaughter, *Exploring Lewis and Clark*, p. 32. Tom Chaffin, *Pathfinder: John Charles Frémont and the Course of American Empire* (New York, 2004), p. 143. Hereafter cited as Chaffin, *Frémont*. Chaffin argues that John Frémont and his amanuensis, wife Jesse, invented narrative, making the account of travels "more literary than empirical." Ibid., p. 144.

[34] James P. Ronda, "'So Vast an Enterprise': Thoughts on the Lewis and Clark Expedition," in Ronda, ed., *Voyages*, p. 23; Bruce Greenfield, *Narrating Discovery: The Romantic Explorer in American Literature, 1790-1855*, (New York, 1992) pp. 11, 19 (qtn.). Hereafter cited as Greenfield, *Narrating Discovery*.

[35] Hayes, *First Crossing*, p. 102; Slaughter, *Exploring Lewis and Clark*, pp. 32, 49, 55 (qtn.), 57.

[36] Allesandro Portelli, *The Death of Luigi Trastulli and Other Stories: Form and Meaning in Oral History* (Albany, NY, 1991), pp. ix, 2. Hereafter cited as Portelli, *Oral History*. Slaughter, *Exploring Lewis and Clark*, p. 64.

[37] Jackson, *Jefferson*, p. 121; Jackson, "United States Army," in Ronda, ed. *Voyages*, pp. 64, 70 n. 9. For treatments of Mackenzie's influence on Jefferson see *JLCE*, 2:3; Ambrose, *Undaunted Courage*, pp. 74-76; Goetzmann, *New Lands*, pp. 111-112.

[38] Lamb, *Mackenzie Journals*, p. 313; *JLCE*, 5:112.

[39] Lamb, *Mackenzie Journals*, p. 314.

[40] Lamb, *Mackenzie Journals*, pp. 314, 321, 455-457; Allen, *Lewis and Clark*, p. 29. Robert Gray did not return to Boston after having discovered and named the Columbia River until late July 1793, precisely when Mackenzie was beginning his return from the Pacific. J. Richard Nokes, *Columbia's River: The Voyages of Robert Gray, 1787-1793* (Tacoma, 1991), p. 257. Hereafter cited as Nokes, *Gray*. Couriers from Vancouver's expedition, including William Broughton who had surveyed the Columbia, did not reach London, England, until June and July of 1793. However, given the British admiralty's penchant for controlling the release of information pending publication of official narratives and charts, it may have been as late as October 1795, when Vancouver himself returned to England, that details about the Columbia River began to circulate. Vancouver's account was published in late August or early September of 1798. Lamb, *Vancouver*, pp. 107, 117, 188, 201, 206, 241-242.

[41] Lamb, *Mackenzie Journals*, p. 318; Ambrose, *Undaunted Courage*, p. 277.

[42] Jackson, *Jefferson*, pp. 192, 194; Chaffin, *Frémont*, p. 188.

[43] Lamb, *Mackenzie Journals*, p. 314.

[45] *JLCE*, 5:88, 106.

[45] *JLCE*, 5:109.

[46] *JLCE*, 5:111, 113.

47 *JLCE*, 5:114-115. Cameahwait also traded names with Clark, or gave Clark a name by which he was called in the Shoshone tongue. This was an honor not bestowed on Lewis and may have reflected the intercession of Sacagawea with her brother in recognition of Clark's generous treatment of her. *JLCE*, 5:115.

48 *JLCE*, 5:113, 115.

49 *JLCE*, 9:204-206. The term "mountain," as used by Ordway and other members of the expedition, was often used as a collective noun in that era, indicating a range of peaks and not just a single detached eminence. Belyea, *Columbia Journals*, p. 196.

50 *JLCE*, 11:272-274.

51 *JLCE*, 10:126-127.

52 *JLCE*, 5:124.

53 *JLCE*, 10:127-128.

54 *JLCE*, 5:170; 9:211, 212 n. 2; 11:284-285.

55 *JLCE*, 5:171-172.

56 *JLCE*, 5:128-131, 131 n. 6; 132 nn. 7, 8.

57 *JLCE*, 5:155.

58 *JLCE*, 5:155-156.

59 *JLCE*, 5:156-157, 157 n. 14.

60 *JLCE*, 5:154-155, 157 n. 5; 10:131.

61 Emphasis in the original. *JLCE*, 5:163, 164 n. 8.

62 *JLCE*, 5:162-163; 10:132.

63 *JLCE*, 5:171, 173; 9:211.

64 *JLCE*, 5:174 n. 4, 175, 178; Coues, *History*, 2:536 n.

65 *JLCE*, 11:290-291.

66 *JLCE*, 9:214.

67 *JLCE*, 5:114, 163. For the editorial effect see Coues, *History*, 2:484, 486, 508 n., 512 n., 522. See also, for example, Thwaites, *Original Journals*, 2:366, and *JLCE*, 5:76 n. 9, 141 n. 11, 157 n. 11; 9:211 n. 1, 215 n. 2. Coues also marked up the original journals themselves in an ill-advised attempt to impose his normative understanding of geography upon that of the explorers themselves, as seen at *JLCE*, 5:169, 170 n. 5.

68 Belyea, *Columbia Journals*, p. xxiv. For her work on Thompson's journals, Belyea employed a less-intrusive style of annotation than Lewis and Clark scholars are used to, leaving Thompson's narrative in the world as he knew it, not the way modern scholars know it.

CHAPTER 3

[1] *JLCE*, 5:183.

[2] *JLCE*, 5:187; 9:216-217; 11:298-299, 305.

[3] Allen, *Lewis and Clark*, p. 298; *JLCE*, 5:191-192. Further evidence that the "Clark's River" designation came later is seen in Clark's own course and distance table where the terminology "The Creek" was crossed out and replaced by "Clark's River." Clark's own field map, sketched on or near 10 October 1805 while the expedition was on the Snake River, still referred to the stream as "Flat head river." John Ordway's table of completed distances from Camp Fortunate on the Missouri River to the Pacific Ocean, and thus inscribed no earlier than the winter *after* the party was on the Bitterroot River, also denominated this stream the "flat head River." Ibid., 5:194, 267; 9:231. The term "Flathead" was nonetheless used loosely by Lewis and Clark over the course of the next few weeks of their trip to refer to the first tribes encountered west of the divide, excepting the Shoshone who were clearly distinct. Lewis's usage resulting in the naming of the river originated with an encounter with three men near Traveler's Rest who were indisputably Nez Perce, given the account rendered. Ibid., 5:196, 198 n. 3. To add to the confusion of historians, Clark later used the term "Flathead River" to describe what's now known as the Lochsa in northern Idaho. This latter act of naming in itself reinforces the interpretation that when the explorers used the term "Flathead," usually the reference was to the Nez Perce tribe, not the Salish of the Montana valleys. Ibid., 5:204, 205 n. 9, 237.

[4] *JLCE*, 5:192; 198 n. 1.

[5] *JLCE*, 5:192, 198 n. 1; Allen, *Lewis and Clark*, pp. 301-302.

[6] *JLCE*, 3:368; 5:196. In fact, as described by the Hidatsa at Fort Mandan, the Blackfoot flows due west from the divide. However, the larger stream into which the Blackfoot flows, the Clark Fork, follows a course north of west, not southerly as noted at Fort Mandan.

[7] Allen, *Lewis and Clark*, p. 302; *JLCE*, 1:map 2; 5:196, 198 n. 1. On the basis of Lewis's faulty memory regarding the direction of the flow of the river opposite the Medicine, John Logan Allen stipulated that Lewis and Clark "now realized... the northward-flowing river the [Hidatsa] had described was the Bitterroot rather than the Lemhi." Allen, *Lewis and Clark*, p. 302. This is a debatable conclusion supported as it is on a likely transposition of the cardinal directions induced by the stress of the moment. Furthermore, William Clark's field map, composed a month later when the party was on the Snake River and well after the Bitterroots had been crossed, shows, unmistakably, the Flathead River system flowing in a southwesterly direction towards the northern fork of the Columbia. *JLCE*, 5:267. Thus, in the end, Lewis and Clark did not think of the Flathead system as one flowing south to north like the Lemhi/Salmon. The Hidatsa had always been thinking of the latter as the path to waters that flowed into the Pacific Ocean.

[8] *JLCE*, 5:197; Jackson, *Letters*, 1:320. Clark also referred to the Nez Perce camps being on the Columbia River but corrected his journal to read "Kooskooske River" when working with Biddle in 1810, having since learned the hydraulic primacy of the northern fork of the Columbia. Ibid., 5:197, 198 n. 5.

[9] *JLCE*, 2:524; 11:306, 309.

[10] *JLCE*, 11:309-310.

[11] *JLCE*, 11:310.

[12] *JLCE*, 5:199 n. 1; 11:311.

[13] *JLCE*, 5:206-207, 215; 11:319-323. For instances of difficulties facing the horses see, Ibid., 5:201, 202, 206, 210, 211, 215, 218, 225, 228; 8:25, 43.

[14] For historians on the starvation myth, see Coues, *History*, 2:599 n. 30, 612 n.; Allen, *Lewis and Clark*, p. 218 n. 300; James J. Holmberg, *Dear Brother: Letters of William Clark to Jonathan Clark* (New Haven, 2002), p. 113. Hereafter cited as Holmberg, *Letters of William Clark*. Stephen Dow Beckham, *Lewis & Clark: From the Rockies to the Pacific* (Portland, 2002), p. 28. Hereafter cited as Beckham, *Rockies to the Pacific*. James P. Ronda, "'So Vast an Enterprise': Thoughts on the Lewis and Clark Expedition," in Ronda, ed., *Voyages*, p. 14. Hereafter cited as Ronda, "Vast Enterprise," Ronda, ed., *Voyages*. Ken Burns, "Lewis & Clark: The Journey of the Corps of Discovery," (PBS, 1997).

[15] Laton McCartney, *Across the Great Divide; Robert Stuart and the Discovery of the Oregon Trail* (New York, 2003), pp. 215-216. Hereafter cited as McCartney, *Robert Stuart*. Chaffin, *Frémont*, pp. 113, 115, 214-220.

[16] Beckham, *Rockies to the Pacific*, pp. 28, 31. The explanation Beckham put forth—Lewis focused on natural history to stave off "despair and hunger" or was simply "rising to President Jefferson's expectations"—is unconvincing. If the latter was true, Lewis had chosen an odd time to be faithful to the charge of keeping a daily journal since gaps abounded heretofore and the largest was about to ensue.

[17] *JLCE*, 5:163, 205, 207.

[18] *JLCE*, 5:209; Nisbet, *Mapmaker's Eye*, pp. 41-42; Chaffin, *Frémont*, p. 218.

[19] *JLCE*, 5:211, 213.

[20] *JLCE*, 5:213, 214 n. 9.

[21] *JLCE*, 5:211, 213, 214 n. 4, 216. The bear's oil and "candles" were probably the same substance, just stored in different containers. The oil would have been previously rendered into tallow and kept in canisters or molds. The tallow was used to cook dry meat and could also be made into candles. Coues, *History*, 2:600; Chaffin, *Frémont*, p. 120. During planning for the return trip at the provisioning camp opposite the Sandy River on the lower Columbia, Lewis determined shortly thereafter to transform the river voyage into a caravan. With horses "we shall not only sucure the means of transporting our baggage over the mountains but that we shall also have provided the means of subsistence; for we now view the horses as our only certain resource for food, nor do we look forward to it with any detestation or horrow, so soon is the mind which is occupyed with any interesting object reconciled to it's situation." *JLCE*, 7:54.

[22] *JLCE*, 5:215.

[23] *JLCE*, 5:219, 222-223.

[24] *JLCE*, 5:217-218.

[25] *JLCE*, 5:225-226.

[26] *JLCE*, 5:226, 228-229.

[27] *JLCE*, 5:230; Jenkinson, "Slaughter's Expedition," p. 626.

[28] *JLCE*, 5:235, 244; 11:336-337, 339.

[29] *JLCE*, 8:21, 24; 9:227.

[30] *JLCE*, 3:65-66.

[31] *JLCE*, 11:315, 317, 322-323.

[32] *JLCE*, 5:229; Portelli, *Oral History*, p. 53.

[33] Belyea, *Columbia Journals*, pp. 137, 141, 262.

[34] Belyea, *Columbia Journals*, pp. 138, 141; Coues, *History*, 2:536 n.

CHAPTER 4

[1] *JLCE*, 5:226.

[2] *JLCE*, 5:226-227, 237, 238, 240, 240 nn. 2-4, 248 n. 2.

[3] *JLCE*, 5:230. Twisted Hair's map appears to have been twice duplicated in Clark's hand amidst his field notes and partially overwritten on 13-14 October entries. See maps in Ibid., 5:267, 270.

[4] *JLCE*, 5:229-230, 231 n. 9; 267; 9:228; Allen, *Lewis and Clark*, p. 305 n. Alternatively, "Clarks River" may have been in Clark's mind one and the same with the northerly, or "Clark fork" of the Columbia, in juxtaposition to the south or "Lewis's fork." This can be deduced from Clark's very next phrase which suggests that from "the mouth of that [Clarks] river" (that is, the Snake/Columbia confluence) it was "5 sleeps" to Celilo Falls. This theory is made more plausible by a comment that Clark made to Jefferson ten years after the expedition concluded when he referred to the Columbia River and the "Lewis & Clarks rivers" by which it was constituted. Jackson, *Letters*, 2:625.

[5] *JLCE*, 5:230; 10:149; Ruby and Brown, *Chinook Indians*, p. 89; Douglas C. Wilson, et al., *Historical Archaeology at the Middle Village: Station Camp/McGowan Site (45PC106), Station Camp Unit, Lewis & Clark National Park, Pacific County, Washington* (Vancouver, WA, 2008), passim.

[6] *JLCE*, 5:229, 231.

[7] Jackson, *Letters*, 2:501, 541; *JLCE*, 11:365.

[8] *JLCE*, 5:232-233; 11:331.

[9] *JLCE*, 5:234 n. 2, 234-235, 241-246.

[10] *JLCE*, 5:248-249, 250 n. 2. Nez Perce elder Allen Pinkham believes that the name "Tetoharsky" is a garbling of "Tee-token-opskop." This insight is from a personal communication with Pinkham, dated 2 June 2006.

[11] *JLCE*, 11:341, 343.

[12] *JLCE*, 5:249, 250 n. 2, 252-253, 255-256. Notwithstanding Clark's map that shows this camp barely downstream from the confluence of the two rivers, to say nothing of a similar description in text, cartographer Martin Plamondon places this campsite in his reconstruction a mile farther down the Snake. See Martin Plamondon II, *Lewis and Clark Trail Maps, A Cartographic Reconstruction* (Pullman, 2001), 2:186. Hereafter cited as Plamondon, *Cartographic Reconstruction*. Clark's last "call" or landmark sighting was to

a bend in the river downstream from the confluence. At the end of that paragraph, Clark notes the expedition "camped." I do not believe Clark meant to imply that the camp itself was that far to the west. *JLCE*, 5:283 n. 1.

[13] *JLCE,* 5:230, 243, 245, 256, 258, 260 nn. 9, 15. Clark's "campfire" journal bound in elkskin never references the "Columbia River" in the narrative until the arrival at the Snake/Columbia rivers confluence on October 16th, unlike his maps which do so earlier in the sequence as found at Ibid., 5:267, 270. Clark's leather-bound notebook journals for the run of the Snake River, prepared weeks or months later, contain numerous erasures and strikeovers relative to the names of Columbian tributaries, reflective of initial confusion and post-dated editing. Clark's notebook entry for October 16th, probably written well after the fact, provides the first differentiation between the "junction of this [Snake] river and the Columbia which joins from the N.W." Ibid., 5:256, 258, 276-277. Clark had a good opportunity to conduct journal conformance and editing at the Rock Fort encampment below The Dalles. The expedition stayed within those friendly confines for two days. On October 26th Clark recorded that he "had all our articles put out to dry" after shooting the famed rapids of the Short and Long Narrows of the Columbia. This probably provided Clark with an opportunity to get the notebooks out from storage where they would have been tucked away for safety in anticipation of running the numerous rapids of the Columbia. Ibid., 5:283 n. 2, 340.

[14] *JLCE*, 9:229, 236; 11:332, 346.

[15] *JLCE*, 5:255, 260 n. 7; Allen, *Lewis and Clark*, p. 309. Clark's leather-bound notebook for October 10th also refers to the Snake alternatively as "Lewis's River," but we know from subsequent events that this name was not settled on any earlier than October 17th and possibly as late as the following May 6th when "Clarks River" was denominated. *JLCE*, 11:357; 7:216. Here, "Lewis's River" appeared written over an erasure that had probably spelled "Kim-moo-e-nem" or Columbia. Ibid., 5:255–256, 260 nn. 7, 11.

[16] *JLCE*, 1:map 123; 5:256; 6:213, 311, 313, 324, 336, 355-356, 359-360. Clark appears to have borrowed his colorful phrasing about "sticks of timber" from Meriwether Lewis, who twice on the Missouri River leg in 1804 had referred to landscapes that contained "not a stick of timber" or "without a stick of timber." Ibid., 4:30, 176.

[17] Allen, *Lewis and Clark*, pp. 307, 309. Confirming Allen's thesis of the verbally challenged explorers, Joseph Whitehouse captured the setting, somewhat rustically, when he wrote of the hills with "not even a tree to be Seen no place." *JLCE*, 11:348.

[18] *JLCE*, 5:263-265, 268; 10:153; Pamela Regis, *Describing Early America: Bartram, Jefferson, Crevecouer, and the Influence of Natural History* (Philadelphia, 1999), p. 30. Hereafter cited as Regis, *Early America*.

[19] *JLCE*, 5:271-272. Whitehouse said the lodge planking "was covred So carefully with Stone." Ibid., 11:352.

[20] *JLCE*, 5:274-275; 9:237-239; 11:353-354. Joseph Whitehouse seems to have been the one journalist to look upon the country most equitably. He wrote on October 12th, "this River is verry handsom and country pleasant but no timber at all." Ibid., 11:349.

[21] *JLCE*, 5:256 (qtn.), 262-263, 268, 271 (qtn.), 274-275.

[22] *JLCE*, 5:263, 265-266 (qtns.); 11:351; Ambrose, *Undaunted Courage*, pp. 181-183. The Snake River once had fifty-one sets of rapids on its 141-mile run from the vicinity of its junction with the Clearwater to that with the confluence with the Columbia. *Snake River and Tributaries*, House Doc. 190, 73rd Congress, 2nd session, p. 121.

23 *JLCE*, 5:268; 9:237.

24 *JLCE*, 5:265, 266; 11:350.

25 *JLCE*, 5:274-275, 276 n. 4; 7:204 n. 6. Whitehouse noted that the Nez Perce accompanying the expedition on horseback had to "ride fast to keep up with us for the current mostly rapid." Ibid., 11:351.

26 *JLCE*, 5:276-277.

27 *JLCE*, 5:271-272.

28 *JLCE*, 5:274-275, 276 n. 2.

29 *JLCE*, 5:263-264, 274-275.

CHAPTER 5

1 C. S. Kingston, "Sacajawea as Guide: The Evaluation of a Legend," *Pacific Northwest Quarterly*, 35:1 (January 1944), pp. 3-4. Hereafter cited as Kingston, "Legend."

2 Kingston, "Legend," pp. 3, 7 n. 16, 9 n. 20.

3 Kingston, "Legend," p. 11; *JLCE*, 8:180 (qtn.), 182.

4 Kingston, "Legend," p. 13; *JLCE,* 8:180 n. 8, 305.

5 Ronald W. Taber, "Sacagawea and the Suffragettes," *Pacific Northwest Quarterly*, 58:1 (January 1967), pp. 7-8. Hereafter cited as Taber, "Suffragettes."

6 Taber, "Suffragettes," p. 9.

7 Taber, "Suffragettes," pp. 10-12, 11 n. 28; James P. Ronda, *Lewis and Clark among the Indians* (Lincoln, 1984), pp. 256-259. Hereafter cited as Ronda, *LCAI*. W. Dale Nelson, *Interpreters with Lewis and Clark: The Story of Sacagawea and Toussaint Charbonneau* (Denton, TX, 2003), pp. 123-131. Other evidence that what Taber once called the "fortress which surrounds that myth" of Sacagawea has not been demolished can be seen in a recent advertisement for "Russell Country, Montana." Titled "Real Men Ask for Directions," the copy reads: "Lewis and Clark had Sacagawea to guide them through their most memorable adventures, including a daunting portage of the Great Falls of the Missouri River." Taber, "Suffragettes," p. 7; *Sunset Magazine* (March 2004), p. 149. In truth Sacagawea was lain prostrate at the onset of the portage by an infection and was hardly in the position to be piloting anyone. *JLCE*, 4:276-277, 279, 281.

8 Kingston, "Legend," p. 16; Slaughter, *Exploring Lewis and Clark*, p. 86. On this rare point Thomas Slaughter agrees with Gary Moulton, the latter having also written that Sacagawea's "presence with a baby calmed the fears of *many* tribes that the party was a war expedition." *JLCE*, 3:229 n. 2. Emphasis added.

9 *JLCE*, 5:268; Ronda, *LCAI*, p. 258; Joyce Badgley Hunsnaker, *Sacagawea Speaks: Beyond the Shining Mountains with Lewis and Clark* (Guilford, CT, 2001), p. 16; www.pbs.org/lewisandclark/inside/saca.html.

10 *JLCE*, 5:268, 269 n. 3; 10:154; Wood, *Prologue*, p. 176.

11 *JLCE*, 5:267, 268 n. 1, 278; 11:349.

[12] Lamb, *Mackenzie Journals*, pp. 314, 317, 337.

[13] Lamb, *Mackenzie Journals*, pp. 317, 340, 364.

[14] *JLCE*, 5:284 n. 8.

[15] *JLCE*, 5:278; 7:203-204. In his miscellaneous notes composed at Fort Mandan, Clark stated in his treatise upon Indian laws, government, and language, that "all nations Harrang." Native elders or others with stature within the tribe usually employed this rhetorical device. Ibid., 3:489-490.

[16] *JLCE*, 5:301, 303.

[17] *JLCE*, 5:146, 222; Coues, *History*, 2:529.

[18] *JLCE*, 5:305-306; Coues, *History*, 2:648; Jackson, *Letters*, 1:317.

[19] *JLCE*, 1:map 75; 5:305-306; William L. Lang, "Lewis and Clark on the Columbia River: The Power of Landscape in the Exploration Experience," *Pacific Northwest Quarterly*, 87:3 (Summer 1996), pp. 145-146. Hereafter cited as Lang, "Landscape." The idea that a stressful voyage led to a destabilized psychological state for Clark, thereby damaging the captain's self-confidence or self-control, is unproven. To the contrary, Clark's notebook recapitulation states that after shooting the crane, he crossed the river to the lodges precisely *because* he could see Lewis approaching the village without any awareness of its existence. Clark hastened to the other side of the Columbia when he became "fearfull that those people might not be informed of us." By this he meant the potentially startling appearance of Lewis. *JLCE*, 5:305. Consider, too, Clark's first contact with some frightened Nez Perce boys when he wandered out of the Bitterroot Mountain wilderness onto Weippe Prairie. To "quiet their fears," James Ronda explains, Clark "gave each one several small pieces of ribbon and then urged them with gestures to announce the arrival of friendly visitors in their village." Ronda, *LCAI*, p. 158. Surely if a formidable landscape encounter was going to test William Clark's capacity for psychological self-control, emerging from the mountains at Weippe was a likelier occasion for failure than floating out of Wallula Gap.

[20] *JLCE*, 5:305; Ronda, *LCAI*, p. 168; Jackson, *Letters*, 2:529-530.

[21] *JLCE*, 5:303; 10:158; 11:360; Robert Conner, "Our People Have Always Been Here," in *Lewis and Clark Through Indian Eyes*, Alvin Josephy Jr., editor (New York, 2006), p. 99.

[22] Goetzmann, *New Lands*, p. 48; Ronda, *LCAI*, p. 168; Greg Dening, *Beach Crossings: Voyaging Across Time, Cultures, and Self* (Philadelphia, 2004), pp. 236, 240. Hereafter cited as Dening, *Beach Crossings*. See Brigitta Hauser-Schäublin, "Witnesses of Encounters and Interactions," in *Life in the Pacific of the 1700's: The Cook/Forster Collection*, Stephen Little and Peter Ruthenberg, editors; Brigitta Hauser-Schäublin and Gundalf Krüger, co-editors, (Honolulu, 2006), 2:32-35, (hereafter cited as Hauser-Schäublin, "Witnesses of Encounters") for an introduction to the academic debate over whether Native Hawaiians truly intended to have Cook understand that they thought of him in divine terms.

[23] Dening, *Beach Crossings*, p. 236; Lamb, *Mackenzie Journals*, p. 351; Coues, *History*, 2:648.

[24] William Layman, "Hawkbells: David Thompson in North Central Washington," *Columbia*, 5:4 (Winter 1991), pp. 18-19; Jack Nisbet, *Sources of the River: Tracking David Thompson Across Western North America*, (Seattle, 1994), p. 203. Hereafter cited as Nisbet, *Thompson*. *JLCE*, 11:377. Ordway makes a comparable observation to Whitehouse's at Ibid., 9:247.

25 *JLCE*, 5:326-328; 11:367.

26 *JLCE*, 5:329; 336 n. 4.

27 *JLCE*, 5:328-329; Gilman, *Across the Divide*, p. 225.

28 *JLCE*, 5:335-336; 9:245; 11:370.

29 *JLCE*, 5:332, 338. Clark does not identify this tribe, but Moulton suspects they may have hailed from the Wishram village above the Long Narrows from which the expedition had just departed, or possibly the village above Celilo Falls. Ibid., 5:340 n. 7.

30 *JLCE*, 5:338-339.

31 *JLCE*, 11:372.

32 *JLCE*, 5:345, 346 n. 3, 349-350.

33 Ronda, *LCAI*, p. 173.

34 Kingston, "Legend," p. 18.

CHAPTER 6

1 *JLCE*, 5:277.

2 *JLCE*, 5:276-277.

3 Allen, *Lewis and Clark*, pp. xxii, 310-311.

4 Coues, *History*, 2:635 n.; Allen, *Lewis and Clark*, p. 311.

5 *JLCE*, 9:239; 11:355. In his own note on sources, Allen said, "Other journals, written by other members of the party, do exist, but since the focus here is on Lewis and Clark and their geographical ideas, these will be cited only occasionally." Allen, *Lewis and Clark*, p. 182 n. 3. The triangulation of perspective made possible by recourse to the journals of Ordway and Whitehouse casts this episode in an entirely more complex context than the one presented by Clark alone.

6 Bernard DeVoto, "'Passage to India:' From Christmas to Christmas with Lewis and Clark," Ronda, ed., *Voyages*, p. 96. Consider, for example, the annotation by Gary Moulton relative to Ordway in which the sergeant "continues to consider the river on which he has been traveling the Columbia; it is actually the Snake." *JLCE*, 9:239 n. 1.

7 Ronda, "Passages," pp. 539-541.

8 Clark's notebook entry for October 16th is also curiously constructed. He refers to the course for that day as being "Seven miles to the junction of this river and the Columbia which joins from the N. W." *JLCE*, 1:10, map 75; 5:267, 276-277, 295. Gary Moulton says the October 13th map is a "somewhat confused sketch… showing the drainage of the Columbia River." Actually, this map seems rather to be a strikingly faithful depiction of the narrative information about the river system as first provided by Twisted Hair and other Nez Perce informants when the expedition first emerged from the Bitterroot Mountains the previous September. Any confusion may be a function of the fact that the inscription "Columbia" is written upside down, making immediate discernment of that word difficult. The "large river" of Twisted Hair's description in September appears as "Big River" coming in from the

north in Clark's field map. Ibid., 5:230, 268 n. 1. Alternatively, instead of drawing this map while coursing the Snake, as he did in other instances, Clark may have simply paged ahead in his field book in September when talking with Twisted Hair at Weippe Prairie and drew this and other maps that were later written over by narrative copy. Ibid, 5:270, 293. I am reliant on Moulton's analysis about the delayed inscription date for Clark's leather-bound notebooks. See Ibid., 2:25-26. Even Nicholas Biddle discerned the anomaly that Clark never provided an Indian name for the Columbia River. Jackson, *Letters*, 2:552. One last vestige of William Clark's original perception along the line that Ordway and Whitehouse explicated can be found later in the voyage. Below Celilo Falls, when the Nez Perce chiefs finally leave the expedition, Clark describes Twisted Hair and Tetoharsky as having "accompanied us from the head of the river." *JLCE*, 5:339.

9   *JLCE*, 5:284-286. The campsite at the forks was on the Columbia just above the confluence of the Snake at the present site of Sacajawea State Park.

10   Lamb, *Mackenzie Journals*, pp. 343-344; *JLCE*, 5:289.

11   Lamb, *Mackenzie Journals*, pp. 400-401; *JLCE*, 5:288; Slaughter, *Exploring Lewis and Clark*, p. 45, offers the tendentious argument about the captains' avoidance of indigenous place names. The journals are replete with native names for places, as any fair reading would allow. The name "Tap teel" may well have been filled in a space left blank in October 1805 and filled the following spring when Lewis and Clark were again at the forks and able to learn much more about the geography of the region from the Indians. On the return trip the expedition encountered a Shoshone captive living among the Walla Walla Indians with whom Sacagawea could communicate and so, thus, the captains as well, through the famous chain of translation. Neither Ordway nor Whitehouse when first at the forks cite a name being given to this "western fork." However, Whitehouse's fair copy does have the word "Columbia" written over an erasure or an illegible word describing the larger northern fork. Might this erased word have been "Mackenzie?" *JLCE*, 7:150, 151 n. 10, 174-175, 177 n. 6, 178; 11:357, 358 nn. 3-5. Also suggestive of the notion that the "Tap teel" or "Tapteet" rivers were synonymous with Mackenzie's "Tacoutche Tesse" is discerned in Clark's geographic deduction from the return trip wherein he referred to "white people who come into the inlets to the North at no great distance from the Tapteet." Mackenzie himself had proved how close his Tacoutche Tesse was to the coast already frequented by fur traders. Moulton surmises that Clark was referring to trade emanating from Grays Harbor or Puget Sound, but the fur trade at those inlets was not as rich as the coastal precincts visited by Mackenzie. Ibid., 7:129, 130 n. 14.

12   James P. Ronda, "'A Darling Project of Mine:' The Appeal of the Lewis and Clark Story," in Ronda, ed., *Voyages*, p. 332. Hereafter cited as Ronda, "Darling Project." Jenkinson, "Slaughter's Expedition," p. 628.

13   Slaughter, *Exploring Lewis and Clark*, pp. 29, 204; Allen, *Lewis and Clark*, p. 175.

14   *JLCE*, 9:240; 11:357. I have used the fair copy of Whitehouse's journal for this date because of its readability. His original field note said more simply: "we now call the north fork as it is the largest the Columbian River, and the other which we came down loose it name from Columba. and we call it after the Indian name kimoo-e-num." The key difference between the two versions is the addition of "Lewis's River" in the fair copy. Since the latter was drafted after the fact, perhaps even after the expedition was completed, the copyist had the benefit of knowing intervening decisions, including the naming of Lewis's River at Fort Clatsop or in the spring of 1806. Ibid., 1:10, map 75; 11:xvi, 356. Though problematic in many respects, it is interesting to note that Robert Frazer's map of the expedition's track shows the Snake/Columbia course as a continuous stream with a vestigial Tacoutche Tesse as a minor tributary. Ibid., 1:map 124.

15 *JLCE*, 8:156, 290; 9:350; Cutright, *Journals*, p. 132 (qtn). Ordway was the senior sergeant in service and authority, and he kept the duty roster and detachment orders. If both Lewis and Clark had met an untimely fate, the command would have fallen to him. When Lewis and Clark were both detached from the command Ordway was left in charge. This first happened during the winter of 1803-1804 when the captains were both in St. Louis at the same time and again on the return voyage when Ordway commanded the squad that conducted the canoes from the upper Missouri cache to the Great Falls. *JLCE*, 2:193; Cutright, *Journals*, p. 134.

16 *JLCE*, 2:19; Coues, *History*, 2:407 n.

17 Portelli, *Oral History*, p. x; Belyea, Barbara, "The Silent Past is Made to Speak," in Juneau and Purviance, eds., *Confluence of Cultures*, p. 39.

18 Portelli, *Oral History*, pp. 2, 53, 113.

19 *JLCE*, 11:191, 263. Though Lewis purported to have named the various forks of the Missouri on 28 July 1805, other journals indicated that this was not done, or at least announced, until August 9th, the date Lewis cut out for Lemhi Pass. Ibid., 5:7, 61; 9:199; 10:123; 11:245, 263.

20 Gilman, *Across the Divide*, pp. 143-144. Ironically, the Snake River *is* longer than the main stem of the Columbia above the forks. The northern fork above the junction is 886 miles in length while the Snake is 1,036 miles long. However, the discharge of the Snake is only one-third that of the main stem. *Columbia River and Minor Tributaries*, House Doc. 103, 73rd Congress, 1st session, pp. 22, 572.

21 Charles Wilkes, *Narrative of the United States Exploring Expedition* (Philadelphia, 1844), 4:459-460. Hereafter cited as Wilkes, *Expedition*.

22 The map can be found at *JLCE*, 1:map 67. Textual changes/insertions fall into three categories. "Lewis's" river is at Ibid., 1:map 75; 5:255-256, 258, 260 nn. 7, 11, and 14, 278, 284 n. 11, 287, 289, 290-291 nn. 7, 9, 11, and 13. "Clarks" river amendments are at Ibid., 5:197, 198 n. 5, 230, 231 n. 9, 237, 240 n. 2. Filled blanks are at Ibid., 5:238, 240, 240 nn. 3, 4, 256, 258, 260 nn. 9, 15. The naming process for the Snake River worked much in the same fashion as when "Tap teel" was initially substituted for Mackenzie's "Tacoutche Tesse." At first, what Clark understood to be the Indian name "Kimooenim" (or variations thereof) was applied to the river they descended, with "Lewis's River" to be added later still. In a curious and related twist, Meriwether Lewis inserted into Clark's 13 October 1805 notebook entry the name "Ki-moo-e-nimm" for the present-day Tucannon River, which flows into the Snake about halfway between the Clearwater and the Columbia confluence. Moulton says the captains named the Snake River "Ki-moo-e-nim" by mistake, intending it for the Tucannon all along. More likely, "Ki-moo-e-nim" was a temporary placeholder name strategy devised by Clark, allowing him time to sort through the problem of not having been on the main stem of the Columbia. The "Lewis's River" naming came later, perhaps at Fort Clatsop. Elliott Coues was also puzzled by the duplicate use of "Kimooenim." Coues asserted it was an editorial oversight on Biddle's part to have allowed "Kimooenim" to appear in print representing two different streams. Coues theorized that with the larger river no longer named "Kimooenim" because it was supplanted by the "Lewis's" usage, Lewis himself allowed a smaller stream, the Tucannon, that honor. Ibid., 5:268, 268 n. 2; 9:240 n. 1; Coues, *History*, 2:635 n.

23 Jackson, *Jefferson*, p. 303.

24 *JLCE*, 1:maps 96, 99-101; 2:25; 5:297, 299; 7:216, 219 n. 1. The Deschutes River of Oregon proved to be too small a stream to honor Clark. On the return voyage up the Columbia

in the spring of 1806, Clark himself first discerned a major river, known presently as the Willamette, and deduced that it and not the Deschutes was the last major affluent to the Columbia. With the realization, as Clark phrased it, that the Deschutes "does not water that extensive Country we have heretofore Calculated on," his name could now be employed on a more strategic river. Ibid., 1:10; 7:149, 216, 219 n. 4. Of course, the Coeur d'Alene Indians lived on or near the present lake of the same name, which flows into the Spokane River, a stream Lewis and Clark did not distinguish from the larger, separate, and more northerly Bitterroot/Clark Fork/Pend Oreille River system. Ibid., 7:219 n. 1.

[25] *JLCE*, 7:216; 10:157.

[26] Allen, *Lewis and Clark*, p. 19; *JLCE*, 7:216, 219 n. 3. David Thompson noted that a "Lake Indian Road" ran from the Kootenai River to the northern end of Lake Pend Oreille and a "Skeetshoo Road" ran from there to Lake Coeur d' Alene. The whole system was also known as the "Great Road of the Flathead." This was undoubtedly the river scheme crudely sketched by Arrowsmith in 1802 showing a river flowing into the Tacoutche Tesse from the northeast, what King called the "Great Lake River" in his map. See also chapter 3 and map at Hayes, *First Crossing*, p. 298. Nisbet, *Thompson*, pp. 142, 144.

[27] Miller, *Native America*, pp. 2-3.

[28] Miller, *Native America*, pp. 3, 11-12, 70-71; Jackson, *Letters*, 1:57.

[29] Miller, *Native America*, p. 109.

[30] Miller, *Native America*, pp. 81, 109, 154; Jackson, *Letters*, 1:65.

[31] Belyea, *Columbia Journals*, pp. xiv, 254.

[32] Belyea, *Columbia Journals*, pp. x, xi, 229; Nisbet, *Thompson*, p. 107. Lobbying from their men in the field like Thompson and Henry prompted North West Company and other Canadian fur-trading officials to appeal to the British ambassador in Washington, DC, in September 1809. The furmen denounced American claims to the Columbia River or any territory west of the Continental Divide. "The right in both cases," the Canadians argued, "belongs to Great Britain by the discoveries of Cook, Vancouver and Mackenzie." D'Arcy Jenish, *Epic Wanderer: David Thompson and the Mapping of the Canadian West* (Toronto, 2003), p. 155. Hereafter cited as Jenish, *Mapping*.

[33] Nisbet, *Mapmaker's Eye*, p. 70.

[34] Belyea, *Columbia Journals*, pp. 152, 165, 249; Nisbet, *Thompson*, p. 226.

[35] Ronda, "Writingest Explorers," in Ronda, ed., *Voyages*, pp. 302, 310. For the insight on how objectives for the expedition were differentiated by whether or not the captains were traversing lands claimed internationally by the United States, I am reliant on Peter J. Kastor, *The Nation's Crucible: The Louisiana Purchase and the Creation of America* (New Haven, 2004), pp. 77-78. Hereafter cited as Kastor, *Nation's Crucible*.

[36] Belyea, *Columbia Journals*, pp. 271-272; Nisbet, *Thompson*, pp. 226-227.

[37] Jenish, *Mapping*, pp. 177, 264.

[38] Nisbet, *Mapmaker's Eye*, p. 139.

[39] Belyea, *Columbia Journals*, p. 207; Ronda, "Writingest Explorers," Ronda, ed., *Voyages*, p. 304; Nokes, *Gray*, p. 267. Jefferson quotation found at James P. Ronda, *Finding the West: Explorations with Lewis and Clark* (Albuquerque, 2001), p. 124. Hereafter cited as Ronda,

Finding the West. When John C. Frémont, a later American geopolitician/explorer, came upon the great forks of the Columbia in 1844, just as the boundary crisis was coming to a head, he invoked Alexander Mackenzie's great strategic insight. Echoing the Nor'Wester's hyperbole, Frémont stipulated that the junction of the Snake and Columbia Rivers opened "two great lines of communication with the interior of the continent." One led to the Athabasca country and Hudson Bay, the other to the Mississippi Valley. This was a central fact of geography, Frémont stated, that "cannot be overlooked." Chaffin, *Frémont*, p. 182.

40　*JLCE*, 5:286-287, 289. Whitehouse records that the Indians at the confluence "made signs to us that there is deer & Elk below this place," which would prefigure forested terrain. Ibid., 11:357.

41　*JLCE*, 5:291-292, 296.

42　*JLCE*, 5:292, 294; Jackson, *Letters*, 1:61-62.

CHAPTER 7

1　Allen, *Lewis and Clark*, p. 374.

2　*JLCE*, 1:3; Cutright, *Journals*, pp. 99-100; Coues, *History*, 2:421 n.

3　Silvio A. Bedini, "The Scientific Instruments of the Lewis and Clark Expedition," in Ronda, ed., *Voyages*, p. 155; Lamb, *Mackenzie Journals*, p. 60. Clark even held onto to his writing desk longer than Lewis did. The latter stashed his in the cache below the Great Falls of the Missouri while Clark had his with him until it was smashed in a trail accident going over the Bitterroot Mountains. *JLCE*, 4:334; 5:206.

4　*JLCE*, 5:298.

5　*JLCE*, 5:294, 298; Allen, *Lewis and Clark*, pp. 253, 312.

6　*JLCE*, 4:386, 431, 432, 433 nn. 5, 82; 5:294-295, 298. For the discussion of the expedition's sighting of the Cascade volcanoes, see Plamondon, *Cartographic Reconstruction*, 3:21. A modern roadside historical marker in Oregon, based on local LEWIS & CLARK lore, ignores Clark's sighting of the "conocal form" from Wallula Gap in favor of the Hat Rock locale farther to the west. This interpretation, based on a slightly more detailed accounting of the Cascade volcanoes that occurred the next day, is dubious. The myth took root in part because the ability to see Mount Hood from so easterly a vantage as Wallula Gap has been made rare in modern times due to the degradation of air quality and transparency. All students of this question assert that Mount Hood is not visible from the modern-day water level in the gap nor could have been with the even lower level of water evident in historic times. Accordingly, to see the mountain, Clark, or someone else in the party, would have had to establish a point of observation on land with a requisite amount of elevation. Though speculative, it is possible that Mount Hood's glaciation could have been appreciably greater 200 years ago as a function of the Little Ice Age. David Thompson's native informants told him in 1801 that they could not remember so much water flowing from the Rocky Mountains as found in that year's spring freshet. Belyea, *Columbia Journals*, p. 34. Under this theory, much like the glaciers in the Alaskan littoral that have receded by dozens of miles since the time of Cook and Vancouver, Mount Hood could have been hundreds of feet higher in 1805 than it appears today. The glaciers on Mount Hood have shrunk 34 percent in the past century alone. Hood's glaciers are especially vulnerable to attrition from global warming due to the mountain's singularity and proximity to temperate oceanic weather. Conversely, for the same reason, Mount Hood would have been unusually susceptible to rapid glaciations during cooling periods, such as the Little Ice Age. See *The Sunday Oregonian*, 26 March 2006, p. 1.

[7] *JLCE*, 5:294, 298, 315. Clark's sketch map for this area contains a word difficult to transcribe placed in the location of the gap's southern bluffs that may be "Clark" or "Climb." Ibid., 5:295. Computer-aided topographical analysis provided by Rob Stratton, a professional land surveyor, in possession of the author, is the source of the mathematical model referenced herein. Of the other journalists, Sgt. John Ordway and Pvt. Joseph Whitehouse make first mention of sighting a snow-capped mountain on the next day, October 19th, lending some credence to the theory that Clark may have misplaced this notation. However, Moulton attributes the Ordway and Whitehouse sightings as most likely being Mount Adams. Ibid., 9:241 n. 2; 11:361 n. 2. Patrick Gass makes no mention of mountain sightings until ten days later. Ibid., 10:163. The fact that Clark was keeping the course for the river voyage strongly suggests that if a terrestrial-based observation of Mount Hood was made, then someone other than him reported on the face of the country and the occurrence of the conical mountain. On the Missouri River Clark once reported on the difficulty of conducting a land traverse concurrent with keeping the river courses. Ibid., 4:385. For an explicated example of courses, see Lewis's entry for 3 May 1805. While on the Missouri River he refers to a landmark having been cited in "the 10th course of this day." Ibid., 4:103. In the instance of seeing Mount Hood, by "2d course" Clark may have meant the second entry on the course and distance table of the 18th, which ends at the island upstream from the Walla Walla River, where the party landed a "few minits." Likelier he meant the second course *direction*, that being his fourth and last call of the day when the path of the Columbia stopped trending to the southeast in favor of a southwesterly orientation. In any event, at some point between the Walla Walla River near the Two Sisters and that night's campsite four miles downstream near today's Port Kelley grain terminal, Clark (or some other member of the expedition) saw Mount Hood. Lastly, it is worth remembering that the Biddle account also keeps the sighting of Mount Hood on this date. We know Biddle spoke to Clark about this day's events because of the editor's expanded narrative about the limitations of using willow for fuel at that night's camp and that the expedition was "not able to burn the drift-log which had tempted us to land." Ibid., 5:298; Coues, *History*, 2:644-645.

[8] *JLCE*, 5:298-300.

[9] *JLCE*, 5:301, 303-304. George W. Aguilar Sr., *When the River Ran Wild: Indian Traditions on the Mid-Columbia and the Warm Springs Reservation* (Portland, 2005), p. 180. Hereafter cited as Aguilar, *Indian Traditions*.

[10] *JLCE*, 7:174; Jackson, *Letters*, 2:544.

[11] *JLCE*, 7:178-179, 187.

[12] *JLCE*, 5:301-302, 304, 307 n. 9.

[13] *JLCE*, 5:301, 304. Clark's confusion between St. Helens and Adams was not resolved until the following spring. Plamondon, *Cartographic Reconstruction*, 3:21. John Ordway's journal also mentions the discovery of a "verry high round mountain a long distance down the River which appears to have Snow on the top of it." Ordway's sentence construction emulates Clark and suggests he and Clark were referring to the same mountain. *JLCE*, 5:304; 9:241; Allen, *Lewis and Clark*, p. 312. Near The Dalles, Ordway again referred to sighting "the round high mountain," but he could only have been referring to Mount Hood in that instance as only the briefest glimpses of Mount Adams avail themselves that far west. *JLCE*, 9:245. Curiously, David Thompson, passing through this district six years later, makes no mention of any of the Cascade peaks until he is nearly twice as far from the forks of the Columbia as Clark's first mention. Nor, when he apparently sights Mount Adams, does he refer to its sister peak, Mount Hood. Belyea, *Columbia Journals*, pp. 152, 272.

[14]   *JLCE*, 5:304-305.

[15]   *JLCE*, 5:302, 304. The critique of local lore about Clark's sighting of Mount Hood is prompted by an interpretive marker at Oregon's Hat Rock State Park. Topographic maps indicate Hat Rock is 478 feet above sea level while the heights immediately to its west have an elevation of 500 feet. Indeed, on the approach to Hat Rock heading in a westerly direction through Wallula Gap, even at today's elevated water level and thus well above Clark's vantage, it is Boat Rock with its distinctive basalt seam that one sees in the distance, not its famed neighbor. Hat Rock is not discernible to the river traveler until virtually parallel to it. See www.TopoMAKER.com for the Hat Rock, WA, [*sic*] locale. Land surveyor Rob Stratton has mathematically confirmed that Mount Hood is not visible from Hat Rock even were it not for the visual block created by Boat Rock to the west. It is, simply, not high enough. Electronic correspondence, Rob Stratton to the author, 20 November 2002. In sum, there is no evidence, as inferred from Oregon State Parks' interpretive signage, that Clark or any member of the expedition climbed Hat Rock. Because of its singularity, worth mentioning because of its similarity to human garb, Clark's comment was a mere gratuity, a statement of the obvious fact that Hat Rock approximates the eastern end of the plain that provides continuous and open views toward the west.

[16]   See *JLCE*, 5:308, 310, 316 for field maps amended with dates associated with the return trek. Also Moulton's note on the dates of entries at Ibid., 2:47 n. 54. J. Russell Harper, ed., *Paul Kane's Frontier* (Austin, 1971), p. 113.

[17]   *JLCE*, 6:11, 13. In this entire discourse about conical peaks, Clark never evidences interest or awareness of the geologic origins of these mountains. Thomas Jefferson had a hand in this. First, Jefferson had no particular interest in geology. His instructions to Lewis emphasized the more utilitarian interest in mineralogy. Accordingly, the journals of Lewis and Clark regularly refer to coal, iron, lead, and salt, but as Donald Jackson noted, they paid "little attention to the vast eruptions, upheavals, and subsidences that formed the face of the West." Jackson, *Jefferson*, p. 33. Clark was continually attempting to make sense of his initial mountain sightings. Further evidence of the confidence he had in his own judgments on the matter is confirmed in his comments of 4 November 1805. Then in vicinity of what is now the Portland metropolitan area, Clark took bearings on "Mount Hellen" to his northeast, later "Mt. *Helien*," and (mistakenly) speculating that it was "perhaps the highest pinical in America." He concluded, "This is the mountain I saw from the Muscle Shell rapid on the 19th of October last Covered with Snow." *JLCE*, 6:16, 18, 21 n. 22.

[18]   *JLCE*, 5:309, 312-313 n. 6, 315, 317, 319 nn. 3, 9. There were other promising signs. Fowl was becoming more plentiful. In this district the Columbia country was "furnished with fine Springs" flowing into the river. Pvt. John Collins, like any number of brewers in Northwest history who have found good water, seized upon this serendipitous development and made what his captain judged "verry good *beer*." Clark was so taken by Collins' accomplishment that he made a note of it on his map for the stretch of the river traversed on October 21st. *JLCE*, 5:314-316, 318. Collins used *aged*, that is to say moldy and soured bread made of camas roots, as a substitute for the conventional grains and other flavoring ingredients such as hops. Microbrewers take note! Collins was one of three "Superindendants of Provision," responsible for his mess's food preparation, portions, and care of utensils. In assuming this responsibility, Collins and the other two "Superintendants" were exempt from guard duty, pitching tents, or collecting firewood. Collins was the provisioner for Sgt. Nathaniel Pryor's mess (or squad). Ibid., 2:188-189, 360.

[19]   *JLCE*, 5:314-315; Slaughter, *Exploring Lewis and Clark*, p. 20.

[20]   *JLCE*, 5:230, 321, 323.

21   *JLCE*, 5:323; 11:365.

22   *JLCE*, 5:323, 325; 7:129.

23   *JLCE*, 5:326-327; 9:244; 11:367-368.

24   *JLCE*, 5:328, 331.

25   *JLCE*, 4:284-285, 288 n. 3, 290.

26   Ronda, *Finding the West,* p. 75.

27   *JLCE*, 4:220 n. 1, 266.

28   Barbara Maria Stafford, *Voyage into Substance: Art, Science, Nature, and the Illustrated Travel Account, 1760-1840* (Cambridge, 1984), pp.14-15. Hereafter cited as Stafford, *Voyage into Substance.*

29   *JLCE*, 4:225; 5:74. For explorers and place, see Greenfield, *Narrating Discovery*, p. 6. Even Patrick Gass seemed inclined to emulate Lewis's style. In describing the lower Snake River, Gass wrote the following: "This river in general is very handsome, except at the rapids, where it is risking both life and property to pass; and even these rapids, when the bare view or prospect is considered distinct from the advantages of navigation, may add to its beauty, by interposing variety and scenes of romantick grandeur where there is so much uniformity in the appearance of the country." This passage is so out of keeping with the general style and manner of Gass's journal to suggest that it may be a paraphrase of Lewis's verbalizations, or actual dictation. *JLCE*, 10:155. For the insights on Lewis's style I am indebted to Regis, *Early America*, p. 41.

30   Regis, *Early America*, p. 92; *JLCE*, 5:322, 324, 331. Early in the journey Clark crossed out the word "Trip" and replaced it with the more scientifically oriented "Voyage" to describe the expedition's purpose. Ibid., 2:399.

31   Coues, *History*, 3:956.

32   The Walter quotation is from Stafford, *Voyage into Substance*, p. 46; Bradbury's is from Jackson, *Letters*, 2:459 n. 1.

33   *JLCE,* 5:328-332.

34   See Clark's maps at *JLCE*, 5:330, 332.

35   *JLCE*, 5:329-331. Ordway and Whitehouse estimated the width of these narrows at only twenty yards, Gass seventy. The average between these two extremes yields Clark's forty-five yards. Ibid., 9:244; 10:161; 11:368.

36   *JLCE*, 5:333.

37   *JLCE*, 5:329, 335, 336 n. 2.

38   Aguilar, *Indian Traditions*, pp. ix, 6, 109, 118.

39   *JLCE*, 5:329, 333, 335; 11:369.

40   *JLCE*, 5:329, 335; Regis, *Early America*, p. 92.

41   *JLCE*, 5:336-338; 9:245; 11:370.

[42] *JLCE*, 5:338; Stafford, *Voyage into Substance*, p. 50.

[43] *JLCE*, 5:339; Regis, *Early America*, p. 30.

[44] *JLCE*, 5:342-343; 9:245; 11:372.

[45] *JLCE*, 5:336 n. 2, 343-344, 346 n. 3.

[46] *JLCE*, 5:346-348.

[47] *JLCE*, 5:345-346, 348, 351.

[48] *JLCE*, 5:349; 11:376.

[49] Stafford, *Voyage into Substance*, p. 59; *JLCE*, 5:350-353.

[50] Allen, *Lewis and Clark*, p. 315; *JLCE*, 5:266, 268, 347-348, 354-356. Observers early in the twentieth century counted as many as 1,800 tree remnants in the river above the rapids. Jim E. O'Connor, "The Evolving Landscape of the Columbia River Gorge: Lewis and Clark and Cataclysms on the Columbia," *Oregon Historical Quarterly*, 105:3 (Fall 2004), p. 408; personal communications from geologist Patrick T. Pringle, 19 August 2002; 3 August 2004.

[51] *JLCE*, 1:map 78; 5:354-356, 360, 362-363, 370, 372. In the nomenclature of Thomas Jefferson, a cascade was a tall waterfall. Thomas Jefferson, *Notes on the State of Virginia*, ed. William Peden (Chapel Hill, 1955), p. 21. Typologically, a smaller fall with low volume (like Multnomah) is a cascade. Falls with a large volume (like Niagara) are cataracts. Stephen Beckham asserts that Clark's map uses the term "cataracts" to describe Multnomah and its sister falls, but clearly the word is "cascades." Beckham, *Rockies to the Pacific*, pp. 57-58; *JLCE*, 1:map 78. Elliott Coues was the first to point out that Lewis and Clark never used the modern place name "Cascades." Coues, *History*, 3:940 n. 15.

[52] *JLCE*, 5:355; Jackson, *Letters*, 2:540. Engineers assessing the hydroelectric capacity of the Columbia River system in the 1930s validated Clark's field assessment that the river displayed minimal current above the Cascades. This was in contrast to the river's mean low-water velocity from the junction of the Snake to Celilo, which averaged 10 miles per hour. Indeed, the flow above the Cascades that struck Clark as being so leisurely in its pace was considerably less than the 3.5 miles per hour flow evidenced once the Columbia reached its tidewater segment. Taken as a whole, the Columbia's slope below the Snake in its pre-engineered state was 2.31 feet per mile, less than the Snake's 2.82 feet per mile from Asotin, Washington to the Columbia confluence. These slopes were five times as rapid as the Ohio. More particularly, the fall from the head of Celilo to below the last rapid at The Dalles was 81 feet over 12 miles, or 6.7 feet per mile. From The Dalles to the head of the Cascades (at low water) the fall was just 4 feet over 43 miles, or .09 feet per mile. The government engineers also concluded that the navigation of the Snake and Columbia rivers was most practicable precisely at the time Lewis and Clark first descended them, the low water months of October and November. *Columbia River and Minor Tributaries*, House Doc. 103, 73rd Congress, 1st session, pp. 567, 571, 667, 1416, 1577. Scholars know this document as the "308 Report," which took its name from a companion instrument, conformed as the *River and Harbor Act of 1925*, House Doc. 308, 69th Congress, 1st session.

[53] *JLCE*, 7:118; 122 n. 4. Nathaniel D. Reynolds, "Dating the Bonneville Landslide with Lichenometry," *Washington Geology*, 29:3/4 (December 2001), pp. 11-16. Hereafter cited as Reynolds, "Bonneville." Donald B. and Elizabeth G. Lawrence, "Bridge of the Gods Legend, Its Origin, History and Dating," *Mazama*, 40:13 (December 1958), p. 33; Robert L. Schuster and Patrick T. Pringle, "Engineering history and impacts of the Bonneville landslide, Columbia River Gorge, Washington-Oregon, USA," in *Proceedings of the First*

European Conference on Landslides, eds. Jan Rybar, Josef Stemberk, and Peter Wagner (Exton, PA, 2002), p. 697. The evidence upstream from the Great Rapids "choke point," namely the sunken forest, betokens what science now calculates as the great volume and speed (33 feet per second) of the landmass that hit the Columbia. It is estimated that the land bridge damming the Columbia was breached one mile south of the river's original channel, thus creating Clark's "Great Rapids" or "The Cascades." Reynolds, "Bonneville," p. 11.

54 *JLCE*, 5:355-356, 358 n. 10.

55 *JLCE*, 5:358, 360-362.

56 *JLCE*, 5:358, 360, 362; 6:7, 9 n. 5; 7:78.

57 *JLCE*, 1:10, map 79; Beckham, Rockies, *Rockies to the Pacific*, p. 57. The change to "Beacon Rock" on the return was probably a function of its enhanced visibility as one approaches it from the west, where it took on the meaning of a beacon, as in a signal, directional guide, or marker. The rock resembles a flaming torch from certain viewing angles, and as Lewis noted on the return voyage, it "rises to a very sharp point and is visible for 20 miles below on the river." *JLCE*, 7:79.

58 Stafford, *Voyage into Substance*, pp. 69, 72, 88.

59 *JLCE*, 5:366-367, 369, 371; 11:378.

60 *JLCE*, 5:370, 372; 6:7, 9.

61 Coues, *History*, 1:260 n. 10; Jenkinson, *Lewis*, pp. 29, 31.

62 Jenkinson, *Lewis*, pp. 54, 114; Lamb, *Mackenzie Journals*, pp. 59-60.

CHAPTER 8

1 *JLCE*, 6:10-11; 11:382-383. In fact, Whitehouse was off in his estimation of the distance to saltwater by nearly a magnitude of two.

2 *JLCE*, 6:11; 10:167 n. 2.

3 *JLCE*, 6:15, 18; 10:166.

4 *JLCE*, 6:21-24. John Ordway also noted that in this district "the natives verry numerous," an expression duplicated by Whitehouse. Ibid., 9:250; 11:386.

5 The texts of news accounts about the expedition are reproduced in facsimile form in *Columbia*, 1:2 (Summer 1987), p. 4. Also see Thwaites, *Original Journals*, 7:347-348.

6 *Columbia*, 1:2 (Summer 1987), p. 4. The actual phrasing in the referenced letter, attributed to Clark but ghostwritten by Lewis, said of the Columbia River Natives that they were "extremely noumerous and generally friendly." Jackson, *Letters*, 1:329.

7 Jackson, *Letters*, 1:320-321. Several other aspects of the expedition's story merited mention in early press accounts. This catalogue included their reappearance dressed in buckskins, the fact that the Rocky Mountains had "eternal snows," the mild climate on the Pacific Coast, and, as related at length in a later chapter, the ritualized engraving of names at the end of the voyage. Thwaites, *Original Journals*, 7:347-348.

8 *JLCE*, 11:390; 6:31, 85; Jackson, *Letters*, 1:65, 105.

9 Jackson, *Letters*, 1:23, 58-59.

10 Jackson, *Letters*, 1:65, 105. Jefferson's instructions to Lewis on this point were a replication of thoughts conveyed to Andre Michaux, a botanist selected for an ill-fated exploration of the West sponsored by the American Philosophical Society that anticipated the Lewis and Clark Expedition. Jefferson told Michaux that when he reached the Pacific he should go to any "settlement of Europeans" if convenient to do so. There, Jefferson instructed Michaux, he was to "commit to writing a narrative of your journey & observations & take the best measures you can for conveying it by duplicates or triplicates thence to the society by sea." The object thereby achieved was to furnish "the best proofs... of the reality & extent of your progress." Ibid., 2:671.

11 *JLCE*, 7:18.

12 *JLCE*, 7:32-33; 10:203-204.

13 *JLCE*, 7:34.

14 Greenfield, *Narrating Discovery*, p. 72.

15 Ibid., pp. 78-79, 83.

16 *JLCE*, 7:55.

17 *JLCE*, 1:map 79; 7:57, 59, 61 n. 17, 70 n. 6, 100 n. 1; Jackson, *Letters*, 2:543.

18 *JLCE*, 7:58.

19 Lamb, *Mackenzie Journals*, pp. 377-378; Slaughter, *Exploring Lewis and Clark*, pp. 12-13.

20 *JLCE*, 7:64; Dening, *Beach Crossings*, pp. 240, 254.

21 *JLCE*, 7:64-65.

22 *JLCE*, 7:66. In his later recounting of Clark's exploration of the Willamette, Lewis said this watershed was "level and wholy destitute of timber," perhaps concluding, mistakenly, that the terrain was akin to the Great Columbia Plain east of The Dalles. Ibid., 7:86.

23 Robert Boyd, *The Coming of the Spirit of Pestilence: Introduced Infectious Diseases and Population Decline Among Northwest Coast Indians, 1774–1784* (Seattle, 1999), pp. 294-295. Hereafter cited as Boyd, *Spirit of Pestilence*. Jackson, *Letters*, 1:35, 64, 130. Clark's list of inquiries to be put to the Indians of the newly acquired Louisiana Territory included this one: "What is their mode of treating the *Small pox* particularly?" Ibid., 1:158.

24 Lamb, *Mackenzie Journals*, pp. 74-75. In a corresponding account from August 1804, William Clark referred to "the ravages of the Small Pox... which Swept off" hundreds of the Omaha Indians. "I am told," Clark wrote, "when this fatal malady was among them they Carried their franzey to verry extroadinary length, not only burning their Village, but they put their *wives* & Children to D[e]ath with a view of their all going together to Some better Countrey." *JLCE*, 2:479. Clark may have been "told" (which is to say instructed) by Mackenzie's account, or by Pierre Cruzatte, a member of the party who was half-Omaha and half-French. Ibid., 2:516.

25 Mark Spence, "*Sayaapo* and the Remaking of Lewis and Clark, *Oregon Historical Quarterly*, 105:3 (Fall 2004), p. 489; Boyd, *Spirit of Pestilence*, pp. 244, 278 (qtn.); *JLCE*, 6:24.

CHAPTER 9

1   *JLCE*, 5:362, 370.

2   Richard J. Nokes, *Almost a Hero: The Voyages of John Meares, R. N., to China, Hawaii, and the Northwest Coast* (Pullman, 1998), pp. 7-8, 61, 69-70, 71 n. 9. Hereafter cited as Nokes, *Almost a Hero*.

3   *JLCE*, 6:58; Ambrose, *Undaunted Courage*, p. 305; Thwaites, *Original Journals*, 3:210 n. 2. One exception to the consensus is Rex Ziak who writes that Clark did in fact have a view of the ocean on the day he wrote that immortal line. However, even Ziak might not go far enough in his reconstruction of events. Rex Ziak, *In Full View* (Astoria, 2002), pp. 186-189. Hereafter cited as Ziak, *In Full View*.

4   *JLCE*, 6:30-33.

5   *JLCE*, 6:31, 34 n. 9; 11:390. The basis for Pillar Rock's name is only evident approaching it by water and not the transverse perspective seen from land. The river currents over eons have shaved its sides to create the narrow pillar-like form.

6   *JLCE*, 6:33, 58. Gary Moulton convincingly argues that Codex H, where these statements are found, was probably composed no earlier than April or May of 1806. Ibid., 2:23, 25-26; 5:300 n. 5; 6:34 n. 6. Several well-known accounts of the Lewis and Clark Expedition have mistakenly attributed *"Ocian in view*! O! the joy!" to Clark's elkskin-bound field notes. See, for example, Ambrose, *Undaunted Courage*, p. 305. Given the line's apparent spontaneity, this seems credible, even though it is the last of the three versions Clark wrote. The error can probably be attributed to Bernard DeVoto's influential abridgement of the journals, where in a footnote he places this quote in "the notebook which he [Clark] kept on his knee to record courses and bearings." Following Thwaites's lead, DeVoto adds that Clark was "mistaken" about seeing the ocean from his camp near Pillar Rock. See Bernard DeVoto, ed., *The Journals of the Lewis and Clark Expedition* (New York, 1973), p. 279 n.

7   *JLCE*, 2:7; 6:35 n. 10; Allen, *Lewis and Clark*, p. 316; Ambrose, *Undaunted Courage*, pp. 307-308; Ziak, *In Full View*, pp. 186-189.

8   Thwaites, *Original Journals*, 3:210 n. 2; *JLCE* 4:295, 297.

9   Lamb, *Vancouver*, 2:752 n. 1. Notwithstanding Broughton's technically correct assertion that a river is constituted by fresh water, Vancouver in his *Voyage of Discovery* stated unequivocally that the Columbia was a "river Mr. Gray had discovered." Ibid., 2:691.

10 Jackson, *Letters*, 1:345; *JLCE* 1:map 82; 6:104.

11 Coues, *History*, 1:xiii, lxxxiv; Jackson, *Letters*, 2:497-545.

12 Coues, *History*, 2:702. Biddle's interlineation found in Clark's journal entry for November 7th is consistent with the theory that the view to the ocean was perceived to have presented itself early in the day, not at its end at camp near Pillar Rock. *JLCE*, 6:33.

13 Personal communication to the author by Harold Lampi, 7 March 2002. Mr. Lampi was born in 1917 and has lived most of his life in Clatsop County, Oregon.

14 Jackson, *Letters*, 2:540-541; *JLCE*, 1:16 n. 21; 6:47 n. 3, 50. The perceived deficiencies in Vancouver's geography were likely compounded by Lewis's "haisty manner" in making his copy. Jackson, *Letters*, 1:53. Stephen Beckham writes that Lewis made a copy of

Vancouver's cartography because the composite map made for the expedition by Nicholas King provided no detail about the mouth of the river. Beckham speculates that when Clark "could not See any Island in the mouth of this river as laid down by Vancouver" he had been misled by Lewis's handiwork, the latter having misinterpreted the cartographic placement of a sandbar for an island *inside* the capes. *JLCE,* 6:50; Beckham, *Literature,* p. 41. However, it's also possible that Lewis mistook the cartographic symbol of an anchorage in the ocean *outside* the capes for an island. Vancouver's master map of the western coast of North America, from Prince William Sound to San Diego, only employs the anchorage symbol once, and very indistinctly, off the mouth of the Columbia River. Its inclusion may have been unintended, since a later edition of the map published in the octavo edition of Vancouver's *Voyage* in 1801 deleted the symbol. Alternatively, Lewis may have hurriedly copied Vancouver's section map, from the northern tip of Vancouver Island to Cape Lookout on the Oregon Coast, which shows a penumbra or intimation of an island to the ocean side of Point Adams. It is this chart that contains an inset view of the map titled "Entrance of Columbia River." George Vancouver, *A Voyage of Discovery to the North Pacific Ocean, and Round the World* (London, 1798) atlas as found in Lamb, *Vancouver,* 1:xiv, back pocket.

[15]   *JLCE,* 6:52; Parkman's quote can be found in E. N. Feltskog, ed., *Parkman: The Oregon Trail* (Madison, 1969), p. 28a. Hereafter cited as Feltskog, *Parkman.*

[16]   *JLCE,* 6:35, 52. It has been suggested that there may have been additional oceanic-related expectations in the minds of Lewis and Clark. As Rex Ziak has pointed out, preparing for a ceremonial arrival at the end of a voyage was a well-established exploratory tradition. The preceding few days the expedition had gotten under way early, but they broke camp late on the 8th "haveing Changed our Clothing." According to Ziak, the captains and others may have dressed up in uniform with the expectation of seeing a naval captain. If so, this may have been in response to the reports conveyed by the Natives on the 7th, as chronicled by Joseph Whitehouse "that there were vessells lying at the Mouth of this River." On the other hand, there could be a simpler explanation. As related in the Biddle narrative, "It rained this morning [November 8th], and having changed the clothing which had been wet during yesterday's rain, we did not set out till nine o'clock." Subsequent and repeated references during the ensuing week to the party's deteriorated leather clothing would be consistent with this interpretation, especially once conjoined with John Ordway's assertion that the party broke camp on the morning of the 8[th] "as us[u]al." Ziak, *In Full View,* p. 9; *JLCE,* 6:35, 39, 42-43, 47; 9:251; 11:390; Coues, *History,* 2:702, 710, 720. Lewis had his officer's coat until 17 March 1806, or just before leaving Fort Clatsop, when it was traded for a canoe. Clark offered his in trade for horses at The Dalles on 20 April 1806. *JLCE,* 6:426; 7:147. I am indebted to Roger Daniels, whose craft allowed Roger Wendlick and me to analyze Clark's writings of 7–8 November 1805 from a river-level perspective.

[17]   *JLCE,* 9:251; 11:390.

CHAPTER 10

[1]   *JLCE,* 6:35-36.

[2]   *JLCE,* 1:maps 82, 89; 6:37-38, 493; 10:168.

[3]   Stephen Ambrose spent about one page of text describing the conditions faced by the party on the north bank of the Columbia River while devoting whole chapters of his book to the rigors of the Great Falls portage and the traverse of the Bitterroot Mountains. This is a function of the fact that Meriwether Lewis, the subject of his biography, was not

writing his journal when the expedition reached the lower Columbia and had not been for nearly two months. Ambrose, *Undaunted Courage*, pp. 241-250, 284-296, 308, passim; Allen, *Lewis and Clark*, p. 300; *JLCE*, 2:23; Dayton Duncan, *Out West: A Journey Through Lewis and Clark's America* (Lincoln, 2000), p. 303. Hereafter cited as Duncan, *Out West*.

4 *JLCE*, 4:325-328.

5 *JLCE*, 4:328-329.

6 *JLCE*, 4:331, 338.

7 *JLCE*, 4:341.

8 *JLCE*, 4:341.

9 *JLCE*, 4:343.

10 *JLCE*, 4:361-362.

11 *JLCE*, 5:201, 203, 205-207, 209; 11:318.

12 *JLCE*, 5:215; 10:145.

13 *JLCE*, 5:229.

14 *JLCE*, 6:38-39; 9:252. Gass says the return from the "point" was "about a mile." Ibid., 10:169.

15 A more careful reading of the journals suggests that the expedition only made eight miles this day since they backtracked two as a consequence of failing to round Point Ellice. Whitehouse records the distance traveled between camps at seven miles. What Clark meant to say, in practice, is that he measured ahead ten miles of terrain by dead reckoning. *JLCE*, 6:39-40; 9:252; 10:169; 11:391.

16 *JLCE*, 8:34; Ambrose, *Undaunted Courage*, pp. 361-362. There was actually a third retrograde movement during the expedition. In the early spring of 1804 Clark named "*retragrade* bend" in the Missouri river after an incident at the "Deavels race ground." The keelboat hit projecting rocks in the Missouri, wheeling the boat around. All hands had to jump in the water, refasten a line, and tow her to shore. The expedition lost two miles. *JLCE*, 2:250-251.

17 *JLCE*, 6:40-41. Similarly Alexander Mackenzie marveled at the navigating skills of coastal Indians, noting: "I had imagined that the Canadians who accompanied me were the most expert canoe-men in the world, but they are very inferior to these people." Lamb, *Mackenzie Journals*, p. 364.

18 *JLCE*, 6:41-42.

19 *JLCE*, 6:42-43, 49, 101 n. 8; 10:170; 11:392. Clark may have been drawing on his familiarity with the Dismal Swamp of southeast Virginia for this place name. Ibid., 9:217 n. 1.

20 *JLCE*, 1:map 82; 2:289-290, 342; 4:63-66; Coues, *History*, 2:706.

21 *JLCE*, 6:42-43; 11:393. Whitehouse has the fishing expedition yielding "16 Salmon trout" on the 11th, partial testimony to the confused, at time chaotic nature of Clark's journal record during the week in question. Ibid., 11:392.

22   *JLCE*, 6:42-43; 11:393. One of Dr. Benjamin Rush's cardinal rules to Lewis "for preserving his health" stipulated that "Flannel should be worn constantly next to the skin, especially in wet weather." Lewis's list of equipage reveals the purchase of forty-five flannel shirts. Jackson, *Letters*, 1:54-55, 97.

23   Ambrose, *Undaunted Courage*, p. 308; Ronda, *LCAI*, p. 157; Duncan, *Scenes*, pp. 123-124.

24   *JLCE*, 6:44-45, 52, 59; 10:170; 11:393. Whitehouse said the canoe Colter, Willard, and Shannon departed in was the smallest at the disposal of the expedition. Ibid., 11:393. Gass said this canoe was acquired from the Indians because it was "excellent for riding swells." Ibid., 10:170; 11:393.

25   James G. Swan, *The Northwest Coast; or, Three Years Residence in Washington Territory* (New York, 1857), p. 44. Hereafter cited as Swan, *Northwest Coast. JLCE*, 11:397. For references to the maritime provinces of the Atlantic and Fort Mandan as geographic benchmarks, see Ibid., 7:234; 9:172, respectively. After a little experience in the vicinity Clark began to rethink these assumptions about snow, ice, and freezing temperatures, actually referring to a "Supriseing Climent." Observing Indians at the coast "Slightly Clothed" and who gave "account of but little Snow," Clark could begin to see that this "neighbourhood" was going to be warmer than expected. On what we know now to be the normally temperate coast of the Pacific Northwest the expedition would not face freezing weather "of any consequence," in Patrick Gass's phrasing, until 25 January 1806. Cold air, snow, and ice endured through the 31st of the month. Ibid., 6:73, 85-86; 10:190.

26   *JLCE*, 6:44-47; 9:253; 10:170. At Harper's Ferry, when equipping the expedition, Lewis bought forty "fish Giggs such as the Indians use with a single barbed point." Jackson, *Letters*, 1:73.

27   *JLCE*, 6:46-47.

28   *JLCE*, 6:46-47, 59 n. 2; 10:170-171; 11:393; Coues, *History*, 2:708.

29   *JLCE*, 6:48-49.

30   *JLCE*, 6:48.

31   *JLCE*, 6:48-50; 11:393.

CHAPTER 11

1   *JLCE*, 6:46; 11:393.

2   Ambrose, *Undaunted Courage*, p. 308; *JLCE*, 6:47, 429.

3   Beckham, *Rockies to the Pacific*, p. 64; Jenkinson, *Lewis*, pp. 9, 50.

4   *JLCE*, 2:6; Jenkinson, *Lewis*, p. 52.

5   Jenkinson, *Lewis*, p. 53; Holmberg, *Letters of William Clark*, p. 72; Jackson, *Letters*, 2:571.

6   Holmberg, *Letters of William Clark*, p. 218.

7   Holmberg, "Fairly Launched," p. 22; Jackson, *Letters*, 1:222; 2:396. See Ibid., pp. 399-407 for McKeehan's critique of Lewis. Allen, *Lewis and Clark*, p. 373 n. 39. The monument at Lewis's gravesite in Tennessee—erected in 1848—cites Lewis as "commander of the Expedition" to Oregon. Coues, *History*, 1:lx.

8 Belyea, *Columbia Journals*, p. xvii; *JLCE*, 4:9-10; Jenkinson, *Lewis*, p. 55; Slaughter, *Exploring Lewis and Clark*, pp. 36, 53.

9 Jenkinson, *Lewis*, p. 99.

10 *JLCE*, 4:66, 70, 77.

11 *JLCE*, 4:132. Moulton suggests that Clark composed this copy of Lewis's journal at Fort Clatsop or on the return trip in 1806. Ibid., 4:200 n. 10.

12 *JLCE*, 4:134, 167-168, 169 n. 2, 189, 191, 192 nn. 4, 6.

13 *JLCE*, 4:198, 200 n. 11, 203-204.

14 *JLCE*, 4:200, 201, 204.

15 *JLCE*, 4:271.

16 Slaughter, *Exploring Lewis and Clark*, p. 29; *JLCE*, 4:271, 274, 275.

17 Slaughter, *Exploring Lewis and Clark*, p. 29; *JLCE*, 4:283.

18 *JLCE*, 4:416-417.

19 *JLCE*, 4:418, 423-424.

20 *JLCE*, 4:427-428, 433 n. 9, 436.

21 *JLCE*, 4:436; 5:8-9, 11, 17, 18, 25, 29 n. 1.

22 *JLCE*, 5:29, 40.

23 *JLCE*, 5:44-45, 51 n. 2.

24 *JLCE*, 5:43, 47, 52, 54.

25 *JLCE*, 5:52-53.

26 *JLCE*, 5:53-55.

27 *JLCE*, 5:59, 62-63.

28 Coues, *History*, 2:471 n.; Ambrose, *Undaunted Courage*, pp. 262, 264.

29 *JLCE*, 9:199.

30 *JLCE*, 5:173; Coues, *History*, 2:584, 585 n.

31 *JLCE*, 8:7, 11, 50-51, 52 n. 1.

32 Holmberg, *Letters of William Clark*, p. 236.

CHAPTER 12

1 *JLCE*, 6:50.

2 To reinforce Swan's observation, consider that St. Helens was sighted and named by Captain George Vancouver at sea off the bar of the Columbia River. In his geographic

memoir, Vancouver wrote that from his "station" at sea he regained the view of the "high round snowy mountain" first seen to the south of Mount Rainier when his expedition was on Puget Sound. Swan, *Northwest Coast*, pp. 103, 109, 293. Lamb, *Vancouver*, 2:694. By way of contrast, the mountain Broughton named Hood on his voyage up the Columbia River was not discernible until it was only forty miles away. Ibid., 2:760.

3   *JLCE*, 1:5; 6:49-50.

4   *JLCE*, 1:4, 10, map 89; 6:29 n. 11, 48-52, 59, 446, 458; 9:232; 10:171; 11:393. Elliott Coues, after his study of this and other data, concluded that Station Camp (though he did not call it that) was midway between Chinook Point (the location of Fort Columbia) and the abandoned Chinook Indian village. Coues, *History*, 2:709 n. Joseph Whitehouse complicates the location of Station Camp somewhat in that he said the move of November 15th was "about 4 Miles." Whitehouse, however, may be the least reliable authority of the three in these matters. *JLCE*, 11:393. James Swan later provided clarity on the meaning of the term for present Chinook Point, "point open Slope." Known in Swan's time as "Scarborough's Hill," it was "one of the most prominent objects seen while entering the Columbia, and which has the appearance of a green field, is a clearing which has been made either by accident or design, and is thickly covered with fern." Swan, *Northwest Coast*, p. 101.

5   *JLCE*, 6:50; 11:394. One of Clark's maps shows a single symbol of Native habitation accompanied by the wording "1 house" just east of the mouth of the present Chinook River. A second shows a similar marking west of the mouth of what Clark termed the "Chin-nook" (present Wallacut) River. Ibid., 1:map 82; 6:52.

6   *JLCE*, 6:48, 50.

7   *JLCE*, 6:50, 74; Lamb, *Mackenzie Journals*, pp. 376, 380. Lewis and Clark purchased hats from the Chinooks on 21 November 1805. They were of such durability that at least one of them lasted on the return voyage as late as the recombination of the separate Clark and Lewis commands near the confluence of the Yellowstone and Missouri Rivers in August 1806—more than eight full months of use. John Ordway, who was coming down the Missouri with Lewis's squad, found the Chinook hat of George Gibson, who was with Clark on the Yellowstone. Ordway's find told him and Lewis that Clark's detachment was near and thus also the reunion of the command. Gary Moulton says Gibson's hat was one of those purchased from Clatsop Indians in February 1806 at Fort Clatsop. This may or may not have been the case given the specific ethnographic attribution of the hat's Chinook origin as recorded by Lewis. It could have been one of the hats acquired earlier at Station Camp. *JLCE*, 8:151, 152 n. 10, 162 n. 1.

8   *JLCE*, 4:111-124; 6:74; Howay, *Voyages of the Columbia*, p. 399.

9   *JLCE*, 6:49-50.

10   *JLCE*, 6:53.

11   *JLCE*, 11:394.

12   *JLCE*, 10:155, 171. Though Lewis did not return to the larger party and therefore into Gass's presence until the next day, Private Shannon, who had been with Lewis, may have conveyed the captain's thoughts along these lines.

13   *JLCE*, 9:232. William Clark's recapitulation of mileage from the mouth of the Missouri River to the Pacific computed at Fort Clatsop is calculated to Cape Disappointment. Clark's post-expeditionary computations conclude with a measurement to Point Adams, in neither case to Fort Clatsop. Ibid., 6:59; 8:387.

14 Jackson, *Letters*, 2:692, 693 n.

15 *JLCE*, 6:73, 112, 458; 10:176.

16 *JLCE*, 1:maps 82, 89; 6:52.

17 *JLCE*, 6:60; 11:395.

18 Swan, *Northwest Coast*, pp. 423-424; Lamb, *Vancouver*, 1:111; 2:765-767; Barry, "Columbia River Exploration," 33:1, p. 34; Nathaniel Philbrick, *Sea of Glory: America's Voyage of Discovery: The U. S. Exploring Expedition, 1838–1842* (New York, 2003), p. 204. Hereafter cited as Philbrick, *Sea of Glory*.

19 Lamb, *Vancouver*, 2:765; Barry, "Columbia River Exploration," 33:2, p. 152.

20 *JLCE*, 4:9, 226, 283; 5:74.

21 *JLCE*, 6:60.

22 *JLCE*, 6:52, 115 n. 13. Lewis considered Clark's Columbia River cartography so important that it is one of the few locales identified in his early planning for the publication of the expedition's narrative as needing its specific map. Lewis also envisioned maps for the "connected falls" of the Missouri (that is, the Great Falls), and for the "falls, narrows, and great rapids of the Columbia." Clark's map of the Columbia estuary is modeled after these "plan" maps, though Lewis seems to have originally envisioned it as a separate item stylistically. As a set defined by their great detail and finished state, the four plan maps are remarkable in their geographic clarity. This is especially true of those maps in the Voorhis collection (kept by Clark and later donated by his Voorhis descendants to the Missouri Historical Society) which are even more polished than those found in the notebook journals of the American Philosophical Society (APS). Clark's finished map of the mouth of the Columbia based on his survey at Station Camp is found in an APS notebook inclusive of entries from 19 November 1805 through 29 January 1806. As discussed in an earlier chapter, Moulton asserts that this is not necessarily indicative of when those inscriptions took place. Clark's plan maps for Celilo Falls, the Long & Short Narrows, and the Great Rapids (that is, the Cascades) of the Columbia are found in Voorhis notebook number 4, which has no other dated entries. This obviates any prospect of determining why or when they may have been prepared as duplicates for the maps in the APS notebooks. One possibility is that Clark readied them for use by an engraver for the published account. Or perhaps he developed them for his own enjoyment. Unlike the other Columbia River plan maps, there is no companion to the Station Camp plan map in the Voorhis notebooks. Jackson, *Letters*, 2:392, 395. *JLCE*, 2:25-29, 538, 551; 4:353; 5:324, 332, 372.

23 Plamondon, *Cartographic Reconstruction*, 1:2.

24 Goetzmann, *New Lands*, pp. 7, 38-39, 47-48, 51 (qtn.), 52, 101-102, 169, 231, 268-269, 297. See also Furtwangler, *Discovery*, p. 56.

25 Goetzmann, *New Lands*, passim, 5, 38-39, 55, 96, 111-112, 268; Jackson, *Letters*, 1:13.

26 *JLCE*, 2:91-92, 262, 269, 305, 325; 3:42 (qtn.), 44 n., 256; 4:71, 173-174, 251, 310-317; 5:7, 292; 11:209.

27 Ziak, *In Full View*, pp. 64, 139. The Moulton edition of the journals cites Clark's first call as follows: "From the m[outh] of the Creek No. 1 40 poles below P[oin]t," and so on. However, there is no discernible physical or historical evidence that a creek has or

currently exists 40 poles below Point Ellice. A close inspection of Clark's original survey field notes at the Missouri Historical Society reveals that the term "40 poles below P[oin]t" was added to neighboring phrasing by editor Moulton, presumably to make sense of what would otherwise constitute a stray notation above the line that in manuscript form reads: "From the m. of the Creek No 1," etc. It is important to note that the previous editor of the journals, Reuben Gold Thwaites, did not make this insertion, reinforcing the idea that the decision by Moulton to include the stray measurement of poles was an editorial judgment over which reasonable people can disagree. Thwaites, *Original Journals*, 6:22. I interpret Clark's outlying note, written in a noticeably smaller script than the rest of the survey data, as a false start of a survey. Emulating good surveying practice as outlined in Jefferson's instructions to Lewis, namely, that places and marks of a "durable kind" be used to fix points of observation, Clark restarted the survey farther west at the mouth of the largest creek in the vicinity. This unnamed creek can be seen today at milepost 1 on Highway 101, west of where the bridge from Astoria lands. This can be further confirmed by reference to the entirety of Clark's cartography which clearly delineates a large creek flowing into the Columbia appreciably farther to the west of Point Ellice than 40 poles (660 feet). *JLCE*, 1:maps 82, 89; 6:113; Jackson, *Letters*, 1:62.

28   *JLCE*, 6:52, 113-114; 9:169-171; 11:201, 209-210; Jackson, *Letters*, 1:52, 69, 96.

29   *JLCE*, 6:112-113, 458. Insights here and the ensuing paragraph are derived from a re-enactment of Clark's survey conducted in 1998 by professional surveyors Pat Beehler and Ken Frazier, to whom I am indebted.

30   *JLCE*, 1:map 89; 6:59, 112-113, 458. In his finished map of the mouth of the Columbia, Clark gave names to what were merely "points" when conducting the survey. There is no deviation from the survey notes and the corresponding named landmarks on the map. Point #1, "Point William" (named for his own self), is known today as Tongue Point and is due east from Station Camp. Point #2, Clark's "Point Meriwether" (for Lewis), now Smith Point in Astoria was S. 47 degrees east. Point Adams was S. 41 degrees west. Finishing the sweep, Clark discerned Cape Disappointment at S. 88 degrees west. Visiting Station Camp today it is easy to discern the immutable landmarks that attracted Clark's attention as a surveyor. *JLCE*, 6:52, 113. The rigor of scientific surveying is also the solution to the mystery "X" found on Clark's early sketch map of the Columbia estuary. Gary Moulton surmised that this cryptic mark symbolized a "move" of the camp on November 16th. As Moulton himself points out, there is no other reference to a relocation of the camp on the sandy beach. In truth Clark's "X" was his standard symbol for places where he conducted a survey or established latitude. Similar marks, numbered sequentially, can be found on several of Clark's maps depicting the party's course down the Columbia River. Two sets of survey "Marks" were created. The first, or eastern, set ran from the confluence of the Missouri with the Mississippi. The second, or western, set of observation points commenced with the mouth of the Little Missouri River, a little above Fort Mandan. Latitude "Mark" 49 was established at the confluence of the Snake and Columbia Rivers. "Mark" 50 was at Celilo Falls, and 51 just past the Long Narrows. "Mark" 52 was denoted at the last great rapids on the Columbia (the present Cascades), and "Mark" 53 was at Station Camp. Each, of course, is a major point of geographic interest, one could say the definitive ones for the voyage down the Columbia. Each "Mark" corresponds to the latitude given to the "remarkeable points" in Clark's "Estimated Distances" catalogued at Fort Clatsop. In compiling this catalogue Clark was being faithful, in practice and in literary terms, to one of the fundamental elements of Thomas Jefferson's instructions to Meriwether Lewis—to "take observations... at all remarkeable points... especially at the mouths of rivers... & other places & objects distinguished by such natural marks & characters of a durable kind, as that they may with certainty be recognised hereafter." Ibid., 1:maps 75, 78, 79, 82; 4:24; 6:59 n. 2, 446, 454-458; Jackson, *Letters*, 1:61-62.

31   Jackson, *Letters,* 1:59; 2:618.

32   Goetzmann, *New Lands,* pp. 5, 12-15, 186.

33   Jackson, *Letters,* 1:227, 230.

34   Jackson, *Letters,* 1:358, 359, 361.

CHAPTER 13

1   *JLCE,* 6:60-61.

2   *JLCE,* 1:maps 89, 91; 6:52, 62, 66.

3   Clark's draft map denotes the location of this tree with a simple initialing of "WC" and "ML." *JLCE,* 1:map 91; 6:66, 107 n. 1; Ruby and Brown, *Chinook Indians,* p. 83; Goetzmann, *New Lands,* pp. 111, 114. Mackenzie first employed the imperial rite of inscription, later emulated by Clark, in 1789 on the Arctic coast. Four years later on Pacific tidewater, Mackenzie's narrative reached a crescendo describing another moment of exploratory triumph. He wrote, "I now mixed up some vermilion in melted grease, and inscribed, in large characters, on the South-East face of the rock on which we had slept last night, this brief memorial—'Alexander Mackenzie, from Canada, by land, the twenty-second of July, one thousand seven hundred and ninety-three.'" Hayes, *First Crossing,* pp. 113, 212-214, 218, 220; Lamb, *Mackenzie Journals,* p. 378.

4   A more complete iteration of the Nor'wester's title is, Alexander Mackenzie, *Voyages from Montreal Through the Continent of North America, to the Frozen and Pacific Oceans... In the Years 1789 and 1793* (London, 1801), heretofore cited as Lamb, *Mackenzie Journals.* Goetzmann, *New Lands,* p. 114.

5   *JLCE,* 2:3; Allen, *Lewis and Clark,* p. 63; Ambrose, *Undaunted Courage,* pp. 74-76; Goetzmann, *New Lands,* pp. 111-112; Hayes, *First Crossing,* pp. 114, 256; Ronda, *LCAI,* p. 1; Lamb, *Mackenzie Journals,* pp. 417-418. The original quarto edition read by Jefferson was quickly succeeded by the publication of a handy two volume octavo set in England in 1802, plus successive American octavos in 1802 and 1803. It was an octavo version that Thomas Jefferson ordered for Lewis on 17 June 1803. See Lamb, *Mackenzie Journals,* p. 35; Jackson, *Letters,* 1:55-56 n. Bibliographic collation by Steve Beckham, et al., suggests that it was the English octavo secured for Lewis, but there is no way to be certain on this point. Jefferson wanted the English octavo for Lewis, not only because the quarto edition was bulky but also because the first American octavo had defective maps. Given the date of Jefferson's letter of inquiry juxtaposed with Lewis's departure on July 5th, there should be some doubt that any copy ordered would have found its way into Lewis's hands on a timely basis. Though it is certain Lewis had a copy of Mackenzie's *Voyages,* it was probably one he secured independently of the president's intercession. Beckham, *Literature,* pp. 53-54; Jackson, *Letters,* 1:106 n.

6   Lamb, *Mackenzie Journals,* p. 418.

7   Beckham, *Literature,* pp. 36, 53; Lamb, *Mackenzie Journals,* p. 107; Barbara Belyea, "Heroes and Hero Worship: Alexander Mackenzie's influence on the Lewis and Clark expedition journals," *Oregon Humanities* (Spring 2004), p. 39. Hereafter cited as Belyea, "Heroes and Hero Worship."

8   Lamb, *Mackenzie Journals,* p. 370 n. Gary Moulton, in his attempt to explain Clark's seemingly extraneous comment, noted that Jefferson and therefore Lewis had been

familiar with Cook's narrative. Certainly inlaid shell decoration would have been an obscure point for Lewis to recollect. Moulton states that Cook's narrative does not make any reference to teeth, which of course raises an interesting question as to the origin of Mackenzie's putative correction. *JLCE*, 7:10, 11 n. 8.

9 Lamb, *Mackenzie Journals*, pp. 266, 302, 372, 389, 406; *JLCE*, 2:79, 82; 4:66, 85, 113, 336, 383, 411; 5:112; Nokes, *Almost a Hero*, p. 13; Philbrick, *Sea of Glory*, p. 159.

10 Ziak, *In Full View*, p. 9; Lamb, *Mackenzie Journals*, pp. 239 n. 4, 359; Belyea, *Columbia Journals*, pp. 155, 284; Chaffin, *Frémont*, pp. 133, 184; Coues, *History*, 2:702, 710, 720.

11 James Mackay's instructions to John Evans included the proviso to mark the "route in all places where there will be a portage to pass from one river to another or from one waterfall to another by cutting or notching some trees or by some piles of stones engraved and cut." Wood, *Prologue*, p. 99; *JLCE*, 4:259, 304; 5:164; 6:66, 70, 72, 81, 107; 8:181, 184, 225, 237; Ambrose, *Undaunted Courage*, p. 75 (qtn.).

12 Slaughter, *Exploring Lewis and Clark*, pp. 40-41; *JLCE*, 5:304; 6:11-12, 14 n., 47, 50; Jackson, *Letters*, 1:53.

13 Allen, *Lewis and Clark*, p. 131; Goetzmann, *New Lands*, p. 114.

14 Beckham, *Literature*, p. 36. Adams, *Travel Liars*, pp. 11, 84-85, 142-161 passim, 229. Though Lewis never had the chance to acknowledge this and other problematic aspects of exploration literature because of his early death, Mackenzie, to his credit, did. The latter warned his readers "not to expect the charms of embellished narrative, or animated description." Nevertheless, Mackenzie, like John Meares before him, was assisted in the preparation of his account by one William Combe. The historian and editor W. Kaye Lamb, after comparing Combe's enhancements to Mackenzie's original wording, determined that the basic chronology and sequence of events went undisturbed, but many grammatical changes were made and "purple patches" added. Lamb, *Mackenzie Journals*, pp. 34-35, 59.

15 Hayes, *First Crossing*, p. 254; Regis, *Early America*, p. 31.

16 *JLCE*, 4:9-10.

17 *JLCE*, 3:285 n. 1; 4:12 n. 1; Lamb, *Mackenzie Journals*, p. 328.

18 *JLCE*, 4:270-271.

19 Lamb, *Mackenzie Journals*, pp. 200-201, 323-324; Hayes, *First Crossing*, p. 112. Mackenzie had actually reached the Arctic Ocean by the time of this incident but had not fully realized that fact yet. Lamb, *Mackenzie Journals*, p. 201 n. 1.

20 *JLCE*, 4:284-285, 290.

21 Lamb, *Mackenzie Journals*, p. 128. Mackenzie's quote is also reminiscent of Lewis's famed "seens of visionary inchantment" episode in the White Cliffs region of the Missouri downstream from the falls. Lewis remarked "so perfect indeed are those walls that I should have thought that nature had attempted here to rival the human art of masonry had I not recollected that she had first began her work." *JLCE*, 4:226.

22 *JLCE*, 4:285; *Mackenzie Journals*, pp. 258-259.

23 Lamb, *Mackenzie Journals*, p. 395.

24 Lamb, *Mackenzie Journals*, p. 407.

25 *JLCE*, 5:88; Lamb, *Mackenzie Journals*, pp. 300, 321.

26 *JLCE*, 5:79, 104, 109; Lamb, *Mackenzie Journals*, pp. 364-365; Gilman, *Across the Divide*, p. 198.

27 Lamb, *Mackenzie Journals*, p. 315; *JLCE*, 5:91-92.

28 *JLCE*, 5:112; Lamb, *Mackenzie Journals*, pp. 313, 389.

29 Jackson, *Letters*, 2:411.

30 *JLCE*, 8:31-32; Lamb, *Mackenzie Journals*, pp. 321-322.

31 Jackson, *Letters*, 2:399-408, quote on p. 401; Slaughter, *Exploring Lewis and Clark*, p. 215 n. 7.

32 Jackson, *Letters*, 2:401-402; Gough, *Mackenzie*, p. 123; Lamb, *Mackenzie Journals*, pp. 21-22.

33 *JLCE*, 11:6.

34 Lamb, *Mackenzie Journals*, pp. 59-60; *JLCE*, 11:7. Regarding Whitehouse see, Ibid., 11:xvi.

35 See Jackson, *Letters*, 2:385-386 n. for a history of the Lewis/McKeehan exchange. Lamb, *Mackenzie Journals*, pp. 518-519. Of course, herein Mackenzie was mistaking the Columbia River for the Fraser, a distinction discerned that same year for the first time by Simon Fraser, after whom the stream took its present name. Ibid., p. 22.

36 On the edited nature of the journals of Lewis and Clark, see Slaughter, *Exploring Lewis and Clark*, pp. 32-33. Also see Barbara Belyea, *Columbia Journals*, pp. ix, xvi, xvii, xxi, for an excellent analysis of the distinctions between "campfire journals" and texts that filter the accounts of exploration for narrative effect. Lewis's essay can be found in Coues, *History*, 3:1215-1243 and Thwaites, *Original Journals*, 7:369-388, as "Lewis's Observations and Reflections on Upper Louisiana, 1809" plus Jackson, *Letters*, 2:696-719.

37 Thwaites, *Original Journals*, 7:377–378. Coues determined that Lewis wrote the "Essay" sometime between his return from the West in September 1806 to as late as July-September of 1807. Coues stipulated, "Nothing like it is found anywhere in the thirty codices I possess, nor do I know whether it was first published in this book [i.e., Biddle's edition], or originally printed in another connection." The original editorial note in Biddle states, "The preceding observations of Captain Lewis, although left in an unfinished state, are too important to be omitted. The premature death of the author has prevented his filling up the able outline that he has drawn." This last phrase has a certain Jeffersonian ring to it, as found in the President's letter to William Dunbar that commits the nation to "fill up the canvas" Lewis and Clark had begun. This comment has become a frequent epigram for the expedition. Coues, *History*, 3:1215, 1219, 1228-1229 n., 1241 n.; Jackson, *Letters*, 1:245.

38 Thwaites, *Original Journals*, 7:379, 380, 382, 385, 388; Lamb, *Mackenzie Journals*, p. 418.

39 Lamb, *Mackenzie Journals*, p. 418.

Chapter 14

1 *JLCE*, 6:65-67.

2 *JLCE*, 1:map 91; 6:68, 70; Furtwangler, *Discovery*, p. 18 (qtn.).

3   *JLCE*, 6:65-66, 72.

4   *JLCE*, 6:72, 73 n. 23; 10:173.

5   *JLCE*, 6:73.

6   *JLCE*, 6:79; 10:176; 11:396-397; Ziak, *In Full View*, p. 100.

7   *JLCE*, 6:81.

8   *JLCE*, 6:81.

9   *JLCE*, 6:83-85, 100; 9:256; 10:177; 11:398.

10   Thwaites, *Original Journals*, 3:246, 246 n. 17; Ronda, *LCAI*, p. 178; *JLCE*, 6:86, n. 3.

11   Duncan, *Out West*, p. 381; Ambrose, *Undaunted Courage*, p. 311; Robert P. J. Cooney Jr.,
     Winning the Vote: The Triumph of the American Woman Suffrage Movement (Santa Cruz,
     2005), pp. 2-3; Duncan, *Scenes*, p. 129.

12   Slaughter, *Exploring Lewis and Clark*, pp. 106, 115-116, 133. As for Sacagawea's role,
     Slaughter says Clark's use of the endearing term "Janey" in recording her vote was the sole
     instance of such familiar usage and was therefore "a slip from the professional voice the
     explorers intended for the journals." Ibid., p. 107. In fact, Clark later referred to "Janey"
     in a note to her husband Toussaint Charbonneau encouraging him to bring his wife and
     child to St. Louis. Jackson, *Letters*, 1:315.

13   *JLCE*, 2:500; 11:186; McCartney, *Robert Stuart,* pp. 244-245.

14   Duncan, *Scenes*, p. 129. Even into the twentieth century, American mountaineering
     expeditions in the Himalayas exemplified this same democratic tradition. Their European
     and Japanese counterparts thought it strange that the Americans believed they could
     "vote their way up a mountain." Personal correspondence from alpinist Nicholas B. Clinch,
     25 July 2005, is in the possession of the author.

15   Kennedy, *Lost Cause*, p. 40; Kastor, *Nation's Crucible*, pp. 85 (qtn.), 95.

16   Kastor, *Nation's Crucible*, p. 83, 219; Kukla, *Wilderness So Immense*, pp. 323-325.

17   Slaughter, *Exploring Lewis and Clark*, pp. 204-205.

18   Ronda, "Darling Project," Ronda, ed., *Voyages*, pp. 329-330.

19   Duncan, *Scenes*, p. 129; Stephenie Ambrose Tubbs, *Why Sacagawea Deserves a Day Off and
     Other Lessons from the Lewis & Clark Trail* (Lincoln, 2008), p. 40.

20   Holmberg, *Letters of William Clark,* pp. 100, 144, 160, 187, 197, 201, 210, 252.

21   Furtwangler, *Discovery*, p. 88; Ronda, "Darling Project," Ronda, ed. *Voyages*, p. 330-331.
     Ronda, "'The Writingest Explorers'" in Ronda, ed., *Voyage*s, p. 321; *JLCE*, 2:370-371;
     3:167–168, 290 n.; 4:70; 5:32.

22   Duncan, *Scenes*, pp. 118, 132; personal correspondence from Dayton Duncan, 11
     December 2005, in the possession of the author; Kastor, *Nation's Crucible,* p. 29.

23   *JLCE*, 6:73-74, 85; 10:176; 11:397.

24   *JLCE*, 6:85-86.

[25] *JLCE*, 6:83-84.

[26] *JLCE*, 6:83-85; Brian Harrison, "Wapato: *Sagittaria Lotifolia*," *Northwest Coast* (Spring 2009), pp. 8-9.

[27] *JLCE*, 6:65, 83-84.

[28] *JLCE*, 6:84; 9:256.

[29] *JLCE*, 6:86.

CHAPTER 15

[1] *JLCE*, 6:88-89.

[2] *JLCE*, 6:90-91.

[3] *JLCE*, 6:91-92.

[4] *JLCE*, 6:92.

[5] *JLCE*, 4:285; 6:94 n. 1.

[6] *JLCE*, 6:93, 95-96.

[7] *JLCE*, 6:103-104; 11:400.

[8] *JLCE*, 6:105.

[9] *JLCE*, 5:213, 215; 6:106-107.

[10] *JLCE*, 6:108-109.

[11] *JLCE*, 6:109, 112, 114, 115 n. 14, 116, 121; 10:180.

[12] *JLCE*, 6:124, 127, 134, 136-138; 9:262; 10:182. Patrick Gass says the fort was formally named on 1 January 1806, as opposed to the Ordway and Whitehouse determination that this took place on Christmas. Gass may have deduced this from Lewis and Clark's formal promulgation of an order "for the more exact and uniform dicipline and government of the garrison." Ibid., 6:152-153; 9:262; 10:185; 11:407.

[13] *JLCE*, 6:112; 9:263, 267; Ronda, *LCAI*, p. 181.

[14] *JLCE*, 6:141, 143, 168-169.

[15] *JLCE*, 6:147, 148 n. 3.

[16] *JLCE*, 6:151-152, 158 n. 1.

[17] *JLCE*, 6:141, 158 n. 2, 172 n. 4.

[18] Indian hats, the practice of head flattening, native tools (such as arrows, bone fishhooks, digging instruments, knives, paddles), and canoes seem to have made a particular impression on the explorers and were recorded pictorially in the journals. *JLCE*, 6:161 (qtn.), 207, 209, 212-213; 232, 234, 245 (qtn.), 246, 247, 249, 250, 252, 264, 266, 268-269, 271; 11:411 (qtn.), 414-415, 417, 419-422, 424-425, 427, 429.

[19] *JLCE*, 6:273 (qtn.), 278-306.

[20] *JLCE*, 6:307-308; Allen, *Lewis and Clark*, p. 325.

[21] *JLCE*, 1:map 123; 6:311.

[22] *JLCE*, 6:333, 337. Beginning February 15th and running through March 17th the journals are replete with information from this biological survey. Ibid., 6:312-428.

[23] *JLCE*, 6:351, 353, 368, 374, 382; 9:273.

[24] *JLCE*, 6:395-396, 407, 413; 9:276; 10:196; 11:427. Whitehouse is the source that Gass was assigned canoe repair. Ibid., 11:426. Gass took the count of moccasins but numbers them at 338 pair. Ibid., 10:197.

[25] *JLCE*, 6:421.

[26] *JLCE*, 6:426.

[27] *JLCE*, 6:429-430. Ordway describes this episode as follows: "our officers Sealed up some papers and letters for Mr. Hailey and gave them to the Savages." Ibid., 9:277. This was a reference to what the explorers concluded was the favorite trader of the local Indians, after whom they attempted to name the bay that faced them from Station Camp. Ibid., 6:50.

[28] *JLCE*, 6:431.

[29] Jackson, *Letters*, 1:319-324, 329-330 n., 334 (qtn.), 335 n. 6. Paul Cutright holds that Lewis prepared the draft of the letter to Clark's family "in recognition of the fact that he was the better journalist and certainly a better speller." Cutright, *Journals*, p. 184.

[30] Holmberg, *Letters of William Clark*, p. 108; *JLCE*, 1:map 82; 6:48-50, 52, 60.

[31] Slaughter, *Exploring Lewis and Clark*, p. 199 (qtn.).

[32] Jackson, *Letters*, 1:327-329, 332-334; *JLCE*, 4:283, 428; 5:73-74, 109, 219. Clark reconfirmed November 17th as the common date denoting the arrival at the Pacific Ocean in a recapitulation of the voyage constructed after the return of the party to St. Louis in September 1806. Ibid., 8:413.

[33] *JLCE*, 4:295.

[34] *JLCE*, 4:66; 6:431; 8:276.

[35] Holmberg, *Letters of William Clark*, p. 107; Jackson, *Letters*, 1:364; 2:385, 401, 406. Another instance of Lewis's habit in this regard can be found at Ibid., 1:369.

[36] Ambrose, *Undaunted Courage*, p. 212; *JLCE*, 4:10; Jackson, *Letters*, 2:589. Interestingly, seven years after Lewis's death, Jefferson himself substantiated a subsidiary criticism of McKeehan's, namely that Lewis regarded his journals and those of his men as private property. They were instead, said the president, "the property of the government." Jackson, *Letters*, 2:612.

[37] Jackson, *Letters*, 2:720.

[38] *JLCE*, 6:430, 432 n. 2.

[39] *JLCE*, 6:441.

[40] *JLCE*, 6:441, 444.

CHAPTER 16

1   *JLCE*, 7:7-8, 8 n. 1; 11:430.

2   *JLCE*, 7:4.

3   *JLCE*, 7:49-50. When Lewis actually reached the rapids on 11 April he concluded, "the natives are not so much distressed for food as I was induced to believe." Ibid., 7:107.

4   *JLCE*, 7:49-50.

5   *JLCE*, 7:50.

6   *JLCE*, 7:75, 80.

7   *JLCE*, 7:105; Wilkes, *Expedition*, 4:360.

8   Ambrose, *Undaunted Courage*, pp. 467-468. Another influential figure in the Lewis-as-suicide camp is Donald Jackson. See Jackson, *Letters*, 2:574-575. Also see Paul R. Cutright, "Rest, Rest, Perturbed Spirit," *We Proceeded On*, 12:1 (March 1986); and Dawson A. Phelps, "The Tragic Death of Meriwether Lewis," *William and Mary Quarterly*, 3:13 (July 1956) pp. 305-318. Among those who subscribe to the view that Lewis was murdered are Vardis Fisher, *Suicide or Murder? The Strange Death of Governor Meriwether Lewis* (Chicago, 1962); Eldon G. Chuinard, "How Did Meriwether Lewis Die? It Was Murder," pts. 1-3, *We Proceeded On*, 17:3 (August 1991), pp. 4-12; 17:4 (November 1991), pp. 4-10; 18:1 (January 1992), pp. 4-10; and most recently J. Frederick Fausz and Michael A. Gavin, "The Death of Meriwether Lewis: An Unsolved Mystery," *Gateway Heritage*, 24:2-3 (Fall 2003/Winter 2004), pp. 66-79.

9   Jenkinson, *Lewis*, passim; Ambrose, *Undaunted Courage*, pp. 471-473.

10   Norfolk (Virginia) *Gazette & Public Ledger*, 20 November 1809, p. 3. The most celebrated postmodernist account is Slaughter, *Exploring Lewis and Clark*. Ronda, "Vast Enterprise," in Ronda, ed., *Voyages*, p. 22 (qtn).

11   *JLCE*, 5:74, 81, 88.

12   Ambrose, *Undaunted Courage*, pp. 284-312; Beckham, *Rockies to the Pacific*, pp. 13-55; Ziak, *In Full View*, pp. 29-49; Lang, "Landscape," p. 146.

13   *JLCE*, 5:175, 177; Jenkinson, *Lewis*, p. 14.

14   *JLCE*, 7:131; Allen, *Lewis and Clark*, p. 326; Regis, *Early America*, pp. 86, 123-129.

15   Coues, *History*, 2:688; *JLCE*, 6:273; Allen, *Lewis and Clark*, pp. 397-398.

16   *JLCE*, 6:151-152; 7:267.

17   *JLCE*, 7:275, 325; 8:31, 56, 61.

18   Greenfield, *Narrating Discovery*, pp. 26-41; *JLCE*, 8:61, 104.

19   *JLCE*, 4:226, 265. Dayton Duncan, one of the great popularizers of the Lewis & Clark story, has made "Scenes of Visionary Enchantment" his epigram for the entire venture. See Dayton Duncan, *Scenes*.

20   Jenkinson, *Lewis*, passim. With fanfare Thomas Slaughter specifically credits William Clark with the observation that, relative to the Nez Perce, "nature seems to have dealt with a

liberal hand." In his favored view of Clark versus Lewis, Slaughter overlooked that it was actually Meriwether Lewis who first made this observation. Slaughter, *Exploring Lewis and Clark,* p. 10; Coues, *History,* 3:959 n.

21 Nisbet, *Thompson,* p. 189.

22 *JLCE,* 7:105.

23 *JLCE,* 7:143-144.

24 *JLCE,* 7:146, 156, 163.

25 *JLCE,* 5:88-92, 94 n. 2, 95 n. 16.

26 *JLCE,* 7:146, 148-149, 151-152; Belyea, *Columbia Journals,* pp. 154, 274.

27 I am indebted to the insights found in Dening, *Beach Crossings,* pp. 240, 254, to explain Native comportment. *JLCE,* 7:151-152; 10:213.

28 Jenkinson, *Lewis,* p. 78. Thomas Slaughter says Clark defused the situation at the Long Narrows, and the captain exercised discretion about the incident in his journal. In fact, Lewis simply left the scene and joined Clark upriver. Clark actually recounted the incriminating tale of Lewis's loss of composure. Slaughter, *Exploring Lewis and Clark,* pp. 179-180; *JLCE,* 7:154.

29 *JLCE,* 7:155-156.

30 Jackson, *Letters,* 1:369; *JLCE,* 7:157.

31 *JLCE,* 7:163.

32 Alan Moorehead, *The Fatal Impact: Captain Cook's Exploration of the South Pacific—Its High Adventure and Disastrous Effects* (New York, 2000), p. 70; Philbrick, *Sea of Glory,* p. 81; Jenkinson, *Lewis,* pp. 42, 102.

33 *JLCE,* 5:301, 303 (Clark's qtn.); 7:210, 226, 230.

34 Beckham, *Rockies to the Pacific,* p. 120; Slaughter, *Exploring Lewis and Clark,* p. 141; *JLCE,* 7:234, 275.

35 McCartney, *Robert Stuart,* p. 219.

36 *JLCE,* 7:38-41; 41 n. 4. This was not the first time one of the captains had seen or visited Indian burials along the banks of the Columbia River. On the westbound trip Clark made several oblique references to Indian graveyards, but in only two instances did he frequent them for the purpose of examination—one was a vault below the Pelican rapids on 20 October 1805, and then again near Beacon Rock. He wrote in regard to the first instance, "our curiosity induced us to examine the methot those nativs practicd in disposeing the dead." More typically, as Clark wrote on 22 October 1805, "on one of those Island I saw Several tooms but did not visit them," no doubt as a function, in part or in whole, of the exigencies of travel and the strong desire to reach the Pacific Ocean. Ibid., 5:263, 268-269, 281-282, 309, 311 (qtn.), 325 (qtn.), 349, 358-361, 380.

37 *JLCE,* 7:106-108.

38 *JLCE,* 7:123, 131-132. When in this vicinity the previous fall, the expedition noted but did not examine Indian tombs on the island. Or, at least, Clark didn't. Ibid., 5:325, 349, 353 n. 5.

[39] Lamb, *Mackenzie Journals*, p. 359; Nisbet, *Thompson*, p. 225; Hauser-Schäublin, "Witnesses of Encounters," pp. 33-34. Lewis visited Indian burial sites, at least in part, in response to Jefferson's direction that the expedition be "acquainted" with the customs of encountered tribes. More specifically, Jefferson instructed, ". . . it will be useful to acquire what knolege you can of the state of morality, religion & information about them." Jefferson himself appears to have been encouraged in this direction by Levi Lincoln, his attorney general, who, along with other members of the President's Cabinet, had been invited to comment upon an early draft of Lewis's instructions. Lincoln asked Jefferson, "may not some new aspects be usefully given to the undertaking, and others made more prominent?" Lincoln answered his own rhetorical question by proposing, among other items, that Lewis look into "the ideas the various tribes or nations possess of a supreme being, their worships, their religion, the agency it has in their respective govts." Lincoln professed the view that new insights on these matters would enhance the government's prospects of "impressing their minds with a sense of an *improved religion* & morality & the means by which it could be effected." Jefferson, following Lincoln's advice, told Lewis that information about Indian morality and religiosity would "better enable those who may endeavor to civilize & instruct them." Jackson, *Letters*, 1:32-36, 62-63.

Thus, Jefferson did not specifically prescribe visiting places of interment. However, the President asked his scientific colleagues in Philadelphia—Benjamin Rush, Caspar Wistar, Benjamin Smith Barton, and Robert Patterson—to help Lewis give dimension to the scientific scope of the expedition. All four received letters advising them that Lewis would shortly appear in their city and asked them "the favor of you to prepare notes of such particulars as may occur in his journey & which you think should draw his attention & enquiry." Of Jefferson's correspondents, Dr. Benjamin Rush's response is germane. Rush prepared for his student what Lewis called "abstract queries under the several heads of *Physical History*, *medicine*, *Morals* and *Religeon* of the Indians, which I will have no doubt will be servicable in directing my inquiries among that people." Two of the questions posed by Rush were: "Is Suicide common among them?" and "How do they dispose of their dead, and with what Ceremonies do they inter them." Ibid., pp. 16-19, 21, 50, 52.

[40] *JLCE*, 7:210-211, 219, 222. Another circumstance that may be probative in this regard was the odd temperament of a previously friendly and enormously helpful Nez Perce chief. Lewis wrote on 8 May, "the Twisted hair received us very coolly an occurrence as unexpected as it was unaccountable to us." Lewis interprets Twisted Hair's indifference as a consequence of a quarrel between Twisted Hair and Cut Nose, ostensibly over the handling of the expedition's horses the preceding winter. Clark seems less certain of this explanation than Lewis but is in general concurrence with it. While Cut Nose may have been critical of Twisted Hair's handling of the horses, there is no plausible reason why this should have made Twisted Hair speak to Lewis and Clark "in a angry manner." There is also no explanation of the comportment of a relation of Twisted Hair's, whom Lewis found, like the man who threw the puppy on his plate, "an impertinent proud supercilious fellow." This observation was made the same day that Cut Nose and Twisted Hair "have become good friends again." All this suggests that some factor besides Twisted Hair's care of horses guided his querulous re-introduction to Lewis and Clark. Ibid., 7:228, 232, 235.

[41] *JLCE*, 8:109-110, 127.

[42] Jenkinson, *Lewis*, passim; Slaughter, *Exploring Lewis and Clark*, p. 20.

[43] Barbara Belyea, "Heroes and Hero Worship," pp. 38-43; Lamb, *Mackenzie Journals*, p. 23; Gough, *Mackenzie*, p. 169; Hayes, *First Crossing*, p. 236.

[44] Lamb, *Mackenzie Journals*, p. 454. Mackenzie seems not to have been as avid in this pastime of visiting gravesites as Lewis was, but he did from time to time. See Ibid., pp. 310, 347, 353-354.

⁴⁵ *JLCE*, 9:235-236; 10:152; 11:344-345.

⁴⁶ *JLCE*, 5:253; Ambrose, *Undaunted Courage*, p. 295. Curiously, the same evening as the incident on the Clearwater, Old Toby, the expedition's Shoshone guide who had served as the pilot through the mountains, left abruptly at dark. Clark wrote, "we Could not account for the Cause of his leaveing us at this time...." Patrick Gass attributed Old Toby's departure to a reluctance to run the river's rapids. *JLCE*, 5:252; 10:152.

⁴⁷ *JLCE*, 5:249, 252-253; 9:235; 10:152; 11:344; Ronda, *LCAI*, p. 162; Aguilar, *Indian Traditions*, pp. 152-153; Gilman, *Across the Divide*, pp. 269-271.

⁴⁸ *JLCE*, 5:232-236, 243; 245-246; 249 (qtn.); Gilman, *Across the Divide*, pp. 271, 278; Aguilar, *Indian Traditions*, p. 150.

⁴⁹ Aguilar, *Indian Traditions*, p. 131; Belyea, *Columbia Journals*, p. 26. For Thompson to consider this "so savage an Action" is no small irony considering how common bloodletting was as a medicinal cure in Euro-American society. Ibid., p. 204 n. Lewis and Clark often bled those under their care. See *JLCE*, 2:356; 3:278-279; 4:276-277, 279, 334; 6:429.

⁵⁰ Belyea, *Columbia Journals*, pp. 144, 146, 265 n. During these dances Thompson noted that the Indians often exhibited "a trait of enthusiasm," what Belyea tells us is a nineteenth-century euphemism for fanatical excitement. Ibid., p. 267 n.

⁵¹ Ambrose, *Undaunted Courage*, pp. 463-465; Jenkinson, *Lewis*, p. 110; Gilman, *Across the Divide*, p. 202. Major Gilbert Russell, commander of the fort at Chickasaw Bluffs where Lewis stayed in the days just before his death and who prepared a statement on the sequence of events in the fall of 1809, described the manner of Lewis's suicide as occurring in a "Barbarian-like manner." Jackson, *Letters*, 2:573.

⁵² Jenkinson, *Lewis*, p. 97; Ambrose, *Undaunted Courage*, pp. 306-307, 430-431, 461-465. On the Warren Commission's "single bullet theory," see Gerald Posner, *Case Closed: Lee Harvey Oswald and the Assassination of JFK* (New York, 1993), p. 327, 410-411.

⁵³ Ambrose, *Undaunted Courage*, p. 306; Jenkinson, *Lewis,* p. 98; personal communications from Dr. David Musto, April 17, 19, 2004; Kay Redfield Jamison, *Touched with Fire: Manic-Depressive Illness and the Artistic Temperament* (New York, 1993), p. 13. Hereafter cited as Jamison, *Touched with Fire.*

⁵⁴ Greenfield, *Narrating Discovery*, p. 71. Hoffhaus is quoted in Wood, *Prologue*, p. 138.

⁵⁵ *JLCE*, 5:229. Donald Jackson argued that Lewis probably kept a journal in 1804 but lost it during the spill of one of the pirogues on 14th May 1805, a month or so west of Fort Mandan. If true, this further weakens the "journal gaps as depression" thesis. In a letter to Jefferson sent nigh upon the departure from Fort Mandan, Lewis said that Clark's 1804 journal, one sent to the president in the same dispatch, "will assist me in compiling my own for publication after my return." Lewis further stated his intention to send his journal to Jefferson from the Continental Divide or the extreme point of navigation on the Missouri, which strategy, Per Jackson, was foiled in part when the pirogue capsized. Jack, *Jefferson*, pp. 194-195; Jackson, *Letters*, 1:232.

⁵⁶ Jamison, *Touched with Fire*, pp. 13, 16, 98, 132.

⁵⁷ Kay Redfield Jamison, *Night Falls Fast: Understanding Suicide* (New York, 1999), pp. 111-112, 127, 142. Hereafter cited as Jamison, *Suicide.*

⁵⁸ Wood, *Prologue*, p. 160; Ambrose, *Undaunted Courage*, pp. 238, 280-384, 431, 437-446, 450-465 (qtn.), 467; *JLCE*, 4:141. See information on PTSD posted by the

National Center for Post-Traumatic Stress Disorder, sponsored by the U. S. Department of Veterans Affairs, at www.ncptsd.ord/facts/general (accessed 25 February 2005). Individuals in even more ambiguous situations than Lewis found himself as the circumstances journalists or peacekeepers face, can also suffer from PTSD. In situations where life and limb may not be at immediate risk, stressors common to war zone experiences may have a cumulative effect and result in PTSD. Those stressors might be "changes in lifestyle, separation from family, exhaustion, unfavorable climatic conditions, uncertainty about the length of the mission, and demoralization about the efficacy of the mission." Lewis's longing for home, his behavioral aggression, exaggeration of threats, the avoidance of writing the expeditionary narrative, his problematic interpersonal relationships, and other personality abnormalities such as excessive drinking and verbal boisterousness—all seen in the captain's behavior from the spring of 1806 forward—seem to point to PTSD symptomatologies. Ibid, www.ncptsd.org/facts/specific, (accessed 25 February 2005), sections titled "PTSD in Journalists," "Traumatic Stress and Peacekeepers," "Forensic Validity of a PTSD Diagnosis," and "Anger and Trauma." For a detailed study on the causative correlation between PTSD and depression, see Darin J. Jackson, et al., "Posttraumatic Stress Disorder and Depression Symptomatology in a Sample of Gulf War Veterans: A Prospective Analysis," *Journal of Consulting and Clinical Psychology*, 69:1 (2001), pp. 41-49.

Complex PTSD, a relatively new diagnosis, may also be applicable to Lewis's case. With this syndrome, rather than a single short-lived event, a chronic or long-term trauma occurs. For example, people who are held in captivity, such as prisoners of war, are victimized because they are unable to flee. Individuals suffering from Complex PTSD exhibit alterations in emotional regulation, such as explosive anger; avoid thinking about trauma-related topics; abuse alcohol and drugs to numb their feelings; and engage in self-mutilation and other forms of self-inflicted harm. See www.ncptsd.org/facts/specific/fs_complex (accessed 25 February 2005).

59 Jenkinson, *Lewis,* p. 97; Feltskog, *Parkman,* pp. 27a, 51a.

60 Jamison, *Suicide,* p. 26.

61 Edwin Arlington Robinson (1869-1935), "Richard Cory," found at the website of the Academy of American Poets, www.poets.org.

62 *JLCE,* 4:10.

Epilogue

1 *JLCE,* 7:156-158; 9:296. See also Loren M. Gibbons, "All Them Horses and One Poor Mule: A Numerical Accounting of the Corps of Discovery's Livestock," *We Proceeded On,* 28:3 (August 2002), pp. 26-32.

2 *JLCE,* 7:159-160, 162, 162 n. 1.

3 *JLCE,* 7:163-164; 10:215.

4 *JLCE,* 7:163, 165-166, 168 n. 1; 9:297; 10:215.

5 *JLCE,* 7:166-167.

6 *JLCE,* 7:167; 10:215.

7 *JLCE,* 2:235-237, 330. Hugh Hall was among those detailed to the expedition from an Army post in Tennessee and, as such, was likely one of those deemed initially by Lewis to be not "in readiness" to serve. Some of Hall's cohorts indeed were eventually rejected

for western duty. In both instances, Hall had company in the conduct of the infractions. John Collins, Hall's mate on the whiskey caper, and Hall himself had gotten drunk on New Year's Eve, 1803, at Camp DuBois in Illinois. Ibid., 2:139 n. 2, 143.

[8] *JLCE*, 5:76, 94. Clark's thoughtful concern was not unique. Lewis gave up his horse on the Lemhi Pass portage to Peter Weiser who was ill and could not march. Ibid., 5:158-159.

[9] Jackson, *Letters*, 1:370 n. 3; *JLCE*, 7:326.

[10] *JLCE*, 11:7.

CONCLUSION

[1] Ephemeral literature, in the possession of the author.

[2] Regis, *Early America*, pp. 33, 36-37 (qtn.).

[3] Kennedy, *Lost Cause*, p. 171; Greenfield, *Narrating Discovery*, p. 10.

[4] Ronda, "Passages," p. 540.

[5] Greenfield, *Narrating Discovery*, p. 42.

[6] Greenfield, *Narrating Discovery*, pp. 89-90, 97.

[7] Greenfield, *Narrating Discovery*, p. 93.

[8] Greenfield, *Narrating Discovery*, p. 93.

[9] Greenfield, *Narrating Discovery*, p. 95.

[10] Greenfield, *Narrating Discovery*, p. 101.

[11] Greenfield, *Narrating Discovery*, pp. 101, 103, 106-107 (qtns.).

INDEX

M

Mackay, James, 16, 24, 33, 85, 264
Mackenzie, Alexander, as exploratory model, 40-44, 148, 149, 176, 191, 197, 200, 203-217 passim, 222, 261, 277; discovery claims for Great Britain, 59, 98, 109, 205, 280; inscriptions, 205; literary style, 40, 116, 209, 211, 212, 330n.; mentioned, 10, 12, 13, 39, 40, 42, 43, 49, 58, 107, 110, 138, 146, 205, 260, 277; north fork Columbia (Fraser) River, 10, 11, 12, 15, 22, 57, 59, 101, 106, 110; plagiarized by LCE, 101, 177, 205, 209, 213, 215; reaches the Pacific Ocean, 191, 205, 209, 210, 214, 216; *Voyages from Montreal* xvi, 5, 12, 42, 57, 86, 90, 101, 205, 206, 208-217 passim, 259, 277, 278, 296n.
Madison, Dolley, 200
Malaspina, Alessandro, 200
Mandan (Indians), geographic information provided by, 16, 17; villages mentioned, 36, 77, 83, 110, 141, 248, 264, 280
Marias River, decision point, 23, 99, 104, 181, 209, 222, 232, 271; mentioned, 124, 260
Marks, Lucy, 21
Marquette, Jacques, 9, 97
McGowan (WA), 199
McKay, Alexander, 214-215
McKeehan, David, 177, 186, 214, 215, 243
McKenzie Head (WA), 219
McKenzie, Roderic, 261
McNary Dam, 118
McNeal, Hugh, 260

Meares, John, 153, 206
"Medicine" (Sun) River, 17, 18, 21, 23, 30, 56
Megler Creek, 168
Megler (WA), 158, 166
Memaloose Island, 183
Merritt, Jim, 38
Methy Portage, 211
Michaux, Andre, 243
Milk River, 178
Miller, Robert, 12, 107, 109
Mississippi River, 24, 97, 198, 215
Missoula (MT), 56, 58
Missouri Historical Society, 199
Missouri River, passim, adjoining plains, 34, 65, 252; "Breaks," 22; Gates of the Mountains, 4, 17, 56; —Great Falls, description by Lewis, 123-125, 130, 175, 181, 195, 211, 232; Indian information about, 17, 181; mentioned, 4, 28, 30, 31, 47, 109, 237, 238, 253, 260, 264-265; other explorers' accounts, 17, 156; portage 164-165, 168, 172, 198, 232— headwaters, 9, 10, 15, 18, 37, 47, 109, 182, 278; headwaters conjecture, 24, 97; navigability, 24, 58, 104; proximity to Columbia River headwaters, 16, 17, 18, 22, 23, 49, 97, 98, 107; Three Forks, 4, 18, 24, 30, 57, 83, 182, 198, 242; White Cliffs, 4, 125, 253, 295n.
Montana, 16, 20
Montreal, xvi
Moulton, Gary, 74, 84, 103, 115, 134, 176, 195, 222, 232, 235, 275; *Journals of the LC Expedition* 4, 38, 52, 199, 221
Mount Adams, 119
Mount Baker, 116

Mount Hood, 11, 13, 30, 116, 117, 119, 120, 132, 133, 141
Mount Rainier, 11, 16
Mount St. Helens, 116, 119
"Multnomah" (Willamette) River, 147, 237, 247
Musselshell River, 30

N

National American Woman Suffrage Association, 84
Nebraska, 223
Ne-cha-co-lee (Indian village), 147
Nevada, 237
New Mexico, 237
Nez Perce (Indians), assistance, 2, 64, 72, 73, 90, 93, 94, 269-270; first encounters with LC, 62, 88, 213, 242; geographic information provided by, 20, 60, 62-63, 69, 99, 132, 194; guides, 57, 79, 253 (also see Twisted Hair and Tetoharsky); location, 86; mentioned, 33-34, 43, 56, 57, 58, 71, 104, 248, 256, 257, 260, 262, 270, 271; relationship with Chinookan tribes, 91-92, 94; spiritual practices, 261-262
Nisbet, Jack, 111
North West Company, xvi, 11, 109, 110, 146, 205, 216, 217, 254
Nova Scotia, 171

O

Ohio River, 104, 149, 198
Okanogan River, 263
Old Toby (Shoshone), 43, 45, 48, 49, 50, 51, 56, 58, 59, 62, 87, 88, 104, 276, 278, 280
Ordway, John, mentioned, 4,

Z